MILITARY

Military Virtues is an outstanding contribution to the growing field of military ethics. It makes a compelling case for the revival of the classical emphasis on character – the seat of moral goodness. In that context it explores such generic leadership qualities that have the flavour of moral excellencies, such as integrity, justice or fairness, compassion and humility. They are the building-blocks of 'good leadership and leadership for good.' Anyone who cares about the ethos of our unique Armed Services will read this pioneering book with interest and profit.

Professor John Adair, Chair of Leadership, United Nations

The concept of 'virtue' in the Aristotelian sense of 'functional excellence' is widespread in the military. Indeed, much of military training follows precisely Aristotle's understanding of how virtues are developed through repetitive practice under supervision and coaching. This volume provides the most thorough and insightful analysis of a wide range of military virtues yet compiled. It skilfully balances examination of the conceptual understanding of these virtues with extremely helpful case studies which make the conceptual analysis concrete and clear. This book should be widely read and used for classroom discussions at all levels of professional military education.

Dr Martin L. Cook, Admiral Stockdale Professor of Professional
Military Ethics (Emeritus), United States Naval War College

Winston Churchill once said, 'Without courage, all other virtues lose their meaning'. After reading this volume, I realize how far I missed the mark focusing on Churchill's most important virtue of courage while expecting to then easily learn the others. Henley writes in *Invictus*, 'I am the Master of my Fate, I am the Captain of my soul'. If a military leader and warrior wants to be 'the Master of their Fate, the Captain of their soul' they need to also read about the other 13 virtues identified in this volume, review carefully the corresponding case studies of each and then strive to master not just one, not just two, but all 14.

Captain Mike Michel, Deputy Commandant for Leadership and
Character Development, United States Naval Academy

At a time of increasing domestic and international complexity and seemingly constant change, the role of ethical leadership has never been more important. This extremely timely and thought-provoking book allows us to re-examine our core virtues as leaders, to study and validate them and critically to ensure that they are not just empty words on a vision paper. The chapter on 'Humility' serves as a reminder of our 'Serve to Lead' heritage: leadership is about maximising the talents of all our people and putting them first in all things. By really understanding these virtues, inculcating them in all that we do and, by constant practice, making them dispositional we give ourselves the 'ethical leadership armour' to tackle the many difficult challenges that face us. Finally, clearly articulated in the 'Courage' chapter, unless we have the hard moral courage to do what is right all of our study of these virtues is meaningless. Hugely readable, fascinating and adept at drawing on both the successes and mistakes of our predecessors, it is a 'must read' for anyone involved in leadership in the military or commercial sector, from those at the 'coal face' to the board room.

Brigadier WSC Wright OBE, Commander Sandhurst Group (RMAS Gp)

ISSUES IN MILITARY ETHICS

Edited by Don Carrick, King's College London,
Michael Skerker, United States Naval Academy, and David Whetham, King's
College London at the Joint Services Command and Staff College

With most officer training schools including military ethics as part of their programme, more than ever there is a need for clarity on ethical decision making. Contemporary military conflict is ever changing and with it military practitioners are confronted by new ethical challenges which often puts additional weight on the professional activity of personnel. At a minimum, military professionals need to have a clear knowledge of the laws that underpin their profession in order to evaluate situations quickly.

The series explores the complexities of acting ethically within the military system. It is not a philosophical debate on military ethics nor is it a general introduction. Instead, this series aims to provide real world guidance for military commanders and leaders. Edited alongside King's College London Centre for Military Ethics and the United States Naval Academy, this series brings a unique and relevant combination of practitioner and academic expertise which profoundly enhances the overall effect of the learning experience from its publications.

Military Virtues

Edited by

MICHAEL SKERKER
United States Naval Academy, U.S.A.

DAVID WHETHAM
King's College London, U.K.

DON CARRICK
King's College London, U.K.

Howgate Publishing Limited

First published in 2019 by
Howgate Publishing Limited
Station House
50 North Street
Havant
Hampshire
PO9 1QU
Email: info@howgatepublishing.com
Web: www.howgatepublishing.com

British Library Cataloguing-in-Publication Data
A catalogue record for this book is available from the British Library

ISBN 978-1-912440-00-9 (pbk)
ISBN 978-1-912440-01-6 (ebk - PDF)
ISBN 978-1-912440-10-8 (ebk - ePUB)

Michael Skerker, David Whetham and Don Carrick have asserted their right under the Copyright, Designs and Patents Act, 1988, to be identified as the editors of this work.

The views expressed in this book are those of the individual authors and do not necessarily reflect official policy or position.

CONTENTS

NOTES ON CONTRIBUTORS

Rear Admiral Alan T. Baker CHC, USN, Retired

Alan 'Blues' Baker is a retired officer who served as the 16th Chaplain of the United States Marine Corps from 2006 to 2009. Dr Baker was the first graduate of the United States Naval Academy and former Surface Warfare Officer selected as a Chaplain Corps Flag Officer. He established and served as principal of Strategic Foundations where he taught, coached, and catalyzed organizations valuing the intersection of learning, leadership and faith. He is a deeply experienced executive with over 20 years of international leadership in complex organizations. His former public service spanned from Dean of the Chapel at the U.S. Naval Academy to the Presidential nomination and Senate appointment as Rear Admiral where he provided executive oversight to a global team of several hundred professionals. Blues brings extensive background in ethical leadership, education, organizational development, and strategic planning.

Colonel David M. Barnes

David Barnes is the Deputy Head of the Department of English and Philosophy at the United States Military Academy. He serves on the Editorial Board for *The Journal of Military Ethics* and on the Board of Directors for the International Society for Military Ethics (ISME). He is a career U.S. Army officer and earned his PhD in Philosophy from the University of Colorado, Boulder. His research interests include the ethics of war, humanitarian intervention, and military privatization, as well as the ethical application of A.I. and other technology.

Dr Edward T. Barrett

Edward Barrett is the Director of Research at the United States Naval Academy's Stockdale Center for Ethical Leadership. A graduate of the University of Notre Dame, he completed a PhD in political theory at the University of Chicago, and is the author of *Persons and Liberal Democracy: The Ethical and Political Thought of Karol Wojtyla/John Paul II* (2010). While in graduate school, he served for two years as speechwriter to the Catholic Archbishop of Chicago. He joined the United States Air Force reserves after serving nine years as an active duty C-130 instructor pilot, and recently retired as a Colonel from the Air Staff's Directorate of Strategic Planning.

Ambassador Reuben E. Brigety

Reuben Brigety II is Dean of the Elliot School of International Affairs at The George Washington University in Washington, D.C. Before joining the faculty at GWU, he most recently served as the appointed Representative of the United States of America to the African Union and Permanent Representative of the United States to the UN Economic Commission for Africa on September 3, 2013. Prior to this appointment, Ambassador Brigety served as Deputy Assistant Secretary of State in the Bureau of African Affairs from November 14, 2011 until September 3, 2013 with responsibility for Southern African and Regional Security Affairs. From December 2009 to November 2011, he served as Deputy Assistant Secretary of State in the Bureau of Population, Refugees, and Migration. Ambassador Brigety previously served as Director of the Sustainable Security Program at the Center for American Progress from January 2008 to November 2009 and as a Special Assistant in the Bureau for Democracy, Conflict, and Humanitarian Assistance at the United States Agency for International Development from January 2007 to January 2008. From November 2008 to January 2009, he also served as a senior advisor for Development and Security to the U.S. Central Command Assessment Team in Washington and in Doha, Qatar. Prior to his work in the policy arena, Ambassador Brigety served as an assistant professor of government and politics at George Mason University and at the School of International Service at American University between August 2003 and April 2009. In addition, Ambassador Brigety was a researcher with the Arms Division of Human Rights Watch (HRW) from August 2001 to May 2003, where he conducted research missions in Afghanistan and Iraq. Before joining HRW, Ambassador Brigety was an active duty U.S. naval officer and held several staff positions in the Pentagon and in fleet support units. Ambassador Brigety is a 1995 distinguished midshipman graduate of the U.S. Naval Academy, where he earned a BS in political science (with merit), served as the Brigade Commander and received the Thomas G. Pownall Scholarship. He also holds an MPhil and a PhD in international relations from the University of Cambridge. The author of many publications, Ambassador Brigety is a member of the International Institute for Strategic Studies, a Life Member of the Council on Foreign Relations, and a recipient of the Council's International Affairs Fellowship.

Mr Don Carrick

Don Carrick is a philosopher specializing in the field of applied ethics and is also a keen amateur military historian. His main interests are in military ethics education, medical ethics, just war theory, and moral and political philosophy. He has co-edited and contributed to several volumes in his field, the latest, with James Connelly and David Whetham, being *Making the Military Moral: Contemporary Challenges and Responses in Military Ethics Education*. Don currently teaches military medical ethics at the University of Leeds and he is also a postgraduate student at King's College London, where he is working on a PhD thesis entitled 'Teaching Ethics to the British Soldier.'

Chaplain (FltLt) Reverend Dr Nikki Coleman

Nikki Coleman is a military ethicist who specializes in space ethics, obedience in the military, military bioethics, military ethics education, moral injury and post-traumatic stress disorder (PTSD). She is a research associate at the Case Western Reserve University Inamori International Center for Ethics and Excellence, as well as currently serving as a Chaplain in the Royal Australian Air Force.

Lieutenant Colonel Rafford M. Coleman

Rafford Coleman enlisted into the Selected Marine Corps Reserve upon graduation from Baltimore City College High School in 1987. While a student and lacrosse player at Rutgers University he was activated for Operations Desert Shield and Desert Storm and upon graduation in 1993, Lt Col. Coleman was commissioned a 2nd Lieutenant and later was designated a Marine Aviator. He would serve in Marine Medium Helicopter squadron-263 at Marine Corps Air Station New River and then as an Instructor Pilot with Helicopter Training squadron 8 at Naval Air Station Whiting Field before joining 8th Marine Regiment at Camp Lejeune in 2004. Following his tour with 8th Marines, Lt Col. Coleman would deploy as a Department Head with Marine Medium Helicopter squadron-61 and would be Marine Medium Tiltrotor squadron 261's first Executive Officer. Lt Col. Coleman and his family were re-assigned to Okinawa, Japan in spring 2008 as a part of the 3rd Marine Expeditionary Force. In 2013, Lt Col. Coleman and his family returned to the U.S. and he assumed command of Helicopter Training squadron 18 at NAS Whiting Field. In 2016, Lt Col. Coleman assumed responsibilities for the 2nd Battalion of the Brigade of Midshipmen.

Dr Stephen Coleman

Stephen Coleman is Associate Professor of Ethics and Leadership in the School of Humanities and Social Sciences, and Program Director, Military Ethics at the Australian Centre for the Study of Armed Conflict and Society with the University of NSW, Canberra, at the Australian Defence Force Academy. He has published on a diverse range of topics in applied ethics, including military ethics, police ethics, space ethics, medical ethics, and the practical applications of human rights. His latest book is *Military Ethics: An Introduction with Case Studies*.

Colonel James L. Cook

James Cook is Professor and Head, Department of Philosophy, U.S. Air Force Academy, Colorado Springs, Colorado. A foreign area officer and cyber officer, his assignments have included the Pentagon and NATO. He serves as a board member of the International Society of Military Ethics and co-editor of the *Journal of Military Ethics*. He earned his doctorate in philosophy at the Universität-Heidelberg and publishes on philosophical topics including the ethics of war.

Lieutenant Colonel Scott Cooper USMC, Retired

Scott Cooper served 20 years on active duty in the Marine Corps. He flew the EA-6B Prowler and also served as a Forward Air Controller, serving five tours in Iraq and two in Afghanistan. Today he is the National Security

Outreach Director at Human Rights First and the Founder and Director of Veterans for American Ideals, a grass-roots, community-based movement of veterans aiming to leverage military veteran voices to bridge divides and regain that shared sense of national community.

Dr Stephen Deakin

Stephen Deakin teaches British Army officers at the Royal Military Academy, Sandhurst. He has published widely especially in the area of military ethics and he is particularly interested in practical ethical dilemmas on the battlefield.

Mr Ian Fishback

Ian Fishback is a PhD student of philosophy at the University of Michigan, where he researches moral and political philosophy. Prior to transitioning to academia he served four combat tours as an infantry and special forces officer in the U.S. Army.

Commander Michael A. Flynn USN

Michael Flynn graduated from the U.S. Naval Academy in 1995 with an English major and French minor, completing an MA degree in English literature from the University of Maryland later that same year. He was designated a Naval Flight Officer in 1998 and assigned to Fleet Air Reconnaissance Squadron Two in Rota, Spain. Next, he planned and coordinated air reconnaissance missions as a staff officer in Naples, Italy. In 2003 he was selected as an Olmsted Scholar and spent the next few years studying Mandarin Chinese and International Relations at Nanjing University and the Hopkins-Nanjing Center in China. He returned to operational duties from 2006–2008, flying reconnaissance missions in the Pacific and Middle East. In 2008 he served as an Electronic Warfare Office for the Army's Civil Affairs Brigade in Iraq, fielding and maintaining their counter-IED electronic warfare program. In 2009 he jointed a NATO staff in southern Italy as the air operations officer. In 2011 he was selected for the Permanent Military Professor program, completed his PhD with a dissertation on literary representations of PTSD in contemporary Colombian fiction in 2015 at the University of Texas at Austin. He teaches in the English department at the United States Naval Academy, specializing in literature of the sea, trauma, and, war, and contemporary Latin American literature, especially from Colombia.

Professor Shannon E. French

Shannon French is the Inamori Professor in Ethics, Director of the Inamori International Center for Ethics and Excellence, and a tenured full professor in the Philosophy Department with a secondary appointment as a professor in the School of Law at Case Western Reserve University in Cleveland, Ohio. She is also the General Hugh Shelton Distinguished Visiting Chair in Ethics for the U.S. Army Command and General Staff College (CGSC) Foundation and has been a non-resident Senior Associate at the Center for Strategic and International Studies (CSIS) in Washington, D.C. Prior to starting at CWRU in July of 2008, she taught for 11 years as a tenured Associate Professor of Philosophy at the United States Naval Academy in Annapolis, Maryland, and served as Associate Chair of the Department of Leadership, Ethics, and Law. Dr French received her B.A. in philosophy, classical studies, and history from Trinity University (San Antonio, Texas) in 1990 and her PhD in philosophy from Brown University (Providence, Rhode Island) in 1997. Her main area of research is military ethics; especially conduct of war issues, ethical leadership, command climate, sacrifice and responsibility, warrior transitions, ethical responses to terrorism and the future of warfare. She is the author of many scholarly publications, and her groundbreaking book, *The Code of the Warrior: Exploring Warrior Values, Past and Present* was re-released in 2017 as an updated and expanded second edition. She is editor-in-chief for the *International Journal of Ethical Leadership* and an associate editor for the *Journal of Military Ethics*. Her additional scholarly interests include business/corporate and organizational ethics, bioethics, environmental ethics, meta-ethics, moral psychology, and ethics and emerging technology, including Artificial Intelligence (AI).

Lieutenant Colonel Kate Germano USMC, Retired

Kate Germano is a 20-year veteran of the Marine Corps and the author of *Fight Like A Girl: The Truth Behind How Female Marines Are Trained*, with Kelly Kennedy. After being relieved from command of the only all-female unit in the entire Department of Defense, she gained notoriety for taking a stand against the Marine Corps for gender bias and lowered standards and expectations for female recruits and Marines. Her writing has been published in national media outlets including the *New York Times*, *New York Post*, *Time* magazine, U.S. News and World Report, and the *Washington Post*. She has also been featured on NPR, Vice News Tonight, CSPAN, and the PBS NewsHour.

Lieutenant Junior Grade Max Goldwasser

Max Goldwasser graduated from the United States Naval Academy in 2016. He holds a Bachelors of Science in Cyber Operations. Upon graduating, Goldwasser reported to Corry Station, Pensacola to attend the Cryptologic Warfare Officer's Basic Course. In fall of 2016, Goldwasser checked in to the Navy Cyber Defense Operations Command in Suffolk, Virginia, where he has served on staff for Task Force 1020, responsible for managing distributed defensive cyberspace operations worldwide. In October of 2017, Goldwasser screened positively for the Tactical Information Officer program at NSW Special Reconnaissance Team Two, where he was due to report to at the end of 2018.

Lieutenant Commander Michael D. Good

Michael Good completed four sea tours and multiple deployments on three different guided missile destroyers in addition to multiple shore tours including the staff of the Chief of Naval Operations, Director of Surface Warfare. Nominated by his subordinates, he was awarded the 2009 Navy and Marine Association Leadership Award in the Department Head Category. He holds an MA in Philosophy of Religion and Ethics from Biola University and is enrolled as a PhD student in Philosophy at University of Maryland. Currently, he is Junior Permanent Military Professor, Department of Leadership, Ethics, and Law, United States Naval Academy. His main academic and practical interest is moral formation.

Dr Carl Jacob

Carl Jacob is attached to the University of Ottawa's Nursing History Research Unit (NHRU). He received his PhD in Education from the University of Québec, Montréal. In addition to writing on stress and resilience, programme and facilitator evaluation, as well as transformative and tacit learning, he is presently contributing to two books, namely: diversity and inclusion (LGBTQIA+) in the Canadian Armed Forces and facilitating and developing leaders as lifelong learners at the Royal Military College of Canada.

Dr Pauline Shanks Kaurin

Pauline Shanks Kaurin holds a PhD in Philosophy from Temple University, and is a specialist in military ethics, just war theory, philosophy of law and applied ethics. She is Associate Professor at Pacific Lutheran University in Tacoma, Washington and teaches courses in military ethics, warfare, business ethics, social and political philosophy and history of philosophy. She served as a Featured Contributor for The Strategy Bridge, and her recent work has appeared in War on the Rocks, Just Security, Newsweek and Real Clear Defense. She also serves as Professor of Military Ethics in the College of Leadership and Ethics at the Naval War College in Newport, Rhode Island.

Colonel Steven M. Kleinman USAF, Retired

Steven Kleinman, U.S. Air Force (Ret.) has 30 years of operational and leadership experience with assignments and deployments across the globe. He is a recognized subject matter expert in human intelligence, intelligence support to special operations, strategic interrogation, and resistance to interrogation. His military service includes combat campaigns in Central America and the Middle East and assignments as the director of the U.S. Air Force Combat Interrogation Course, the Department of Defense Senior Intelligence Officer for special survival/resistance to interrogation training, and as the Senior Intelligence Officer at both the Air Force major command and joint combatant command levels. He was a senior advisor to the Educing Information Study, the Director of National Intelligence-sponsored research effort tasked with studying the science that underpins strategic interrogation. He is also a founding member and current chairman of the research advisory committee for the High-Value Detainee Interrogation Group (HIG). He was called to testify on interrogation and detainee policy before five U.S. Congressional committees. He continues to serve as a senior advisor and subject matter expert for interrogation-related research conducted by government agencies and academic institutions worldwide. He has authored or co-authored nearly 30 professional papers that have appeared in major peer-reviewed journals. He earned a BA in psychology from the University of California, Davis, an MSc in Strategic Intelligence from the National Intelligence University, Washington, D.C., and an MSc in Forensic Sciences from National University, San Diego, California. He is also a graduate of the U.S. Air Force Air War College, the Air Command and Staff College, and the Strategy and Policy Program at the U.S. Naval War College.

Dr Daniel Lagacé-Roy

Daniel Lagacé-Roy is an associate professor at the Royal Military College of Canada (RMC) and the Head of the Military Psychology and Leadership (MPL) Department. At RMC, he teaches, amongst other courses, Military Professionalism and Ethics, Advanced Leadership, Military Psychology, and Psychology of Religious Conflicts. He previously taught Ethics at the Université du Québec in Rimouski, and at the University of Alberta in Edmonton. He served in the Canadian Forces from 1987 to 1995 (Regular) and from 1998 to 2001 (Reserves). He published *Ethics in the Canadian Forces: Tough Choices* (workbook and instructor manual), a *Mentoring Handbook*, and articles addressing various topics such as identity development, leadership, and cultural intelligence. He is also the co-editor of a book on *Military Ethics* and one on *Military Stress and Resilience*. Dr Lagacé-Roy received his PhD from the Université de Montréal, Québec.

Dr Peter Lee

Peter Lee is a Reader in Politics and Ethics at the University of Portsmouth, U.K. His academic interests include: the ethics and ethos of lethal military drone operations; the politics and ethics of war and military intervention; and the politics and ethics of identity. Peter's main research focus is the human dimension of drone operations in the U.K.'s Royal Air Force Reaper squadrons, with an emphasis on the place of personal ethics in the use of lethal force. From 2001 to 2008 he served as a Royal Air Force chaplain, and from 2008 to 2017 lectured in the ethics of war at Royal Air Force College, Cranwell.

Special Operations Chief Daniel Luna

Daniel Luna is the current SEAL Program Manager at the United States Naval Academy. SOC Luna classed up and graduated with BUDS class 228 and he was assigned to SEAL Team One where he served ten years completing five deployments. The deployments included two tours to Iraq, two to Afghanistan, one to PACOM and various other countries for joint training. In 2010 he screened positive for the Naval Special Warfare Development Group and continued various training and deployments while at that Command. His decorations include the Bronze Star Medal with Valor x 2, Purple Heart, Defense Meritorious Service Medal, Joint Commendation Medal, Navy Commendation Medal with Valor x 4, and other various unit and service awards. SOC Luna has an associate degree in Oceanography Technology from Coastline Community College, a bachelor's degree in Organizational Leadership from the University of Charleston and recently completed an executive master's degree in leadership from Georgetown University's McDonough School of Business.

Reverend Professor Philip McCormack MBE

Philip McCormack is the Principal of Spurgeon's College, London. Established in 1856 by Charles Haddon Spurgeon, the college is one of the leading Higher Education Theological Colleges in the U.K. Previously, Professor McCormack was an Assistant Chaplain General in the British Army and its academic lead on ethics nationally and internationally. An accredited minister of the Baptist Union of Great Britain, Professor McCormack holds PhDs from The Queen's University of Belfast in New Testament Studies and from Cranfield University in Philosophy and Strategic Studies. He is the Chair of an International Prize Committee for Military Ethics, an Honorary Professor of Practical Ethics in the Institute of Health and Society, University of Worcester, a Principal Fellow of the Higher Education Academy and President of the Naval Military & Air Force Bible Society.

Lieutenant Colonel Thomas McDermott DSO

Thomas McDermott is an Australian Army officer who also served 15 years in the British Army. He has worked in the U.K. Ministry of Defence, the EU Headquarters in Brussels, the Australian Army's HQ Forces Command in Sydney, and as the Chief of Staff of Australian amphibious forces. He took part in the 2003 Iraq invasion as a tank officer, and served three tours in Afghanistan (for which he was awarded the U.K.'s Distinguished Service Order). He holds fellowships at the Centre for Military Ethics (King's College London) and the Australian Centre for the Study of Armed Conflict and Society (University of New South Wales), and has published works on strategy and ethics. He is currently a PhD candidate at the Australian National University, studying strategic decision-making in Iraq.

Professor Peter Olsthoorn

Peter Olsthoorn is Associate Professor in Military Leadership and Ethics at the Netherlands Defence Academy, Breda. Besides leadership and ethics, he teaches on armed forces and society, war and media, and on ethics and fundamental rights in the European Joint Master's in Strategic Border Management. His research is mainly on topics such as military virtues, military medical ethics, and the ethics of border guarding. Among his publications are *Honor in Political and Moral Philosophy* (2015) and *Military Ethics and Virtues: An Interdisciplinary Approach for the 21st Century* (2011).

Mr Erik Phillips

Erik Phillips is a former U.S. Army Special Operations and contract interrogator and Arabic linguist. He has earned both a BA in Psychology and an MA in Psychological Science from the University of Colorado, Colorado Springs. With an overarching aim to validate and translate scientific research into meaningful best practices, Mr Phillips consults and provides in-depth interviewing and interrogation training to federal and local law enforcement. Mr Phillips currently serves as the Projects Manager of the 'What Works' Project, a program designed to identify and summarize leading-edge research for practitioners, policy makers, and behavioral scientists.

Dr Michael Robillard

Michael Robillard is a postdoctoral research fellow at the Uehiro Centre for Practical Ethics at the University of Oxford. He received his PhD from the University of Connecticut in 2016. Prior to that, he was a resident research fellow at the Stockdale Center for Ethical Leadership at the United States Naval Academy. His research focuses on a variety of philosophical topics which include: collective responsibility and global terrorism, the ethics of military recruitment, autonomous weapons, soldier enhancement, war and its relationship to future generations, and veteran/civil dialogues. Michael is an Iraq War veteran, a West Point graduate, and a former Airborne Ranger.

Professor Paul Robinson

Paul Robinson is a professor in the Graduate School of Public and International Affairs at the University of Ottawa. He is the author and editor of numerous works on Russian and Soviet history, military history, military ethics and defence policy. His latest book, *Grand Duke Nikolai Nikolaevich: Supreme Commander of the Russian Army,* was awarded the Distinguished Book Award for Biography by the Society of Military History. He has served as an officer in both the British and Canadian armies.

Brigadier General Benoit Royal, Retired

A research fellow closely associated with professional ethics at the Research Centre, Saint-Cyr Coëtquidan School, General (Ret.) Royal has accumulated significant command experience during his career. He has spent more than ten years of his career working outside of France: Germany, Polynesia, Reunion as well as the Ivory Coast, and he has completed several overseas courses (U.K., Nepal, U.S.A.). General Royal is a graduate of the War College and attended both the Centre for Higher Military Studies (CHEM) as well as the Institute for Higher Studies in National Defence (IHEDN). He spent three years as the Head of Army Corporate Communications and this was followed by three years as the Deputy Director Army Recruiting. He also was the Commandant of the School of French Artillery and Infantry for three years. Additionally, since June 2012, General Royal has been the President of the International Military Ethics Society in Europe (Euro-ISME). He is the author of numerous articles published in civilian and military periodicals, as well as several books, notably, *The Ethical Challenges of the Soldier – The French Experience.*

Captain Rick Rubel USN, Retired

Rick Rubel grew up in a navy family and graduated from the Naval Academy in 1972. He completed a 30-year career in which he had two commands. Capt. Rubel has taught the Core Ethics Course at the Naval Academy for 20 years. In 2002 he was appointed to be the first Distinguished Military Professor of Ethics at the Naval Academy. Since that time he has served as the Course Director of the Core Ethics Course for 16 years. In this capacity, he has co-authored and co-edited two textbooks and had several articles published in journals and encyclopedias. His textbooks and class notes are also in use by all of the 59 Naval Reserve Officer Training Corps (NROTC) universities in the country to teach the Ethics Course. He trains all of the new NROTC Professors of Naval Science around the country each summer, and he conducts a three-week summer seminar for all of the 41 Captains and Commanders at USNA who teach the course. In 2004 and 2006, the Chief of Navy Chaplains asked him to travel around the world with a team of Ethicists to train the Navy Chaplain Corps in Military Ethics. Between the 2004 and 2006 Seminars he wrote 18 case studies about navy Chaplains and the dilemmas that they face. He has given seminars to the Navy Chaplain School, Command Leadership School, and the Navy Judge Advocate General Corps (JAG), Navy Supply School, and Officer Candidate School (OCS) in Military Ethics. He has served on the Maryland State Board for Character Education the past ten years, and takes midshipmen out to Maryland schools to give talks on character to students. In his spare time, he has written several books for children on character and moral development.

Lieutenant General John F. Sattler USMC, Retired

John Sattler served as the Director of Strategic Plans and Policy (J5) on the Joint Staff from September 2006 until his retirement in August 2008. Prior to joining the Joint Staff, he was the Commanding General of the First Marine Expeditionary Force and Commander, Marine Corps Forces Central Command from September 2004 to August 2006. During this period, he commanded all forces in Al Anbar Provence in Iraq from September 2004 through March 2005. Prior to Commanding I MEF, he was the Director of Operations (J3) for Central Command from August 2003 to July 2004. In November 2002, he stood up and commanded the initial Combined Joint Task Force-Horn of Africa and established the Headquarters in the Country of Djibouti. He commanded the Second Marine Division, Camp Lejeune, North Carolina prior to sailing to the Horn of Africa. He is currently the Distinguished Chair of Leadership in the Stockdale Center for Ethical Leadership at the U.S. Naval Academy.

Associate Professor Michael Skerker

Michael Skerker is an associate professor in the Leadership, Ethics, and Law department at the U.S. Naval Academy. His academic interests include professional ethics, just war theory, moral pluralism, theological ethics, and religion and politics. Publications include works on ethics and asymmetrical war, moral pluralism, intelligence ethics, police ethics and the book *An Ethics of Interrogation* (2010). His most recent book *The Moral Equality of Combatants* is forthcoming.

Dr David G. Smith

David Smith is the co-author of *Athena Rising: How and Why Men Should Mentor Women* (2016) and Associate Professor of Sociology in the National Security Affairs Department at the United States Naval War College. As a sociologist trained in military sociology and social psychology, he focuses his research in gender, work, and family issues including dual career families, military family diversity, women in the military, retention of women, and performance evaluation bias.

Air Vice-Marshal J.J. Stringer CBE MA RAF

Johnny Stringer was born in Sale, Cheshire and educated at Watford Boys' Grammar School and New College, Oxford. Johnny was sponsored by the RAF through both Sixth Form and University, and after officer and pilot training, joined the Jaguar Force at RAF Coltishall in 1993. A Qualified Weapon Instructor, he flew operationally over the Former Yugoslavia and helped enforce the Northern Iraq No Fly Zone. His staff experience at Sqn Ldr and Wg Cdr encompassed tours in the Equipment Capability area of the U.K. Ministry of Defence, the RAF's HQ No. 1 Group, and as Military Assistant to Director General Typhoon. From 2007 to 2009, Johnny commanded 29 Squadron, the Typhoon Operational Conversion Unit at RAF Coningsby; leaving on promotion, he spent two years as Deputy Assistant Chief of Staff Joint Effects in the J3 Current Ops Division of the U.K. Permanent Joint Headquarters at Northwood. He returned to New College as a visiting Trenchard Fellow on the Oxford Changing Character of War programme in Autumn 2011. Between October 2012 and September 2014, Johnny commanded RAF Coningsby and its Typhoon Wing, supporting national and overseas Typhoon operations, and displayed the Spitfire and Hurricane with the Battle of Britain Memorial Flight. He was posted as ACOS Ops to HQ Air Command in August 2015 before commanding No. 83 Expeditionary Air Group as the U.K. Air Component Commander between October 2016– October 17, in charge of all national air operations in the fight against Daesh (Op SHADER) and across the Middle East. Promoted in February 2018, Johnny is currently Chief of Staff Joint Forces Command; he was awarded the CBE in the May 2018 Operational Honours List. Johnny is a graduate of the U.K. Advanced and Higher Command and Staff Courses, the Royal College of Defence Studies and holds Masters degrees from Oxford and Kings College London. Johnny is married to Lisa and has two sons. His interests include history, literature, food and drink, and cycling.

Air Commodore John Thomas RAF, Retired

John Thomas served in the Royal Air Force for 32 years, retiring as an Air Commodore. His responsibilities included being the U.K. MOD's first coordinator for policy matters with the UN in New York, serving as a Director in the U.K.'s Joint Services Command and Staff College, and as a Deputy Director of the Air Staff in the U.K. MOD. He was subsequently the U.K.'s Deputy Military Representative to the European Union in Brussels and the Defence and Air Attaché at the British Embassy, Paris. He is currently co-Executive Director of the International Society for Military Ethics in Europe (Euro-ISME).

Professor David Whetham

David Whetham is Professor of Ethics and the Military Profession in the Defence Studies Department of King's College London, based at the U.K.'s Joint Services Command and Staff College where he coordinates or delivers the military ethics component of courses for between two and three thousand British and international officers a year. David has held Visiting Fellowships at the U.S. Naval Academy, Annapolis, the Australian Defence College, Canberra, the University of Glasgow, the University of New South Wales and he was a British Academy Mid-Career Fellow in 2017–18. He is the Director of the King's Centre for Military Ethics, which has the aim of promoting best practice in the delivery of military ethics education worldwide.

Professor Jessica Wolfendale

Jessica Wolfendale is Professor of Philosophy at Marquette University. Prior to her current position, she was Associate Professor of Philosophy at West Virginia University. Her most recent book is *War Crimes: Causes, Excuses, and Blame* (with Matthew Talbert), (forthcoming). In addition, she is author of *Torture and the Military Profession* (2007), co-editor with Paolo Tripodi of *New Wars and New Soldiers: Military Ethics in the Contemporary World* (2011), and has published numerous articles and book chapters on topics including security, torture, terrorism, bioethics, and military ethics. Her work has appeared in journals including *Ethics and International Affairs, Journal of Political Philosophy, American Journal of Bioethics, Studies in Conflict and Terrorism*, and the *Journal of Military Ethics*.

PREFACE

What does Aristotle have to teach a fighter pilot? Most of the ethics professors included in this volume have heard this question from students at service academies and staff colleges at one time or another. It is not a question of simple sophomoric insouciance. After all, the study of character, once the dominant mode of academic moral reflection, fell out of favor in the seventeenth century. No one disputed the idea that people had to be honorable, temperate, brave, patient, generous, honest, and so on, but the more pressing questions during the Enlightenment were about the state's relationship with its citizens. Today, one might reasonably ask if a mode of thought developed in ages of the phalanx and the mounted knight is really relevant to adjudicate questions about civilian liability in counter-insurgent battlespaces, the permissibility of targeted killing by drone, and the advisability of covert offensive cyber operations.

Virtue always had a place in just war thinking, not only as a natural application of the dominant moral framework in classical and medieval times, but a purposive inquiry led by thinkers recognizing the moral hazards presented by war. A renewed interest by some scholars in the 1980s led to serious work on the topic of virtue, broadly – about the same time Michael Walzer's *Just and Unjust Wars* led to a resurgence in just war thinking. Curiously, this twin development did not result in a profusion of texts about *military* virtue. This is a significant gap. The basic conundrum of military virtue was never solved. How can someone cultivate character traits leading to success on the battlefield that are not maladaptive in the civilian world? The general idea associated with the cultivation of virtue is that a virtuous person will be a good person, good spouse, good neighbor, good citizen, and good professional, because virtues lead one to do the right thing "to the right person, to the right extent, at the right time, with the right aim, and in the right way." (*Nicomachean Ethics*, Bk II). Since virtues dispose one to respond excellently to all situations we might think that one needs to be a good person to be a good warfighter. Yet Aristotle himself speculates that the best soldiers might not be the best men. Someone living the good life of virtuous activity knows his life is valuable and therefore, may not be so quick to obey orders and charge into dangerous situations. Contemporary anecdotes have been related by officers who marveled at the technical brilliance of some peers and subordinates who are miserable people to deal with or who are liabilities ashore, literally, dangers to the community. Are these people anomalies or must one cultivate traits that are destructive in civilian life in order to flourish on the battlefield?

What does Aristotle have to teach a fighter pilot? There is a clear need to explore how the classical account of the virtues applies to the modern military environment characterized by high technology, asymmetrical warfare, gender integration, and religious extremism. For example, what does courage mean in the modern military for drone pilots launching weapons from thousands of miles away from their targets? In an integrated military, would it be unjust to treat male and female service personnel exactly the same? Is the virtue of truthfulness actually a liability for interrogators who are trained to use deceptive stratagems? How can an officer handle all the power she is given without becoming hubristic? Is there any room at all for compassion on the battlefield?

This volume is unique in the just war / military ethics literature in that it brings together academics and service personnel to address these questions in a format that is accessible and relevant to military professionals. Its 14 chapters each contain an overview article about a military virtue and case studies applying the virtue in modern military life. The reader will find Aristotle has much to teach fighter pilots as well as SIGINT analysts, artillery gunners, submariners, ordnancemen, snipers, linguists, and logisticians.

Michael Skerker
Annapolis, March 2019

INTRODUCTION

Military Virtues and Moral Relativism

Peter Olsthoorn

Introduction

Herodotus claimed that what we deem good and proper ultimately depends on where we stand: every society and epoch believes that the way it does things is the best way. To illustrate his argument, Herodotus described how at Darius's court Herodotus own Greek countrymen, who burned their dead, met with the Indian tribe of the Callatiae, who ate them. They were all convinced that their way was the best way (and appalled by the idea of having to perform the burial rites of the other). Only a madman, Herodotus concluded, would ridicule the customs of another people.[1] But what was an insight for Herodotus – that what we consider just and proper is relative – has become a commonplace today: those who teach ethics at a military institution will, sooner or later, encounter students who point out to their teacher that the Taliban stand as firm in their values as we do in ours.[2] This, then, should prove that our (and everyone else's) values are relative. 'One man's terrorist is another man's freedom fighter,' as the platitude goes. Clearly, such relativism effectively reduces ethical judgments to matters of opinion. Although most students who advance such relativistic views think that their argument is rather nuanced and philosophical, most moral philosophers hold that such a position is ultimately untenable – even if their opinions differ as to how exactly, and to what extent, full-blown

---

1 Herodotus, *The Histories Book 3*, chapter 38.
2 As a Taliban fighter famously remarked, "they love Pepsi-Cola, but we love death," Ian Buruma and Avishai Margalit, *Occidentalism: The West in the Eyes of Its Enemies* (New York: Penguin Books, 2004), 49.

relativism is wrong. Most agree with philosopher Simon Blackburn that the claim 'kicking babies for fun is wrong' is both true and objective, and think that the same claims can, equally true and objective, be made about apartheid, slavery and the torture of puppies.[3]

This introductory chapter looks at moral relativism from the perspective of virtues, especially military virtues.[4] Owing to the increased interest for virtues as an alternative to rule-based ethics, military virtues are increasingly seen as the best way to underpin the ethics education of military personnel. Virtues are typically described as stable character traits that are worth having, often working as correctives to our self-regarding inclinations.[5] Where duty-based ethics focuses on the act, that is, on what is wrong, right, permitted, or obligatory, the emphasis in virtue ethics is on terms that describe the actor, such as good and praiseworthy. This focus on the kind of person one wants to be makes that it has a much broader range than rule-based ethics. Being friendly, for instance, is a virtue, but it is not a duty.[6] Motives, emotions, character formation, personality and emotions are important in virtue ethics, something until recently allegedly overlooked by other schools in moral philosophy. That does not mean that there is anything radically new about an approach that centers on virtues, though. Most virtue ethicists draw on Aristotle, who held that performing virtuous acts makes us virtuous. Doing courageous deeds grows courage, for instance. It is this Aristotelian view on virtues that also underlies most literature on military virtues. What makes virtue ethics especially interesting for the military is its concern with character formation. It assumes that character can be developed, and that virtues are not to be understood as inborn or God-given qualities, but as dispositions that can be acquired through training and practice. Such an approach also fits the tendency of many Western militaries to move away from a largely functional approach towards a more aspirational approach that aims at making soldiers better persons, mainly based on the view that bad persons are not likely to form morally good soldiers – although they could still be effective ones.[7]

---

3   Simon Blackburn, *Ruling Passions* (Oxford: Oxford University Press, 1998), 317–18.

4   David Whetham has already briefly sketched what utilitarianism and deontology have to say on the topic, D. Whetham, "The challenge of ethical relativism in a coalition environment," *Journal of Military Ethics* 7 (2008): 307–308.

5   Philippa Foot, *Virtues and Vices and Other Essays in Moral Philosophy* (Oxford: Clarendon Press, 2002), 8–12.

6   Stan van Hooft, "Introduction," in *The Handbook of Virtue Ethics*, ed. S. van Hooft and N. Saunders (London: Routledge, 2014), 3.

7   P. Robinson, "Ethics training and development in the military," *Parameters* (Spring 2007), 22–36.

A question that lies at hand in the context of this volume is whether what counts as (military) virtues is place and time dependent, and at first sight a convincing case can be made that it is not. Some virtues are valued in all times and places[8] – mainly because they perform an important function in society. The disposition to tell the truth and keep our promises, for instance, has important beneficial consequences. Justice is another example of a universal virtue, but so is the more martial virtue of courage, because justice is of little value if we lack the courage to defend it. But if we take a closer look at courage, it also becomes clear that we should not overestimate the consensus on virtues: although all societies value courage, the kind of courage they prize may vary greatly. Aristotle, for instance, famously defined courage in his *Nicomachean Ethics* as the mean between rashness and cowardice,[9] and thought that this virtue is especially needed in battle – a brave man does not fear a noble death in war.[10] This conception of courage as a mean fitted the Greek phalanx very well, as an excess or a deficiency of courage would likewise destroy the organized whole it was. But this notion of courage is clearly worlds apart from what Gandhi envisioned when he pleaded for courageous but non-violent resistance to British colonial rule.[11] More generally, Aristotle believed he provided us with an objective description of human nature and the moral and intellectual virtues that spring from it, but in fact mainly described the traits an Athenian gentleman from fourth-century BC would ideally possess.[12] That supposedly objective account of human nature also motivated his defence of slavery. Apparently, arguments against slavery are mainly convincing to those who subscribe to the modern Western idea that all people are equal – a notion that was alien to Aristotle.[13] His idea that people are not equal also informed his hierarchical conception of justice, which is markedly different from our egalitarian conception of that universal virtue.

The question that underlies the remainder of this chapter is not about the relativity of virtues, however, but about whether some virtues themselves further (or lessen) moral relativism. An illustrative example is respect, a virtue that can induce military personnel to adopt a morally

---

8 Jack Donnelly, "Cultural relativism and universal human rights," *Human Rights Quarterly* 6 (1984): 414.

9 Aristotle, *Nicomachean Ethics* (Indianapolis: Bobbs Merrill Company, 1962), 1115.

10 Aristotle, *Nicomachean Ethics*, 1107b, 1115a, 1115b.

11 Christopher W. Gowans, "Virtue Ethics and Moral Relativism," in *A Companion to Relativism*, ed. S. D. Hales (Malden, MA: Wiley-Blackwell, 2011), 397.

12 Gowans, "Virtue Ethics and Moral Relativism," 394.

13 See also Emrys Westacott, "Moral Relativism," in *Internet Encyclopedia of Philosophy*, ed. J. Feiser and B. Dowden (2012).

relativistic position. In recent years Western military personnel faced situations "in which the conduct of the local population in a deployment area (a different culture) [was] experienced as conflicting with one's own personal moral and cultural values."[14] In preparation for such situations, pre-deployment training teaches Western military personnel knowledge of and respect for other cultures. And for good reasons: Western forces can be involuntarily offensive in their dealings with the local population if they have insufficient knowledge of local sensitivities, and "a lack of cultural relativity in their occupation 'technique.'"[15] But there is another side to this: emphasizing the relativity of our values, and the need to respect other people's mores, provides Western soldiers in, for example, Sudan, Afghanistan or Mali with a ground for not intervening in cases of corruption or the cruel treatment of women and children.

In Afghanistan, Western military personnel regularly witnessed a now well-documented practice called *bacha bazi*. That last phrase translates as 'boy play,' and involves the sexual molesting of what are euphemistically called dancing boys: men in positions of power 'own' femininely dressed boys who serve tea, dance – and have to perform sexual services. That the success and perhaps even safety of the mission to some extent depended on good relations with the same local leaders who may be involved in *bacha bazi* probably explains why now and then military personnel were instructed to look away.[16] At other times such instructions stemmed from the belief that showing cultural respect was by itself instrumental to the democratization and restoration of security in contested areas.[17] And sometimes soldiers had to do without guidelines about how to act: David Whetham describes how in recent missions soldiers from Australia, Great Britain, Canada and the United States "… kept asking for guidance when faced with situations that they knew

---

14   Michelle Schut, *Soldiers as Strangers: Morally and Culturally Critical Situations during Military Missions* (doctoral dissertation, University of Nijmegen, 2015), 106.

15   Victoria Fontan, "Polarization Between Occupier and Occupied in Post-Saddam Iraq: Colonial Humiliation and the Formation of Political Violence," *Terrorism and Political Violence* 18 (2006): 219.

16   David Pugliese, "Former soldier still fights to protect Afghan boys from abuse," *Ottawa Citizen*, September 21, 2009; J. Goldstein, "U.S. Soldiers Told to Ignore Sexual Abuse of Boys by Afghan Allies," *New York Times*, September 20, 2015.

17   Marcus Schulzke, "The Antinomies of Population-Centric Warfare: Cultural Respect and the Treatment of Women and Children in U.S. Counterinsurgency Operations," *Studies in Conflict & Terrorism* 39 (2016): 410–11. At first sight, such straightforward instructions could turn potential moral dilemmas into tests of integrity: it is clear what is the correct way to proceed, yet there are reasons (in this case one's own moral repugnance) to follow a different course of action. S. Coleman, "The problems of duty and loyalty," *Journal of Military Ethics* 8 (2009): 105–106.

'just weren't right'" but did not receive it.[18] For Dutch military personnel guidelines about how to deal with *bacha bazi* were equally absent.[19]

When the political and military leadership fail to provide guidelines on how to act in such situations, responsibility shifts to the men and women on the ground. For soldiers, an encounter with *bacha bazi* can then become a moral dilemma: the wish to further human rights and the rule of law, and to improve the situation of the boys in question, conflicts with their feeling that it is not legitimate to impose Western values on members of other cultures. But even with guidelines in place, proscribing for instance that one should not interfere, there still might be a dilemma: it brings personal principles into conflict with laws, rules and procedures, and soldiers have to choose between following the rules and following conscience.[20] If military personnel subsequently decide to look away, their respect for other cultures comes not only at the cost of one's own values and of values most people consider to be universal; it evidently also harms the human dignity and physical integrity of the victims. To put it somewhat polemically: more culturally competent soldiers are sometimes less morally competent, that is, more prone to look away and put aside their own values.[21] A soldier deployed to Afghanistan explained: "During mission-specific training, we didn't discuss this subject at all. But we did learn that we must respect local culture."[22] Yet exactly how respectful for local cultural practices should a soldier be?

Why Moral Relativism is Probably Wrong

Moral philosophers routinely do away with undiluted moral relativism (yet at the same time make sure not to identify themselves with a too objectivistic position), and although this chapter does not intend to delve too deeply into the philosophical nuances of the matter, it is worthwhile to briefly recap their line of argument. Moral relativism consists of an empirical claim, stating that there is deep and widespread moral disagreement, and a meta-ethical claim, holding that the truth or justification of moral judgments is

---

18 David Whetham, "ABCA Coalition Operations in Afghanistan, Iraq and Beyond: Two Decades of Military Ethics Challenges and Leadership Responses," in *Military Ethics and Leadership*, ed. P. Olsthoorn (Leiden: Brill, 2017), 98.

19 Schut, *Soldiers as Strangers*.

20 But even if 'guidelines' mitigate the dilemma, military personnel might still suffer from feelings of guilt and failure; Schut, *Soldiers as Strangers*.

21 Schut, *Soldiers as Strangers*.

22 Schut, *Soldiers as Strangers*, 116.

"relative to the moral standard of some person or group of persons."[23] Students forwarding a relativist position subscribe to both claims, and will feel that the empirical claim substantiates the metaethical one. But does it? And is that initial empirical claim really true? The answer to the latter question is not necessarily affirmative; just think of the near universal prohibition on killing and stealing, the golden rule 'do unto others as you would have them do unto you' and the more or less global appeal of human rights.[24] We already noted that also some virtues enjoy universal support. Perhaps there is more consensus than meets the eye. Most of what looks like disagreement about values is in fact disagreement about the norms that we derive from these values, and about what a person has to do to live up to these values: both those who eat their dead, and those who burn them, do what they think amounts to paying respect to the dead.[25]

What is more, our idea that the sexual molestation of dancing boys and corruption are part of Afghan culture is misguided; like everyone else, most Afghans think both practices immoral – according to one research eighty per cent of the Afghan population disapproves of the practice of *bacha bazi*.[26] Similarly, Western military personnel might see a superior who withholds part of a police officer's salary as merely confirming to local cultural mores, but the officer involved sees it as corruption. That most Afghans do not think dancing boys and corruption are morally acceptable or part of their culture suggests that there is some basic morality that most people will agree on. Afghan law, by the way, forbids both practices. Clearly, corruption and the sexual molestation of children do not stand up against internal evaluation: they are not defensible within the value framework of Afghan society.[27] Often, such practices, sometimes defended by claiming that the idea of human rights is too Western, have only the loosest of connections with local culture.[28]

---

23 Christopher Gowans, "Moral Relativism," *The Stanford Encyclopedia of Philosophy* (Winter 2016 Edition), ed. Edward N. Zalta. https://plato.stanford.edu/archives/win2016/entries/moral-relativism/.

24 Gowans, "Moral Relativism." These examples belong by and large to the rule-based domain; the utilitarian credo of the greatest happiness to the greatest number suggest there is also a consequentialist *summum bonum* we can all agree on.

25 Michael Sheenan, "Moral Relativism," in *Principles of Health Care Ethics*, Second edition, ed. R. E. Ashcroft, et al. (Chichester: John Wiley & Sons, 2007), 94. See also Donnelly, "Cultural relativism," 404–405.

26 The West ousted the Taliban for a variety of reasons, but their poor human rights record was certainly among them. However, the Taliban did suppress the practice of *bachi bazi* during their years in power; it resurfaced after the Taliban reign ended. To complicate things even further: most Afghans, although opposed to *bacha bazi*, do not think that Western military personnel should intervene. Schut, *Soldiers as Strangers*.

27 See also Donnelly, "Cultural relativism," 406.

28 Donnelly, "Cultural relativism."

But even if most or all Afghans thought that child molestation was right, would that really imply that we should respect their position? Most will hold not, because they believe child molesting is a clear violation of important external standards; condoning every practice that meets internal standards would overlook that we are also member of a more cosmopolitan moral community.[29] That the majority in certain societies endorsed or endorses certain practices – say slavery, or female genital mutilation – does not make these practices right. Thinking that a practice is 'right' if a majority in a society agree with it would, first of all undercut any criticism we might want to level at a society (and that could be our own society) that permits slavery or any other abhorrent practice. As long as the majority supports slavery, they will represent the norm, and from a relativist position those who oppose it would be mistaken. Until, of course, for some reason the abolishers have become the majority.[30] In the same way, if relativists were right we could not reasonably say that the small minority of U.S. southerners that opposed slavery in the nineteenth century, or the equally small minority in Germany that resisted the Nazi regime a century later, were acting morally in doing so. That is an outlandish point of view for many reasons, one of the more important ones being that it is criticism from within a society that can work as a catalyst for moral progress.[31] Soldiers on mission sometimes end up believing that "the situation is culturally determined and therefore unchangeable," when it is in fact not.[32] Gradual moral disengagement plays a role to: referring to *bacha bazi*, a member of the Dutch military explained that "[t]he peculiar thing is that it becomes more and more 'normal,' which is a phenomenon known as 'mission creep.' ... After six months, you start to adjust and start to assimilate local customs and we practically never talked about it, you get used to it."[33]

Embracing the relativist position would not only make moral progress less likely to happen, however; it would also effectively do away with the idea that moral progress exists in the first place.[34] We would have no ground to say that a society that has abolished slavery, or the use of the rack

---

29 Donnelly, "Cultural relativism," 407.

30 See also William H. Shaw, *Utilitarianism and the Ethics of War* (London and New York: Routledge, 2016), 12; Whetham, "ABCA Coalition Operations," 93.

31 Kwame A. Appiah shows in his book *The Honor Code* how something that was once thought honorable can be turned relatively quickly into something to laugh about, as happened to the practice of dueling in Great Britain, or as something backward, which was the fate of foot binding in China. See K. A. Appiah, *The Honor Code* (New York: W. W. Norton, 2010), especially 51, 100, 162.

32 Schut, *Soldiers as Strangers*, 94.

33 Schut, *Soldiers as Strangers*, 116.

34 See also Shaw, *Utilitarianism and the Ethics of War*, 12; Whetham, "ABCA Coalition Operations," 93.

on suspects and the drawing and quartering of those who confess, is better than a society that still permits these practices. In *The Code of the Warrior* Shannon French gives us the (in the debate about moral relativism more often used) example of Tsujigiri: after receiving a new sword, a samurai tests whether it is sharp enough to cut an adversary in two by trying it out on a random peasant passing by.[35] It is difficult to see how abandoning such a practice could *not* amount to moral progress. Only the most radical forms of relativism do not see a role for at least some very basic rights to serve as a check on all too particularistic practices.[36] Not speaking out against such practices also overlooks that tolerance is, like respect, a matter of reciprocity: there is no obligation to 'bear' the intolerant.[37]

But although all-out moral relativism is unattainable, a certain modesty is in place when we are confronted with cultural practices that are alien to us – as Herodotus already reminded us, our own deeply held convictions might be more a product of our cultural surrounding than we like to think. That courage meant very different things to Aristotle and Ghandi, as we noted earlier, points in the same direction. That leaves us with the not so spectacular yet probably correct conclusion that the truth lies somewhere between radical relativism and radical universalism.[38] But which virtues would fit such a middle position best?

Virtues Needed (and Not Needed)

Established virtues such as courage dominate the lists of virtues and values of most militaries.[39] It is also these virtues that will typically be in the foreground in the literature on military virtues – with chapters on wisdom, patience, temperance, humility and compassion, this volume is partly an exception to that rule. But although there is evidently still an important role for the conventional soldierly virtues, it is equally evident that, however instrumental in attaining the objectives of the military, they are not particularly helpful to military personnel confronted with "morally and culturally critical situations"[40] such as corruption or child abuse. Because military personnel today have to deal with more than just opposing forces,

---

35 Shannon E. French, *The Code of the Warrior: Exploring Warrior Values Past and Present* (Lanham: Rowman & Littlefield, 2003); see also Sheehan, "Moral Relativism," 95.

36 See also Donnelly, "Cultural relativism."

37 Rainer Forst, "Toleration," *The Stanford Encyclopedia of Philosophy* (Fall 2017 Edition), ed. Edward N. Zalta. https://plato.stanford.edu/archives/fall2017/entries/toleration/.

38 See also, for instance, Donnelly, "Cultural Relativism."

39 Robinson, "Ethics training."

40 Schut, "Soldiers as Strangers."

that is a cause for some concern. The virtues we teach military personnel should suit their task, and today they are not only the more martial ones. But we have also seen that a less archetypical military virtue like respect does more harm than good if it provides soldier with grounds to look away. It is therefore important that respect is balanced by other virtues that can function as correctives to too much relativism. To that purpose, we first examine another military virtue that has a less bellicose ring to it, moral courage, and briefly juxtapose it against another possible candidate, the somewhat related virtue of integrity.

We already noted that Aristotle equated courage with physical courage on the battlefield.[41] But although physical courage is an important and for a soldier a defining virtue, it primarily benefits colleagues and the larger organization. Aristotle paid no attention to the just as important virtue of moral courage, which has a much wider reach. Where military virtues such as physical courage are rather functional (loyalty, obedience and discipline are other examples) and aim mainly at good outcomes for the military, moral courage is a more outward looking virtue the beneficiaries of which are the outsiders the military is there to protect.[42] Although some will hold physical courage in higher regard than moral courage because in the case of the latter it is 'only' one's reputation that is at risk, this underrates the degree to which people fear the censure of those whose judgment matters to them. Moral courage asks us to uphold our principles even if others disagree, and perhaps hold us in contempt for sticking to them; it requires "the capacity to overcome the fear of shame and humiliation in order to admit one's mistakes, to confess a wrong, to reject evil conformity, to denounce injustice, and to defy immoral or imprudent orders."[43] This ability to withstand censure from friends and colleagues if that is what doing right requires is an important subspecies of courage. A paradigmatic example of some time ago is Hugh Thompson, Jr., the helicopter pilot who did everything in his power to stop his fellow U.S. soldiers from killing Vietnamese villagers in My Lai in 1968 and reported the incident to his superiors afterwards.

On first sight, moral courage is somewhat akin to integrity, as they both expect us to uphold our principles when others disagree. But there is an important difference between integrity and moral courage: the latter aims at a moral end outside oneself, whereas integrity is in its everyday meaning (which is somewhat different from the meaning it has in the

---

41 Aristotle, *Nicomachean Ethics*, 1115a.

42 In the end this is in the interest of soldiers too: the inability to prevent unethical conduct can cause moral injury. B. T. Litz, et al., "Moral injury and moral repair in war veterans: A preliminary model and intervention strategy," *Clinical Psychology Review*, 29 (2009).

43 William I. Miller, *The Mystery of Courage* (Cambridge, MA: Harvard University Press, 2000), 254.

chapter on integrity in this volume) about standing up for one's personal beliefs – meaning that committed slave holders and devout Nazis could also claim to possess this good quality as long as they live by their own principles. Although we *could* say that such persons possess integrity, we reserve the term morally courageous for those who speak out against them. Whether integrity works out for the good depends on the values someone actually adheres to. That makes integrity intrinsically subjective, and no doubt there have been soldiers who were clearly in the wrong when they acted from personnel principles (and at least *some* conscientious objectors fall under that heading). Integrity is not the antidote to moral relativism we seek, because it is itself a virtue with a clear relativistic core.

So moral courage does a better job as a check on too much moral relativism; there is undeniably something morally objectivistic about exercising moral courage. It is hard to envisage how the just mentioned My Lai hero Hugh Thompson could have stood up for what he believed in if he had at the same time been convinced of the relativity of these beliefs. Thompson acted on ideas about what his country and organization should stand for, not on merely personal values. He later stated in a lecture on moral courage that the soldiers involved in the massacre "were not military people," suggesting that it was a military – and hence not a personal – ethos that was guiding him.[44] One could say that moral courage can fulfill the role often designated for integrity, without having its manifest shortcomings.

Moral courage can only perform that function if militaries allow room for it, however. Although most militaries claim to deem it a plus to have among its personnel principled people who dare to blow the whistle if necessary or to stop a colleague who is about to commit a wrong, in reality military organizations too often offer a fairly unfriendly environment for acting on moral principles, especially when these principles conflict with organizational interests. The emphasize militaries put on loyalty, another quintessential military virtue and subject of a later chapter, might very well be to blame for that. As a consequence, soldiers who take a principled stance sometimes end up as martyrs for a good cause rather than as models for their colleagues. Thompson became the victim of orchestrated slander after the My Lai scandal broke out. More recently, Joe Darby, the sergeant who in January 2004 went to the U.S. Army Criminal Investigation Command with the Abu Ghraib pictures, had to live in protective custody after his name became public. Some soldiers who did intervene to stop child abuse in Afghanistan saw their careers within the military jeopardized.[45]

---

44 Thompson's remarks can found at http://www.usna.edu/Ethics/_files/documents/ThompsonPg1-28_Final.pdf.

45 Goldstein, "Soldiers Told to Ignore Sexual Abuse."

Conclusion

That there exists disagreement on what is right and what is wrong does not mean that we have to embrace the position of the moral relativist. That some might think that kicking babies for fun or torturing puppies is all right does not imply that we are wrong in condemning these practices. According to Thomas Scanlon, thinking about right and wrong is "thinking about what could be justified to others on grounds that they, if appropriately motivated, could not reasonably reject."[46] Clearly, the puppy torturer, the samurai who cuts a farmer in two, the slaveholder and the police commander with a young boy chained to his bedpost all fail that test. As human rights expert Jack Donnelly writes: "Failure to act or even speak out against the grossest affronts to human dignity overseas on the grounds of cultural relativism would be widely – and I believe correctly – perceived as moral cowardice."[47] One could say that the military has a role in addressing flagrant violations of human dignity on the macro level: it is increasingly used for the promotion of democracy, the rule of law, and human rights, sometimes among people who do not yet count these things among the values of their culture.[48] But how does that translate for the men and women on the ground? And how do we prepare them?

Militaries traditionally found the answer to that last question in providing clear rules. That emphasis on rules makes sense in many aspects, most of all because it provides both military personnel and outsiders, say the local population in a mission area, with some security regarding the way they are treated. Such a confidence in the salutary power of rules has its downsides, though, for instance that rules are impotent when no one is around and lack the flexibility necessary in today's missions. Also, rules are often more about inducing people to refrain from unethical behavior than about motivating them to behave humanely.[49] But perhaps the most important drawback of an overreliance on rules is that it can impede the ability to see the moral aspect of what one is doing (or not doing), while that

---

46 Thomas M. Scanlon, *What We Owe to Each Other* (Cambridge, MA: The Belknap Press of Harvard University Press, 1998), 5.

47 Donnelly, "Cultural relativism," 404.

48 "'The reason we were here is because we heard the terrible things the Taliban were doing to people, how they were taking away human rights,' said Dan Quinn, a former Special Forces captain who beat up an American-backed militia commander for keeping a boy chained to his bed as a sex slave," Goldstein, "Soldiers Told to Ignore Sexual Abuse." Somewhat similar: "'It's disgusting,' said Schouten, now retired after eight years in the military. 'We're telling people that we're trying to build a nation there and we let this happen?'" Pugliese, "Former Soldier Fights to Protect Afghan Boys."

49 Albert Bandura, "Selective moral disengagement in the exercise of moral agency," *Journal of Moral Education* (2002), 31.

ability is evidently an important prerequisite for morally sound decision making. Soldiers should have some leeway in that decision making to keep them from committing so-called "crimes of obedience."[50]

Making good use of this leeway presupposes a virtuous disposition, and many militaries hence see a virtue-based approach to ethics as an important complement to rules imposed from above in their effort to make their personnel behave ethically. This volume aims to help militaries in that effort. Virtues such as those elaborated on in the following chapters can provide guidance to military personnel in ambiguous situations, where providing general rules and guidelines for such complex situations will not work – and where militaries are hence disinclined to give them. We have seen how moral courage is an example of a virtue that can form an antidote to too radical forms of relativism, and the accompanying tendency to put aside one's own values. It can be of help in morally complicated missions, but so can some of the other essential virtues developed in this book.

Some might feel we need a more cosmopolitan set of militaries virtues. If true, that still does not mean we have to design a new set of virtues from scratch. Of the four time-proven cardinal virtues of courage, wisdom, temperance and justice, only courage has made it to the traditional lists of military virtues and values. Wisdom, temperance and justice have not, but are today probably as necessary as courage is. Happily, all three have their own chapter in this volume. Another way forward would be to interpret the existing virtues somewhat less narrowly. Conceptions of courage should include moral courage, as we have seen, but likewise militaries could, for instance, interpret loyalty in such a way as that it includes loyalty to a profession, not just loyalty to one's group and organization. The following chapters provide ways forward for more such comprehensive interpretations too.

References

Appiah, K. A. *The Honor Code*. New York: W. W. Norton, 2010.
Aristotle. *Nicomachean Ethics*. Indianapolis: Bobbs Merrill Company, 1962.
Bandura, A. "Selective moral disengagement in the exercise of moral agency," *Journal of Moral Education* 31 (2002): 101–19.

---

50 Herbert C. Kelman and V. Lee Hamilton, *Crimes of Obedience: Toward a Social Psychology of Authority and Responsibility* (New Haven, CT: Yale University Press, 1989). A recent handbook on military ethics states that "in any situation where law and ethics set different standards, a member of the military profession will follow the higher standard, inevitably the one required by ethics," S. Coleman, *Military Ethics* (Oxford: Oxford University Press, 2013), 268.

Blackburn, S. *Ruling Passions*. Oxford: Oxford University Press, 1998.

Buruma, I. and A. Margalit, *Occidentalism: The West in the Eyes of Its Enemies*. New York: Penguin Books, 2004.

Coleman, S. "The problems of duty and loyalty," *Journal of Military Ethics* 8 (2009): 105–15.

Coleman, S. *Military Ethics*. Oxford: Oxford University Press, 2013.

Donnelly, J. "Cultural relativism and universal human rights," *Human Rights Quarterly* 6 (1984): 400–419.

Fontan, V. "Polarization Between Occupier and Occupied in Post-Saddam Iraq: Colonial Humiliation and the Formation of Political Violence," *Terrorism and Political Violence* 18 (2006): 217–38.

Foot, P. *Virtues and Vices and Other Essays in Moral Philosophy*. Oxford: Clarendon Press, 2002.

French, S. E. *The Code of the Warrior*. Lanham, MD: Rowman & Littlefield, 2003.

Goldstein, J. "U.S. Soldiers Told to Ignore Sexual Abuse of Boys by Afghan Allies," *New York Times*, September 20, 2015.

Gowans, C. "Moral Relativism," *The Stanford Encyclopedia of Philosophy* (Winter 2016 Edition), edited by Edward N. Zalta. https://plato.stanford.edu/archives/win2016/entries/moral-relativism/.

Gowans, C. "Virtue Ethics and Moral Relativism," in *A Companion to Relativism*, edited by S. D. Hales. Malden, MA: Wiley-Blackwell, 2011, 391–410.

Hooft, S. van, "Introduction," in *The Handbook of Virtue Ethics*, edited by S. van Hooft and N. Saunders. London: Routledge, 2014, 1–14.

Kelman, H. C., and Hamilton, V. L. *Crimes of Obedience: Toward a Social Psychology of Authority and Responsibility*. New Haven, CT: Yale University Press, 1989.

Litz, B. T., Stein, E. Delaney, L. Lebowitz, W. P. Nash, C. Silva and S. Maguen, "Moral injury and moral repair in war veterans: A preliminary model and intervention strategy," *Clinical Psychology Review* 29 (2009): 695–706.

Miller, W. I. *The Mystery of Courage*. Cambridge, MA: Harvard University Press, 2000.

Pugliese, D. "Former soldier still fights to protect Afghan boys from abuse," *Ottawa Citizen*, September 21, 2009.

Robinson, P. "Ethics training and development in the military," *Parameters*, Spring 2007, 22–36.

Scanlon, T. M. *What We Owe to Each Other*. Cambridge, MA: The Belknap Press of Harvard University Press, 1998.

Schulzke, M. "The Antinomies of Population-Centric Warfare: Cultural Respect and the Treatment of Women and Children in U.S. Counterinsurgency Operations," *Studies in Conflict & Terrorism* 39 (2016): 405–22.

Schut, M. *Soldiers as Strangers: Morally and Culturally Critical Situations during Military Missions*, doctoral dissertation, University of Nijmegen, 2015.

Shaw, W. H. *Utilitarianism and the Ethics of War*. London and New York: Routledge, 2016.

Sheenan, M. "Moral Relativism," in R. E. Ashcroft, A. Dawson, H. Draperband and J. R. McMillan, *Principles of Health Care Ethics*, Second Edition. Chichester: John Wiley & Sons, 2007.

Westacott, E. "Moral Relativism," in *Internet Encyclopedia of Philosophy*, edited by J. Feiser and B. Dowden, 2012.

Whetham, D. "The challenge of ethical relativism in a coalition environment," *Journal of Military Ethics* 7 (2008): 302–16.

Whetham, D. "ABCA Coalition Operations in Afghanistan, Iraq and Beyond: Two Decades of Military Ethics Challenges and Leadership Responses," in *Military Ethics and Leadership*, edited by Peter Olsthoorn. Leiden: Brill, 2017, 86–103.

Virtues or Values?

Philip McCormack

Introduction

When an organisation produces and issues its code of ethics, often specific to the needs of that particular organisation or institution, it frequently contains a brief introduction from the Chief Executive, Chairman or within the military, a Service Chief. The British Army's *Values and Standards* booklet is a classic example. This is a top down exercise. Very good reasons why this should be so can be easily imagined. In some instances, the 'brand' of the organisation will be inextricably linked with the professional behaviour of its people. In others, the conduct of its personnel outside of the workplace might affect public perception of the 'brand.' The approach taken by institutions regarding a code of ethics, however, is frequently premised upon certain assumptions: firstly, that personnel within an organisation/ institution will understand the ethical language used; secondly, that the shared, societal frameworks necessary for ethical concepts to be understood are known, recognised and accepted; and thirdly, that those using the code of ethics understand the moral landscape they have to navigate. This chapter will explore the problem of this approach, before setting the question of virtues or values in an operational dimension. It will contend that a virtue ethics approach is better suited to equip preparing professional militaries for operational service, especially in hostile and contested environments.

Virtues and Values: A Brief Description

The Greek word for virtue is arete (ἀρετή), which means excellence. Virtue ethics focuses upon the person and what their action(s) or behaviour reveals about the moral character of that individual.[1] This theory therefore, looks at the virtue or moral character of the person carrying out an action, rather than at ethical duties and rules, or the consequences of particular actions. Unlike the other major ethical theories, virtue ethics is concerned with the whole of a person's life, rather than particular episodes or actions. The creation of moral character was thought by the Greeks to enable *Eudaimonia*, which can be translated as 'well-being,' 'happiness' and in the context of virtue ethics, 'human flourishing.' *Eudaimonia* in this sense is not subjective but an objective state. It characterises, to the community that espouses a virtuous life, the well-lived life. It is in Plato's *The Apology of Socrates*, that we find that a virtuous life is the product of an examined life. In the *Apology*, Socrates is on trial for his life. He is charged, among other things, with corrupting the youth of Athens. Towards the end of the trial he makes his famous statement 'that the unexamined life is not worth living for a human being.' Socrates' commitment to life lived according to virtue, or moral excellence, compelled him to live an examined life. An unexamined life was not worth living because it would not be *his* life but one already determined by others. Although Socrates expounded the virtuous life, he would not have desired anyone, especially the youth of Athens to embrace his theory of an examined life unthinkingly.

Each individual has natural tendencies: some positive and some negative. These can be encouraged, developed or discouraged by a range of influences. In Greek culture it was understood that moral development relied upon good role models. The virtuous agent acts as a role model and the student emulates his or her example, from which 'right' habits could be developed. In virtue ethics, the moral agent does not act merely out of an unreflective response, but has come to recognise the value of virtue and why it is the appropriate response. Virtue is chosen knowingly for its own sake. In this regard, good habits shape the growth of character, which in turn influences decisions. The Greeks understood that the development of moral character takes time: many viewed it as a lifetime exercise. But once it is firmly established, one will normally act consistently, predictably and appropriately in a variety of situations. There are four cardinal virtues:[2]

---

1   The reader should note that classical and modern conceptions of virtue are, by necessarily, somewhat conflated in this short overview piece.
2   The Greeks recognised many virtues but it is common to refer to four cardinal virtues. The definitions offered above are not exhaustive. The Greek words are capable of bearing several nuances or shades of meaning.

- Prudence (φρόνησις, *phronēsis*) or the practical application of wisdom
- Justice (δικαιοσύνη, *dikaiosynē*) meaning that which is right or fair
- Temperance (σωφροσύνη, *sōphrosynē*) the practice of self-control or moderation'
- Courage (ἀνδρεία, *andreia*) the ability to act in the face of fear.

When taken together the virtues provide a moral framework[3] from which an individual can construct their unique character. The Greeks believed that a life lived according to virtue was a life well lived.

For any culture or society to exist there must be some ethical standards that are shared and these are often reflected in the common values of that culture or society. Frequently there are common values that do not vary substantially from culture to culture.[4] In their work to create a meta-inventory of values, Cheng and Fleischmann identified 16 value concepts from 12 different value inventories created by leading experts from a wide range of disciplines that focus on human values.[5] These 16 value concepts were: 1) *freedom*, 2) *helpfulness*, 3) *accomplishment*, 4) *honesty*, 5) *self-respect*, 6) *intelligence*, 7) *broad-mindedness*, 8) *creativity*, 9) *equality*, 10) *responsibility*, 11) *social order*, 12) *wealth*, 13) *competence*, 14) *justice*, 15) *security*, and 16) *spirituality*.[6] This list indicates that values may have a moral content (honesty or equality) or they may be morally neutral (intelligence or creativity). In this chapter, the word 'values' is employed in the context of 'moral value': i.e., that this value has a moral or ethical good. In a post-modern age[7] values are often understood as being subjective, and therefore they can mean whatever an individual or group wants them to mean.[8] Unless values are ground upon and derived from an ethical good they can become morally subjective, even within a social group that claims to adhere to them.[9] This fluidity of meaning in combination with multifaceted societal changes has created profound problems for any military wishing to prepare its professional forces for service in complex operational environments.

---

3   The limitations of this paper prohibit any further exploration of how the moral framework may be applied.

4   David Whetham, "Ethics, Law and Conflict," in *Ethics, Law and Military Operations*, ed. D. Whetham (Basingstoke: Palgrave Macmillan, 2011), 17.

5   An-Shou Cheng and Kenneth R. Fleischmann, "Developing a Meta-Inventory of Human Values," *Proceedings of the American Society for Information* 47, no. 1 (2010): 1–10.

6   Cheng and Fleischmann, "Developing a Meta-Inventory," 9.

7   Ulrich Beck, *World Risk Society* (Cambridge: Polity, 1999), prefers to use the term 'late-modernity' rather than 'post-modern.'

8   Stephen Deakin, "Ethics and the British Army's Values and Standards," *The British Army Review* 140 (2006): 40 makes the same point.

9   See Phillip McCormack, "Grounding British Army Values Upon an Ethical Good," March 30, 2015. http://www.cgscfoundation.org/wp-content/uploads/2015/04/McCormack-GroundingBritishArmyValues.pdf.

Stating the Problem

The Fragmentation of Ethical Language

In 1981, the Scottish philosopher Alasdair MacIntyre published his well-known work *After Virtue*.[10] Although it has gone through several editions, apart from his response to criticism, he stated in the 2007 edition that "I have found no reason for abandoning the major contentions of *After Virtue*."[11] It is his claim concerning the use of ethical language that is a particularly relevant starting point to sketching out a significant problem. MacIntyre's 'Disquieting Suggestion' in Chapter 1 is based upon an imaginary world he constructs where a

> … Know-Nothing political movement takes power and successfully abolishes science teaching in schools and universities, imprisoning and executing the remaining scientists. Later still there is a reaction against this destructive movement and enlightened people seek to revive science, although they have largely forgotten what it was. But all they possess are fragments: a knowledge of experiments detached from any knowledge of the theoretical context which gave them significance; parts of theories unrelated to the other bits and pieces or theory.[12]

In this imagined world the language of natural science although used, "is in a grave state of disorder."[13] MacIntyre uses his allegory to explain the impact of Enlightenment philosophy, from his perspective, upon moral theory, maintaining that it was doomed from the start precisely because it used ethical language that had been detached from its source, namely Aristotelianism with its teleological idea about human life. He states that "the language and the appearances of morality persist even though the integral substance of morality has to a large degree been fragmented and then in part destroyed."[14] MacIntyre's argument is a carefully constructed critique of moral discourse emerging from Enlightenment philosophy, which from his perspective was a failure. The point he makes is that Enlightenment philosophers were the inheritors of both a moral language and the substance that gave that language meaning and shape. The rejection of Aristotelian virtue ethics with its teleology, led to the fragmentation of moral language and the substance from which it is derived being ignored and then destroyed.

---

10   Alasdair MacIntyre, *After Virtue: A Study in Moral Theory* (London: Duckworth, 2007).
11   MacIntyre, *After Virtue*, vii.
12   MacIntyre, *After Virtue*, 1.
13   MacIntyre, *After Virtue*, 2.
14   MacIntyre, *After Virtue*, 5.

This is not the occasion to engage fully with MacIntyre's overall argument. What is important to highlight, however, is the suggestion that moral language has become fragmented. I contend that, not only has the process of fragmentation continued, but even the ethical frameworks created by Enlightenment philosophers and their successors are now largely unknown. What little knowledge of them that remains among the general public, is disjointed at best. Abundant evidence may be discerned through watching a television debate purporting to examine an ethical subject. When organisations/institutions issue their organisational ethic, it is done so with the implied assumption that their personnel will understand: 1, the ethical language used; and 2, the authority underpinning it that gives it moral force. It is not at all certain that personnel within an organisation will understand the language used in ethical codes and comprehend it in the manner the organisation expects. One only has to consider how problematic the concept of loyalty has been and continues to be for militaries.[15]

The Changing Social Imaginary

A second aspect to the problem lies in the assumption that the shared, societal frameworks necessary for ethical concepts to be understood are known, recognised and accepted by the personnel working for that organisation or institution. I want to go much further than MacIntyre and suggest that not only is moral/ethical language fragmented and detached from the substance that gives it meaning, but that the shared societal frameworks within which ethical concepts must be understood are unknown, forgotten by many or have been transformed without much social awareness that this has taken place.

The philosophical observations concerning modern social imaginaries by Charles Taylor are pertinent.[16] According to Taylor, "the social imaginary is not a set of ideas; rather, it is what enables, through making sense of, the practices of a society;"[17] it is "the ways people imagine their social existence," he contends, "how they fit together with others, how things go on between them and their fellows, the expectations that are normally met, and the deeper normative notions and images that underlie those

---

15 One example is 'wall of silence' that confronted the Judge in the Baha Mousa case. See, *The Aitken Report: An Investigation into Cases of Deliberate Abuse and Unlawful Killing in Iraq in 2003 and 2004.* January 25, 2008, http://data.parliament.uk/DepositedPapers/Files/DEP2008-0229/DEP2008-0229.pdf.

16 Charles Taylor, *Modern Social Imaginaries* (Durham, NC and London: Duke University Press, 2004).

17 Taylor, *Modern Social Imaginaries*, 2.

expectations."[18] His focus is primarily Western history and the social imaginary that underpinned the rise of Western modernity.[19]

One of the characteristics of a social imaginary, according to Taylor, is that it "can eventually come to count as the taken-for-granted shape of things too obvious to mention"[20] and "seems the only one that makes sense."[21] Social imaginaries can change over time. How "people imagine their social existence, how they fit together with others, how things go on between them and their fellows, the expectations that are normally met" has evolved in the past. The point is not that social imaginaries change but that the societal frameworks from which our ethical frameworks emerged is unknown to many, perhaps even the majority, and that a process of transformation has occurred without much social awareness that this has taken place. The "taken-for-granted shape of things too obvious to mention" has been forgotten or has become unknown, precisely because it had the characteristic of being "too obvious to mention."

The Fluidity of Ideas and Concepts

The sociologist Zygmunt Bauman introduced the idea of *Liquid Modernity* into our modern vocabulary[22] using it as a powerful metaphor to articulate the changes taking place within our everyday lives. [23] Bauman's phrase captures the increasingly rapid changes that have taken and are continually taking place to 'solid' structures that underpinned Western modernity. He argued that Modernity melted the foundational 'solids' that gave pre-modern social structure its essential character in order to reshape and mould them to fit its needs.[24] The consequence of globalisation and what Bauman referred to as individuality, has resulted in societal 'solids' being thrown into the melting pot of fluid modernity.[25] Concepts like love, fear, social structure resemble the characteristic of a liquid in that they do not stand still for long and keep its shape for long.[26] The idea of liquid modernity

---

18   Taylor, *Modern Social Imaginaries*, 23.
19   Taylor, *Modern Social Imaginaries*, 2.
20   Taylor, *Modern Social Imaginaries*, 29.
21   Taylor, *Modern Social Imaginaries*, 17.
22   Zygmunt Bauman, *Liquid Modernity* (Cambridge: Polity, 2006).
23   Mark Davis, "Liquid Sociology – What For?" in *Liquid Sociology: Metaphor in Zygmunt Bauman's Analysis of Modernity*, ed. Mark Davis (Farnham: Ashgate, 2013), 1.
24   Bauman contended that "the first solids to be melted and the first sacreds to be profaned were traditional loyalties, customary rights and obligations which bound hands and feet, hindered moves and cramped the enterprise." Bauman, *Liquid Modernity*, 3.
25   Bauman, *Liquid Modernity*, 6.
26   Davis, "Liquid Sociology," 2.

can be illustrated in the topical issue of gender fluidity. ABC News has identified 58 different gender options currently being used.[27]

Not only are once fixed societal solids becoming increasingly fluid, a hollowing out of traditional ideas may also be occurring. One eye-catching example of this phenomenon is the striking idea of the eminent sociologist Ulrich Beck and what he referred to as 'zombie categories' in twenty-first-century life.[28] He explained his idea of 'zombie categories' in an interview with Jonathan Rutherford in London on February 3, 1999. Beck uses what he describes as 'individualization' to explain the "disembedding of the ways of life of industrial society," for example class, family, gender and nation. Individualization does not, he maintains, mean individualism.[29] Individualization creates a lot of zombie categories.[30] When asked for illustrations Beck cited family, class and neighbourhood as examples.[31] It is sobering to think that one of the most distinguished sociologists of our age, described institutions traditionally understood as being critical to modern life, as husks whose life has been hollowed out: transformed into the living dead.

An Increasingly Unknown Moral Landscape

The moral beliefs and moral reasoning among 'emerging adults' may offer an insight into the impact of the fragmentation of ethical language, the 'unknownness' of historical social foundations, the fluidity of concepts and the hollowed out nature of social categories like family and neighbourhood. This subsection is indebted to the impressive sociological research by Christian Smith and his collaborators that resulted in their book *Lost in Transition: The Dark Side of Emerging Adulthood*.[32] The main conclusion from this important book "is that – not withstanding all that is genuinely good in emerging adulthood – emerging adult life in the United States today is beset with real problems."[33] Smith and his colleagues choose the phrase

---

27 See Russell Goldman, "Here's a list of 58 gender options for Facebook users," February 13, 2014. http://abcnews.go.com/blogs/headlines/2014/02/heres-a-list-of-58-gender-options-for-facebook-users/.

28 Ulrich Beck and Elisabeth Beck-Gernsheim, *Individualization: Institutionalized Individualism and its Social and Political Consequences* (London: Sage, 2001), Chapter 14 "Zombie categories: Interview with Ulrich Beck," 202–13. See also, Ulrich Beck, "The Cosmopolitan Society and its Enemies," *Theory, Culture & Society* 19, nos. 1/2 (2012): 17–44.

29 Beck and Beck-Gernsheim, *Individualization*, 202.

30 Beck and Beck-Gernsheim, *Individualization*.

31 A zombie category for Beck was a social phenomenon that was dead, in his view, but which was perpetuated in common language. Zombie categories have no steady referent.

32 Christian Smith, Hilary Davidson and Kari Christoffersen, *Lost in Transition: The Dark Side of Emerging Adulthood* (Oxford: Oxford University Press, 2011).

33 Smith, et al., *Lost in Transition*, 3.

'emerging adulthood' from the array of labels used to describe the period in an individual's life between 18 and 30. While one should exercise caution in transposing an academic study from one country to another, the themes are identifiable in the U.K. and I suspect in other Western democracies. Sociological studies have demonstrated that "the transition to adulthood today is more complex, disjointed, and confusing than it was in the past decades."[34]

The first thing that struck Smith and his team was how strongly individualistic most emerging adults were when it came to morality.[35] Sixty per cent of those interviewed thought that morality was a personal choice, entirely a matter of individual decision. Moral rights and wrongs were essentially a matter of individual opinion.[36] The majority also expressed the belief that it is wrong for people to morally judge other people.[37] What became very clear to the researchers was that the majority had a live-and-let-live lifestyle, underpinned by a profound moral relativism.[38] Despite this, more than half of emerging adults wanted to resist moral relativism.[39] What Smith and his team realised, however, is that they appeared "to possess few moral-reasoning skills with which to do that."[40] This became evident whenever the sociologists asked questions on the source of morality. "Where does morality come from? What is morality's basis"?[41] Thirty-four per cent of emerging adults interviewed said that *they simply did not know what makes anything morally right or wrong* [emphasis in original]. They had no idea about the basis of morality."[42] Some of those questioned did not understand the question. For others it was framed by their understanding of what other people might think about their action or choice,[43] or whether or not it functionally improved their situation (like cheating in an exam). [44] Emerging adults demonstrated a clear distinction between hurting individuals, which they thought was wrong, and organisations, such as a business or social groups.[45]

Smith and his team are at pains to stress that are not suggesting that all or most emerging adults are reprobates.[46] Rather, they contend that

---

34 Smith, et al., *Lost in Transition*, 15.
35 Smith, et al., *Lost in Transition*, 21.
36 Smith, et al., *Lost in Transition*.
37 Smith, et al., *Lost in Transition*, 23.
38 Smith, et al., *Lost in Transition*, 25.
39 Smith, et al., *Lost in Transition*, 33.
40 Smith, et al., *Lost in Transition*.
41 Smith, et al., *Lost in Transition*.
42 Smith, et al., *Lost in Transition*, 36.
43 Smith, et al., *Lost in Transition*, 37.
44 Smith, et al., *Lost in Transition*, 38.
45 Smith, et al., *Lost in Transition*, 40–41.
46 Smith, et al., *Lost in Transition*, 68.

emerging adults live in a world where very little counts as moral and where their moral blindness has been learned.[47] Emerging adults are not therefore morally corrupt but they are morally lost. Smith argues that "they do not adequately know the moral landscape of the real world that they inhabit. And they do not adequately understand where they themselves stand in that real moral world."[48] What they need according to Smith are "better moral maps and better equipped guides to show them the way around."[49] They lack, and neither have they been given, sufficient moral tools with which to make genuine moral choices.

Virtues or Values: An Operational Dimension

For the majority of Western militaries, the question of 'Values or Virtues' is not a metaphysical enquiry for academics to debate. Western societies are increasingly sceptical about the use of military force in interventions of choice that have only a tenuous link with national interests. The ethical and legal justification underpinning these operations is vital ground, before and during the operation. When ethical language is used to justify how a calculation for armed intervention is made (e.g., doing the 'right thing' by Britain and the people of Afghanistan)[50] morality and ethics become major factors in that conflict. This is not to suggest that morality and ethics have not been major factors in war up to this point; that would be absurd. However, a paradigm shift has occurred.[51] Ethics and morality have become weapons used by non-state players against states (who are signatories to international humanitarian law) but who may well, because of ideological reasons, have repudiated or ignored accepted international conventions.[52] The ethical behaviour of soldiers, particularly from Western democracies, is vital ground in any contested operational environment. The question of 'Virtues or Values' cannot be abstracted from embedded life when preparing modern military personnel for operational service, particularly in hostile situations.

Moral shallowness can be hemmed in, at least to some degree, by the residual moral consciousness contained in societal behavioural norms, although this residual moral consciousness cannot survive, in my

---

47   Smith, et al., *Lost in Transition*, 60.

48   Smith, et al., *Lost in Transition*, 69.

49   Smith, et al., *Lost in Transition*.

50   See, the former British Prime Minister Gordon Brown's speech, "Afghan aims 'realistic'," September 4, 2009, http://news.bbc.co.uk/1/hi/8237207.stm.

51   See Phillip J. McCormack, "You've been silent Padre," in *Military Chaplains in Contention* (Aldershot: Ashgate, 2013).

52   See Mary Habeck, *Knowing the Enemy: Jihadist Ideology and the War on Terror* (New Haven and London: Yale University Press, 2006), 74.

view, without a rediscovery of the substance that once provided moral authority. Whether this is a realistic possibility or even if it is possible for a society to achieve this, is beyond the scope of this chapter. There is a profound practical implication here for Western militaries. While military personnel operate within, or in close proximity to, the residual moral consciousness that is still located in societal behavioural norms, the vast majority of military personnel will conduct themselves appropriately and professionally. The issue of ethical shallowness is mitigated by societal pressures. On operational deployment, however, when military personnel are deployed in unfamiliar societal and cultural environments, the behavioural practices of the indigenous population may appear strange or confusing to young, inexperienced Service personnel.

Jonathan Glover comments in his book *Humanity: A Moral History of the Twentieth Century* that before the atrocity at My Lai there had been an erosion of moral resources among the American soldiers who would commit this infamous massacre. Moral restraints had been eroded by degrees, which appeared to be relatively small at first.[53] An incremental ethical drift had occurred in which the perceived abnormality of the lived experience of the soldiers began to give rise to the notion that the normal moral reference points did not apply. Every soldier and officer who has served on operations in hostile environments will be familiar with this particular and consistent challenge. Can senior military commanders really expect soldiers, living at small isolated checkpoints in a foreign country, to wash and iron their uniforms every day or every couple of days when the forward line of enemy troops is only a few hundred metres away and soldiers endure daily sniper and regular rocket attacks? What about washing and shaving, or cleaning their living areas? What about the retention of normal military protocols regarding rank and seniority? Many of the normal reference points can begin to fade or appear irrelevant in austere conditions. This is explored throughout Jim Frederick's book *Black Hearts: One Platoon's Descent into Madness in Iraq's Triangle of Death*. Frederick's careful analysis is an excellent depiction of the lived context out of which one of the most heinous war crimes of the Iraq conflict was committed.[54] In a strange and hostile operational environment, the norms of daily routine were whatever the soldiers thought were appropriate. It is essential, however, to note that it was only one platoon's decent into madness. In the recent Iraq and Afghanistan conflicts the conduct of the

---

53 Jonathan Glover, *Humanity: A Moral History of the Twentieth Century* (London: Pimlico, 2001), 60.

54 Jim Frederick, *Black Hearts: One Platoon's Descent into Madness in Iraq's Triangle of Death* (London: Pan, 2010).

overwhelming majority of Western military personnel serving there gave little cause for concern.

The uncomfortable thought that emerges is that evil can reside in the everyday and the ordinary. This is a modern slant on the banality of evil.[55] Of themselves, the mundane and commonplace are usually the unnoticed structural components that comprise significant elements of our lives. This is the lived context within which the moral agent acts. The gradual ethical drift that both Glover and Frederick describe is compounded by the failure to do the basic elements of professional military life well. Each reinforces the other in a continual spiral of descent. When soldiers deliberately choose to stop, or simply can't be bothered, doing the basic elements of daily life well on operations, why should anyone be surprised if this attitude is then manifested in their approach to other areas of life: for example, respect for others, displaying integrity and when required, courageous restraint? If evil can reside in the everyday and the mundane, so too does ethical behaviour. The concept of consistently doing small things well is vital. The concept of repetitiveness is a well-known and established principle in military training. What is repetitive in training can become habit forming in practice. Being repetitive is not of itself a basis for moral action. An individual can develop unethical behaviours that are consistently repeated. Neither would militaries wish to view their military personnel as variants of Pavlov's dogs, classically conditioned into unthinking behavioural traits that effectively remove individual moral agency. It is within this context that the question of Virtues or Values comes into clearest focus.

Virtues or Values: Preparing Professional Militaries for Operational Service

Militaries that rely solely upon a 'values' based approach to preparing personnel for operational service in complex, contested environments do their Service personnel a huge disservice. Unless values are grounded upon and derived from an ethical good, they are increasingly fluid and malleable in Western societies. The fragmentation of ethical language, the hollowing out of societal structures and the unknown moral landscape of 'real life' for many emerging adults, means that unless 'values' are anchored upon a universal good they will always be susceptible to moral drift. The language may be retained and the institution's code of ethics may have its glossy booklet but the underpinning substance has been and continues to be substantially eroded. An institution's moral code should

---

55 See Hannah Arendt, *Eichmann in Jerusalem: A Report on the Banality of Evil* (New York: Viking Press, 1964).

not simply descend from 'above.' It must begin from the ground up, with the individuals who are expected to embody and live out the principles contained in the institution's code of ethics.

In contrast, what makes virtue ethics ideal for military personnel is that it begins with the individual, unlike many ethical codes that descend from an executive.[56] It is a moral framework that focuses upon the individual as a moral agent with the capacity for ethical decision making. Individuals are encouraged to incorporate the practice of moral daily habits into a larger holistic framework recognising the lifelong benefits of a well-lived life. Drawing from his own experiences in World War I, Lord Moran maintains in his book, *Anatomy of Courage*,

> that a man of character in peace becomes a man of courage in war. He cannot be selfish in peace and unselfish in war. Character as Aristotle taught is a habit, the daily choice of right instead of wrong; it is a moral quality which grows in maturity in peace and is not suddenly developed on the outbreak of war. War ... has no power to transform, it merely exaggerates the good and evil that are in us, till it is plain for all to read; it cannot change, it exposes. Man's fate in battle is worked out before war begins.[57]

Those who have experienced combat will recognise what Lord Moran is describing. An individual's character is exposed for all to see when it is placed under the intense scrutiny of contact with the enemy. War does not transform, it merely provides the canvas upon which character is displayed. Will Durant, the American historian and philosopher summed up virtue ethics when he said that "excellence is an art won by training and habituation ... We are what we repeatedly do. Excellence, then, is not an act, but a habit."[58] If you want an insight into a person's character, look at their habits. There is a direct and inescapable link between, the habits we choose to ingrain, the behaviour that is shaped by those habits and the character that is displayed in times of crisis. Perhaps this is why many of those who win their nation's highest awards for valour do not recognise themselves as heroes, preferring to view themselves as just ordinary people who did what any other member of the team would do. We who read of their actions recognise something much deeper and see evidence of a character that shone in extremis.

---

56   For example, like the U.K. Police *Code of Ethics*, July 2014. http://www.college.police.uk/What-we-do/Ethics/Documents/Code_of_Ethics.pdf.

57   Lord Moran, *The Anatomy of Courage* (London: Constable, 1945), 170.

58   Will Durant, *The Story of Philosophy* (New York: Time, 1926), 74.

Scholars such as John Doris[59] and Gilbert Harman,[60] however, have questioned the empirical basis for the concept of character as presented within virtue ethics. They are content to accept that virtue or character can exist as a fleeting feature but this, according to Harman this "must be distinguished from virtue or character as an enduring characteristic of a person."[61] If Doris and Harman are correct, virtue ethics is rendered as unstable as a values based approach for professional militaries. The evidence they present from social psychology is both depressing and striking: that moral behaviour can be effected by surprisingly small situational factors.[62] The weakness of their argument, however, is that the cohort that took part in the various social psychology experiments had not been brought up in a social setting underpinned by Socratic, Platonic and Aristotelian ideas of virtue. This is the thrust of MacIntyre's critique. Although the language has been retained it has been dislocated from the essence that gave it substance. For example, the idea of character is retained but the philosophy underpinning the idea of character in Aristotelian thought is largely absent in modern life. Life in the late twentieth and early twenty-first century has been marked by a consumption of disposable products.[63] Instant access and use is the ordinary and everyday lived experience for the many, not the lifelong dedication to the slow and methodical growth of a consistent character.

Conclusion

Values are important. In modern Western societies, however, they have become increasingly fluid and susceptible to cultural fluctuation. Consequently, they can appear situationally irrelevant to military personnel in operationally challenging environments when the societal context in which they had a particular meaning for those military personnel has radically changed. Any military ethic that is overly reliant upon a values-based approach is, in the view of this author, not only inadequate but inherently susceptible to ethical drift. Young people recruited into

---

59 For example, see J. M. Doris, *Lack of Character: Personality and Moral Behaviour* (Cambridge: Cambridge University Press, 2002); "Heated agreement: Lack of Character as Being for the Good," *Philosophical Studies* 148, no. 1 (2010): 135–46.

60 For example, see Gilbert Harman, "No Character or Personality," *Business Ethics Quarterly* 13, no. 1 (2003): 87–94; and "Skepticism about Character Traits," *The Journal of Ethics* 13, nos. 2/3 (2009): 235–42.

61 Harman, "Skepticism about Character Traits," 242.

62 See the section on "Compassion."

63 See Greg Kennedy, *An Ontology of Trash: The Disposable and its Problematic Nature* (New York: State University of New York Press, 2007).

militaries, will be in the vanguard of the forces deployed in service to their country, possibly in places of extreme danger. The question is: Will they deploy with sufficient moral resources to enable them to navigate complex moral situations?

If we are what we repeatedly do and Lord Moran is correct that war has no power to transform, then ethical behaviour on the battlefield is grown and developed in the daily habits of normal 'peace-time' military service. The ethical armour necessary for military personnel, who find themselves in contested operational environments, is forged in the everyday, mundane tasks and life of the Service person in barracks or in training. The simple but vital task of doing small things consistently well is essential to developing good behavioural patterns. There is, in my view, a causal relationship between the thoughts that a person may have, the actions that may occur as a result, the behavioural habits that result from repeated actions and the behavioural traits that become character forming. Each of us becomes what we repeatedly do. Excellence is not a one-off act it is the product of good habits.

One striking example of the concept that excellence is not an act, but a habit is frequently referred to as the Miracle on the Hudson. On 15 January 2009, U.S. Airways Flight 1549 was struck by a flock of Canadian geese shortly after take-off from LaGuardia airport, New York. The bird strike rendered both engines on the Airbus A320 inoperative. The pilot Chesley 'Sully' Sullenberger took the decision to land the stricken plane on the Hudson River. All 150 passengers and five crew were rescued from the plane as it floated intact on the river. It was an incredible feat of judgement and professional skill in the context of impending disaster. After the incident, Sullenberger told CBS News anchor Katie Couric,

> One way of looking at this might be that, for 42 years, I've been making small regular deposits in this bank of experience: education and training and on January 15, the balance was sufficient so that I could make a very large withdrawal.[64]

Ensuring that professional military personnel have sufficient moral resources capable of withstanding and enduring the relentless attrition of deployment in a potentially hostile setting is of critical importance. The moral dimension to any operational deployment in a contested environment is vital ground to strategic and campaign success. Historically, virtue ethics was, and in the opinion of this author should be, the code of the warrior/

---

64 See "Capt. Sully Worried About Airline Industry," February 10, 2009. https://www.cbsnews.com/news/capt-sully-worried-about-airline-industry/.

soldier. It is not a set of rules to be learned so that they can be repeated upon request. Rather it is the embrace of a way of life that is lived through personal, daily examination and as a consequence can contribute to moral and spiritual resilience in even extreme conditions.

References

Arendt, H. *Eichmann in Jerusalem: A Report on the Banality of Evil*. New York: Viking Press, 1964.

Bauman, Z. *Liquid Modernity*. Cambridge: Polity, 2006.

Beck, U. *World Risk Society*. Cambridge: Polity, 1999.

Beck, U. "The Cosmopolitan Society and its Enemies," *Theory, Culture & Society* 19 (1–2) (2012): 17–44.

Beck, U. and E. Beck-Gernsheim. *Individualization: Institutionalized Individualism and its Social and Political Consequences*. London: Sage, 2001.

Cheng, A. and K. R. Fleischmann. "Developing a Meta-Inventory of Human Values," *Proceedings of the American Society for Information* 47, no. 1 (2010): 1–10.

Davis, M. "Liquid Sociology – What For?" in *Liquid Sociology: Metaphor in Zygmunt Bauman's Analysis of Modernity*, edited by Mark Davis. Aldershot: Ashgate, 2013.

Deakin, S. "Ethics and the British Army's Values and Standards," *The British Army Review* 140 (2006).

Doris, J. M. *Lack of Character: Personality and Moral Behaviour*. Cambridge: Cambridge University Press, 2002.

Doris, J. M. "Heated agreement: Lack of Character as Being for the Good," *Philosophical Studies* 148, no. 1 (2010): 135–46.

Durant, W. *The Story of Philosophy*. New York: Time, 1926.

Frederick, J. *Black Hearts: One Platoon's Descent into Madness in Iraq's Triangle of Death*. London: Pan, 2010.

Glover, J. *Humanity: A Moral History of the Twentieth Century*. London: Pimlico, 2001.

Habeck, M. *Knowing the Enemy: Jihadist Ideology and the War on Terror*. New Haven and London: Yale University Press, 2006.

Harman, G. "No Character or Personality," *Business Ethics Quarterly* 13, no. 1 (2003): 87–94.

Harman, G. "Skepticism about Character Traits," *The Journal of Ethics* 13, nos. 2/3 (2009): 235–42.

Harman, G. "Skepticism about Character Traits," November 15, 2008, https://www.princeton.edu/~harman/Papers/GH-Situ.pdf.

Hsieh, N. "Incommensurable Values," *The Stanford Encyclopedia of Philosophy* (Fall 2008 Edition), edited by Edward N. Zalta, http://plato.stanford.edu/archives/fall2008/entries/value-incommensurable/.

Kennedy, G. *An Ontology of Trash: The Disposable and its Problematic Nature.* New York: State University of New York Press, 2007.

Lord Moran, *The Anatomy of Courage.* London: Constable, 1945.

MacIntyre, A. *After Virtue: A Study in Moral Theory.* London: Duckworth, 2007.

McCormack, P. J. "Grounding British Army Values Upon an Ethical Good," March 30, 2015. http://www.cgscfoundation.org/wp-content/uploads/2015/04/McCormack-GroundingBritishArmyValues.pdf.

McCormack, P. J. "You've been silent Padre," in *Military Chaplains in Contention* Aldershot: Ashgate Publishing, 2013.

Shramko, Y. and Wansing, H. "Truth Values," *The Stanford Encyclopedia of Philosophy* (Summer 2014 Edition), edited by Edward N. Zalta, http://plato.stanford.edu/archives/sum2014/entries/truth-values/.

Smith, C., H. Davidson and K. Christoffersen, *Lost in Transition: The Dark Side of Emerging Adulthood.* Oxford: Oxford University Press, 2011.

Taylor, C. *Modern Social Imaginaries.* Durham, NC and London: Duke University Press, 2004.

Whetham, D. "Ethics, Law and Conflict," in *Ethics, Law and Military Operations,* edited by D. Whetham. Basingstoke: Palgrave Macmillan, 2011.

1

JUSTICE

Overview: Just (and Unjust) Warriors: Nature and Causes

Edward T. Barrett

The Traditional Account: Just Persons

With apologies to Plato, the traditional account of the virtue of justice most relevant to modern conflict is that of Aristotle. Aristotle's empirically-derived virtue ethics was teleologically-grounded: experience reveals that acts should be directed not simply toward the possession of possible pleasures, but instead toward a more complex state of being referred to today as 'flourishing.' The goods constitutive of flourishing include not only bodily and material goods such as health and property, but also various 'good of the soul' – the intellectual and moral virtues. The latter are dispositions to feel and act in fulfilling ways. Aristotle argues that in order to flourish in the real world, with its pleasures, dangers and social interactions, persons must become inclined to act in many of the ways explored in this volume – temperately, courageously, justly – by repeatedly acting in such ways. Repetition is crucial because unfulfilling acts and dispositions can seem fulfilling, at least in the short-term. Moral formation thus requires proper habituation through good exemplars and the persistent constraints of parents, schools and the state. Ultimately, a well-formed and flourishing person freely acts justly – in ways that give others their due.

However, Aristotle provides relatively little concrete guidance about the acts that form and are chosen by just persons.[1] He does offer an abstract

---

1 On whether virtue ethics can give an account of right action, see Ramon Das, "Virtue Ethics and Rights Action," *Australasian Journal of Philosophy* 81, no. 3 (2002): 324–39; and

political and social model of justice as fairness: one ought to receive benefits in proportion to contributions made ('distributive justice') and suffer harms commensurate with harms inflicted ('corrective justice').[2] He also asserts that murder, stealing and adultery are never fulfilling for the agent. But instead of supplementing his virtue ethics with a rule-oriented natural law or deontological account that more robustly specifies which goods and harms are justified and why, he emphasizes that we know what persons are due by observing how a just and flourishing person treats others.[3] We can only speculate about the reason for this emphasis. Perhaps it was epistemological: Aristotle considered it easier to recognize a flourishing and just person than a just act. Or perhaps it was cultural, the result of ancient Greek society's inegalitarian obsession with greatness and defense of natural inferiority.

The Turn Toward Norms: Just Acts and Human Rights

Whatever the reason for Aristotle's emphasis on the virtue of justice and relative neglect of the norms of justice, the next two millennia of Western ethical thought worked to correct this imbalance. In the process, virtue ethics – especially concerning the virtue of justice – became less agent-centered and eudaimonistic, and more target-centered.[4] In other words, just and flourishing persons do not define just acts, but instead are inclined to act in ways deemed just according to criteria that are independent of the agent.

This thought on exactly what others are due was initially dominated by Christianity's concern with identifying sins against others that could jeopardize one's salvation, but evolved in two ways. First, it became more philosophical. While early Christian moral theologians concentrated on Biblical exegesis and divine commands, the Scholastic tradition – influenced by Stoicism and finding its fullest expression in Thomas Aquinas' writings – strongly defended a reason-derived natural law that specified just acts. In response to both the Enlightenment challenge to religion and the utilitarian challenge to natural law, Immanuel Kant's philosophy offered an influential

---

Frans Svensson, "Virtue Ethics and the Search for an Account of Right Action," *Ethical Theory and Moral Practice* 13, no. 3 (2010): 255–71.

2   Aristotle, *Nicomachean Ethics*, Book V. For a full and insightful treatment, see David Johnston, *A Brief History of Justice* (Chichester: Wiley-Blackwell, 2011).

3   For an extended discussion of this issue, see Terrence Irwin, *The Development of Ethics, Volume 1: From Socrates to the Reformation* (Oxford: Oxford University Press, 2011).

4   On this distinction, see Christine Swanton, *Virtue Ethics: A Pluralistic View* (Oxford: Oxford University Press 2003), chapter 11.

deontological theory of justice grounded in the imperative to always treat persons as ends.

Second, as Kant's formulation suggests, Western thought on what others are due became less concerned with the sinner and more attentive to the recipient of acts. The primary reason for this shift lies in the gradual acceptance of the concept undergirding Kant's imperative: human dignity or worth. Throughout its history, dignity as a personal quality has been defined in at least three ways: high social rank, virtuous character and behavior, and high intrinsic worth.[5] In these first two understandings, dignity is the result of one's acts and therefore conditional and unequal. The third meaning – high intrinsic worth – is the Kantian and contemporary one, and conceives of dignity as unaffected by acts, irreducible and equally high.

The historical causes of this deeper and broader sense of human worth are highly speculative and beyond the scope of this chapter. Certainly the long period between the abuse of indigenous Americans criticized by Bartolomé de las Casas and the soul-searching after Second World War atrocities was decisive.[6] More certain and important for our purposes is the effect of this development: the human rights revolution. Increasingly, just acts were defined in terms of human rights. With irreducible and equal dignity providing the normative foundation, the goods necessary for flourishing are now widely construed as inalienable and universal moral rights that should be secured through various means, including the liberal state.

Human Rights and Warfare

Concomitantly, and encouraged recently by the work of 'revisionists,' our understanding of retributive justice and the *jus ad bellum* and *jus in bello* criteria of the venerable just war tradition have become more explicitly anchored to the logic of human rights.[7] Most of the criteria can be grounded in the assertion that persons normally possess an inviolable right to life.[8]

---

5   Helpful treatments of the history and meaning of dignity include: Michael Rosen, *Dignity: Its History and Meaning* (Cambridge, MA: Harvard University Press, 2012); George Kateb, *Human Dignity* (Cambridge, MA: Harvard University Press, 2011); and Jeremy Waldron, *Dignity, Rights, and Rank* (Oxford: Oxford University Press, 2012).

6   See Bartolomé de las Casas, *A Short Account of the Destruction of the Indies* (1552).

7   Seminal revisionist works include David Rodin, *War and Self-Defense* (New York: Oxford University Press, 2003) and Jeff McMahan, *Killing in War* (New York: Oxford University Press, 2009).

8   For the purposes of this chapter, the *ad bellum* criteria are right intention, proper authority, just cause, last resort, reasonable chance of success, and broad proportionality; and the *in bello* criteria are discrimination, necessity and due care.

In the context of war, the existence of human rights means not only that aggression is impermissible, but also that defensive uses of lethal force are impermissible unless an aggressor has forfeited their right to life. This 'principle of forfeiture' has a Thomistic pedigree and recently has been developed by revisionist philosophers under the rubric of 'liability to lethal defensive harm.'

While the preconditions for such liability are contested, I would argue that they include the aggressor's threat level and culpability, and the response's effectiveness and necessity – all of which are grounded in the diminished worth and rights of the wrongdoer. Grave and culpable rights violations such as attempted murder compromise one's right to life to the requisite degree, and are the basis for the *ad bellum* just cause criterion. Effectiveness and necessity are internal to liability because even murderous acts do not eliminate a person's potentialities and worth. The effectiveness precondition generates the just war tradition's reasonable chance of success criterion, while the necessity requirement creates the *ad bellum* last resort and the *in bello* prohibition against killing combatants unnecessarily.

Finally, the existence of human rights in war gives rise to the discrimination and due care criteria. Because civilian bystanders in a war zone have forfeited none of their rights and are not liable to any harm, defenders must target only liable combatants. And when doing so, they must treat innocents with due care. In accordance with the principles of double intention and effect, soldiers must incur acceptable risks to avoid killing bystanders and then cause only a proportionate amount of unintentional but foreseeable harm to them.[9]

Just Warriors: Enduring Challenges

Clarifying the underpinnings of the just war criteria illuminates exactly what the virtue of justice entails for soldiers. Most fundamentally, it requires sensitivity to the dignity of all persons, and a disposition to respect the rights of those associated with military operations.

However, combat presents at least three enduring challenges to creating and sustaining just warriors. First, understanding aids one's disposition, and soldiers manage complex rights-related duties that are difficult to understand. On the one hand, they have a special duty to defend the lives of their own citizens, who are not only innocent victims of aggression, but also have a right to be defended by their soldiers based

---

9 On the principle of double intention, see Michael Walzer, *Just and Unjust Wars: A Moral Argument with Historical Illustrations* (New York: Basic Books, 1977), chapter 9.

on consent and reciprocity.[10] On the other hand, they have general or cosmopolitan duties to respect the rights of adversary combatants and bystanders, duties that are embodied in the *in bello* discrimination, necessity and due care criteria.[11] These general duties in war can be especially vexing. Even the most dispassionate soldier might struggle to affirm the dignity and right to life of an incapacitated or surrendered combatant who was recently trying to kill him. Arguments against torture are compelling but complicated. Regarding civilians, given the conventional association of risk and sacrifice with the special duty to help, officers strain to explain why the general duty to minimize foreseeable harm to bystanders requires acceptance of additional risk. Perhaps more difficult to explain is the fact that violent efforts to satisfy special duties are limited by the cosmopolitan duty to refrain from disproportionate collateral damage.

A second enduring challenge to one's disposition to respect others' rights is combat stress. Assisted by emotional attachments, most soldiers have no trouble fulfilling their special obligations to compatriots. But the levels of fatigue, fear and anger found in war can overwhelm the good will and judgment of already aggressive soldiers, and lead to the dehumanization of adversaries and war crimes.

Finally, the virtue of justice can be undone by war's likeness to a lawless 'state of nature.' As political theorists from Aristotle to James Madison have argued, human beings have two mechanisms for governing behavior: law and virtue. In war, positive law is temporarily absent; domestic police and courts disappear. Contemporary international courts and military justice systems provide some regulation, but they have limited effects. The former are often eschewed by sovereign states and focus on the transgressions of senior leaders. The latter rely heavily on the self-policing of soldiers whose loyalty toward each other can trump their commitment to reporting wrongdoing. Because of these limitations, societies who care about justice in war admirably strive to produce just warriors. However, one does not have to be a situationist – who insists that character traits are mostly ineffectual determinants of behavior – to acknowledge the importance of incentives and law for virtue.[12] The deterrent function of law helps prevent the weak moments experienced by even virtuous characters from becoming bad habits. Lacking this deterrent, and given the moral

---

10 For the sake of simplicity, this chapter will assume soldiers are engaged in a just war.

11 The literature on special versus natural duties is vast. For a pertinent summary, see Jonathan Seglow, "Associative Duties and Global Justice," *Journal of Moral Philosophy* 7 (2010): 54–73; and Simon Caney, "Humanity, Associations, and Global Justice: In Defence of Humanity-Centred Cosmopolitan Egalitarianism," *The Monist* 94 (2011): 506–34.

12 On situationism, see John M. Doris, "Persons, Situations and Virtue Ethics," *Noûs* 32, no. 4 (1998): 504–30.

complications and stresses of combat, warriors are always at risk for developing the vices lamented by Augustine: "The passion for inflicting harm, the cruel thirst for vengeance, an unpacific and relentless spirit, the fever of revolt, the lust for power."[13]

This occupational moral hazard has been documented in recent analyses of 'moral injury.'[14] Soldiers returning from wars in which they have committed culpable injustices experience not only morally relevant emotions such as guilt and shame, but also profound character changes. More pointedly, they develop a callous attitude toward the value and rights of others. The phenomenon raises important questions. When are emotions cognitively significant for ethics? What is the relationship between emotions such as guilt and the vice of injustice? For example, is the lack of remorse indicative of an unjust person? Is guilt an injury, and should the focus instead be on character harm? Finally, which acts are harming our soldiers' characters? While accumulating data indicates that the answer to the last question includes usual suspects such as killing combatants unnecessarily, other possibilities and their implications warrant further research. These include fighting in an unjust war, fighting for an illiberal regime, killing child soldiers (who may lack culpability and liability), torturing, and justifiably killing combatants when motivated by revenge or pleasure.

Just Warriors: New Challenges

At least four contemporary and future aspects of warfare could further challenge soldiers' sensitivity to human dignity and rights, and undermine a virtue necessary to their flourishing as persons.

The first challenge is posed by distance warfare. Although not a new phenomenon, its modern forms present new concerns. Killing from a distance is not inherently unjust; if *ad bellum* criteria are met, aggressor liability is such that defending soldiers need not be immediately threatened. In fact, societies have a duty to avoid unnecessary risks to their combatants. Additionally, physical distance can create emotional distance that benefits adversaries, reducing fear-induced haste, anger levels and force protection anxieties. But distance weapons might undermine the virtue of justice in a few ways. Soldiers who are completely detached from the battlefield – for example, cruise missile operators and cyber attackers – probably lack sensitivities possessed by those who are in the battlespace and not threatened,

---

13   Augustine, *Contra Faustum*, Book XXII, para. 74.
14   For a seminal work on the topic, see Jonathan Shay, *Achilles in Vietnam: Combat Trauma and the Undoing of Character* (New York: Simon & Schuster, 1995).

but eventually see the aftereffects of engagements. Although operators of unmanned systems witness the effects of their devastating strikes in real time, they do so through images that may mediate their psychological relationship with reality in morally significant ways.[15] Finally, training and fighting in safe and comfortable conditions can indirectly weaken one's commitment to others' rights. Moral virtues are causally related. The self-abnegation associated with habitually foregoing bodily safety and pleasure – the virtues of physical courage and temperance, respectively – enhances one's capacity to give others their due, especially when risks are involved. While traditional combat requires and cultivates courage and temperance, some forms of distance warfare do not.[16] Overall, more empirical research is required to assess these situations' effects on character.

A second challenge to the virtue of justice is the rapid expansion of special operations forces (SOF). Because of difficulties associated with counterinsurgency and nation building strategies, SOF are increasingly essential to steady state operations against non-state actors. Their missions include direct action, 'targeted killing' in conjunction with air assets, and training, advising and assisting local state forces. While elite, clandestine and intensely loyal small units possess obvious advantages, these same characteristics can create temptations and viciousness. Recent reports of rights violations suggest that improvements to growth-strained institutional safeguards against character and cultural problems might be warranted.[17]

Third, human enhancement technologies could create character issues. All future conflict scenarios include the use of soldiers whose physical, cognitive and emotional capacities have been enhanced through exoskeletons, implants, drugs and genetic alterations. Efficiency, force protection, and mission effectiveness would be possible benefits. But these promising technologies might undermine the justice of soldiers in at least two ways. Emotional 'enhancements' that reduce fear and increase aggression might not only compromise the soldiers' freedom and safety; they might also corrupt their judgment and inclinations regarding the rights of others, including their own civilians. Additionally, given the assumption that capacities such as reason are the basis of human worth

---

15 See Robert Sparrow, "War without Virtue?" in *Killing by Remote Control: The Ethics of an Unmanned Military*, ed. Bradley Jay Strawser (New York: Oxford University Press, 2013), 101.

16 On "post-heroic" warfare sans courage, see Edward N. Luttwak, "Toward Post-Heroic Warfare," *Foreign Affairs* 74, no. 3 (1995): 109–22, and Sibylle Scheipers, *Heroism and the Changing Character of War: Toward Post-Heroic Warfare?* (Basingstoke: Palgrave Macmillan, 2014).

17 See Mark Mazzetti, et al., "SEAL Team 6: A Secret History of Quiet Killings and Blurred Lines," *New York Times*, June 6, 2015.

and rights, radically superior soldiers "might think themselves so superior that they would treat (mere) persons as if they had a lower status than they have."[18] If radical enhancements were widely distributed within militaries, the effects on civil-military relations and the treatment of adversaries could be appalling.

Finally, the 'civil-military gap' could create problems for the fulfillment of special duties to citizens and even cosmopolitan duties to adversary bystanders. Decades ago, Samuel Huntington identified durable differences between civilians and the military.[19] Compared to civilian elites and average citizens, the military tends to be more pessimistic about human nature and threat levels, more supportive of increased military budgets and power, less individualistic, less cosmopolitan, more data-driven and methodical in planning, and less eager to resort to war. Huntington called this constellation of attributes 'conservative realism.' In the past several years, a conversation has emerged in the United States about a widening gap created by new developments: the two groups are less familiar with one another because of the all-volunteer force and the consolidation of military bases in the South and West; civilian elites and the electorate have become more liberal, the military more conservative; and the latter possess a sense of moral superiority based on their sacrifices. Especially if combined with fiscally-driven military spending cuts and high deployment requirements, these developments could affect a military's perspective on acceptable sacrifices.

The High Demand for Just Warriors

While these enduring and new challenges threaten to weaken the virtue of justice, several phenomena will increase the demand for it. First, innocent civilians will increasingly be caught in the crossfires of future battlefields. Urban counterinsurgency and counterterrorism missions to subdue combatants hiding amidst civilians will continue. Additionally, forecasts about conditions that will drive conflict – demographic, ideological, geographic, economic, technological, environmental and military – predict that the bulk of future violence will occur in crowded urban areas beset by weak governance, social cleavages, high youth unemployment, poor

---

18   Allen Buchanan, "Moral Status and Human Enhancement," *Philosophy and Public Affairs* 37, no. 4 (2009): 369. Buchanan focuses on whether enhanced persons would possess a higher moral status, but mentions this behavioral point, which he calls "the Practical Worry."

19   See Samuel P. Huntington, *The Soldier and the State: The Theory and Politics of Civil-Military Relations* (Cambridge, MA: Belknap Press, 1957), chapter 3.

infrastructure and bad water.[20] Second and related, the success of military operations will increasingly depend upon whether the military can limit collateral damage. Afforded by various forms of media and the internet, transparency of the effects of war has expanded. At the same time, liberal democratic societies' sensitivities to collateral damage and their soft power have intensified. Respecting the rights of bystanders has thus become a crucial determinate of public support and the resulting chance of success in otherwise just wars.

Third, soldiers will use new technologies whose compliance with *in bello* criteria is unproven. For example, the ability of autonomous strike systems to adequately recognize those liable to harm and then comply with necessity and due care requirements is hotly debated. Similarly, questions remain about whether cyber weapons are discriminate and have predictable effects. The weaponization of outer space is likely, and the use of nuclear weapons is more possible than during the Cold War. In all of these situations, soldiers will be intimately familiar with these systems' capabilities and the first to use them in real conditions, and must have the justice and moral courage to highlight ethical problems.

Finally, soldiers will have to be just in qualitatively different ways than their predecessors. On the one hand, as the following case study suggests, they may have to make *ad bellum* decisions. In liberal democracies, where civilians control their militaries, military members are not considered a proper authority for initiating justified wars. But the predicted growth of intrastate conflict and subsequent use of military in humanitarian aid and peacekeeping roles may result in situations in which time and/or communications limitations require officers to decide between inaction and preventing a massacre by using potentially escalatory lethal force. On the other hand, this chapter's second case study argues that all military members' characters must be finely tuned not only to the demands of retributive justice, but also to distributive justice. Liberal democracies regularly pursue fairness-related goals through their militaries – for example, policies concerning women, homosexuals and transsexuals. Unit cohesion and effectiveness will depend upon respect for the rights of these groups.

Cultivating Just Warriors

My analysis of the challenges to and demand for just warriors has implied or stated many of the ways this virtue can be created and sustained. Responses

---

20 On the prevalence of intrastate war, see National Intelligence Council, *Global Trends: The Paradox of Progress* (2017).

to enduring aspects of combat include more rigorous education to deepen and broaden officer and enlisted understandings of war's complex moral demands; training that produces aggressive soldiers who nevertheless grasp the regretful nature of their work, and produces loyal brothers/ sisters-in-arms who do not tolerate ethical lapses; and serious research on the nature and causes of moral injury. Mitigating the new challenges will require improved study and monitoring of distance warfare's effects on acts and character, better oversight of SOF activities and culture, a cautious approach to the use of enhancement technologies, and efforts to ameliorate the civil-military gap.

But most fundamentally, given the nature of the virtue of justice, the cultivation of just warriors will require the cultivation of sensitivity to the dignity and rights of all persons. Because the worth of (and special duties to) one's compatriots is more readily felt, the more pressing task is imbuing an appreciation for the dignity of 'the Other.' And in service of this goal, the military should reexamine the place of the humanities in the undergraduate and professional education of its officers. For modern warriors, courses in the sciences, technologies, engineering and math (STEM) are essential. But given the moral stakes that accompany future technologies and battlespaces, a deep exposure to disciplines that infuse a deep knowledge and commitment to human fulfillment is imperative. These include history, philosophy, literature, art, and music – and not only those of Western provenance. Of all the arguments for the importance of the humanities, this is one of the most compelling.

Case Study 1:
Doing a Just Deal with the Devil?
Just Cause, David Richards and the
Case of Operation PALLISER

Thomas McDermott

Introduction: Just Cause, Proper Authority and Soldiers

Just cause is the first and most fundamental principle of Just War Theory (*jus ad bellum*). Dating back to the first conceptions of military ethics in the writings of Aristotle in the fourth century BC, this norm demands that protagonists (who over the years have increasingly become states) must only engage in warfare when their cause is just.[21] The list of 'just' causes has ebbed and flowed over the centuries. Aristotle, for example, suggested in his *Politics* that force could be used justly for the enslaving of 'naturally servile' people, a concept that would be abhorrent by today's western standards.[22] Today it is generally accepted that the only real recourse to war is in the resistance to aggression, enshrined since 1945 in international law within Chapter VII of the United Nations Charter.[23]

The next natural question that follows on is 'who decides that a particular cause is just'? This query links *just cause* with another important principle

---

21 Stephen Coleman, *Military Ethics: An Introduction with Case Studies* (New York: Oxford University Press, 2013), 72–77.

22 Aristotle, *Politics*, trans. T. A. Sinclair (London: Penguin Books, 1962), Book 1, Ch VI and VII, 70–75.

23 The full text of the UN Charter may be found at http://www.un.org/en/sections/un-charter/un-charter-full-text/. Accessed April 29, 2018.

of *jus ad bellum*: the idea of *proper authority*. *Proper authority* argues that the decision to go to war must only be made by an appropriate authority, and only after due process.[24] Increasingly over the centuries this right has been reserved for the rulers and governments of sovereign states. It now generally falls to Prime Ministers, Presidents and Cabinets to make those hardest of decisions: whether to risk lives, and take lives, in the national interest. To do this they must rely not only on law and convention, but on their own sense of the value of *justice* as part of a personal, and often societal, virtue ethic. Like war itself, the practical ability to do this well – to make the right choices under adversity – has a long history. To the Ancient Greeks, the fathers of philosophy, such a skill was known as *phronesis*, or 'practical wisdom,' and was highly prized.[25] So, in modern *just wars* politicians choose who to fight. The soldier, the one whose blood may be spilt, generally plays no more than an advisory role: indeed in most cases a civilian / military relationship has developed to the point where politicians debate whether to go to war (*jus ad bellum*), and soldiers in turn examine the right way to fight it (*jus in bello*).[26]

Sometimes, however, the clean progression between political decision and military action becomes blurred. There are times where soldiers are faced with a crisis where they must personally make a choice: expand or change the war, or face a potentially terrible outcome. In these situations there is no time or capacity to pass this responsibility to government. Either the distance is too great, or the government is simply not interested. For military practitioners it is here that the seam between *jus ad bellum* and *jus in bello* seems to become theirs alone. But, in ethical terms, what right do they have to commence, expand or cease hostilities? Can an individual soldier act as a *proper authority*? To what extent can they trust their own sense of *justice* to aid their "practical wisdom" about *just cause*? And what if, bound in their inherently individual and human flaws, they get it wrong?

Brigadier David Richards and a New Ethical Foreign Policy for the U.K.

British Brigadier David Richards faced just such a decision at the turn of the twentieth century. Richards, who would later become the professional

---

24 Coleman, *Military Ethics*, 80–81.

25 The concept of virtue ethics, and the ideas around *phronesis*, are simply and articulately explained by Professor Tom Frame in chapter 4 of Deane Peter Baker, *Key Concepts in Military Ethics* (Sydney: University of New South Wales Press, 2015).

26 Readers interested in a deeper understanding of the concept of civilian/military relationships should examine Eliot A. Cohen, *Supreme Command: Soldiers, Statesmen and Leadership in Wartime* (New York: Simon & Schuster, 2002), Peter D. Feaver, *Armed Servants: Agency, Oversight and Civilian Military Relations* (Cambridge, MA: Harvard University Press, 2005), and Samuel P. Huntington, *The Soldier and the State: The Theory and Policy of Civilian-Military Relations* (Cambridge, MA: Belknap Press, 1957).

head of the British military, was serving as the commander of the U.K.'s newly-formed Joint Rapid Reaction Force (JRRF). The JRRF represented a fresh cosmopolitan turn for British foreign and defence policy. In 1997 the recently-elected Labour government, self-branded as 'New Labour,' declared their intent for the U.K. to act as a 'force for good' in the world. Robin Cook, the new Foreign Secretary, declared with confidence that "our foreign policy must have an ethical dimension."[27] This included the use of the armed forces. The 1998 Strategic Defence Review, commissioned by New Labour, was clear in its conclusion that "our forces must ... be able to back up our influence as a leading force for good in the world ... by helping to prevent or manage crises."[28]

Richards and his team were the tip of Britain's new ethical spear. His role was simple in definition but challenging in execution: to be the first senior officer and decision-maker on the ground to any U.K. response to an emerging crisis. Richards, supported by no more than a handful of officers, would rush to the situation, secure a foothold, make a plan, communicate with London, and then command any resulting inflow of forces. With little time to assess the situation, he had to be trusted by the British government to work on the best of his instincts and character; his capacity for *phronesis*. By 1999 the JRRF command team had already cut their teeth in planning for Kosovo, Macedonia and Montenegro, and in major operations with the Australian Defence Force in East Timor.[29] As these successes built, the British government's commitment to their interventionist, ethical foreign policy deepened – reaching its height in Prime Minister Tony Blair's 1999 Chicago speech where he outlined his now well-known "Doctrine of the International Community."[30]

To Richards, who held a reputation as a deeply political officer, the government's intent for the JRRF was clear. It was to uphold this new ethical foreign policy. This personal perception only solidified as his involvement in the U.K.'s interventions deepened. In 1999, just before the Prime Minister delivered his Chicago speech, Richards first visited

---

27 For the background of Labour's new cosmopolitan approach to foreign policy, see Stephen Deakin, "Britain's Defence and Cosmopolitan Ideals," *Sandhurst Occasional Papers*, No. 3 (2010): 7.

28 United Kingdom Ministry of Defence, *Strategic Defence Review* (London: Ministry of Defence, 1998), para. 201. July 1999. http://webarchive.nationalarchives.gov.uk/20121018172816/http://www.mod.uk/NR/rdonlyres/65F3D7AC-4340-4119-93A2-20825848E50E/0/sdr1998_complete.pdf#page68.

29 For a description of the early activities of the JRRF, see David Richards, *Taking Command* (London: Headline Publishing Group, 2014), 87–111.

30 See the United Kingdom National Archives record of the Prime Minister's speech at Chicago, April 24, 1999. http://webarchive.nationalarchives.gov.uk/+/http://www.number10.gov.uk/Page1297.

the small West African state of Sierra Leone on a routine reconnaissance for the British government. He found a country in crisis. The brutal experience of this first visit, and the imprints it left on his own sense of the importance of *justice* as a core virtue within his ethical framework, would later drive him to bold action: to disobey his orders, to potentially over-reach his authority, and to commit the U.K. to a unilateral intervention in West Africa.

Sierra Leone, a History of Brutal Wars and the Moral Framing of David Richards

Sierra Leone is a small, impoverished sovereign nation on the west coast of Africa. Granted independence from the United Kingdom in 1961, its population of under five million people has always been and remains deeply diverse – consisting of over eighteen ethic groups. A nominal parliamentary democracy was put into place post-independence, but between 1961 and 1999 the country was increasingly controlled by a series of autocratic regimes who exploited the country's natural riches in diamonds and other raw materials for their own benefit, and to the cost of the population at large.

The situation came to a head in 1991 when Foday Sankoh, a former corporal in the Sierra Leone Army (SLA), raised a force called the Revolutionary United Front (RUF). Funded by the notorious Liberian regime of Charles Taylor, Sankoh and the RUF steadily grew in power, seized critical diamond mines, and began to threaten the capital of Freetown. In 1996 the new President, Ahmad Kabbah, signed a peace agreement with the RUF and the situation briefly settled. Kabbah however was overthrown in 1997 by allies of the RUF. In response to the threat of even worse instability the Economic Community of West African States (ECOWAS) deployed Nigerian troops to reinstate him. Fierce fighting ensued, with the RUF gaining a deep reputation for brutality.[31] The rebels sought to terrify the population into submission, their tactics typified by the use of child soldiers, widespread amputations, mutilations, and even cannibalism. In 1999 this brutality reached Freetown and during their self-named "Operation No Living Thing," the RUF killed at least 7,000 people (with at least half being civilians). The RUF briefly held Freetown, and the entire country, before being ejected by ECOWAS troops.[32]

---

31 Andrew Dorman, "The British Experience of Low-Intensity Conflict in Sierra Leone," *Defence and Security Analysis* 23, no. 2 (2007): 186–88.

32 Celina Schocken, "The Special Court for Sierra Leone: Overview and Recommendations," *Berkeley Journal of International Law* 20, no. 2 (2002): 439, and Human Rights Watch, *Sierra*

It was in this environment that David Richards first saw Sierra Leone. His memoirs record a deeply scarring experience.[33] Arriving into the country as part of a small team of no more than five British soldiers, they sailed into the port through waters full of bodies. 25,000 starving refugees had taken shelter in the Kobe sports stadium, which Richards visited during his interactions with senior Sierra Leonean and Nigerian officers. He witnessed RUF gunman execute unarmed civilians in the streets. Perhaps most impactful was his visit to the Milton Margai School for the Blind, where 60 profoundly blind children aged between five and 20 sang to him, "no more guns, no more killing, no more crying and fear of living … no more hunger, no more pain, no more hiding in the rain … peace and democracy that is what we want to see … here in Salone, Sierra Leone, wherever you roam … in this, my West African home." As he left the school, and Freetown, it was clear to him that he had to help if he could. To do anything less would be an affront to his sense of *justice*. He said to himself "come on, you have to bloody well do it and f**k the consequences."[34] The experience of his first visit, and the imprint it left on his moral framework, would prove to have major implications on his *jus ad bellum* decision-making not a year and half later.

Freetown Catches Fire, the British Respond, and Richards Makes a Choice on Their Behalf

In 1999 President Kabbah signed the Lome Peace Agreement with the RUF, giving them a share of the power in Sierra Leone. The UN deployed a peacekeeping force (UNAMSIL) of more than 11,000 soldiers, operating under a seemingly robust Chapter VII mandate outlined in UNSCR 1289. For a brief but uncomfortable period the situation seemed to stabilize. Disarmament, Demobilization and Rehabilitation (DDR) even commenced among both the RUF and the SLA. In April 2000, however, the situation violently collapsed. RUF soldiers detained hundreds of UN observers and peacekeepers and moved again against the capital using captured UN armoured vehicles. With the SLA reduced by the UN's own demobilization process, and with the UN seemingly unwilling to executing its full mandate, little seemed to stand between Freetown and the RUF. The roads seemed open for the RUF to conduct a brutal cleansing of the capital. Both the intent and capacity seemed evident.[35]

Leone: Getting Away with Murder, Mutilation, Rape. New Testimony from Sierra Leone 11, no. 3(A), July, 1999. https://www.hrw.org/legacy/reports/1999/sierra/.

33 Richards, *Taking Command*, chapter 7, 113–29.

34 Richards, *Taking Command*, 122–23.

35 Dorman, "British Experience of Low Intensity Conflict in Sierra Leone," 187–90.

International eyes turned to the British for a response, a demand borne of both colonial history and the U.K.'s more recent involvement in the 'Arms to Africa' scandal. With hundreds of British citizens in Sierra Leone, and with British soldiers among the UN hostages, the Government had little choice but to act. Richards rapidly found himself back in the country, with limited orders to prepare a Non-Combatant Evacuation Operation (NEO) of British citizens under the label of Operation PALLISER. But Richards had his own ideas. As Whitehall's bureaucratic wheels labored, he was already acting. Based on his previous experience in the country, the moral imprint of the horrors he had seen, and his own sense of what was *just* and *unjust* in conflict, Richards formed a plan to prevent the RUF seizing Freetown and repeating the violence of 1999. This self-generated plan had two streams. First, he was determined to use British troops to drive the UN cohort to the outer edges of their mandate, taking them from a peacekeeping to a peace-enforcement mindset, and pushing them to take aggressive action against the rebels. Second he sought to develop a home-grown alliance to fight the RUF, consisting of the SLA, a group of irregular soldiers called the Kamajors, and a notorious gang called the West Side Boys. He and his team would increasingly call this group the 'Unholy Alliance.' With these two lines of effort Richards would stop the RUF.[36]

Richards executed his plan with all the skill and efficiency that would lead to him becoming Chief of the Defence Staff. Supported by the U.K.'s spearhead 1st Battalion the Parachute Regiment, a sizeable special forces contingent and the British High Commissioner, Richards rapidly seized and secured Lunghi Airport. He deployed special operators to the south and east of Freetown, and started to push soldiers from the Parachute Regiment out to bolster UN and SLA positions. Through sheer confidence and reputation he co-opted the Indian commander of UN forces, persuading him and senior UN officials to adopt a more aggressive posture. Richards personally found and visited Johnny Paul Koroma, the notorious leader of the West Side Boys, bargaining him into supporting the Government instead of the rebels. He even contracted a mercenary-flown Mi-24 Hind attack helicopter, using it to strike RUF forces with rockets and machine guns. He did all of this at his own volition, and without consultation with his chain of command at the U.K.'s Permanent Joint Headquarters. Richards' plan was not one of peacekeeping. Tens of RUF fighters were killed by British soldiers in fierce firefights, albeit mostly in self-defence.[37]

---

36   Richards, *Taking Command*, 132–233. On the "Unholy Alliance" see 131.

37   Richards, *Taking Command*, chapter 8 and chapter 9, 130–63.

The Richards plan was markedly effective. Foday Sankoh, the leader of the RUF, was rapidly captured by the SLA.[38] The powerful combination of Government forces, local militias, over 4,500 British troops, a U.K. Amphibious Ready Group of warships and Harrier jets, and an energized UN force suffocated the RUF's forward momentum. By May 2000 this pause had given the UN time to pass Resolution 1299, which bolstered UN troops in the region and re-armed the Sierra Leonean forces.[39] The British Government, finally fully aware of all Richards' actions and originally under pressure to sack him, chose to approve his orders after the fact and accept the credit.[40] Eventually a permanent International Military Assistance Training Team was put in place. Operation PALLISER would enter British history as an example of a remarkably successful, unilateral intervention. Richards' personal reputation was made. But what would *jus ad bellum* theory say about his actions? Were they *just*? Did they demonstrate *phronesis*?

Analysis: Richards, Proper Authority and Just Cause

By his own record of events it is clear that Brigadier David Richards made an individual, unilateral decision to use military force in Sierra Leone. He did this not only without consulting with his political masters in London, but often in direct contravention of the orders he was given.[41] With this in mind, can the British intervention in Operation PALLISER be seen as a *just war*? Can Richards (or any individual soldier) alone rely on their own character to act as a *proper authority*, and therefore make a legitimate judgment on *just cause*? Or does the unilateral nature of his action fundamentally undermine the *justice* of the use of force?

To answer these questions one must perhaps look at *proper authority* and *just cause* in turn. There is a logical step from one to the next: you have to be a *proper authority* before you can make judgments on *just cause*. Whether Richards was *proper* or not is an argument that can swing both ways. History likely stands with the Brigadier. The separation of the military from political authority is a relatively new phenomenon, and

---

38 Schocken, "Special Court for Sierra Leone," 442.

39 The full text of UN Security Council Resolution 1299 can be found within UN archives. May 19, 2000. http://unscr.com/en/resolutions/1299.

40 For Richards' own view, see *Taking Command*, 159. For the formal view of the British government, see the statement of the Foreign Secretary, Robin Cook, delivered to Parliament on May 15, 2000. https://api.parliament.uk/historic-hansard/commons/2000/may/15/sierra-leone#column_24.

41 In *Taking Command*, Richards states that "it has been said that my decision to ignore my order from London and intervene militarily in the civil war – which is what happened over the next days and weeks – was cavalier." See *Taking Command*, 131.

for the bulk of the two thousand year tradition of *jus ad bellum* soldier and politicians have been one and the same. Uniformed, highly-ranked and carrying the Queen's commission, he was certainly a *bone fide* representative of the United Kingdom. In civil-military terms this case was helped by his close association with the British High Commissioner in Sierra Leone, Alan Jones, who supported (but did not order) his actions.[42] There is, however, far shakier ground. Richards based much of his decision to disobey and expand his orders on a chance meeting with the Foreign Secretary, Robin Cook, at Sydney airport in late 1999 where Cook reportedly told him that "Sierra Leone mattered to the Government in an exceptional way."[43] Richards translated this chance meeting, and his own impression of Tony Blair's personal interests, into government policy – using it as justification to overrule the lawful orders he received from London and to order his soldiers to fight the RUF rebels. Arguably this far outreached his authority, dangerously undermining any position he might hold as a *proper authority* in the use of force. Such hubris can be fatal.

If we assume Richards *was* a *proper authority*, can it be said that his cause was just? The instinctive, first glance answer is probably 'yes.' As someone who had seen the horrors of the previous RUF attack on Freetown, Richards was well placed to make a virtue-based judgment about the need to stop them – perhaps more so than the distant, disconnected planners in the U.K. His justification seems to be broadly based on preventing what he perceived to be an imminent humanitarian disaster. Indeed he expended British blood and treasure to do so with little demonstrable gain for the national interest. To him it was the right thing to do, in line with his own sense of *justice* as a core virtue worth defending, and of the U.K.'s stated aim that the British military should be a 'force for good.' The challenge, however, lies in the inherently human limitations of Richards' individual *perception* and the potential bias in his decision-making. He may well have believed that a massacre in Freetown was imminent – but how accurate was this belief? Both the United Nations and the British High Commission had sent alarmed reports back to their headquarters, but there were doubts as to the veracity of the intelligence and the true urgency of the situation.[44] Richards arrived in Freetown on Saturday May 6, and he allowed himself no time to verify the true urgency of the threat. Indeed in his memoirs he admits that he was developing his plan of action before his aircraft even

---

42   Richards, *Taking Command*, 140.
43   Richards, *Taking Command*, 132.
44   Paul Williams, "Fighting for Freetown: British Military Intervention in Sierra Leone," *Contemporary Security Policy* 22, no. 3 (2001): 153.

touched down. By the afternoon of the same day he was acting.[45] With a shallow picture of the situation, and with conceptual pre-planning already complete, to what extent can Richards really argue that he was acting preventively and not pre-emptively? Was the strength of his own virtue ethic driving an unfair urgency to act? Incomplete intelligence, individual bias and personal interests might all threaten his *just cause* credentials.

In the end, like many choices around the use of force, the actions of David Richards are weighed by their consequences. Whether the threat was as serious as he felt or not, Richards certainly prevented the threat of a massacre in Freetown from becoming a reality. Through a relatively tailored and proportionate use of force he stabilized a rapidly deteriorating situation for long enough that the international community could come together and step in. However this did not come without cost. Tens of RUF fighters were killed by British soldiers and the 'Unholy Alliance.' Their deaths must to an extent rest on Richards' shoulders, his sense of the comparative importance of *justice*, and the accuracy of his perceptions. The deal he made with the devil of the West Side Boys, perhaps the most morally questionable of his acts,[46] would eventually bite back with the rebels.kidnapping soldiers from the Royal Irish Regiment and a special forces soldier dying in the rescue.[47] Richards himself admits he was lucky that more British soldiers did not die. If they had, the morality of his decision-making would perhaps seem far more questionable.

As a final point, the longer term impacts of Richards' decisions – and those like his – must also not be ignored. International norms around the use of force are ever malleable, shaped over time by every tactical choice made and shot fired. Richards' actions in Sierra Leone arguably reinforced a broader pattern of intervention and regime change adopted by the British Labour Government; a deepening pattern that would eventually lead to the gateways of the Iraq War. Dr Hans Blix, in his evidence to the U.K.'s Chilcot Inquiry into Iraq, used the British intervention in Sierra Leone as an example of how the UN's custodianship of the use of force, enshrined in Chapter VII of the Charter, was steadily (and perhaps terminally) degraded after 1991.[48] Richards could never have foreseen

---

45 Richards, *Taking Command*, 131–33.
46 Richards, *Taking Command*, 143.
47 The rescue of the Royal Irish soldiers from the West Side Boys (known as *Operation BARRAS*) took place on September 10, 2000, some three months after Richards had left Sierra Leone. See Richard Connaughton, "Operation BARRAS," *Small Wars and Insurgencies* 12, no. 2 (2001): 110–19.
48 Iraq Inquiry, *Public Hearing of Dr Hans Blix*, 19, line 16 at http://webarchive. nationalarchives.gov.uk/20171123123302/http://www.iraqinquiry.org.uk/the-evidence/witness-transcripts/, accessed April 29, 2018.

these long-term implications of his actions, but that does not mean they can be wished away. Like a rock thrown in the *jus ad bellum* pond, the ripples of the decision of this single soldier reached far and wide. All professional soldiers who find themselves in Richards' shoes should keep such things in the back if their mind as they choose whether it is better to act, or to stand by and watch.

Case Study 2:
Gender Equity as Fairness in the Military Institution

Kate Germano and David G. Smith

Introduction

Gender equity refers to the fairness of treatment for women and men based on their respective needs. Generally, people understand this to mean equal treatment, but this also includes different treatment when appropriate that is considered equivalent in terms of rights, benefits, obligations, and opportunities. To examine gender equity as a form of justice, it is important to recognize longstanding institutional challenges.

In modern terms, gender is often understood as a social construct, yet there remains an underlying assumption that gender differences are equated with biological sex. This biological assumption continues to influence political thought and in particular, the Western tradition relies on natural explanations of the roles of women and men (e.g., division of labor) in social institutions.[49] These natural explanations of gender roles continue to reinforce the dichotomy that men work in the public sphere to shape society, and women serve as caregivers in the private sphere.[50]

---

49 Susan M. Okin, "Justice and gender: An unfinished debate," *Fordham L. Rev.* 72 (2005): 1537–67.

50 Joan Acker, "From sex roles to gendered institutions," *Contemporary Sociology* 21, no. 5 (1992): 565–69; F. Mackay, M. Kenny and L. Chappell, "New institutionalism through a gender lens: Towards a feminist institutionalism?" *International Political Science Review* 31, no. 5 (2010): 573–88.

This normative and widely-held gendered hierarchy is infused into every social institution from the family to the state that influences and challenges institutional change to create gender equity.

In the military, gender equity has historically been unattainable based on legal restrictions and constraints placed upon women's military participation. In the United States, these legal restrictions were completely removed in 2016. However, structural barriers, social norms and formal and informal policies remain that prevent the U.S. military from achieving gender equity to the detriment of the institution and its functional imperative.

Nowhere is the lack of gender equity more evident than in the Marine Corps, which is the only service to maintain sex-segregated training. The gendered standards of Marine Corps entry level training are divisive and antithetical to the purpose of bootcamp-transforming individuals and civilians into fighting units and warriors ready for combat. The separation of men and women at recruit training also sets the stage for misperceptions about the abilities of women and perpetuates negative stereotypes about female Marines that then follow them throughout their careers. We analyze the experiences of male and female Marine Corps recruit training battalions providing a structural and social normative account of gender inequity.

Beyond the structural barriers and social norms in military recruit training, throughout their careers women face a continuing informal and formal message that they do not fit in the military institution that paradoxically may be worsened by the meritocratic value of the military. We examine formal and informal personnel policies that reinforce gender bias against women, privilege men's careers and ultimately undermine the recruitment and retention of talented women.

We argue that the military's lack of fairness weakens the foundation of civic republicanism and the citizen-soldier tradition. Implications may include a widening civilian-military divide and continued erosion of the civic obligation of service.

USMC Bootcamp – Separate But Not Equal

The U.S. military espouses meritocratic ideals, promising young men and women that no matter their family history or income level, they will have every opportunity for advancement and growth based on ability and talent. It is one of the only professions that pays men and women with the same experience and seniority equally and transparently, and on the surface, it would appear that the military is one of the few professions where men and women have an equal chance of success and fair treatment. However, structural barriers, social norms, and formal and informal policies continue to prevent the U.S. military from achieving gender equity – to the detriment of the institution and its functional imperative.

While the legal construct of 'separate but equal' has consistently been struck down by U.S. courts, the Marine Corps maintains gender segregated entry-level training for men and women. Senior Marine leaders have consistently defended the practice of gender segregation at bootcamp, arguing that women inherently lack the confidence necessary to train alongside their male counterparts. They claim that the training is exactly the same as that for men, and that the female training compound and female drill instructors provide the same advantages to women. Yet segregation and the size of the female training battalion have both artificially limited the size of the female population and created doubt about whether women can perform to the same levels as men. As a result, the gender divide in the service is both literal and figurative.

There are seven male recruit training battalions in the Marine Corps, and men train both at the Recruit Depot Parris Island, South Carolina, and the Recruit Depot in San Diego, California. In contrast, all women complete recruit training at the Fourth Recruit Training Battalion on Marine Corps Recruit Depot Parris Island. Because women are isolated from their male counterparts in training and female recruits are only assigned one recruit depot, from a cultural perspective, segregated bootcamp ensures women remain 'the Other.' This creates doubt in the minds of male Marines that female recruit training is as challenging and demanding as it is for men. Segregation thus perpetuates negative stereotypes about Marine women by reinforcing the idea that they are not capable of physically and mentally measuring up to the men. Thus, male leaders set the tone at the most foundational level of training for what the predominantly male population should expect from women Marines throughout their careers.

There is no data to demonstrate that segregated training actually increases the confidence and effectiveness of women recruits. In fact, despite the Marine Corps recruitment mantra of 'Earned, never given,' at segregated bootcamp women arguably can do less and still achieve the title of U.S. Marine. Rather than a practice grounded in evidence-based data, segregated bootcamp is more likely a reflection of benevolent sexist tendencies by senior Marine leaders who believe that women require coddling as they are mentally and physically fragile. Because of low expectations and assumptions about physiology, there has been little scrutiny of female recruit performance by Marine leaders. In fact, decades of female recruit graduation scores in categories such as rifle range qualification, close order drill, and physical fitness, demonstrate that the female recruits have consistently underperformed compared to their male counterparts, with no questions asked.

Yet because more female recruits possess college credits when they enlist, many women are automatically promoted ahead of their male peer group upon graduation from bootcamp, regardless of their actual success in training. Thus, from the start of their careers, men and women learn that promotions are not necessarily a reflection of the meritocratic ideal of competence, and that clear double standards exist for women Marines. This breeds resentment and distrust of women Marines. It also sets them up to fail as they leave recruit training with an inflated sense of their accomplishments, only to find out once they attend integrated follow-on training that they are far behind their male counterparts in terms of their knowledge, physical fitness, and shooting abilities.

There are also specific structural barriers to gender equity in the Marine Corps due to segregated bootcamp. The recruit living spaces on the female training compound are much smaller than those in the male training battalions. As a result, there are fewer bed spaces for female trainees, limiting the annual throughput to approximately 3,500 female recruits per year. Because of the constraints presented by the battalion's squadbay size, the Marine Corps is unable to increase the size of the female population past 10 percent, despite women being 51 percent of the recruitable population.[51] In addition to perpetuating cultural problems because most male Marines never serve with women, the small population limits the potential for women to attain high ranking positions that would allow them to influence policies related to gender. Thus, policies that impact gender are formulated by mostly male senior leaders. Additionally, with less than 30 percent of America's youth qualified to join the military, Fourth Battalion's architecture prevents the Marine Corps from drawing upon the available talent pool to the greatest extent possible.

---

51 The Department of Defense considers the recruitable population to include men and women between the ages of 17–29 who are mentally, morally, and physically qualified to enlist. According to DoD data, less than 30 percent of American youth meet the qualifications to join the military (http://cdn.missionreadiness.org/NATEE1109.pdf cited in *2018 Heritage Foundation Report – The Looming National Security Crisis* – available at https://www.heritage.org/defense/report/the-looming-national-security-crisis-young-americans-unable-serve-the-military). The National Academies of Sciences, Engineering, and Medicine states qualifications for military service include "education, aptitudes, physical or medical attributes, moral character, and certain demographic characteristics." Moral disqualifications include drug use and criminal behavior. Demographic qualifications include citizenship, age, and dependents (children and/or marriage). See *Attitudes, Aptitudes, and Aspirations of American Youth*, ed. Paul Sackett and Anne Mavor, available at https://www.nap.edu/read/10478/chapter/6.

Fourth Battalion's architecture also negatively impacts the performance of women in key graduation events, which then impacts their credibility. Because the construction of the compound predated women qualifying with the service rifle, the catwalks connecting living, dining, and academic spaces are too narrow to allow recruits to march with their weapons unless slung across their shoulders or carried in front of them at port arms. The male recruits all attend classes and meals at facilities not co-located with their battalions, requiring them to march to and from each location every training day. Having the opportunity to march in unison not only builds esprit de corps and discipline, but it allows the recruits to practice precision marching movements with their weapons along the way, building their upper body strength and their confidence in their weapons handling skills. Conversely, the architecture of the women's compound has historically negatively impacted the performance of female recruits in their close order drill assessments as well as on the rifle range.

Thus, segregated Marine Corps bootcamp results in lowered expectations for performance, but also inhibits growth of the female population of Marine women. The two factors combine to create a culture where women are considered inferior, untrustworthy, and anything but equal.

The Military as a Meritocracy and Impact on Gender Equity

The military has often been described and does indeed exhibit characteristics of a meritocratic institution such as Equal Employment Opportunity policies reinforced by senior leadership, gender-integrated work environments (with the notable exception previously discussed), social hierarchy based on rank instead of social status characteristics, and a professional ethos that emphasizes competence and expertise in terms of warrior excellence.[52] For example, since the official integration of blacks as a racial minority in the military in 1948, they have had a higher representation within the military as compared to civilian society largely due to the perception that the military provided more equal opportunity

---

52 Jennifer H. Lundquist, "Ethnic and gender satisfaction in the military: The effect of a meritocratic institution," *American Sociological Review* 73, no. 3 (2008): 477–96; C. Moskos, "From citizens' army to social laboratory," *The Wilson Quarterly (1976-)* 17, no. 1 (1993): 83–94; Robert J. Sampson and John H. Laub, "Socioeconomic achievement in the life course of disadvantaged men: Military service as a turning point, circa 1940–1965," *American Sociological Review* 61, no. 3 (1996): 347–67.

and less discrimination.[53] Partially because of the traditionally masculine culture of the military, gender integration continues to be more challenging than racial integration despite the formal removal of all official occupational sex segregation with the opening of all ground combat military occupational specialties in 2016. Contributing to the military's gender integration challenge are gender stereotypes, and conscious and unconscious bias, which are likely impediments to important professional career milestones and outcomes related to performance evaluations, advancement and retention.

The military's emphasis on objective performance, especially as it relates to mission accomplishment and teamwork, is the foundation of merit-based organizational practices related to evaluations, advancement and retention. Continuation in military service is connected to retention through both the service member's desire to continue service as well as the ability to advance in the military's 'up or out' promotion system. In examining the military performance evaluation and promotion systems, we can begin to understand how institutional cultural values, organizational practices, decision makers' biases, and their interrelationships may be the sources of gender integration challenges.

Ironically, research clearly shows that organizations like the military that emphasize meritocracy as a cultural value show greater gender bias in performance evaluations and fail to produce gender neutral employment outcomes despite the good intentions of these merit-based practices.[54] In Castilla and Benard's 2010 research on meritocracy and performance outcomes, this 'paradox of meritocracy' is explained through the unintended activation of stereotypes and schemas for decision makers who feel they are not prejudiced. Decision makers who feel that they have established their "moral credentials" in being non-prejudicial, and that these moral credentials are reinforced through meritocracy as an organizational value, are more prone to unknowingly express prejudiced attitudes.[55] Indeed, these leaders feel they are more objective, confident in their beliefs, more likely to act on these beliefs and are less likely to examine their own biases and motivations when they are not likely to be questioned.

53   J. S. Butler and C. C. Moskos, *All That We Can Be: Black Leadership and Racial Integration The Army Way* (New York: Perseus Book Group, 1996).

54   Emilio J. Castilla, "Gender, race, and meritocracy in organizational careers," *American Journal of Sociology* 113, no. 6 (2008): 1479–1526; E. J. Castilla and S. Benard, "The paradox of meritocracy in organizations," *Administrative Science Quarterly* 55, no. 4 (2010): 543–676; E. J. Castilla, "Gender, race, and the new (merit-based) employment relationship," *Industrial Relations: A Journal of Economy and Society* 51, s.1 (2012): 528–62.

55   Benoit Monin and Dale T. Miller. "Moral credentials and the expression of prejudice," *Journal of Personality and Social Psychology* 81, no. 1 (2001): 33–43.

In organizations like the military that have work-relevant negative stereotypes of women based on a traditional hegemonic masculine culture, leaders are more likely to express these stereotypes in employment-related evaluations and decisions.

Performance evaluations serve two basic purposes in the military: advancement in the promotion system and developmental feedback. Gendered language in performance evaluations subtly (or not) sends signals and reinforces the message that women do not belong or fit in the organization. These messages start early in military women's careers in their indoctrination and are reinforced through performance standards, professional development, peers, senior leaders, lack of role models and mentors that are associated with lower career intentions and outcomes.[56] Specifically, gender bias is apparent in performance evaluations when women are penalized with more negative attributes related to a lack of agentic competency (not qualified to do the job) and usurping agentic dominance (backlash for being assertive) despite performing similarly to men on objective performance measures.[57]

While performance evaluations are potentially one source of bias, military promotion boards are conducted separately by another set of decision makers and therefore a second opportunity for bias to enter into employment-related decisions and particularly in meritocratic organizations. Because military promotion board members believe that the military performance evaluation system is based on merit, they are more likely to relax awareness of their own biases and discount performance evaluations based on gender through the performance-reward bias.[58] In effect, women may suffer the penalty of gender bias twice in the performance evaluation and promotion system in meritocratic organizations like the military.

Evidence shows that overcoming these biases in employment decision-making can be achieved through designing process interventions related to perceived managerial discretion, transparency and accountability.[59] In organizations where decision makers perceive they have less discretion (subjectivity) in employment decisions, research evidence shows fewer

56 David G. Smith and Judith E. Rosenstein, "Gender and the military profession: Early career influences, attitudes, and intentions," *Armed Forces & Society* 43, no. 2 (2017): 260–79.

57 David G. Smith, J. E. Rosenstein, M. K. Nikolov, and D. A. Chaney, "The power of language: Gender, status and agency in performance evaluations." *Sex Roles* (2018): 1–13, available at https://doi.org/10.1007/s11199-018-0923-7.

58 Emilio J. Castilla, "Gender, race, and meritocracy in organizational careers," *American Journal of Sociology* 113, no. 6, (2008): 1479–1526.

59 Iris Bohnet, *What Works: Gender Equality by Design* (Cambridge, MA: Harvard University Press, 2016).

negative employment effects based on bias. As an example, managers with discretion have been shown to perceive that procedural justice will be influential in justifying biased decisions to women employees using readily available social accounts.[60]

Organizations with increased transparency for employment decisions and decision-maker accountability are associated with reduced gender bias effects. Considering the example of military promotions boards, board members' decisions are confidential as are the promotion board proceedings. There is overall accountability of the conduct of the board, but individual decisions are anonymous by design. Board results are publicly disclosed, but justification for decisions remains undisclosed as part of the board proceedings. Board members are sworn to secrecy and are therefore protected from having to provide explanation for their individual decisions. The high level of discretion, lack of transparency and accountability could potentially create an environment for bias to influence employment outcomes such as advancement. Paradoxically, the meritocratic cultural values of the military could be working against efforts to increase gender diversity and reduce inequities.

Implications and Conclusion

The ban on women serving in ground combat roles such as the infantry was considered by many to be the last barrier to equality for military women. However, even with the lifting of the ban by the Secretary of Defense in December 2016, structural barriers like segregated bootcamp in the Marine Corps, as well as social norms, and formal and informal policies prevent military women from achieving true gender equity. In fact, despite the meritocratic values espoused by the services, the failure of military leaders to recognize their own implicit biases may prevent women from being fairly considered for unique leadership opportunities, assignments, and promotion. Further, because they do not fit the stereotypical warrior archetype, women often feel out of place in the military, making them less likely to remain on active duty. The failure of the military to address systemic obstacles to the success of service women serve as a barrier to the available recruitment talent pool. With less than 30 percent of American youth qualified to serve in the military, the failure or unwillingness of the services to see young women as necessary to military readiness could very well have a damaging impact on our national defense in the not so

---

60   Maura A. Belliveau, "Engendering inequity? How social accounts create vs. merely explain unfavorable pay outcomes for women," *Organization Science* 23, no. 4 (2012): 1154–74.

distant future. Gender equity in the military is a form of civic justice that promotes the obligation of all qualified Americans to serve in the spirit of the citizen-soldier tradition. American society and our democratic values demand military accession, training, and promotion policies and practices that reinforce civic equality, not undermine it.

References

Acker, J. "From sex roles to gendered institutions," *Contemporary Sociology* 21, no. 5 (1992): 565–69.

Augustine, *Contra Faustum*, Book XXII.

Belliveau, M.A. "Engendering inequity? How social accounts create vs. merely explain unfavorable pay outcomes for women," *Organization Science* 23, no. 4 (2012): 1154–74.

Bohnet, I. *What Works: Gender Equality by Design*. Cambridge, MA: Harvard University Press, 2016.

Buchanan, A. "Moral Status and Human Enhancement," *Philosophy and Public Affairs* 37, no. 4 (2009): 369.

Butler, J. S. and C. C. Moskos, *All That We Can Be: Black Leadership and Racial Integration The Army Way*. New York: Perseus Book Group, 1996.

Castilla, E. J. "Gender, race, and meritocracy in organizational careers," *American Journal of Sociology* 113, no. 6 (2008): 1479–1526.

Castilla, E. J. "Gender, race, and the new (merit-based) employment relationship," *Industrial Relations: A Journal of Economy and Society* 51, s.1 (2012): 528–62.

Castilla, E. J. and Benard, S. "The paradox of meritocracy in organizations," *Administrative Science Quarterly* 55, no. 4 (2010): 543–676.

Caney, S. "Humanity, Associations, and Global Justice: In Defence of Humanity-Centred Cosmopolitan Egalitarianism," *The Monist* 94 (2011): 506–34.

Cohen, E. A. *Supreme Command: Soldiers, Statesmen and Leadership in Wartime*. New York: Simon & Schuster, 2002.

Coleman, S. *Military Ethics: An Introduction with Case Studies*. New York: Oxford University Press, 2013.

Connaughton, R. "Operation BARRAS," *Small Wars and Insurgencies* 12, no. 2 (2001): 110–19.

Das, R. "Virtue Ethics and Rights Action," *Australasian Journal of Philosophy* 81, no. 3 (2002): 324–39.

de las Casas, B. *A Short Account of the Destruction of the Indies* (1552).

Deakin, S. "Britain's Defence and Cosmopolitan Ideals," Sandhurst Occasional Papers, No. 3 (2010): 7.

Doris, J. M. "Persons, Situations and Virtue Ethics," *Noûs* 32, no. 4 (1998): 504–30.

Dorman, A. "The British Experience of Low-Intensity Conflict in Sierra Leone," *Defence and Security Analysis* 23, no. 2 (2007): 186–88.

Feaver, P. D. *Armed Servants: Agency, Oversight and Civilian Military Relations.* Cambridge, MA: Harvard University Press, 2005.

Frame, T. "Virtue Ethics" in *Key Concepts in Military Ethics*, edited by Dean-Peter Baker, Chapter 4. Sydney: University of New South Wales Press, 2015.

Human Rights Watch, *Sierra Leone: Getting Away with Murder, Mutilation, Rape. New Testimony from Sierra Leone* 11, no. 3(A), July 1999. https://www.hrw.org/legacy/reports/1999/sierra/.

Huntington S. P. *The Soldier and the State: The Theory and Policy of Civilian-Military Relations.* Cambridge, MA: The Belknap Press of Harvard University Press, 1957.

Irwin, T. *The Development of Ethics, Volume 1: From Socrates to the Reformation.* Oxford: Oxford University Press, 2011.

Johnston, D. *A Brief History of Justice.* Chichester: Wiley-Blackwell, 2011.

Kateb, G. *Human Dignity.* Cambridge, MA: Harvard University Press, 2011.

Lundquist, J. H. "Ethnic and gender satisfaction in the military: The effect of a meritocratic institution," *American Sociological Review* 73, no. 3 (2008): 477–96.

McMahan, J. *Killing in War.* New York: Oxford University Press, 2009.

Mackay, F., M. Kenny, and L. Chappell, "New institutionalism through a gender lens: Towards a feminist institutionalism?" *International Political Science Review* 31, no. 5 (2010): 573–88.

Mazzetti, M., N. Kulish, C. Drew, S. F. Kovaleski, S. D. Naylor and J. Ismay. "SEAL Team 6: A Secret History of Quiet Killings and Blurred Lines," *New York Times*, June 6, 2015.

Mission Readiness: Military Leaders for Kids. *Ready, Willing, And Unable to Serve.* Report, http://cdn.missionreadiness.org/NATEE1109.pdf. Accessed April 29, 2018.

Monin, B. and D. T. Miller. "Moral credentials and the expression of prejudice," *Journal of Personality and Social Psychology* 81, no. 1 (2001): 33–43.

Moskos, C. "From citizens' army to social laboratory," *The Wilson Quarterly (1976-)* 17, no. 1 (1993): 83–94.

Okin, S. M. "Justice and gender: An unfinished debate," *Fordham L. Rev.* 72 (2004): 1537–67.

National Intelligence Council, *Global Trends: The Paradox of Progress* (2017).

Richards, D. *Taking Command.* London: Headline Publishing Group, 2014.

Rodin, D. *War and Self-Defense*. New York: Oxford University Press, 2003.

Rosen, M. *Dignity: Its History and Meaning*. Cambridge, MA: Harvard University Press, 2012.

Sackett, P. and A. Mavor. *Attitudes, Aptitudes, and Aspirations of American Youth: Implications for Military Recruitment*. Report, https://www.nap.edu/read/10478/chapter/6. Accessed April 29, 2018.

Sampson, R. J. and J. H. Laub, "Socioeconomic achievement in the life course of disadvantaged men: Military service as a turning point, circa 1940–1965," *American Sociological Review* 61, no. 3 (1996): 347–67.

Scheipers, S. *Heroism and the Changing Character of War: Toward Post-Heroic Warfare?* Basingstoke: Palgrave Macmillan, 2014.

Schocken, C. "The Special Court for Sierra Leone: Overview and Recommendations," *Berkeley Journal of International Law* 20, no. 2 (2002).

Seglow, J. "Associative Duties and Global Justice," *Journal of Moral Philosophy* 7 (2010): 54–73.

Shay, J. *Achilles in Vietnam: Combat Trauma and the Undoing of Character*. New York: Simon & Schuster, 1995.

Smith, D. G. and J. E. Rosenstein. "Gender and the military profession: Early career influences, attitudes, and intentions," *Armed Forces & Society* 43, no. 2 (2017): 260–79.

Smith, D.G., J. E. Rosenstein, M. K. Nikolov and D. A. Chaney. "The power of language: Gender, status and agency in performance evaluations," *Sex Roles*, 1–13 (2018).

Spoehr, T. and Handy, B. *The Looming National Security Crisis: Young Americans Unable to Serve the Military*. Report, February 13, 2018. https://www.heritage.org/defense/report/the-looming-national-security-crisis-young-americans-unable-serve-the-military.

Svensson, F. "Virtue Ethics and the Search for an Account of Right Action," *Ethical Theory and Moral Practice* 13, no. 3 (2010): 255–71.

Swanton, C. *Virtue Ethics: A Pluralistic View*. Oxford: Oxford University Press, 2003.

Waldron, J. *Dignity, Rights, and Rank*. Oxford: Oxford University Press, 2012.

Walzer, M. *Just and Unjust Wars: A Moral Argument with Historical Illustrations*. New York: Basic Books, 1977.

Williams P. "Fighting for Freetown: British Military Intervention in Sierra Leone," *Contemporary Security Policy* 22, no. 3 (2001): 153.

2

OBEDIENCE

Overview: Is Obedience a Virtue?

Jessica Wolfendale

In the United States, all enlisted military personnel swear to obey "the orders of the President of the United States and the orders of the officers appointed over me."[1] Military personnel must obey orders promptly in order to facilitate effective military functioning. Obedience is touted as an essential military virtue, and disobedience to orders is a punishable offense in most, if not all, military forces.

Yet, obedience to orders has been associated with war crimes. Military personnel of all ranks have committed torture, rape, genocide, and murder under orders. 'I was just following orders' (*respondeat superior*) is no longer accepted as a complete defense to a charge of war crimes. In the words of the Nuremberg court: "The obedience of a soldier is not the obedience of an automaton. A soldier is a reasoning agent."[2]

This means that military personnel cannot evade responsibility for the actions they perform under orders. But when and under what conditions should military personnel disobey orders? If obedience is sometimes morally wrong, how can obedience be a military virtue?

In this overview I argue that only *reflective obedience* can be a military virtue: obedience governed and constrained by the ends of the military profession serving a legitimate state and by the laws of armed conflict. Section 1 explains the concept of obedience and outlines the idea of virtuous obedience. Section 2 explores when the military has legitimate

---

1 U.S. Army, "Oath of Enlistment," https://www.army.mil/values/oath.html. Accessed April 16, 2018. Interestingly, officers take an oath to uphold the Constitution, rather than obey the President.

2 Martha Minow, "Living Up to Rules: Holding Soldiers Responsible for Abusive Conduct and the Dilemma of the Superior Orders Defence," *McGill Law Journal* 52 (2007): 17.

authority to compel obedience. Section 3 concludes by exploring the limits on obedience that derive from the military's status as a profession and the legitimacy of the military's authority to issue orders.

What is Obedience?

According to the philosopher Benjamin McMyler, obedience involves "rationally subjecting oneself to the will of another."[3] Obeying a person is not just a matter of doing what a person commands; it is following their command for a particular reason. In contrast to taking a person's advice into account in my deliberations about what I should do, when I obey someone I permit her judgment to *replace* my deliberations: I allow her to make up my mind for me.[4]

But why would I allow someone else's judgment to replace my own? How could doing so ever be virtuous? According to the Aristotelian tradition, virtue requires *phronesis*, or practical wisdom: the exercise of judgment and deliberation. As Rosalind Hursthouse explains, the virtues are felt: "on the *right* occasions, towards the *right* people or objects, for the *right* reasons."[5] Thus, the idea of virtuous obedience seems to be an oxymoron. But this is too quick. Obedience can be governed by reason: virtuous obedience is *reflective* obedience.[6] If I have reason to believe that a person has legitimate authority in a particular realm of action, it may be permissible (and rational) for me to defer to her judgment. This is what McMyler calls *deferential obedience*,[7] where I comply with a speaker's demand because I acknowledge her "practical authority"[8] over me – and it is my recognition of her authority to issue these demands that provides my reason for acting. The justification for deferential obedience depends on what it means for a person (or an institution) to possess legitimate practical authority. In relation to military obedience, then, we will have to explore what it means to say that the military has legitimate authority[9] – a question I take up in Section 2.

---

3 Benjamin McMyler, "Obedience and Believing a Person," *Philosophical Investigations* 39, no. 1 (January 2016): 59.

4 McMyler, "Obedience," 66.

5 Rosalind Hursthouse, *On Virtue Ethics* (Oxford: Oxford University Press, 1999), 108–109.

6 Jessica Wolfendale, *Torture and the Military Profession* (Abingdon: Palgrave Macmillan, 2007), 95–96.

7 McMyler, "Obedience," 63.

8 McMyler, "Obedience," 63.

9 McMyler's uses "practical authority" to describe the moral authority to issue demands ("Obedience," 66). Since "legitimate authority" expresses the same idea, so I will use "legitimate authority" in the remainder of this chapter, since that term is more familiar within the military ethics literature.

A second form of obedience is *coerced obedience*.[10] I display coerced obedience when I comply with someone's demands not because I recognize her authority over me but because I fear the consequences of disobedience, such as when I comply with a mugger's demand to hand over my wallet. Coerced obedience may be rational, if the costs of disobedience are high, but it cannot be morally obligatory in the absence of practical authority.

Coerced obedience and deferential obedience often occur in tandem. For example, many people believe that states (at least democratic states) have the legitimate authority to make and enforce laws.[11] Yet states also use the threat of punishment to coerce obedience to the law. So, I might obey the law because I acknowledge the state's legitimate authority to make law *and* because I fear the consequences of breaking the law.[12]

The military, like the state, enforces obedience through the threat of punishment. Yet, the military is also presumed to have practical authority. Military personnel are often thought to have a duty to obey all legitimate orders from their superiors – not just because they might be punished for disobedience, but because their superiors have the *right* to their obedience. This means that the question of the scope and basis of legitimate authority arises for the military as it does for the state. If the military lacks legitimate authority, military personnel might have no duty to obey orders.

The Military and Legitimate Authority

The military in most states views itself as a profession, and many military forces have codes of honor. However, this is not sufficient to establish that the military has legitimate authority. After all, some organized crime groups have codes of honor, yet such groups do not possess any form of legitimate authority.

Unlike organized crime groups, however, the military serves the state and protects the state's national security interests. Those ends define the scope of the military's professional expertise. This means that the military's legitimate authority is tied to that of the state which it serves. There are

---

10 McMyler, "Obedience," 65.

11 The basis and justification of the state's right to make and enforce laws is at the heart of debates about political obligation. See Richard Dagger and David Lefkowitz, "Political Obligation," *The Stanford Encyclopedia of Philosophy* (Fall 2014 Edition), ed. Edward N. Zalta, https://plato.stanford.edu/archives/fall2014/entries/political-obligation/.

12 McMyler, "Obeying a Person," 67.

two central questions regarding a state's legitimate authority:[13] Firstly, what is the *justification* of a state's authority to coerce its citizens? And, secondly, what are the *constraints* on that authority? That a state is justified in coercing its citizens does not mean that the scope of the state's authority is unlimited. There is broad consensus, for example, that no state has the authority to torture and murder its citizens, or subject them to indefinite detention without trial.[14]

We do not need to settle the question of the basis and scope of the state's authority here. For the purposes of this chapter, I propose the following minimal standard of legitimacy: A state has legitimate authority if it protects citizens' basic human rights (including a commitment to upholding basic principles of justice) and involves a governing process subject to some form of regular and transparent review. A state that met these conditions would be a minimally just state,[15] and state institutions such as the military (and the criminal justice system) would have *prima facie* legitimacy as well. In contrast, a tyrannical state that violated citizens' basic rights would lack legitimacy, and military forces that served such a state would also lack legitimacy. This would mean that military personnel in such a state would have no moral obligation to obey orders.

However, just as there are moral constraints on what a legitimate state may do to its citizens, there are moral constraints on how institutions serving a legitimate state may pursue their aims. For example, the criminal justice system of a legitimate state has the authority to punish citizens found guilty of committing a crime. This means that employees of the criminal justice system, such as prison guards, have a duty to obey orders even if they disagree with them. However, as David Estlund argues, this duty is contingent on the criminal justice system meeting a minimal standard of procedural justice, such as a "legitimate procedure for determining who

---

13 A discussion of state legitimacy is beyond the scope of this chapter. See John Simmons, *Justification and Legitimacy: Essays on Rights and Obligations* (Cambridge: Cambridge University Press, 2000); Michael Walzer, "The Moral Standing of States: A Response to Four Critics," *Philosophy and Public Affairs* 9, no. 3 (1980): 209–29, and Stephen Perry, "Political Authority and Political Obligation," in *Oxford Studies in Philosophy of Law: Volume 2*, ed. Leslie Green and Brian Leiter (Oxford: Oxford University Press, 2013), 1–74.

14 David Estlund makes a similar point in relation to punishment: "some acts are too objectionable to be sanitized by being officially commanded" even by a just state. David Estlund, "On Following Orders in an Unjust War," *The Journal of Political Philosophy* 15, no. 2 (2007): 220.

15 See Brian Orend, *The Morality of War*, 2nd edition (Peterborough, Ontario: Broadview Press, 2013). Orend defines a minimally just state as one that is "1) is recognized as legitimate by its own people and most of the international community; 2) avoids violating the rights of other legitimate states; and 3) makes every reasonable effort at satisfying the human rights of its own citizens" (2013, 86).

gets punished."[16] In the absence of such a procedure, there is no duty of obedience. For example, if a legitimate state implemented a popular vote system to decide who gets punished and how severely, those working for the punishment system would no longer have a moral obligation to carry out its commands.[17]

In relation to the military, these constraints mean that a military force serving a legitimate state has the authority to compel obedience to commands related to the *legitimate* ends of military service, in a context where decisions to use military force are governed by a decision-procedure that is committed to 'getting it right.' In other words, for the military to have practical authority over its members, it is not enough that it serves a legitimate state; there must also be evidence that the "justice of the war is being duly looked after" by the state and military leaders.[18]

When is Disobedience Justified?

I argued above that, in the absence of legitimate authority, military personnel have no moral obligation to obey orders. However, there may be grounds for disobedience even in military forces that possess legitimate authority and where the use of military force is governed by a commitment to justice.

Constraints on the Scope of Military's Legitimate Authority

Military officers serving a legitimate state have the authority to order subordinates to perform any actions necessary for the achievement of military goals. But, a military officer does not have the authority to (say) order her subordinates to marry each other, clean her house, or cook her dinner. Orders that are unrelated to military objectives are not orders that military personnel have a duty to obey.

The moral rights of military personnel also impose constraints on the military's practical authority. While military personnel give up many rights when they join the military, they do not give up *all* rights. The military owes a duty of care to military personnel (what Brian Orend describes as an internal *jus in bello*).[19] For example, the military has an obligation to

---

16   Estlund, "On Following Orders," 221.
17   Estlund, "On Following Orders," 221.
18   Estlund, "On Following Orders," 226. Estlund is not claiming that such procedures must always "get it right," but that any mistakes must be "honest mistakes." (Estlund, "On Following Orders," 221.)
19   See Orend 2013.

adequately house, feed, and provide medical care for its members and, arguably, an obligation not to expose them to excessive or unnecessary risk.[20] While the extent of the military's duty of care is a matter of debate, orders that *clearly* expose military personnel to a significant risk of unjustified harm (such as an order to fly a plane that failed a maintenance test) violate this duty of care and need not be obeyed.

The moral rights of the targets of military violence, as encoded in treaties and conventions such as the Geneva Conventions, impose a third set of constraints. The military's practical authority does not extend to orders that violate the laws of armed conflict. As stated in the *U.S. Army Field Manual*, the *U.S. Naval Handbook*, and the *U.S. Soldiers Handbook*, military personnel are bound to "only obey lawful orders."[21] While identifying lawful and unlawful orders is a difficult issue, the principle is correct: there is no duty to obey illegal orders.

Selective Conscientious Objection

What if a combatant in a legitimate military force believes that a war is unjust? Selective conscientious objection (SCO) refers to an objection to a *specific* use of military force, rather than an objection to serving in the military in general.

Early just war scholars, such as Francisco de Vitoria and Suarez, disagreed profoundly over whether soldiers may refuse to fight in wars they believe to be unjust.[22] One argument in favor of a right to SCO appeals to the moral stakes of fighting in a war. In de Vitoria's words, "if the war seems patently unjust to a subject, he must not fight, even if he is ordered to do so by the prince. One may not kill an innocent man on any authority."[23] A different argument appeals to the value of integrity.[24] If we believe that "individuals should be allowed to live in accordance with their own conceptions of the good and the right,"[25] then it may be wrong to force a combatant to violate her deeply-held moral beliefs, particularly

---

20 See Nikki Coleman, *Does the Australian Defence Force have a compelling justification for the duty to obey orders?* (UNSW Canberra School of Humanities and Social Sciences, 2016): 60.

21 International Committee of the Red Cross, IHL Database: Customary IHL, "United States of America Practice Relating to Rule 154. Obedience to Superior Orders," https://ihl-databases.icrc.org/customary-ihl/eng/docs/v2_cou_us_rule154. Accessed May 14, 2018.

22 See George Lucas "Advice and Dissent: "The Uniform Perspective," *Journal of Military Ethics* 8, no. 2 (2009): 141–61 for an overview of this debate.

23 Quoted in Lucas, "Advice," 142.

24 Paul Robinson, "Integrity and Selective Conscientious Objection," *Journal of Military Ethics* 8, no. 1 (2009): 34–47.

25 Mark Navin, "Sincerity, Accuracy and Selective Conscientious Objection," *Journal of Military Ethics* 12, no. 2 (2013): 112.

since integrity is (as many believe) a military virtue. Thus, the military ought not punish soldiers for exercising a moral virtue that the military itself praises.[26]

There are two main arguments against a right to SCO. The first argument focuses on the impact of permitting a right to SCO on military effectiveness. George Lucas, for example, argues that "[w]e simply cannot have a military organization grounded in dissent and disobedience."[27] However, this objection is not an in-principle objection to SCO but rather an empirical objection, the validity of which requires empirical study that is beyond the scope of this chapter.[28] A second argument questions whether military personnel have the *right* to usurp the authority of their superiors. Lucas again: "it is fundamentally opposed to the very structure, purpose, and function of military forces that those in the rank and file should retain a right of veto over procedural decisions of their superiors and legitimate sovereign masters."[29]

The key phrase in the above quote is '*legitimate* sovereign masters.' The duty of military personnel to defer to the military's authority depends on the legitimacy of the military institution. But, firstly, not all military forces are or serve 'legitimate sovereign masters.' And, secondly, even when a military force serves a legitimate state, military personnel cannot just accept on faith that all the state's uses of the military are legitimate. Given the moral costs of war, blindly "trusting the process" is not acceptable. Military personnel have a duty to check that the decision to go to war meets the procedural commitment to justice discussed by Estlund. While the strength of this duty might depend on a combatant's rank (those of a higher rank have greater access to information about the relevant decision-procedures, for example), even the lowest-ranking combatant has access to some information about decisions to use military force. If there is reasonable[30] evidence that the 'justness of a war' is not being looked after by military and political leaders, then I argue that military personnel may permissibly prioritize their personal judgment and refuse to fight.

---

26   See Robinson, "Integrity."

27   Lucas, "Advice," 152.

28   Although see Orend 2008 for a critique of the effectiveness argument.

29   Lucas, "Advice," 152.

30   "Reasonable" here does not mean "reasonable from the perspective of the combatant." Rather, I mean a "reasonable person" standard of evidence. I cannot provide a complete account of a "reasonable person" standard here, but the central idea is that, if a combatant can point to evidence that a reasonable person would agree demonstrates a lack of care in ensuring the justness of a war, such as evidence of a state's failure to seek legal advice about a war, or evidence that the state is misrepresenting or withholding relevant information about a conflict, then that combatant may refuse to fight.

Conclusion

Virtuous military obedience is not blind obedience. The duty of military personnel to obey orders depends on the military's practical authority to compel obedience. Not all military forces possess this practical authority, however, and the duty to obey is not absolute even in those that do. In a legitimate military force, the duty of obedience is constrained by the military's legitimate professional aims, and by the moral rights of military personnel and the potential targets of military force. Virtuous military obedience therefore requires the exercise of moral reflection on the part of military personnel regarding how decisions to use military force are made, as well as the legal and moral status of specific orders.

Case Study 1:
Strategic Dissent in the Military

Reuben E. Brigety and Shannon E. French

The strategic importance of obedience within the military is well recognized and long understood. Without 'good order and discipline' a military organization cannot function and complete its core missions. Foundational military training begins with indoctrination aimed at securing the obedience of troops, both to those above them in rank and to all applicable rules and laws. Therefore, it may seem counterintuitive to suggest that there is also a place for strategic dissent in the military. At first look, dissent seemed to be antithetical to the entire military endeavor. Yet in fact, providing the right opportunity, conditions, and culture for certain forms of dissent in the military, both by those in uniform and civilians who may also be involved in the defense and national security enterprise, can be as vital to strategic success as obedience.

Obedience and discipline are at the core of the military profession not simply arbitrarily, but because, discipline, which implies obedience to orders (certainly obedience to legal orders, at least), is necessary in order to break through or control the behavior of troops in the midst of the so-called fog of war and the chaos that happens in combat. Obedience is necessary in order to achieve victory in any domain. It is also necessary in order to achieve the political objectives for which one uses force in the first place, if we define war in the usual Clausewitzian way as having political ends.

Might it be the case, however, that on certain occasions, one can actually more effectively help achieve the political objectives for which one is engaging in the use of force, not by obeying, but by dissenting? It is not difficult to imagine such occasions. Indeed, they do not need to be merely imagined. One has only to consider the very well known, well-publicized examples of My Lai on the one hand and Abu Ghraib on the other to see instances where strategic ends would have been better served by troops dissenting against their leadership. There are other, less legally obvious cases, as well. There have been any number of U.S. drone strikes in recent years that may have led to civilian casualties in environments where the stated U.S. strategic goal had been to try to cultivate the civilian population to support American political objectives, even while prosecuting a conflict against known or suspected terrorist subjects in the same territories. Nor do these issues arise only when reflecting on high stakes, high profile uses of force. Many militaries have been weakened by scandals that cost the careers of high-ranking individuals whose misguided actions might have been prevented or the damage from them curtailed by well-timed dissent.

The readiness of the fleet may depend on the ability of a junior officer to dissent against a senior officer or other superior known to be taking illegal or unethical action, whether it be accepting the bribe of a lavish dinner party, or access to prostitutes, or Lady Gaga tickets.

There is a third dimension in which dissent may be strategically necessary, as well: that of policy. What role is there for the officer who thinks, 'I am not sure that the intelligence actually suggests that there are weapons of mass destruction (WMDs) in this particular location,' against the sweeping assessments of others with influential voices? Or the senior enlisted who recognizes independently that her unit will never win the trust of the local population unless they protect nearby cultural sites from collateral destruction? Or the chaplain who wonders if his commanders are doing the right thing in handing over prisoners to an allied military who may not maintain the same human rights standards? Can anyone address the real obligations of the now-cliché 'strategic corporal' without considering the importance of dissent?

The formidable challenge is how to allow dissenting voices or perspectives to be heard in ways that can preserve strategic interests without sacrificing good order and discipline. As is often noted, the military cannot operate "as a democracy," with urgent actions delayed until a consensus is formed and a vote is taken. Where can the time and space for dissent be found in a military setting? One answer is that it must be deliberately created.

The U.S. State Department was modeled in many ways on the U.S. military. Thus, although Foreign Service officers do not wear uniforms, they do exist in a fairly rigid hierarchy. There are ranks that must be respected and there is a firm understanding there has to be some level of discipline between what is decided in capitals and what is actually executed on the ground. Yet precisely because questions of policy can often be quite complicated, there is a formal dissent channel within the State Department, through which any diplomat can raise questions or concerns about the policy that he or she is meant to execute. Not only is there a formal channel for dissent, there is (at least there used to be in the previous administration and there traditionally has been) a formal reward for the best dissent report in the State Department on any given year. Why is that important? Because it shows to the institution what respectful dissent ought to look like, and how it ought to be rewarded, and what the expectations are of the institution for how dissent can be valuable to the mission of the institution as a whole.

Medicine provides another example of how to nurture healthy dissent in a hierarchical organization. Hospitals typically have tight discipline, particularly in the context of surgery or triage, and there is hierarchy from physicians to nurses to physician assistants, etc., where there is an expectation that a doctor's requests for the patient will be followed by everyone else. Those requests are even called 'orders' in the medical environment. There is the assumption that in the operating theater, the surgeon is the highest authority, not only as a matter of law, but because the surgeon has the most in technical experience about the procedure being performed.

As a result of a series of challenges with regard to medical mistakes in the United States over the last decade, it is now common practice in operating theaters across the country for everybody in the room, whether they are the surgeon, or a nurse, or a surgical tech, to be empowered to stop or raise their hand at any given time to say, 'I see something that does not look right,' even if they may not happen to be the most senior person in the room. The senior person may still overrule the less experienced individual's objection or concern, but there is no penalty attached to the dissent and all ranks are reminded of the value of it. If the most junior person in the room notices a problem that was overlooked by everyone else and speaks up about it, it is understood that everyone benefits – most of all, the patient. Similar structures of allowed dissent through many ranks have been adopted within aviation, as when a mechanic can ground a commander's flight for something as small as a missing pen that could have been dropped inside essential machinery. This is the same approach to safety that is behind the idea of having stop buttons all along assembly lines in manufacturing plants. In light of the Deepwater Horizon fiasco, such measures have also been adopted in the drilling industry. In each case, rules for respectful, well-timed, and constructive dissent are a bulwark against any erosion of good order and discipline. Many professions have recognized not only that dissent is not inherently bad, but that dissent supports their mission, and so they have enabled systems to make it possible.

Nevertheless, the question remains of what such a system could actually look like in the military context. How does one simultaneously train a person to charge the hill, to take out the machine gun nest, and to obey the lawful orders of those appointed over them, and also train them not only to be comfortable with, but indeed to embrace the necessity of speaking up with dissent when they see that something is antithetical to the mission, values, or laws that govern the organization? Even for the most wise and experienced person, living with such a fundamental tension in one's head can be incredibly challenging. It is even more stressful under the strains of real world operations, such as when one is deployed at sea or engaged in combat, when the people against whose judgment one must dissent are the same people on whom one's own life depends.

However difficult, finding a balance between obedience and dissent is not impossible. Indeed, the human ability to manage this kind of internal tension is part of what enables us to be responsible moral agents. If we were incapable of dissent, we would have no autonomy. By the same token, if we were incapable of obedience, we would be mere moral patients, like infants. The judgment at the Nuremburg trials that "just following orders" was not an acceptable defense for crimes against humanity was an acknowledgment of the fact that, whatever struggle it may take to achieve, moral duty demands that those given orders decide intentionally and deliberately which orders to obey and which to refuse.

As is often the case, the solution can be found in a positive command climate. While a formal dissent channel might not make sense in every unit, informal channels should always exist, and generally do, so long as those in command are not too insecure in their own authority to allow them. A healthy relationship between a seasoned NCO and a junior officer will include elements of obedience and dissent (sometimes in equal measure), and the best senior officers will find XOs who will provide them with useful push-back and sounding boards to prevent the kind of echo chambers that can make bad or dangerous ideas seem wise.

None of this is unnatural for the military, nor should it be unfamiliar. A number of traditional military virtues strongly complement and encourage the notion of respectful dissent. Most notably, both honesty and courage (in this case, moral courage) often demand dissent. An honest, forthright soldier will have the courage to tell even a general that he has misjudged the placement of the enemy's guns. A courageous squadron commanding officer will close out every pilots' briefing by saying they should follow the mission as briefed, "unless it doesn't look right."

The samurai of feudal Japan – whom no one ever accused of lacking good order and discipline – even tied respectful dissent to the military virtue of loyalty. Their requirements for expressing dissent were a bit extreme, as they believed true loyalty could sometimes best be shown by committing ritual suicide to protest the unwise action of one's lord. Thus they should not be thought of as an ideal model for the modern military. However, the point remains that strategic dissent in the military should not be viewed as unprecedented or disruptive.

The presence of dissent within the command structure is something that fits with the martial values, aids good decision-making, and can prevent strategic harm. While no one is suggesting the measures taken by samurai, maintaining command climates that avoid retribution for disagreement while still fostering confidence in the carrying out of lawful orders (no matter how deeply the contrary position is held by the dissenter) should not present a threat to good order and discipline. Healthy and productive dissent within the military may not best be achieved by formal means as seen within the Foreign Service, but rather through an informal or semi-formal understanding, woven by the commander into the fabric of his or her relationships with subordinates. A culture that permits and values respectful dissent cannot be imposed from the outside, but it can be grown from within the unique structures of military units, and its emergence can prevent tragedy.

Case Study 2:
Should Service Personnel Refuse to Fight in Unjust Wars?

David Whetham

The idea that a soldier is expected to disobey a manifestly illegal order is widely accepted. Today, every professional military around the word acknowledges that there is a duty to disobey an order that is recognized as being blatantly illegal. So for example, "if a lieutenant in a fit of rage orders a sergeant to bayonet a baby to 'inspire' villagers to provide information ... [t]here is no ambiguity. The order is a clear assault against human decency, a clear violation of *jus in bello* proscriptions."[31] The Nuremberg trials following World War II confirmed that there are ethical and legal lines that it is so wrong to cross that one cannot claim the defence of following superior orders.[32] One has a duty – as a soldier and as a human being – to disobey certain orders if they go against the very core of human decency.

Does it make any sense that such widely recognized duties are limited to purely tactical or *in bello* level considerations? What if one was given, not a specific order to do something wrong, but a general order to participate in a conflict that appeared to be unjustified, or even criminal in its purpose? Would there be the same kind of obligation to refuse to fight

---

31 Dan Zupan, "Selective Conscientious Objection and the Just Society," in *When Soldiers Say No*, ed. A. Ellner, P. Robinson and D. Whetham (Farnham: Ashgate Publishing, 2014).

32 George R. Lucas, "Advice and Dissent: The Uniformed Perspective," *Journal of Military Ethics*: "Saying No: Selective Conscientious Objection," 8, Edn 2, June 2009.

in such a war? It would seem strange that an order to do something wrong such as "bayonet that baby" should be disobeyed by an individual, but that an order to participate in a much larger criminal or immoral enterprise in which presumably many more innocent people (including babies) will die should be accepted and obeyed without question.[33] And yet, it is also widely accepted that it is not up to the soldier to question the policy of his or her government. There is a perceived difference between these two levels of moral responsibility. At the local level, soldiers are expected to exercise their moral autonomy and refuse to do the wrong thing. A great deal of time, money and effort is invested in the training and education of the modern soldier to ensure that they have the skills and judgement to be able to do the right thing, even in very stressful environments.[34] But that level of moral autonomy is not generally seen to extend to questioning a government decision. Why is this?

Surely, one cannot be excused from knowingly doing wrong on the basis of "she told me to do it," even if the "she" is the state, no matter what level of action one is referring to.[35] Why should we accept some kind of line above which moral responsibility is magically transferred to another agent leaving the perpetrator blameless? While the thug hired to rough up a rival lover is not the only actor to be guilty, he cannot claim it was all someone else's fault as he stands in the court accused of assault. "I was told to do it" doesn't work in any other situation, so why should a soldier be any different if they know what they are being ordered to do is wrong?

The question as to whether soldiers should be expected to examine their consciences before fighting in the name of a particular cause is not a new one. Nor is the question that immediately follows on – if I am supposed to think about such matters, how sure should I be before obeying? Vitoria, writing in the 16th century, suggested that different people have to make different types of moral decision because of their role and the information that was available to them in carrying out that role. Unlike policy-makers, the assumption is that most soldiers are simply not in a position to know all of the relevant facts about the decision to go to war. As such, it is not possible to expect everyone to be able to make an informed judgment on the justice or injustice of a war. If the state had

33 I accept it is logically possible to fight a war, just or unjust, without the death of innocent people. However, I would suggest we have yet to see such a conflict in practice.

34 See, for example, Don Carrick, James Connelly and David Whetham, *Making the Military Moral: Contemporary Challenges and Responses in Military Ethics Education* (Abingdon: Routledge, 2017).

35 David Whetham, "Do Some Soldiers Deserve to Die More Than Others?" in *Who Should Die? The Ethics of Killing in War*, ed. B. J. Strawser, M. Robillard and R. Jenkins (Oxford: Oxford University Press, 2017).

to explain to all service personnel all of the details about the threat that they were being sent to face, before they could each make their individual decisions about whether or not they were going to join this particular struggle, the state (and its people) could be put in terrible danger. How is a ruler supposed to keep their state and people safe if they are obliged to explain everything before the state's protectors could be motivated to act? The defence of the realm requires a certain level of obedience if everyone is to be safe: "if subjects cannot serve in war except they are first satisfied of its justice, the State would fall into grave peril."[36] The same argument seems pertinent today.

The soldier was therefore obliged to do the job and, as a consequence, was also not responsible for the actual war if it turned out that it was not justified after all. This thinking was captured by Shakespeare in the play Henry V where two soldiers discuss the rights and wrongs of the war on the eve of the Battle of Agincourt:

BATES: If [the King's] cause be wrong, our
obedience to the king wipes the crime of it out of us.

WILLIAMS: But if the cause be not good, the
King himself hath a heavy reckoning to make when
all those legs and arms and heads, chopp'd off in a
battle ...

Henry V Act 4 Scene 1

The attitude captured here led to a very clear separation of moral responsibility – traditionally it was the ruler that would face any Divine retribution for waging an unjust war rather than the soldiers who were simply obeying their orders to participate in it. This moral separation stood even if a soldier had doubts about the justness of their cause.[37]

There is, surely, also a qualitative difference in the type of decision that one has to make at different levels of war. Assessments about international situations, diplomacy and high politics are inherently more complex and therefore "at a higher level of abstraction than the scenario about stabbing the baby."[38] At the local, tactical level, right and wrong is in much clearer focus. But that cannot be true for most wars when thinking about the rights and wrongs of the whole conflict due to the complexity of the situation and the lack of objective evidence upon which to base one's opinions. The

---

36 Vitoria, De Indis De Jure Belli, Part III.31. From Michael Walzer, *Just and Unjust Wars: A Moral Argument with Historical Illustrations, Second Edition* (New York: Basic Books, 1992), 39.

37 Alex J. Bellamy, *Just Wars: From Cicero to Iraq* (Cambridge: Polity Press, 2006), 28.

38 Zupan, "Selective Conscientious Objection," 90.

traditional view is that the access to the knowledge that is required for a definitive answer at the *ad bellum* level is often simply beyond the scope of most people in the chain of command, apart from those at the very top who may have access to the 'bigger picture.' The common military institutional expectation is therefore that for the vast majority of people involved, "they should exercise humility and ... defer to those who are in a better position to judge."[39]

It flows from this that it is not up to the soldier to question the policy of his or her government, monarch or president. The individual soldier was therefore traditionally expected, on moral as well as practical grounds, to give their leaders the benefit of the doubt and obey their orders to go to war. While that might make sense from the point of view of the ruler, of even the society that the soldier is supposed to be serving, but how does that square with one's individual conscience, and does the state really deserve a blank check?

Even when Vitoria was writing, insisting on unqualified obedience was seen as morally problematic. While in many situations there were too many things to take into account for a soldier to be able to have certainty about the rights and wrongs of a conflict, there were still going to be cases which really were a lot more black and white. Vitoria argued that it was possible that someone could be faced with

> arguments and proofs of the injustice of war so powerful, that even citizens and subjects... may not use ignorance as an excuse for serving as soldiers... if the war seems patently unjust to the subject, he must not fight, even if he is ordered to do so by the prince.[40]

If in doubt, then the prince deserves the benefit of that doubt. If you *know* what you are being ordered to do is wrong, then one should not do it. But certainty is going to be a lot harder to find at the *ad bellum* level than at the *in bello* one, so in most situations the soldier will find themselves obeying orders, and should not be blamed for doing so.

Professional soldiers in the contemporary era are expected and indeed trained to ask questions. However, it is important to understand that the type of moral certainty that some newspaper editorial or international affair pundits are able to generate is very different to the reality that most people face.

---

39 Andrea Ellner, Paul Robinson and David Whetham, "Sometimes they'll give a war and nobody will come," *When Soldiers Say No*, 8.

40 Vitoria, On the Law of War, Qu. 2, Art.1.1. in *The Ethics of War: Classic and Contemporary Readings*, ed. Gregory M. Reichberg, Henrik Syse and Endre Begby (Oxford: Blackwell, 2006), 318–19.

The perfect knowledge that may be presented in a philosophical thought experiment is not always realistic in the messy reality of everyday life, let alone the extraordinary circumstances surrounding a decision to go to war.[41]

Certainty about whether one's government has got it right is rarely going to be available. One of the duties of senior military officers who do have access to more information is precisely to engage with these sorts of questions on behalf of the people they are leading. They should be "speaking truth to power" to ensure that "intended operations satisfy *jus ad bellum* and to be prepared to reassure the members of the force that this is the case through the chain of command."[42] As long as the soldier has confidence that such questions have been genuinely asked, those further down the chain of command who are not privy to the comprehensive picture, should be able to trust their prince. This is as much a question about the health of a state and its political processes as it is about epistemology and objective knowledge claims. An executioner is not personally to blame if the court has come to the wrong decision. But if the executioner knows for a fact that he has executed five innocent men this week already because there's something wrong with the court processes or the judge, the executioner can no longer claim they are entirely blameless if they carry on turning up to work. Obedience, when appropriately qualified, is a virtue. Blind obedience is not.

References

Bellamy A. J. *Just Wars: From Cicero to Iraq*. Cambridge: Polity Press, 2006.

Carrick, D., J. Connelly and D. Whetham. *Making the Military Moral: Contemporary Challenges and Responses in Military Ethics Education*. Abingdon: Routledge, 2017.

Coleman, N. "Does the Australian Defence Force have a compelling justification for the duty to obey orders?" A thesis in fulfilment of the requirements for the degree of Doctor of Philosophy, UNSW Canberra School of Humanities and Social Sciences, 2016.

Dagger, R. and D. Lefkowitz. "Political Obligation," in *The Stanford Encyclopedia of Philosophy* (Fall 2014 Edition), edited by Edward N. Zalta, https://plato.stanford.edu/archives/fall2014/entries/political-obligation/.

---

41 David Whetham, "My Country Right or Wrong: If the Cause is Just, is Anything Allowed?" in *Ashgate Research Companion to Military Ethics*, ed. E. Patterson and J. T. Johnson (Farnham: Ashgate, 2015), 291.

42 Peter Wall, "The Ethical and Legal Challenges of Operational Command," in *Ethics, Law and Military Operations*, ed. D. Whetham (Basingstoke: Palgrave, 2010), 222.

Ellner A., P. Robinson and D. Whetham. "Sometimes they'll give a war and nobody will come," in *When Soldiers Say No*, edited by A. Ellner, P. Robinson and D. Whetham. Farnham: Ashgate Publishing, 2014, 8.

Estlund, D. "On Following Orders in an Unjust War," *The Journal of Political Philosophy* 15, no. 2 (2007): 213–34.

Hursthouse, R. *On Virtue Ethics*. Oxford: Oxford University Press, 1999.

Lucas G. R. "Advice and Dissent: The Uniformed Perspective," *Journal of Military Ethics*: "Saying No: Selective Conscientious Objection," 8, Edition 2, June 2009: 141–61.

McMyler, B. "Obedience and Believing a Person," *Philosophical Investigations* 39, no. 1 (January 2016): 58–77.

Minow, M. "Living Up to Rules: Holding Soldiers Responsible for Abusive Conduct and the Dilemma of the Superior Orders Defence," *McGill Law Journal* 52 (2007): 1–54.

Navin, M. "Sincerity, Accuracy and Selective Conscientious Objection," *Journal of Military Ethics* 12, no. 2 (2013): 111–28.

Orend, B. *The Morality of War*. 2nd edition. Peterborough, Ontario: Broadview Press, 2013.

Reichberg, G. M., H. Syse and E. Begby (eds.) *The Ethics of War: Classic and Contemporary Readings*. Oxford: Blackwell, 2006.

Robinson, P. "Integrity and Selective Conscientious Objection," *Journal of Military Ethics* 8, no. 1 (2009): 34–47.

U.S. Army. "Oath of Enlistment," https://www.army.mil/values/oath.html. Accessed April 16, 2018.

Wall, P. "The Ethical and Legal Challenges of Operational Command," in *Ethics, Law and Military Operations*, edited by D. Whetham. Basingstoke: Palgrave, 2010.

Walzer, M. *Just and Unjust Wars: A Moral Argument with Historical Illustrations, Second Edn*. New York: Basic Books, 1992.

Whetham, D. "My Country Right or Wrong: If the Cause is Just, is Anything Allowed?" in *Ashgate Research Companion to Military Ethics*, edited by E. Patterson and J. T. Johnson. Aldershot: Ashgate Publishing 2015.

Whetham, D. "Do Some Soldiers Deserve to Die More Than Others?" in *Who Should Die? The Ethics of Killing in War*, edited by B. J. Strawser, M. Robillard, and R. Jenkins. Oxford: Oxford University Press, 2017.

Wolfendale, J. *Torture and the Military Profession*. Basingstoke: Palgrave, 2007.

Zupan, D. "Selective Conscientious Objection and the Just Society," in *When Soldiers Say No*, edited by A. Ellner, P. Robinson and D. Whetham. Farnham: Ashgate Publishing, 2014.

3

LOYALTY

Overview

David Whetham

"If you were to write a model universal military code, would you put loyalty in it?" I was asked this question on an episode of BBC Radio 4's *The Moral Maze* during a wider discussion regarding whether or not loyalty is always a virtue. After being asked the question by the panel, I committed the cardinal sin of live radio – I paused for thought for what, in the complete silence that followed – must have felt like an eternity to the host.[1]

Why did it take me so long to think about my answer before responding? I work with professional militaries from all around the world. I understand how important loyalty is and recognise how many institutions signal how much they value it by including it in the values and standards statements they make and the lists of virtues they require their personnel to exhibit. However, I also understand the problems it causes when it is poorly understood or misapplied. Is loyalty an appropriate military virtue?

Many countries appear to think so. Loyalty can be found in the list of core values for the British Army and Royal Navy.[2] It is the first virtue listed for the U.S. Army, also appearing in the codes of the Australian Defence Force, and the Canadian militaries, among many others.[3] Even where it is not mentioned as a 'headline' virtue, it is often still mentioned. The U.S. Navy focuses on just the three 'Honor, Courage and Commitment,'

---

1 "Loyalty," November 15, 2014. https://www.bbc.co.uk/programmes/b04nv97d#play.
2 See, https://apply.army.mod.uk/what-we-offer; https://apply.army.mod.uk/what-we-offer/what-we-stand-for and https://www.royalnavy.mod.uk/our-organisation/where-we-are/training-establishments/hms-raleigh/initial-naval-training-ratings. Accessed January 25, 2019.
3 Paul Robinson, Nigel de Lee and Don Carrick (eds), *Ethics Education in the Military* (Aldershot: Ashgate Publishing, 2008), 7.

although loyalty is mentioned under Courage.[4] In the same way, although the Royal Air Force do not list it as a separate core value, it is mentioned under the title of Service, along with physical courage, commitment and teamwork.[5] The Norwegians do something similar, placing loyalty under the idea of Respect.[6]

The British Army's own website explains the core value by stating "Loyalty is about supporting your team, looking after and helping them even when the going gets tough. In return, they do the same for you."[7] This makes a lot of sense and one can easily see how a strong sense of identity and camaraderie can be generated by the knowledge that whatever happens, your team will support you. This is where the 'leave no-one behind' mentality of the U.S. military is generated and there is little doubt that this feeling of solidarity promotes team work and the desire, in extremis to make the ultimate sacrifice if the team needs you to.

Core values statements for militaries around the world do tend to look very similar. Given the functional nature of what military organisations need to be able to do, this is hardly surprising. What is perhaps surprising therefore, is that loyalty is not seen universally as one of the essential headline virtues that military organisations state as part of their core values statement. How and why should loyalty be regarded as anything other than a good thing? While it is rarely unpacked, explored or explained in any depth, loyalty is actually a very complex concept. One can have multiple loyalties and this means that they can collide or conflict and thus generate the type of challenges that both Coleman and McCormack note in the case studies that follow.

Loyalty is both relational and it can also be multi-directional, having both horizontal and vertical manifestations. Horizontal loyalty is the type of loyalty that is referred to in the British Army explanation above – it's about the team around you. Vertical loyalty runs upwards to the chain of command, the broader institutional, the government, state and people. It also runs downwards, to the men and women that you are responsible for. Pauline Kaurin argues that loyalty is about "privileging the moral claims of some people, groups or ideas over others."[8] It comes with ethical obligations and duties and also involves a degree of trust (thus the breaking of that trust being so important in many cases of moral injury). Just as you need to

4   See http://www.navy.mil/navydata/nav_legacy.asp?id=193.
5   RAF (Royal Air Force) (2017) Air Publication (AP) 1: *RAF Ethos, Values and Standards. Second Edition.*
6   Core Values of Norway's Defence Sector S-1015E, Norwegian Ministry of Defence (2013).
7   https://apply.army.mod.uk/what-we-offer/what-we-stand-for.
8   Pauline Kaurin, *The Warrior, Military Ethics and Contemporary Warfare: Achilles Goes Asymmetric* (Abingdon: Routledge, 2014), 28.

trust your team, and they you, you need to trust that the chain of command is looking after your interests and acting for the greater good even as it may be obliged to place you in harm's way. You should also be able to trust that you are being tasked with doing something legitimate. For example, "Only on the basis of absolute confidence in the justice and morality of the cause, can British soldiers be expected to be prepared to give their lives for others."[9] That is the same trust that generates the loyalty of those you are charged with leading – lose that trust, and ultimately loyalty itself will also be undermined.

Horizontal loyalty is therefore an important part of promoting effective teamwork. But, when taken in isolation and removed from the complex broader structure of loyalty, it can also be the source of major problems. Being loyal to one's team does not extend to covering up wrong doing, or letting friends do things that you know are wrong and can prevent. The 'friends don't let friends drive drunk' slogan has been used to promote awareness of the dangers of drunk driving in the U.S. since 1983. It is also a useful reminder that one is not being disloyal to a friend if you take her car keys away from her when she is clearly drunk but, due to a moment of impaired judgement, wants to drive anyway. Real loyalty would be demonstrated by making sure she gets home without putting herself and others at risk. If you are asked to cover up a violation of rules or an illegal action, then it is important to understand that it is the person who is putting you in that situation who is being disloyal, not you when you 'do the right thing.' The person who is asking for your help, is actually asking you to become an accomplice, complicit in their wrong doing rather than having the moral courage to own up to it and resolve the situation themselves. It is a gross breach of trust to place somebody in such a position. The "Green Wall of Silence" that met the investigators into the death of Baha Mousa, discussed in McCormack's case study, is a demonstration of just how dangerous that misplaced loyalty can be. Somebody in that unit beat a prisoner to death, but to date, no-one has been held accountable for that murder because no-one would give meaningful evidence to the inquiry. I would suggest that this is hardly surprising if you re read the way this virtue is explained by the same British Army. Of course, allowing people to get away with murder is not what this articulation of the virtue was supposed to promote, but it is not difficult to see how they were just doing exactly what they had been trained to do – "Loyalty is about supporting your team, looking after and helping them even when the going gets tough. In return, they do the same for you." And this, therefore,

---

9 Army Doctrine Publication, Vol. 5, *Soldiering, the Military Covenant* (2002), 3–13.

is the danger of assuming that people know what you mean when you ask them to recite the values and standards. As long as they mention loyalty, they must understand it, right? However, loyalty is a much more complex virtue than this approach can acknowledge. Without understanding both the gross failure of loyalty exhibited by the cowards who left Baha Mousa with 93 separate injuries when his hooded, manacled body was beaten by his captors, and then expected their peers to cover for them, it also ignores the complete lack of loyalty demonstrated to the wider organisation, the mission itself (there can be little doubt that public confidence in an already unpopular conflict was further strained by this event), and the society that they were supposed to be serving. General Sir Mike Jackson, a former head of the Army, told the subsequent inquiry that Mousa's death remains "a stain on the character of the British Army."[10]

It is not just horizontal loyalty that can cause problems if it is not understood properly. Unthinking vertical loyalty can also be counter-productive or even dangerous in some circumstances. Obedience to orders is required for military organisations to work and be able to carry out the kind of difficult and dangerous tasks that they are assigned. But, in some situations, being disobedient may not only by the right thing to do, it might also be both the loyal and the professional course of action. How could this be?

If circumstances have changed, if you are aware of new information, and you are convinced that it would be counter-productive to follow the given orders, "disciplined disobedience" may be called for to "achieve the larger purpose of the mission."[11] Nelson putting the telescope to his blind eye to avoid having to acknowledge the order to retreat from the battle of Copenhagen might be a good example of this. Had he followed the well-meaning order (Admiral Sir Hyde Parker believed that the attack had stalled and was trying to give Nelson an honourable way out), he would actually have had to retrace his path past still-active Danish defences. Instead, he persevered and scored a major victory, denying a major source of support to Napoleon.[12] In this type of situation, the full richness of the idea of loyalty must be appreciated. This comes back to the idea of trust. Loyalty is built on this, which is one of the reasons it is different to the simpler notion of obedience. Just as one demonstrates loyalty in the chain of command, so that chain of command, should be able to trust that

10 See Rachel Stevenson and Matthew Weaver, "Timeline: Baha Mousa case," September 8, 2011. https://www.theguardian.com/uk/2008/may/14/mousa.timeline.

11 As quoted in Lt Gen. David Barno and Dr. Nora Benashel, "Three Things the Army Chief of Staff Wants You to Know," War on the Rocks, May 23, 2017.

12 See Royal Museums Greenwich, "Admiral Nelson the Leader," https://www.rmg.co.uk/discover/explore/nelson-leader. Accessed January 25, 2019.

their personnel will not knowingly jeopardise the mission by uncritically following out-of-date or counter-productive orders. They should be able to trust in the professional discretion of their subordinates to be just as disobedient as is required. But this also requires any disobedience to be carefully considered and judicially applied. One will, of course, normally have to explain such actions after the event.

This all adds up to making loyalty a very complex virtue in any context, but particularly in a military one. Its overlapping and multi-dimensional nature means that it is, without doubt, the most poorly understood of the 'values and standards' found in so many of the armed forces around the world. It can lead to enormous damage when the source of the loyalty does not warrant or deserve it. It can lead to cover-ups and evil being unchallenged out of misplaced understanding. At the same time, when understood in its more sophisticated sense, it underpins the type of 'disciplined disobedience' that is a key professional requirement and can be the difference between success and failure in many critical situations.

So, after my long pause for thought, what was my answer to the question during the radio interview? Would I include loyalty as a virtue for a model universal military code of conduct? At the time, I argued that as it is such a complex concept, involving horizontal and vertical relationships and understandings, and is almost universally badly taught and badly understood by those who need to apply it, no, I would not include it on the list as a simple single word precisely because that simple word is trying to capture something that is actually enormously complex. It is a concept that needs to be unpacked and thought about if it is to be understood and applied in a positive way.

I have since revised that answer as I think it does belong there, whether it is explicitly stated or implicit in the other stated values of an organisation. The fault, after all, is not with the virtue of loyalty itself, but with the way that it is taught and therefore understood. I believe its relationship with obedience needs to be articulated clearly and unambiguously, with examples that are pertinent and relatable to the people it is taught to at each level of an organisation. These lessons must then be reiterated as people move through, up or around their institution so they are never in any doubt about who and what they should be loyal to, what loyalty looks like, and also, how to determine in what order it should be prioritised by a military professional applying their professional judgement. That means the lessons taught must be approached differently at phase one basic training with 18-year-olds than it will be for 45-year-old staff officers, not because the virtue differs, but because the way it must be understood will change with context. It is the job of professional military training and education, and the task of leaders at every level, to ensure that this is done adequately. If someone in your command does not understand how to apply loyalty in a professional military context because they have never been given cause to think about it, the fault lies with you just as much as it does with them.

Case Study 1:
Levels of Loyalty: Country, Service, Mission, Troops

Philip McCormack

This short case study will begin by briefly considering the death of Baha Mousa paying particular attention to an infamous expression of loyalty associated with this case. It will broaden out to consider William James' notion of 'sub-universes of reality' as a useful vehicle to view the issues of levels of loyalty.

The Aitken Report: An Investigation into Cases of Deliberate Abuse and Unlawful Killing in Iraq in 2003 and 2004[13] was the British Army's response to a number of cases of serious abuse and unlawful killings in Iraq in 2003 and 2004. It did not focus entirely upon the death of the Iraqi Baha Mousa, a hotel receptionist who was arrested by soldiers and taken to a British Army base manned by the Queen's Lancashire Regiment (QLR). *The Aitken Report* also considered the death of Ahmed Jabber Kareem, who drowned in the Shat' al-Arab River,[14] the death of Nadhem Abdullah who died after being allegedly assaulted by British soldiers,[15] the abuse of prisoners at Camp Breadbasket, the death of

---

13 *The Aitken Report: An Investigation into Cases of Deliberate Abuse and Unlawful Killing in Iraq in 2003 and 2004*, January 25, 2008. http://data.parliament.uk/DepositedPapers/Files/DEP2008-0229/DEP2008-0229.pdf, 2.

14 Four soldiers were found not guilty of his murder by court martial in May/June 2006, *The Aitken Report*, 3.

15 Charges of murder against seven soldiers were dismissed by court martial on November 3, 2005. *The Aitken Report*, 3.

Sa'eed Shabram,[16] and the video footage of Iraqi youths being beaten by British soldiers inside a British Army base.[17] While the behaviour of the overwhelming majority of British soldiers on operations in Iraqi and Afghanistan was in the finest tradition of a highly respected, professional Army, there were a number of incidents that challenged the reputation of the British Army and how it trains soldiers.[18]

The Baha Mousa Public Inquiry Report[19] conducted by Sir William Gage and published in 2011 made for deeply uncomfortable reading for the Army's senior leadership and Government officials. Dr Liam Fox, the Defence Secretary when the Gage Report was published, said that

> What happened to Baha Mousa and his fellow detainees in September 2003 was deplorable, shocking and shameful... It was avoidable and preventable, and there can be no excuses. There is no place in our armed forces for the mistreatment of detainees. And there is no place for a perverted sense of loyalty that turns a blind eye to wrongdoing or erects a wall of silence to cover it up.[20]

The professional head of the Army at the time, General Sir Peter Wall, said "the 'shameful circumstances' of the innocent civilian's death cast a 'dark shadow' over the reputation of the service."[21] It is important to note that in 2011, British forces were heavily engaged in combat operations in Afghanistan and had a large detention centre located in Camp Bastion, their Main Operation Base in Helmand Province. The Gage Report highlighted appalling abuse of prisoners by British soldiers while in their custody and in the case of Baha Mousa the deliberate refusal of soldiers on trial to answer questions in a British court. This became known as the 'wall of silence.' This particular expression of loyalty will be considered later.

Baha Mousa was arrested by British soldiers from the QLR as part of a planned, targeted search of a number of hotels looking for individuals who were suspected of being Former Regime Loyalists.[22] In the course of

---

16 Shabram drowned in the Shat' al-Arab. Three soldiers were investigated, and no charges were preferred. See *The Aitken Report*, 3.
17 No disciplinary or administrative action was taken. See *The Aitken Report*, 3.
18 For example, see Andrew T. Williams, *A Very British Killing: The Death of Baha Mousa* (London: Vintage, 2013).
19 Rt Hon. Sir William Gage, *The Report of the Baha Mousa Inquiry*, 3 vols. September 8, 2001. https://www.gov.uk/government/publications/the-baha-mousa-public-inquiry-report.
20 See BBC News, "Baha Mousa inquiry: 'Serious discipline breach' by army," September 8, 2011. https://www.bbc.co.uk/news/uk-14825889.
21 BBC News, "'Serious discipline breach' by army."
22 *The Report of the Baha Mousa Inquiry*, vol. 1, part I, 5.

this operation Baha Mousa was taken along with five other men, on the 14 September 2003 to the QLR main base. On the night of 15 September, Baha Mousa stopped breathing. In the post mortem carried out by Dr Ian Hill, a Home Office accredited pathologist, 93 separate surface injuries were identified on Mr Mousa's body. The Public Inquiry into the events of this particular incident was given evidence that,

He [Payne] stood up and gave Baha Mousa a *'good kicking'*, punching and kicking him to his head and the area of his ribs. The force of the kicks was such that Baha Mousa's head was banged against the wall. In addition, he said with his hands Payne deliberately banged Baha Mousa's head against the wall a few times.[23]

An innocent Iraqi civilian had been beaten to death in British custody. The immediate response of those involved was to close ranks in an attempt to frustrate the official investigation into this death. Indeed, in the opening page of the Gage Report it states that "But for Baha Mousa's death it is possible that the events with which this Inquiry has been concerned would never have seen the light of day."[24] Referring to the court martial of those originally changed with the murder of Baha Mousa, the Gage Report also says that,

The Judge Advocate, Mr Justice McKinnon, made clear that some soldiers who had abused the Detainees had not been charged with offences '... because there is no evidence against them as a result of a more or less obvious closing of ranks.'[25]

There had been a closing of ranks that had been consistently maintained regardless of the level of investigation into the circumstances of what had happened to Baha Mousa. In his report Brigadier Aitken observed that:

The evidence from the cases of deliberate abuse with which this report is concerned suggests that there was a failure to live up to those Values and Standards by some of those involved – not just the accused, but also some of the other individuals involved on the periphery of the investigations; and not just the soldiers, but some of their commanders as well. A particular example of this failing was the lack of co-operation experienced by the Service police in conducting investigations, and what the judge in the Baha Mousa case referred to as the 'wall of silence' from some of those who gave evidence. This is not a form of behaviour limited only to the Army; but it is perhaps

---

23 *The Report of the Baha Mousa Inquiry*, vol. 1, part II, 259.
24 *The Report of the Baha Mousa Inquiry*, vol. 1, part I, 1.
25 *The Report of the Baha Mousa Inquiry*.

exacerbated in an organisation that trains its people in the virtues of loyalty, and which stresses the importance of cohesion. The challenge is to educate our people to understand that lying to the Service Police, or having 'selective memory loss' in court, in order to protect other members of their unit, are not forms of loyalty, but rather a lack of integrity. Respect for others means respecting all others – and that includes people who may be your enemies. Courage includes having the moral courage to challenge unacceptable behaviour whenever it is encountered.[26]

Many reading this extract might be inclined to agree with Brigadier Aitken's assertion that 'selective memory loss,' which was referred to as the 'wall of silence' in court, was not a form of loyalty. The problem is that it was a form of loyalty, at least to the soldiers involved. What it was not was the form of loyalty the senior command of the Army, or a majority of the country, found acceptable.

One of the major problems with the value of loyalty is that it can be extremely fluid as a concept. The loyalty expressed by those involved in the unlawful killing of Baha Mousa was a display of a strong bond of loyalty to each other; the kind of loyalty that one finds in small team settings. Richard Holmes in his book *Acts of War: The Behaviour of Men in Battle* specifically highlights the small four-man ('brick') multiple patrols that the Army employed in Northern Ireland during the troubles.[27] As a former soldier who served in Northern Ireland during this period and did many 'foot patrols' in Belfast, this author knows personally that loyalty at the level of the small team is essential. Each member of the patrol must be able to trust and rely on every other member doing their part consistently. One problem, however, is that our enemies can have their own version of the values we espouse.[28] For example, the *Schutzstaffel* or SS had as its official motto 'Meine Ehre heißt Treue' [My Honour is Loyalty]. Given the tenacity of their fighting spirit during World War II, it is doubtful whether any could question their loyalty as soldiers either to each other or to their cause. For example, in the death camps, according to Peter Haas, the SS had a coherent ethic in which some lives were valued and others not;[29] an ethic that underpinned the dehumanisation of millions of people. Loyalty was honour bound, in this grotesque example, to embrace the belief that some were worthy of life and others extermination.

---

26   *The Aitken Report*, 24.
27   Richard Holmes, *Acts of War: The Behaviour of Men in Battle* (London: Random House, 2003), 297.
28   Jack E. Hoban, *The Ethical Warrior: Values, Morals & Ethics* (Spring Lake: RGI, 2012), 60.
29   Peter J. Haas, *Morality after Auschwitz: The Radical Challenge of the Nazi Ethic* (Philadelphia, PA: Fortress Press, 1992).

In September 2015, the Army launched its *Leadership Code* to bolster its approach to inculcating its Values and Standards within every aspect of its life.[30] In this Leadership Code it states,

> We know what good looks like. But we know that at times we don't all get it right – this is why we need the Army Leadership Code. These ideas are not new; the Code simply pulls together what has been proven to work throughout history and most recently on operations in Iraq and Afghanistan.[31]

The phrase 'we know what good looks like' is the Army's way of actively avoiding defining what good is and relying on those reading the words filling the concept with the same content as the Higher Command who articulated it. The same imprecision can be detected in what the Leadership Code says about loyalty,

> Loyalty binds all ranks of the Army together, creating cohesive teams that can achieve far more than the sum of their parts. The Nation, Army and Chain of Command rely on the continuing allegiance, commitment and support of all who serve. But, loyalty is not blind and must operate within the parameters of the other Values; it should not stop appropriate action to prevent transgressions by subordinates, peers or seniors.[32]

One wonders if the *Schutzstaffel* or SS could have agreed with the British Army's statement on loyalty. What it does introduce, however, is the notion that there are levels of loyalty: 'The Nation, Army and Chain of Command.' William James introduced the idea that modern societies are replete with 'sub-universes of reality.'[33] Some scholars prefer to use Schütz's concept of 'provinces of meaning'[34] rather than sub-universes. The main difference between the two ideas is that the change of terminology emphasises "that it is the meaning of our experiences and not the ontological structure of the objects, which constitutes reality."[35] In other words it is not the sub-universe itself that constitutes reality for an individual but the experience of life while viewing the world from the perspective of that sub-universe.

30 *Army Leadership Code*, https://www.army.mod.uk/media/2698/ac72021_the_army_leadership_code_an_introductory_guide.pdf. Accessed June 11, 2018.

31 *Army Leadership Code*, 5.

32 *Army Leadership Code*, 9.

33 William James, *Principles of Psychology* (Cambridge, MA: Harvard University Press, 1981).

34 Alfred Schütz, *On Phenomenology and Social Relations* (Chicago: University of Chicago Press, 1970).

35 *The Modes of Being, Doing, Teaching, and Discovering*, 1995 Report to the Joint Meeting of the American Academy of Religion and the Association of Theological Schools, published by *the Association of Theological Schools* in 1996. http://www.illuminos.com/mem/select Papers/modes.html. Accessed July 11, 2018.

The U.K. Armed Forces is a small, though vital, aspect of the life of the nation. The Armed Forces are comprised of Naval, Land and Air components. If a young person chooses to join one of the single Services, in this case the Army, they first of all have to choose a trade within the Army: for example, Infantry, Armour, Artillery, Combat Services Support etc. Then our imaginary young person joins a Regiment within the Army. Many Regiments have Battalions of between 300–600 soldiers, that are composed of companies of about 100 soldiers and each company has, on average, three to four platoons of about 30 soldiers. Each platoon will have, on average, three sections of eight soldiers. If the U.K. Armed Forces are a sub-universe within the life of the U.K., this sub-universe is repeatedly divided until for the private soldier, the smallest social grouping is the section of eight soldiers. Utilising the idea of the sub-universe, the individual soldier's experience is framed from the perspective of the sub-universe that appears closest to them. The closest ties will be with the other members of the section, then the platoon and then the company. Many soldiers also form close bonds with their regiment or 'cap badge.' Holmes has noted the particularly strong bonds that members of the Royal Marines and Parachute Regiment have with the Regimental ethos of these 'elite' units.[36] There is a very real sense in which members of specialist major units can identify with the history and battle honours of that unit.

In World War II, many British soldiers maintained that they fought for their country.[37] World War II presented an existential threat to the United Kingdom. In this instance the whole country was at war and the members of the U.K. military were essential in determining the outcome for the nation. Today, however, the U.K. does not face an imminent existential threat from a foreign power planning a full-scale invasion of Britain. The recent policy of interventions of choice presents a different operational context for soldiers. In 2009, I deployed with 19 Light Brigade to Helmand Province, Afghanistan. Before the Brigade deployed, the senior staff officers and the Commanding Officers, of the major units within the Brigade, visited Helmand on a recce. Until British involvement in Helmand, few had any real knowledge of either Afghanistan and in particular Helmand Province. It was literally and metaphorically a world away from my personal experience. This is a key point. When training in the U.K. we were conscious that 19 Brigade would become the main component in the British Task Force Helmand. We saw the various 'homecoming' parades that numerous towns and cities granted to the

---

36 Holmes, *Acts of War*, chapter 7, "Competition, Diffidence and Glory."
37 Holmes, *Acts of War*, 278.

major units that returned from their operational service in Helmand. This emphasised the military covenant between the Army and civil society and the bond of loyalty this represented.

Once 'in country' the focus immediately shifted to the very real and pressing operational demands of Operation HERRICK 10. Levels of loyalty and the strength of bond associated with a particular level were mirrored in the manner of how British forces were deployed 'on the ground.' Camp Bastion was the main U.K. base in Helmand. Moving out from Bastion there were a number of Forward Operating Bases (FOBs). The next level down would be Company sized locations, and then platoon sized locations down to British troops embedded with Afghan soldiers at 'checkpoints.' While one must not exclude the normal cut and thrust of interpersonal relations, by and large, the close bonds were formed by those who lived and fought side-by-side in extreme and austere conditions. I personally believe that it is true to say that strong patriotic pride played second to the loyalty of those immediately beside you.

Had someone suggested to the Commanding Officer, Officers, Warrant Officers and Soldiers of the Queen's Lancashire Regiment that their regiment would bring shame upon the U.K. and bring the reputation of the British Army into disrepute because of their actions before they deployed to Iraq, one might expect that the whole regiment would have been deeply insulted. But that is exactly what happened. The 'wall of silence' erected by members of the QLR was an expression of loyalty that shocked and horrified the Army and the nation. Unless the value of loyalty is firmly anchored to an external ethical good,[38] it will continue to be inherently fluid and susceptible to forms of expression that the Army's Higher Command will find unacceptable. This will continue to be a particular problem if militaries deploy their forces in small force packages in contested operational environments against asymmetric opponents. The sub-universe through which a soldier will invariably interpret the world, will be the one immediately around them. If deployed in support of local government in the U.K., for example assisting with civic emergences like flooding, their understanding of loyalty will be framed by that sub-universe. If, however, they are deployed in a hostile environment in a small isolated checkpoint thousands of miles from the U.K., the soldier's understanding of loyalty will be framed by that sub-universe. Vague statements like 'we know what good looks like' are not a solid foundation upon which to stand or interpret the value of loyalty.

---

38 In this instance, an external good refers to an ethical norm or standard against which behaviour or action may be evaluated.

Case Study 2:
Good Loyalty and Bad Loyalty

Stephen Coleman

Loyalty can, and does, take many forms and those in the military will inevitably exhibit more than one form of loyalty. The patriotism that virtually all members of the military can be expected to share is one form of loyalty, another is the close semi-familial relations that military personnel share with those with whom they have served, especially when that service involves personal physical danger. Since loyalty takes many forms a person can easily have many different loyalties, to family, friends, colleagues, organisations, countries and to themselves, and these loyalties can sometimes come into conflict with each other. I have argued elsewhere that loyalty, as a virtue, is only ever an instrumental virtue, in that loyalty is only good as a consequence of the effects that it brings about and not good in and of itself.[39] In this case study I will discuss some cases that show some of the obvious ways that loyalty in the military can be a good thing, but also some of the ways in which loyalty, especially unconsidered loyalty, can be a very bad thing.

When loyalty is discussed within the military, the type of loyalty which immediately comes to mind for most people is what is commonly referred to as 'horizontal' loyalty, since it is mainly displayed towards those of similar rank or position, or those under one's direct command. It is this sort of loyalty which is being displayed when military personnel risk their lives for their comrades on the battlefield, but when a group closes ranks

---

39 Stephen Coleman, "The Problems of Duty and Loyalty," *Journal of Military Ethics* 8 (2009): 105–15.

to protect against other, more mundane types of attacks, such as criticism from superiors, it is this same type of loyalty which is being displayed. The loyalty displayed when protecting the organisation as a whole against external attacks is characterised as vertical loyalty, since all layers of the organisation tend to band together to protect themselves against this external threat.[40] I would argue that the patriotism which leads a person to volunteer for military service, and to risk their own life in that service, is also a type of vertical loyalty.

Loyalty is highly prized within military circles, for obvious reasons. Both horizontal loyalty and vertical loyalty are vital to combat effectiveness; without vertical loyalty, to the state and its people, personnel are unlikely to go into battle at all, and once there are unlikely to focus on achieving the mission they have been entrusted with. Without horizontal loyalty, troops in the field may well focus on self-preservation, rather than on protecting each other. Both of these types of loyalty can be seen in the countless tales of extraordinary heroism being displayed on the battlefield. In these circumstances loyalty, of both types, is obviously a good thing. But on other occasions, even on the battlefield, displays of loyalty can be much more problematic.

Loyalty, particularly horizontal loyalty, often poses problems for military personnel because the demands of loyalty can easily come into conflict with the duties required by military service. A good example of this is when a soldier finds out that another soldier in his or her section has been engaged in some form of misconduct. In such a situation loyalty seems to demand one course of action, in this case to help the other soldier to avoid punishment for their misconduct, while the duties of military service seem to require that the misconduct be reported. A perfect illustration of this sort of problem can be found in the surveys of Soldiers and Marines serving in Iraq and Afghanistan, which were conducted by the U.S. Army's Mental Health Advisory Team IV between August and October 2006.[41] As well as the usual questions related to mental health, this particular survey also included questions about battlefield ethics, broken up into sections on attitudes, behaviours, reporting and training. In the section on reporting, those surveyed were asked whether they would report a member of their unit for various offences, with the results broken up by service between Soldiers (S) and Marines (M).

I would report a unit member for: Injuring or killing an innocent non-combatant (S=55%, M=40%); Stealing from a non-combatant (S=50%, M=33%);

---

40   See John Kleinig, *The Ethics of Policing* (Cambridge: Cambridge University, 1996), 70.
41   The results were presented to the Commandant of the Marine Corps in a briefing.

Mistreatment of a non-combatant (S=46%, M=32%); Not following general orders (S=46%, M=35%); Violating ROEs (S=47%, M=34%); Unnecessarily destroying private property (S=43%, M=30%). The overall results show a clear reluctance to report a unit member, even for serious offences; perhaps an unsurprising result given the extremely strong bonds of horizontal loyalty which exist between members of a combat unit, but of serious concern to the U.S. military hierarchy nonetheless.[42]

As I have argued in more detail elsewhere,[43] one of the problematic aspects of this sort of display of loyalty is that it represents a fundamental misunderstanding of both the requirements of both duty and the real requirements of loyalty, especially in situations where loyalties come into conflict.

> It is hard to think of a single military situation like this that does not involve the decision-maker (A) becoming aware of the wrong doing of another person (B) who they feel some bond of loyalty with, and then either (1) ignoring (2) covering up, or (3) colluding in the wrong doing of B. If this is the case, then B really cannot be demonstrating loyalty to A; it is a situation … where loyalty is being demanded by someone who by the very act of demanding loyalty is demonstrating their own disloyalty.[44]

I admit that in cases of wrongdoing like this, it is certainly not always going to be the case that B will actually ask A to ignore/cover up/collude in the wrongdoing. However, I have been speaking about these sorts of issues in my teaching for 20 years[45] and it does seem clear that even in cases where A is not explicitly asked to do anything with regard to the misconduct there is, at least in a great many cases, still an implicit expectation that A will show loyalty to B by acting in a manner which helps prevent the misconduct from being discovered. I have often had students say, for example, that 'of course it would be wrong for B to actually ask A to cover up the wrongdoing, but A should do it without being asked.' Situations such as this illustrate what might be thought of as the 'ordinary' case, where vertical loyalty and horizontal loyalty come into conflict, with the apparent demands of horizontal loyalty being the cause of problems. Since such cases are so common, it is tempting to think that it is always horizontal loyalty which causes problems, and thus that vertical loyalty should always be considered more important. But while

---

42   The results were presented to the Commandant of the Marine Corps in a briefing.

43   Coleman, "Problems of Duty and Loyalty," 105–15.

44   Coleman, "Problems of Duty and Loyalty," 112.

45   I have taught ethics to military personnel for 13 years, and for 7 years before that taught ethics to police officers, where almost identical issues of duty and loyalty arise.

this is certainly the most common, there are cases where the situation is reversed and where it is vertical loyalty which becomes problematic. This is probably illustrated most clearly by what has become known in Australia as the F-111 Deseal/Reseal (DSRS) case.

The Royal Australian Air Force (RAAF) ordered 24 specially modified F-111s in 1963, and while the first was delivered in 1968, a series of crashes and technical problems meant that the Australian F-111s were kept in storage for five years and were not used by the RAAF until late in 1973. One of the main reasons that the aircraft was chosen, apart from its versatility, was its long range. One factor which added to the range of the F-111 was the amount of fuel it could carry, which was achieved by abandoning the fuel bladder used in many other aircraft. Instead, all available spaces in the wings and fuselage were coated with a sealant, thus allowing these spaces to be used for the storage of fuel; "It is in one sense a 'flying fuel tank' with armaments attached and a cockpit for the pilot."[46] Within three months of the final F-111s arriving in Australia, "the RAAF discovered deteriorating sealant while investigating fuel leaks. Shortly after this, the RAAF became aware of serious fuel leak issues being experienced by the United States Air Force (USAF) in their F-111 aircraft."[47] Because of the extended delays in design and delivery and the amount of time some of the aircraft had spent in storage, the RAAF took on the task of dealing with these fuel leak problems 'in-house' rather than sending the entire fleet of aircraft back to the manufacturer. This maintenance was of two types. The first, known officially as 'fuel tank leak repair,' but colloquially as 'pick and patch' work, was carried out from 1973–2000 by squadron ground crew as part of the maintenance work on the F-111s and involved picking or scraping out, then replacing, sections of deteriorated sealant. The second, and more major, type of maintenance involved completely removing the sealant (deseal) and then applying new sealant in its place (reseal), with four formal DSRS programs carried out between 1977 and 1999.

All of this maintenance work required the workers to enter the fuel tanks and spend many hours inside, in close proximity to a range of seriously harmful chemicals; for those undertaking 'pick and patch' work, this also often included leftover fuel which proved difficult to fully drain from the tanks. With regard to the formal DSRS programs, the Department of Defence has stated that:

---

46 Joint Standing Committee on Foreign Affairs, Defence and Trade, *Sealing a Just Outcome: Report from the Inquiry into RAAF F-111 Deseal/Reseal Workers and their Families* (Canberra: Parliament of the Commonwealth of Australia, 2009), 5. Hereafter referred to as *Parliamentary Report*.

47 *Parliamentary Report*, 6.

... workers re-entered the fuel tanks to 'hand pick' and physically remove any remaining sealants. This was achieved by using an assortment of dental picks, wire brushes, scrapers and rags ... This process used a general purpose solvent and took approximately 28 days for 24 hours per day utilising three shifts a day to complete. Similar tasks using general purpose solvents were undertaken during squadron pick and patch activities, but were generally of much shorter duration than the hand pick and cleaning phase of the Deseal/ Reseal programs and significantly less intensive in terms of the amount of sealant needing to be removed ...[48]

Almost as soon as these types of maintenance began, workers involved complained about a range of medical problems which they thought may have been caused by their work inside the aircraft fuel tanks. These problems included (among other things) skin rashes, gastro-intestinal symptoms, headaches, memory loss, and erectile dysfunction.[49] There were clear early signs that the DSRS program might be causing medical problems. "On two occasions during the first reseal program workers were dragged unconscious from the fuel tanks and taken to the medical section."[50] Yet none of these issues were taken seriously, nor were other complaints about working conditions voiced by maintenance personnel. Rather, the superiors of those who complained about doing such work suggested that "people who complain are simply trouble makers who are looking for ways of avoiding work which everyone acknowledged was very unpleasant but which nevertheless had to be done."[51] One airman who reported unsafe working conditions to his superior was told to "shut up and mind your own business or be on a charge" and "vividly remember(s) walking out of the office to a hallway of safety posters telling airmen 'if you see something wrong, report it' and 'Safety is your priority.'"[52] The threat of being placed on a charge was not an empty one; one worker who refused to re-enter the fuel tanks was charged with refusal to obey orders, convicted and sentenced to seven days detention.[53] After being released from the cells, he was ordered back to work inside the fuel tanks.[54]

The overriding view of all of those in command of the range of DSRS operations seemed to be that unpleasant, and sometimes unsafe, working

---

48 Department of Defence, Submission No. 83, quoted in *Parliamentary Report*, 14.
49 Nikki Coleman, *Does the Australian Defence Force have a compelling justification for the duty to obey orders?* (UNSW Canberra PhD Thesis, 2016), 164.
50 RAAF, *The F111 Deseal Reseal Board of Inquiry* vol. 1, 6. Hereafter *RAAF BOI*.
51 *RAAF BOI*, 16.
52 Coleman, *A compelling justification*, 216.
53 *RAAF BOI*, 33.
54 Coleman, *A compelling justification*, 1.

conditions were simply part of life in the military, that service involved sacrifice, and that the unconditional priority at all times was to ensure that Defence, in this case RAAF, capability was not compromised in any way. There are times when such an attitude might be understandable, even acceptable, but it is impossible to make such a claim about the circumstances surrounding the F-111 DSRS program, especially when one considers the fact that throughout their entire period of service, from 1973–2010, none of Australia's F-111s ever saw combat. This is, I would argue, a clear example of highly problematic vertical loyalty. The results for personnel who worked in the various DSRS maintenance programs were both wide-spread and extremely serious. "Those affected suffered irreparable health problems and many contracted fatal conditions"[55] and by 2008 the Department of Veteran's Affairs (DVA) had received over 500 claims for compensation for a combination of medical conditions including neurological, psychiatric, and various rare forms of carcinomas.[56] The Senate enquiry into the handling of the matter, published in 2009, notes that; "this Inquiry went well beyond broad policy issues. At its core, has been a consideration of specific cases directly impacting on upwards of 2000 ex-personnel and many more family members."[57]

It is interesting that the very same case also illustrates an example of highly virtuous horizontal loyalty in the face of this problematic vertical loyalty. The problems of the entire DSRS program were essentially brought to light by the actions of a single (publicly unnamed) RAAF Sergeant, who took charge of the fuel tank repair section (FTRS) in September 1999. Concerned with the health problems being experienced by his maintenance crew as a result of their work on the F-111s, in December 1999 he organised for all of his staff who were experiencing medical problems to make individual appointments with the doctor on base. This action made the sheer volume of problems immediately apparent, and the issue could no longer be ignored; over 80 percent of the staff in FTRS had requested appointments by February.[58] This resulted in a unit inquiry, which soon determined that the health problems being examined went back decades.[59] The formal DSRS program was immediately suspended and a Board of Inquiry (BOI) was convened by the Chief of Air Force.

Though vertical loyalty is not explicitly discussed in the report, some of the key findings of the RAAF BOI further highlight the problems

55 Mark Lax, *Australia's Strategic Weapon: How the F-111 Changed the Royal Australian Air Force and Australian Defence Policy* (Canberra: Air Power Development Centre, 2011), 235.
56 Lax, *Australia's Strategic Weapon*, 239.
57 *Parliamentary Report*, 3.
58 *RAAF BOI*, 6.
59 Lax, *Australia's Strategic Weapon*, 237.

which unthinking vertical loyalty can cause. The report specifically states, for example, that

> Air Force workers are loyal to the organisation they serve and it was evident to the Board that they recognised that there are unpleasant jobs that have to be done. But using the discipline system to override grievances has the potential to undermine this loyalty and even, in extreme circumstances, to provoke mutiny.[60]

Other key themes within the BOI report also touch on these problems: the RAAF's "priority of operations over logistics; the priority of platforms (particularly aircraft) over people; ... a failure within the chain of command ... as well as the failure of the command system itself."[61]

It is clear that loyalty, both horizontal and vertical, is essential to military effectiveness. But this loyalty needs to be discussed and clearly understood since unconsidered loyalty, both horizontal and vertical, can also be highly toxic in the military environment.[62]

References

Army Doctrine Publication (ADP), Volume 5, *Soldiering, the Military Covenant* (2002).

The Aitken Report: An Investigation into Cases of Deliberate Abuse and Unlawful Killing in Iraq in 2003 and 2004, January 25, 2008. http://data.parliament.uk/DepositedPapers/Files/DEP2008-0229/DEP2008-0229.pdf.

Army Leadership Code, https://www.army.mod.uk/media/2698/ac72021_the_army_leadership_code_an_introductory_guide.pdf. Accessed June 11, 2018.

Association of Theological Schools. "The Modes of Being, Doing, Teaching, and Discovering," Report to the *Joint Meeting of the American Academy of Religion and the Association of Theological Schools*, 1996, accessed 11 July 2018, http://www.illuminos.com/mem/selectPapers/modes.html.

Barno, D. and N. Benashel, "Three Things the Army Chief of Staff Wants You to Know," *War on the Rocks*, May 23, 2017.

BBC News, "Baha Mousa inquiry: 'Serious discipline breach' by army," September 8, 2011. https://www.bbc.co.uk/news/uk-14825889.

---

60   *RAAF BOI* p. 34.
61   Coleman, *A compelling justification*, 165.
62   Thanks to FLTLT Kierryn Higbed for suggestions, and enormous thanks to Revd Dr Nikki Coleman for her suggestions, especially with regard to the F-111 DSRS case.

Coleman, N. *Does the Australian Defence Force have a compelling justification for the duty to obey orders?* (UNSW Canberra PhD Thesis, 2016).

Coleman, S. "The Problems of Duty and Loyalty," *Journal of Military Ethics* 8 (2009).

Gage, The Rt Hon. William. *The Report of the Baha Mousa Inquiry*, 3 vols. September 8, 2001. https://www.gov.uk/government/publications/the-baha-mousa-public-inquiry-report.

Haas, P. J. *Morality after Auschwitz: The Radical Challenge of the Nazi Ethic.* Philadelphia, PA: Fortress Press, 1992.

Hoban, J. E. *The Ethical Warrior: Values, Morals & Ethics.* Spring Lake: RGI, 2012.

Holmes, R. *Acts of War: The Behaviour of Men in Battle.* London: Random House, 2003.

James, W. *Principles of Psychology.* Cambridge, MA: Harvard University Press, 1981.

Joint Standing Committee on Foreign Affairs, Defence and Trade. *Sealing a Just Outcome: Report from the Inquiry into RAAF F-111 Deseal/Reseal Workers and their Families* (Canberra: Parliament of the Commonwealth of Australia, 2009), 5.

Kaurin, P. *The Warrior, Military Ethics and Contemporary Warfare: Achilles Goes Asymmetric.* Abingdon: Routledge, 2014.

Kleinig, J. *The Ethics of Policing.* Cambridge: Cambridge University, 1996.

Lax, M. *Australia's Strategic Weapon: How the F-111 Changed the Royal Australian Air Force and Australian Defence Policy.* Canberra: Air Power Development Centre, 2011.

Robinson, P., N. de Lee and D. Carrick (eds.), *Ethics Education in the Military.* Aldershot: Ashgate Publishing, 2008.

Royal Australian Air Force (RAAF). *The F111 Deseal Reseal Board of Inquiry* Vol. 1, 6. Hereafter *RAAF BOI.*

Schütz, A. *On Phenomenology and Social Relations.* Chicago: University of Chicago Press, 1970.

Williams, A. T. *A Very British Killing: The Death of Baha Mousa.* London: Vintage, 2013.

4

COURAGE

Overview

Pauline Shanks Kaurin

Definition

> One day Alpha Company was strung out in a long line, walking from one
> village near Pinkville to another. Some boys were herding cows in a free-fire
> zone. They were not supposed to be there; legal targets for our machine guns
> and M-16s. We fired at them, boys and cows together, the whole company,
> or nearly all of it, like target practice at Fort Lewis. The boys escaped, but
> one cow stood its ground. Bullets struck its flanks, exploding globs of flesh,
> boring into its belly. The cow stood parallel to the soldiers, a wonderful
> profile. It looked away, in a single direction, and it did not move. I did not
> shoot, but I did endure, without protest, except to ask the man in front of me
> why he was shooting and smiling.[1]

The above narrative from Tim O'Brien raises an interesting question:
Is this an example of courage? One might say no, since the cow is only
standing there, and as an animal does not have a sense of the danger
or risk involved in the situation; it is not overcoming fear or acting
positively. On the other hand, one might say that endurance, not running
away, does take a kind of courage and in the passage O'Brien compares
himself to the cow who just stands there, witnessing the horrible event
without running away or protesting. This example is interesting as it
opens up questions about knowledge, risk and action that will all be
important in giving an overview to the virtue of courage. This overview
will look at 1) the aspects of courage, 2) offensive courage, 3) courage of
endurance, 4) the politics of courage and 5) courage in community.

---

1   Tim O'Brien, *If I Die in a Combat Zone* (New York: Dell Publishing, 1977), 139.

First, like the philosopher Plato in his dialogue *Laches*, we are looking for what is distinctive and constitutive in the virtue of courage. What is it that all instances of courage have in common? It is the project in this overview to develop such a definition and highlight areas of tension and disagreement, as well as major important views and authors engaging this topic.

Second, there is a range of questions to consider in the search for this definition.

1. Is courage overcoming fear and still acting? Is fear necessary for courage? What about those who act in ways we consider courageous, but who say they have or felt no fear?
2. How is courage different from cowardice on one hand and recklessness on the other?
3. Does courage involve more than a relation to fear? Is it the ability to act against pressure and influence?
4. Can we think of courage as some kind of overcoming of obstacles, pressures, fears, challenges? Is every instance of overcoming courage?
5. Is courage an act or disposition? Is courage reflected in one action, or do we think it requires habitual and regular courageous actions, which would reflect courage as a part of a person's character?
6. Is Plato right that courage cannot be action alone, but knowledge is necessary? What degree of deliberation is necessary, and can there be too much deliberation and can lead to cowardice?[2]
7. Is courage a matter of knowledge and intention on the part of the agent or does the outcome matter? Is an action only courageous if it has the desired/intended effect?

Out of these questions, a key idea emerges: risk.[3] Risk, the assessment of it and the facing of risk is central to the definition of courage, without it there cannot be courage. In this overview, I will define courage as overcoming or persistence through a significant obstacle or issue that would threaten an important/significant mission or life aim/project. The obstacle and the mission must be significant not only in the eyes of the agent, but to others as well.

Courage also requires intention and knowledge, but there can be different kinds of knowledge. In the military, knowledge is often rooted in training and habit which may look like an automatic or instinctual

---

2 Chris Walsh, *Cowardice* (Princeton, NJ: Princeton University Press, 2014), 181.
3 See Pauline Kaurin, *The Warrior, Military Ethics and Contemporary Warfare: Achilles Goes Asymmetric* (Farnham: Ashgate Publishing, 2014), 17–21 and William Ian Miller, *The Mystery of Courage* (Cambridge, MA: Harvard University Press, 2000), 21 for two instances.

response. The agent must be able to 1) recognize and assess the obstacle/threat/resistance as significant and related to some project/mission/aim of import; 2) have an intent to overcome it; and 3) carry out in some action or series of actions. Assessing courage solely on outcome is problematic because it may be to some degree out of control of the agent. The Courage of Endurance, Moral Courage and Existential Courage all feature limited agency.

Aspects of Courage

Physical Courage

Courage, particularly in the context of the military, produces first images of physical courage, as documented in war stories like the *Iliad*, of great warrior feats of physical strength, overcoming the warrior's own fatigue, weakness and fear. Further, the warrior overcomes these things in relation to also overcoming the physical obstacle of the enemy, their fortifications or other implements of war to win the day. Medal of Honor citations often reflect such actions, but also see courage as sacrificing one's self for comrades against the enemy. Rescuing can be a form of physical courage given the physical risks involved, and frequently rescuers are not armed.

Martial courage (the courage of the warrior) is a particular version of physical courage and changes in technology (the longbow, nuclear weapons, long-range artillery and UAVs) raise the question about to what degree martial courage can be maintained. William Ian Miller, for example, notes that physical courage decays under the demands of combat, but martial courage needs daily practice to be effective.[4]

Moral Courage

On the other hand, there is moral courage, which Clausewitz notes alongside physical courage as being important in war.[5] Moral courage is harder to define since it does not necessarily involve the body and physical acts, but mental and spiritual perseverance and commitment to principles in the face of outside pressure. As Eliot Cohen notes, this pressure is very often not in opposition to the enemy, but in opposition to members of one's own group who are exerting social pressure to conform, even if that means

---

4 Miller, *The Mystery of Courage*, 65.
5 Carl von Clausewitz, *On War*, Book I, Chapter 3, https://www.clausewitz.com/readings/OnWar1873/BK1ch03.html, accessed June 9, 2018.

violating some principle or value.[6] Moral courage involves a different kind of risk than physical courage, social risk and risk posed not by the enemy but by one's peers. Along these lines institutional/professional courage may well be a kind of moral courage, where the specific pressures are related to one's institutional or professional role.

Existential Courage

Existential courage may also be related, but is often more about metaphysical pressures (which can manifest in a variety of ways, including through the social context) that threaten one's sense of authentic selfhood and fulfillment. Paul Tillich's argument in *The Courage to Be* and Albert Camus' discussion of suicide in *The Myth of Sisyphus* fit into this framework. This could be seen as a specific variant of the moral courage, or its own category since it is really about an individual and their entire sense of themselves relative to existence as a whole, not just their moral commitments. Paul Tillich sees courage as more associated with strength of mind and courage is an affirmation of one's rational nature (following the Stoic tradition), while other traditions, including existentialism, may focus on emotion and embodiment.[7]

Offensive Courage

When we think of courage, we think of the courage of going over the top at dawn in trench warfare, throwing oneself on the grenade to save comrades or innocents or the courage of rescuing. This is what William Ian Miller calls the "courage of dishing it out" or offensive courage, as opposed to the courage of endurance.[8] This distinction is important and will help us think through some important issues about the definition of courage.

Medal of Honor citations, like the below from Petty Officer Michael Monsoor, often reflect this conception of courage:

> The grenade hit him in the chest and bounced onto the deck. He immediately leapt to his feet and yelled "grenade" to alert his teammates of impending danger, but they could not evacuate the sniper hide-sight in time to escape harm. Without hesitation and showing no regard for his own life, he threw himself onto the grenade, smothering it to protect his teammates who were

---

6 Eliot Cohen, "America's Crisis of Courage," November 8, 2017. https://www.theatlantic.com/politics/archive/2017/11/americas-crisis-of-courage/545063/.

7 Paul Tillich, *The Courage to Be* (New Haven, CT: Yale University Press, 1952), 9.

8 Miller, *The Mystery of Courage*, 7, 21, 23.

lying in close proximity. The grenade detonated as he came down on top of it, mortally wounding him.

Petty Officer Monsoor's actions could not have been more selfless or clearly intentional. Of the three SEALs on that rooftop corner, he had the only avenue of escape away from the blast, and if he had so chosen, he could have easily escaped. Instead, Monsoor chose to protect his comrades by the sacrifice of his own life. By his courageous and selfless actions, he saved the lives of his two fellow SEALs and he is the most deserving of the special recognition afforded by awarding the Medal of Honor.[9]

This kind of courage is associated with 1) quick, decisive physical action impacting others or the course of battle events in a positive way; or 2) involves the protection of innocents or comrades as opposed to the enemy (rescuing or placing oneself in harm's way to deflect or mitigate harm to others at one's own expense.) While the stories are different, they share an overt and physical display of a moral commitment to facing risk and require agency/intentionality of action, with an actual, beneficial effect.

Given these ideas of courage, we should consider whether character of war changes the possibilities of offensive courage. Tim O'Brien noted that the war in Vietnam made traditional courage impossible, while Rob Sparrow is skeptical about the possibility of physical (in this case martial) courage in UAV warfare.[10] These arguments are rooted in concerns about the nature of risks faced, and the fact that courage is a social virtue, requiring a sense of physical community in which to learn, practice and be judged.

Courage of Endurance

Turning now to the Courage of Endurance, Miller sees this as the courage of taking it, of enduring, as opposed to the courage associated with impactful actions. If courage requires a high degree of agency (especially Offensive Courage), Courage of Endurance is more prevalent in conditions (like asymmetric war) where agency is limited. The literature and poetry from World War I (trench warfare), Vietnam, Afghanistan and Iraq show themes of an elusive, invisible enemy, more distant leadership, failing public support and a sense of limited control or agency.[11] In addition, the nature of the threat and risk that are faced are related to this issue: Does Courage of

---

9   See http://www.navy.mil/ah_online/moh/monsoor.html, accessed June 9, 2018.

10 Tim O'Brien, *The Things They Carried* (New York: Broadway Books, 1990), 147, 153. Rob Sparrow, "Drones, Courage and Military Culture," *Routledge Handbook of Military Ethics,* ed. George Lucas (New York: Routledge, 2015), 383.

11 Kaurin, *The Warrior, Military Ethics and Contemporary Warfare,* 18–19.

Endurance involve facing less physical risk and more moral, psychological, existential risks?

How is this kind of courage different from cowardice? Chris Walsh affirms Tim O'Brien below in noting that courage often comes not wanting to be shamed as a coward.[12] One critical difference with Walsh is that the coward fails to put the Common Good and others ahead of self; the coward is selfish.[13] The coward can be self-deceptive and often avoids action, which is different with the Courage of Endurance. The Courage of Endurance still requires action and there is a great degree of self-reflection and understanding. Regarding his decision to go to war, O'Brien observes, "I couldn't make myself be brave, it had nothing to do with morality, Embarrassment, that's all it was ... I would go to the war. I would kill and maybe die because I was embarrassed not to."[14]

Courage of Endurance is a common theme in the Ken Burns/Lynn Novick documentary *The Vietnam War* related to the issue of moral injury.[15] (Moral injury, as distinct from PTSD, is the idea that there are moral harms in war resulting from a sense of betrayal of one's moral values and/or commitments often by someone in a position of authority, related to an issue of import or value.)[16] This kind of courage could be a species of moral courage, but existential courage also seems to fit into this category, as a kind of resistance and persistence against oneself and also other forces (not physical) that threaten the self.[17] Knowledge and deliberation fit well here; they may play more of a role in moral and existential courage, less with physical and martial courage.

Politics of Courage

William Ian Miller uses the term 'Politics of Courage' to denote the ways in which courage is a virtue, a communal virtue which is publicly judged, rewarded or its lack punished, and is in large part motivated by the fear of adverse public judgment. Chris Walsh echoes many other authors in arguing that courage is motivated, at least in part, from a fear of being viewed a coward. He also notes that courage seems tenuous and can

---

12   Walsh, *Cowardice*, 11.
13   Walsh, *Cowardice*, 49, 181.
14   O'Brien, *The Things They Carried*, 59–60.
15   Ken Burns and Lynn Novick, *The Vietnam War*, see http://www.pbs.org/kenburns/the-vietnam-war/home/, accessed June 9, 2018.
16   Jonathan Shay, in *Achilles in Vietnam: Combat Trauma and the Undoing of Character* (New York: Simon & Schuster, 1994), coined the term and uses the rage of Achilles as his example of moral injury.
17   Tillich, *The Courage to Be*, 3.

be easily undone by one cowardly act while the reverse does not hold; cowardice is viewed as a disposition, not temporary weakness.[18]

For example, there are very different public judgments, rewards and punishments accorded to two Vietnam veterans, John McCain and John Kerry. Both served honorably; McCain was shot down and endured years of torture, while Kerry served in combat and returned home to become active (along with other Vietnam veterans) in the anti-war protest movements. McCain is accorded public acclaim as a hero in general, while the judgment of Kerry's courage has been much more mixed.[19] Why is Kerry's service and record not accorded with same acclaim as a hero who served his country? McCain is seen as demonstrating Courage of Endurance in surviving torture, while Kerry's service seems to fit Offensive Courage and his anti-war work could be seen as an example of moral courage. If anything, we would expect Kerry to receive more acclaim, while McCain is showing the less conventionally valued Courage of Endurance. What this shows is that the public makes judgments about courage that may or may not match conventional ideas of courage as we have discussed.

In addition, the relations between military and civilian communities play a role in these judgments. These judgments of courage are based upon an assessment of the kind and nature of the risk that is faced.[20] In an era when there is increasing distance from the military on the part of civilians and general deference and a reluctance to be critical in any way, how do civilians make these judgments? Increasingly there is a reluctance to do so, to defer to an assumption of courage and in fact, to inflate and overestimate the kinds and severity of risks faced.

Related is the character of current conflicts, which seem more asymmetric and more removed from the kinds of war civilians are used to seeing through popular culture. The public has a preference for Offensive Courage, since that is the kind of courage reflected in the decisive, morally clear wars that are preferred.[21] However, as the actual wars fought fail to reflect that model, and have more in common with wars like Vietnam where Courage of Endurance is the model we see a shift and ambivalence about who is courageous.

Finally, there is an important link between martial virtue and the civic virtue needed to support it. If civic courage is fading, this has implications for the Politics of Courage; those who are doing the judging do not have

---

18   Walsh, *Cowardice*, 31.
19   Kaurin, *The Warrior, Military Ethics and Contemporary Warfare*, 21.
20   Kaurin, *The Warrior, Military Ethics and Contemporary Warfare*.
21   Kaurin, *The Warrior, Military Ethics and Contemporary Warfare*, 23.

or do not understand courage. This would account for the shift to Courage of Endurance and the increasing deference and reluctance to judge the military on the part of the civilian public.

Courage in Community

To conclude, consider the role of community (beyond the Politics of Courage) in the virtue, especially the role of communal norms. Sebastian Junger argues that courage is a communal virtue, a virtue not of the individual person but of individuals lived out in tension and community with others.[22] First, this communal nature is clear in the response to courageous action: 'I was only doing what anyone in my situation/position would do.' The historical case of Le Chambon, a small French Huguenot town that was involved in rescuing and resistance activities against the Nazi's and Vichy French during World War II is one place reflecting this response.[23] The activities of the villagers happened within a religious and historical context, in particular an understanding of Biblical hospitality, which rendered these things natural and already habituated in a sense. They did not see what they were doing as ethically unusual, but as what one would do, even though they took large risks (both death and imprisonment) and violated conventional norms against lying, forgery and other forms of deception. This shows the power of habituation, norming and community expectations in conditioning courage, both as a virtue and in producing and maintaining courageous actions.

Second, there is the role of technology in relation to these social norms. While not a new issue, UAV warfare has raised issues about whether traditional martial courage is possible due to the lack of physical presence on the battlefield, and the physical risk often taken as necessary for courage. Some have pointed to psychological and moral courage as being more appropriate here, but Rob Sparrow raises important issues about the role of community in martial courage seen not as individual acts of courage, rather as having courageous character, with the latter requiring moral community.[24] On this view, others need to understand the risks and nature of warfare. If this is missing, what becomes of martial courage, even if moral courage becomes more important, but you are not in the

---

22 See the following discussion at https://shankskaurin.wordpress.com/2016/06/29/courage-and-obedience-virtues-of-the-tribe/.

23 For more, see Philip Hallie, *Lest Innocent Blood Be Shed* (New York: Harper, 1994) and the film, *Weapons of the Spirit*.

24 Rob Sparrow, "Drones, Courage and Military Culture," *Routledge Handbook of Military Ethics*, ed. George Lucas (New York: Routledge, 2015), 383.

same proximity to that moral community. Are these effectively individual decisions, which undermines the idea of courage as a communal virtue?

Third, it would be remiss not to acknowledge the gendered nature of courage, as tied to warrior and masculine, where women are the enforcers in relation to ideas of masculinity.[25] 'Come home with your shield or on it' is the infamous statement of the Spartan Queen, while in *The Four Feathers* it is the female character who renders the judgment of cowardice that must be resisted and redeemed.[26] Here courage is not so much about action, but about courageous character which is tied to suitability for marriage and social respectability where war is a masculine rite of passage. Given the asymmetric nature of war now, this may need reconsideration, and Tim O'Brien suggests that there might be degrees of courage, where the difference between courage and cowardice seems small.[27]

Finally, it is necessary to return to moral courage and social risk. Is contemporary warfare eroding civic courage and institutional courage? In many ways contemporary warfare (especially since it tends to be morally fraught and drawn out) requires more moral courage, since it becomes less about the adversary and more about endurance and also standing up against our own social group. Reed Bondonna notes that the ancient Greeks viewed warfare as a test of character, which was why they foregrounded courage as the primary virtue.[28] If this is still true, and the Politics of Courage seems to suggest that it is, then discussions about courage need to be framed in terms of how contemporary warfare tests character and what courage we extol and expect.

---

25   Walsh, *Cowardice*, 57.

26   A. E. W. Mason, *The Four Feathers* (London: Macmillan, 1902).

27   O'Brien, *The Things They Carried*, 147.

28   Reed Bonadonna, *Soldiers and Civilization: How the Profession of Arms Thought and Fought the Modern World into Existence* (Annapolis, MD: Naval Institute Press, 2017).

Case Study 1:
Courage in an Age of Technology

Peter Lee

Introduction

Throughout history, developments in weapon technology have consistently prompted new ways of war: from the longbow to the rifle; from the cannon to the long-range bomber. In the twenty-first century, advanced air forces have deployed weaponised Remotely Piloted Aircraft (RPA) – 'drones' in popular terminology – in Afghanistan, Iraq, Syria and beyond. The most high-profile of these RPA have been the MQ-1 Predator and the MQ-9 Reaper. The two key functions of the MQ-1 and MQ-9 are to provide both ISR – Intelligence Gathering, Surveillance and Reconnaissance – and Attack – Close Air Support and Interdiction – capabilities. Both systems have been operated by the United States, with the latter also being operated by the U.K.'s Royal Air Force, their crews based thousands of miles from the battlespace.

At the same time – on the ground in Afghanistan, Iraq and Syria – Taliban, ISIS jihadists and other insurgent fighters have also become more technologically proficient. Tactics that previously involved the laying of passive anti-personnel mines or Improvised Explosive Devices (IEDs) – complete with trip wire or pressure-plate detonation – evolved to include armour-piercing shaped explosive charges and remote-controlled detonation.

Both of these technological developments – RPA and sophisticated IEDs – have challenged conventional understandings of physical and moral courage in modern domains of war and counter-insurgency. This case study will consider two examples from Afghanistan that address both conventional battlefield courage and moral courage in the operation of the RPA. The first incident examines physical courage and occurred in a routine ground patrol by a squad of U.S. Marines from Golf Company, 2nd Battalion, 8th Marine Regiment (2/8) and ultimately cost the life of Corporal Matthew Richard. The second incident considers the moral courage of a newly qualified Senior Mission Intelligence Coordinator on 39 Squadron, the Royal Air Force's Reaper Squadron. However, before the two incidents are examined, first consider a brief outline of the emergence of conventional understandings of physical and moral courage as they relate to the U.S. Marine Corps and the Royal Air Force.

Physical Courage and Moral Courage

For more than 2,500 years, since Homer wrote the *Iliad*, Achilles has been held up as the ultimate example of the strong, determined and relentless warrior: "Through blood, through death, Achilles still proceeds, O'er slaughtered heroes, and o'er rolling steeds."[29] He is the archetypal model of courage on the battlefield, relentless hand-to-hand combat. Gallantry medals for extraordinary courage in the face of the enemy are still awarded in the twenty-first century. Over millennia, another form of courage – moral courage – has existed in the shadow of its physical counterpart.

Almost 1,600 years ago, Augustine, a towering figure in the just war tradition, alluded to these two different forms of courage: moral and physical. Writing to Boniface, a rebellious Roman Army commander, Augustine said, "When you are arming yourself for battle, then, consider this first of all, that your courage, even your physical courage, is a gift from God ... When one makes a promise, one must keep faith, even with an enemy against whom one is waging a war."[30] For Augustine, moral courage – the character of the soldier that enabled him to conduct himself honourably on the battlefield – was more important, even, than physical courage.

By the twenty-first century, armies, navies and air forces around the world would define the core values that guide the actions of their personnel in war. The U.S. Marine Corps has a comprehensive definition of courage that includes both the physical and moral dimensions: "courage

---

29 Homer, *The Iliad of Homer*, trans. Alexander Pope, 1899th edition (Project Gutenberg, 2006), 636.

30 Augustine, "Letter 189 to Boniface," in *Political Writings*, ed. Margaret Atkins and Robert Dodaro, Cambridge Texts in the History of Political Thought (Cambridge, U.K.; New York: Cambridge University Press, 2001), 217.

is the mental, moral, and physical strength ingrained in Marines that sees them through the challenges of combat and the mastery of fear, and to do what is right, to adhere to a higher standard of personal conduct, to lead by example, and to make tough decisions under stress and pressure."[31]

Addressing similar themes, in the U.K., the Royal Air Force defines moral courage as "the conviction to do what you believe to be right, even though it might be unpopular or dangerous and the personal cost might be high."[32] Separately, physical courage is defined as a preparedness to "directly take the lives of others or knowingly risk our own, or to witness the injury and death of our comrades but still continue with the task in hand."[33] In the example of physical courage in the U.S. Marine Corps to follow, and in the subsequent example of moral courage from the RAF Reaper Force, the challenges of technology to these established definitions of courage will be considered.

Physical Courage – U.S. Marine Corps, Afghanistan 2011

On June 9, 2011, U.S. Marine Sergeant Seth Hickman, Golf Company Squad Leader from the 2/8, prepared his men to deal with sporadic Taliban gunfire that was regularly threatening foot patrols as they returned to Patrol Base Lambert.[34] Shots were coming from a small hamlet of houses and compounds approximately 1.5 kilometres to the south. Five men would be positioned several hundred metres west of Lambert. Initially, they would provide overwatch for an assault team that Hickman would lead a 12-man assault team south down a canal to the suspected source of the incoming gunfire. Once the assault team was in position, the overwatch team would then walk back towards Patrol Base Lambert to draw the incoming fire that would expose the shooters to the assault team.

Marine Rosperich took point as the assault team made its way down the canal towards their target, using a metal detector to check their path for landmines or IEDs. Everyone was on edge, looking for potential threats and waiting for the sound of incoming rounds. Golf Company had taken heavy losses in 2009, a thought that was never too far away from those who had lived through it.

31 U.S. Marine Corps, "Marine Corps Values," *What Are the Marine Corps Values?*, accessed June 9, 2018, http://www.hqmc.marines.mil/hrom/New-Employees/About-the-Marine-Corps/Values/.

32 Royal Air Force, "Ethos, Core Values and Standards," *Air Publication 1*, January 2008.

33 Royal Air Force, "Ethos, Core Values and Standards."

34 More extensive accounts of the two incidents in this chapter can be found in Peter Lee, *Reaper: The Inside Story of Britain's Drone Wars* (London: John Blake Publishing, 2018).

Several hundred metres down the canal, Hickman and most of the assault team paused, while Corporal Matthew Richard and Rosperich moved a bit further on to get a better view and see if they could spot possible enemy. A few metres from the team, a huge explosion broke the calm. Marine Hunt was knocked over by the blast, briefly losing consciousness. Marine Hollar, the radio operator, took a piece of shrapnel in the hand. Once he was patched up his hand still worked so he would carry on. Richard ran back from his advance position, closely followed by Rosperich. If someone in Richard's team was hurt, he was responsible and wanted to look out for them.

A quick assessment showed the blast to have come from a Remote Control Directional Fragmentation Improvised Explosive Device (RCDFCIED). The assault team had got lucky. Whoever had remotely detonated the explosion had narrowly missed the point of maximum potential lethality when the Marines were closest to the seat of the blast. Once everyone checked out ok, Hickman got the assault team moving forward. They now knew that both remote-controlled IEDs, plus at least one gunman, were in the vicinity. Also playing on several minds – although nobody mentioned it – was an explosion that happened only a few weeks before. Another member of Golf Company had stepped on an IED and lost both legs in the blast.

When they arrived at the two suspect compounds, the assault team split into two smaller teams. Rosperich once more took point on Cpl Richard's team. Rosperich edged his way round the compound wall with his metal detector. A couple of metres around the first corner, he got a 'hard hit' from his detector at an entrance to the compound – a favourite Taliban location to place IEDs for foot patrols like theirs. The ground had also been disturbed, a sign that there was probably something buried there. Retracing his steps, Rosperich reported to Richard what he had found.

Cpl Richard, always keen to look after his team, took it upon himself to deal with the potential threat. He would use his standard-issue KBar knife to 'feel' – probing the earth an inch at a time – for whatever was buried around the corner. Unbeknown to the squad below, a Royal Air Force Reaper flown by a crew situated in Creech Air Force Base, Nevada, had just arrived on station 20,000 feet overhead to provide overwatch for them. As Richard moved forward, the Reaper camera was trained on him. Only seconds later the Reaper screens filled with a huge blast that shook the earth below. Despite the immediate efforts of the squad members to apply emergency first aid, Cpl Matt Richard died instantly and could not be saved. Sgt Hickman and his assault team, reinforced by explosives and intelligence specialists, went on to search the suspect compounds. Bomb-making equipment was found and two suspected IED-makers were detained.

Every stage if this incident involving these Marines of the 2/8 in Helmand Province, Afghanistan, highlights the enduring need for physical courage on the battlefield in an age of technology. Marines and soldiers from earlier eras would recognise the actions as familiar. The initial plan called for the five members of the overwatch team to expose themselves and draw gunfire, so that the assault team could pinpoint the shooter. Rosperich had only a metal detector to identify landmines or IEDs underfoot – if they contained metallic, detectable elements. The first blast that hit Hollar was undetected and potentially lethal. Yet Hickman led the assault team forward, knowing that they faced unseen but real threats to their lives. Rosperich kept searching with the detector until he found an IED, then Cpl Richard stepped forward to deal with it. The U.S. Marine Corps definition of courage ends with the words: "It is the inner strength that enables a Marine to take that extra step."[35] Neither new technologies like the overhead Reaper, nor new threats have changed that reality for Marines – or other combat forces – on the ground in a twenty-first century operational environment. It was that courage which enabled Cpl Matthew Richard to take that extra, final step. And after his death, that same courage carried his surviving squad members back out on patrol to face the same dangers all over again. Every day.

Moral Courage – No. 39 Squadron, RAF Reaper Force, Afghanistan

Royal Air Force crews based in Nevada had been using Reaper Remotely Piloted Aircraft (RPA) to track a high priority Taliban target for several days, looking for the opportunity to strike him when no civilians would be harmed in the process. He had been involved in the killing of Coalition personnel and Afghan civilians. Over the course of the day in question, the duty crew, together with their relief crew, had observed him moving around the area on his motorbike. Clearance to target him with a Hellfire missile had so far been granted six times. On each occasion, the risk to civilians prevented a shot from being taken. From the crew in the Reaper Ground Control Station, to the Operations Room next door, to the Combined Air Operations Centre and the joint terminal attack controller (JTAC), the pressure was steadily increasing to ensure he did not escape to continue his deadly work.

---

35   U.S. Marine Corps, "Marine Corps Values," *What Are the Marine Corps Values?*, accessed June 9, 2018. http://www.hqmc.marines.mil/hrom/New-Employees/About-the-Marine-Corps/Values/.

As the Reaper crew watched their target get on his motorbike at a bazaar and begin the ride home, clearance to shoot was given again. The crew was made up of one of the most senior and experienced combinations of pilot, sensor operator and mission intelligence coordinator available on the Squadron. As the strike was being prepared, an item was spotted on the back of the bike. Was it a parcel or possibly a child? The sensor operator zoomed in the camera and they concluded it was a parcel. The time and distance available for a strike was receding quickly. The pilot, formerly a Harrier fast jet pilot, was satisfied that the item was a parcel. He later said that had he been alone in his Harrier, having met the Law of Armed Conflict requirements, he would already have shot against this valid target. A second aircraft was asked to check, and its crew concluded that there was only one person on the bike.

As the strike was being lined up, a call to the pilot from the Authorising Officer in the Operations Room next door said that the supervising, senior mission intelligence controller (SMIC) had stated, "That's a kid." The SMIC was an Acting Sergeant, newly qualified, and on her first day in a supervisory role.

Video footage was quickly reviewed again, and more checks and double checks followed, with the same outcome: it is a parcel, and the man on the bike is a valid target. Everyone but the SMIC was convinced. Under pressure from every quarter, and with the ambiguous evidence apparently against her, she refused to change her assessment of the situation. A helicopter strike was called in, then aborted for collateral risk (potential civilian harm).

At this point, the target arrived back at his home on the bike. The presence of family members once more precluded an attack on him. He was now being watched – as a minimum – by the Reaper crew in the Ground Control Station, the Authorising Officer and the SMIC in the Squadron Operations Room, the JTAC, and multiple others at the CAOC. With all those eyes on him, the target got off his bike, turned around and lifted his parcel from the back of the bike. The 'parcel' was a child around two years old, who he put on the ground.

During subsequent exhaustive analysis of all the video footage, it was still not clear – because the footage was not high definition quality – how the SMIC made her judgement about the child. However, the crew involved were extremely relieved and grateful that she not only made her judgement but would not be swayed from it under pressure.

Therein lies the significance of moral courage in an age of technology. Remotely piloted aircraft like the Reaper function as part of a large and complex system. A major advantage of such a system is the crew having access to second, third or fourth opinions where required. Video footage can be reviewed even as an incident is proceeding. A potential disadvantage is that with so many people involved, groupthink might take over. Everyone could wait for someone else to speak up about a problem. In such systems – now and in the future – moral responsibility is increasingly shared by everyone involved. Anybody who has concerns about any aspect of an operation will have to speak up, as the SMIC did on this occasion. Crews will also need to have the trust and confidence to listen to those who speak up – as this crew did.

New technology and advance weapon systems do not remove or reduce moral responsibility and accountability: they increase and redistribute that moral responsibility to individuals who might previously have been separated from the use of lethal force in the battlespace. The emergence of that technology, similarly, does not reduce the requirement for physical courage on the part of those who must fight to hold ground, as soldiers and Marines have always done. From the time of Achilles to the present, and into the future, military technology has always advanced and will continue to do so. Meanwhile, physical and moral courage have always remained, and will continue to remain, at the heart of military virtues.

Case Study 2:
Moral Courage

Scott Cooper

Military virtues – loyalty, competence, selflessness, integrity, courage, judgment, dependability, initiative – if rank-ordering them, most people would place courage near the top. Soldiers since time immemorial point to and hold up stories of physical courage in battle, from Achilles at Troy to the heroism of Medal of Honor winners we revere today. We are enamored of the tales of derring-do – sinking ships, explosions, and charges into enemy fire.

What motivates someone to be courageous? All young people who ponder their potential military service wonder how they will perform when tested. Henry Fleming, the young soldier in Stephen Crane's coming-of-age Civil War novel, *The Red Badge of Courage,* spends much of the novel wondering if, when facing the enemy and the possibility of imminent, painful death, he will stand tall and fight or retreat in shame. Richard Holmes in his classic 1986 book, *Acts of War: The Behavior of Men in Battle,* studies the individual experience of soldiers in battle. He concludes that for many of soldiers the greatest fear was not of being killed or wounded, but of 'bottling out' or showing cowardice.

Sociologists have extensively analyzed what induces people to be courageous, and many have concluded that people will fight and die not for ideologies or for economics, but rather they will stand and fight for one very simple reason: fear that their peers will hold them in contempt.

The root of this motivation is the natural human desire to belong, to be respected and to be held in high esteem by one's peers. There is a strong group dynamic in military service, not unlike a sports team, which pushes others to strive to achieve. Military service, especially in combat, conjures images and memories of enduring shared hardship together, of fighting together, of people displaying individual courage that they otherwise might not have displayed in service to their unit. There is a bond mysterious and almost beyond definition, binding people together forever by pride and respect and love: 'we few, we happy few, we band of brothers.'

But what of moral courage? In contrast to the courage that is enabled and encouraged through the bonds of comradeship, moral courage is an act of standing apart from and often in opposition to the group. Moral courage is the will to take action in spite of the risk of adverse consequences. It is putting into practice the axioms: 'stand up for what is right,' 'have integrity,' and other such platitudes that underpin the philosophies of leadership, and not just military leadership. While the physical courage displayed on the battlefield often receives the most praise, moral courage may be the more important virtue and also the more difficult virtue to put into practice.

Standing apart from the group, overcoming the fear of being ostracized – that runs counter to our instincts, including the virtue of loyalty, and encapsulated by other adages which are also part of military parlance: 'never leave the pack,' 'if the heat is on someone else, it's not on me,' 'when in trouble, deny, deflect, and make counter accusations.' These are humorous, satirical expressions, but they each have an element of truth to them.

In thinking about displays of moral courage, we can easily relate to the experiences of youth. We remember the kid who got picked on in school, and the leader who led those picking on him. It is the metaphorical (or not) bully snapping a towel in the locker room, and the poor and weak object of those taunts enduring them. Moral courage is the other kid who stands up to the bully snapping the towel. It is much easier to just be silent, because pushing back against the bully places one at risk and likely will not result in a positive outcome. More often than not the bully is a popular kid, a good athlete, the kid who wears the right clothes and who possesses significant power and influence among classmates.

But that is the playground, not the battlefield. One of the most renowned examples of moral courage on the battlefield is that of Hugh Thompson in Vietnam. Thompson was an Army warrant officer and helicopter pilot. On the morning of March 16, 1968, he and his gunner, Larry Colburn, and his crew chief, Glenn Andreotta, were flying a Hiller OH-23 Raven in support of search and destroy operations in Son My village. During their mission:

they spotted the bodies of men, women and children strewn over the landscape. Thompson landed twice in an effort to determine what was happening, finally coming to the realization that a massacre was taking place. The second time, he touched down near a bunker in which a group of about 10 civilians were being menaced by American troops. Using hand signals, Mr. Thompson persuaded the Vietnamese to come out while ordering his gunner and his crew chief to shoot any American soldiers who opened fire on the civilians.[36]

When Thompson and his crew had to return to base because of their fuel status, he immediately reported the massacre to his superiors. He filed an official report of the killings and met personally with the commander of the 11th Infantry Brigade.

As news of the My Lai massacre became public, Thompson found himself the object of severe criticism. He was summoned to appear at a closed hearing of the House Armed Services Committee, and was sharply criticized by members of Congress, among them Chairman L. Mendel Rivers (D-SC), who stated that Thompson was the only soldier at My Lai who should be punished (for threatening U.S. soldiers when he protected the civilians). Rivers also attempted unsuccessfully to have Thompson court-martialed.

It is an ironic turn of history that Congressman Rivers had a submarine named after him, the *USS L. Mendel Rivers* (SSN-686), and that Hugh Thompson's actions went unrecognized until 1996, when he was awarded the Soldier's Medal (the highest award for valor not involving combat).

Thompson's example is extreme. Young leaders in the military will inevitably ask themselves 'would I have the courage to stand up like Hugh Thompson did?' It is easy to romanticize Thompson's case, picturing oneself bravely doing what's right. And yet moral courage is called for in situations far less dramatic than a battle in Vietnam, situations that seem mundane or everyday, when a young leader may be called to stand up and stand apart.

An episode from my early years in the Marine Corps stays with me. I was tasked with conducting an investigation in my flying squadron. One of the Marines, a young lance corporal whom I shall call Lance Corporal X, had written to his Congressman alleging that he had been hazed. We had to investigate this and provide answers to Congress. I was a young captain, and I worked in the Operations section of the squadron. The alleged hazing occurred within the avionics division of the maintenance department.

---

36 Richard Goldstein, "Hugh Thompson, 62, Who Saved Civilians at My Lai, Dies." *The New York Times*, January 7, 2006. https://www.nytimes.com/2006/01/07/us/hugh-thompson-62-who-saved-civilians-at-my-lai-dies.html?mtrref=en.wikipedia.org.

My investigation revealed a situation of toxicity because of poor leaders and of people lacking moral courage when it was called for. Lance Corporal X was unpopular, socially awkward, overweight, introverted, and performing poorly as a maintenance technician. He had on numerous occasions sought to be placed on 'light duty,' seeking treatment from the flight surgeon for shin splints, a twisted ankle, a stomach bug, headaches, and other minor injuries and illnesses. Most of the Marines believed he was faking these ailments in order to avoid taking the physical fitness test (which he couldn't likely pass), to avoid coming to work, and also to avoid the bi-annual weigh-ins that ensure each Marine is within height and weight standards. Moreover, the Marines felt that they were picking up his slack. This disaffection with Lance Corporal X metastasized to such an extent that the enlisted leader of the work center, a staff sergeant whom I shall call Staff Sergeant W, believed and publicly stated that the lance corporal was a malingerer.

But it wasn't just that this lance corporal's fellow Marines were hostile to him and believed he wasn't carrying his share of the load. Staff Sergeant W was a cruel and malevolent bully. He gave Lance Corporal X the nickname 'Whiskey Sierra,' which stood for 'Weak Sister.' He encouraged the Marines to 'harden him up,' which led to constant push-ups in the work center, twice daily room inspections of his barracks room, middle-of-the-night wake-ups for random physical training, and consistent tongue-lashings from not just the staff sergeant, but from nearly every Marine in the work center.

During my investigation I listened as sergeants and corporals stated during private interviews 'I felt like maybe we were crossing some lines, and I did kind of feel sorry for Lance Corporal X but you can't cross Staff Sergeant W. And we like the staff sergeant. He works hard, and he plays hard.'

I remember the conversation I had with the division officer in charge of the avionics division (the immediate superior of Staff Sergeant W). He was a fellow captain with roughly the same experience and time in the Marine Corps as I. He stated: "Staff Sergeant W gets results. The work gets done. He's hard on them, but he gets upset if I get in his business. He has on more than one occasion told me, 'Sir, you don't need to worry about this. It's below your noise level. Staff NCO's lead. We got this. What goes on in the barracks, stays in the barracks.' And so I've felt like I can't question him, because he's just such a strong personality. I mean, he did do a tour on the drill field."

I have often thought about that investigation. The failures were many – a mean-spirited and cruel leader in the staff sergeant who encouraged others to mistreat a weaker team member. A feeble leader in the captain who failed to stand up to a strong personality. Many young and impressionable aspiring leaders who perhaps could not be expected to stand up to the staff sergeant, but who also went along, some because they resented having to carry Lance Corporal X's load, some because they feared 'leaving the pack.'

This is not a case of life-or-death as that of Hugh Thompson, but it was a moment when people at various levels could have displayed the moral courage we seek to inculcate, and such opportunities occur at all levels, from ones like the above, to the very highest levels.

For instance, in November 2005 General Peter Pace was only a few months into his tenure as the Chairman of the Joint Chiefs. He was standing next to Secretary of Defense Donald Rumsfeld at a press briefing at the Pentagon. Secretary Rumsfeld was asked a question about reports of Iraqi Interior Ministry and Ministry of Defense personnel who were abusing people in their custody, and the obligations of U.S. military personnel to stop such abuses. Secretary Rumsfeld responded that "Obviously, the United States does not have a responsibility when a sovereign country engages in something that they disapprove of; however, we do have a responsibility to say so and to make sure that the training is proper and to work with the sovereign officials so that they understand the damage that can be done to them in the event some of these allegations prove to be true."[37] He then turned to General Pace. The transcript is as follows:

GEN. PACE: It is absolutely the responsibility of every U.S. service member, if they see inhumane treatment being conducted, to intervene to stop it. As an example of how to do it if you don't see it happening but you're told about it is exactly what happened a couple weeks ago. There's a report from an Iraqi to a U.S. commander that there was possibility of inhumane treatment in a particular facility. That U.S. commander got together with his Iraqi counterparts. They went together to the facility, found what they found, reported it to the Iraqi government, and the Iraqi government has taken ownership of that problem and is investigating it. So they did exactly what they should have done.

SEC. RUMSFELD: But I don't think you mean they have an obligation to physically stop it; it's to report it.

GEN. PACE: If they are physically present when inhumane treatment is taking place, sir, they have an obligation to try to stop it.[38]

---

37 See https://www.globalsecurity.org/military/library/news/2005/11/mil-051129-dod01. htm.

38 See https://www.globalsecurity.org/military/library/news/2005/11/mil-051129-dod01. htm.

General Pace took a stand there. He publicly contradicted his superior, at personal risk. One can imagine the conversation after the press conference.

Another example from the same kind of issue, only at a lower level and some two years earlier, is similarly instructive. In the summer of 2003 as the insurgency in Iraq was just beginning to grow, one of the human intelligence officers at the joint task force headquarters wrote an email to all subordinate divisions in Iraq stating that because 'casualties are mounting,' the 'gloves are coming off regarding these detainees.' He then went on to ask recipients for a 'wish list' of interrogation techniques they believed might make their interrogators more effective.[39]

In response to this thread, Major Nathan Hoepner, the Operations Officer of the 501st Military Intelligence Battalion wrote a response in a 'reply to all':

> We have taken casualties in every war we have ever fought – that is part of the very nature of war. We also inflict casualties, generally many more than we take. That in no way justifies letting go of our standards. We have NEVER considered our enemies justified in doing such things [torture] to us. Casualties are part of war – if you cannot take casualties then you cannot engage in war. Period. BOTTOM LINE: We are American soldiers, heirs of a long tradition of staying on the high ground. We need to stay there.[40]

Major Hoepner took a significant risk. He publicly (at least in an email that would be seen by his entire community of peers as well as general and flag officers) took a stand. He left the pack. He opened himself up to criticism, and as this episode played out, he endured a backlash among many in his peer group.

Major Hoepner's actions show another aspect of acts of moral courage – they are not results-focused. A soldier who charges a machine gun nest is likely to say afterward that someone had to do it, or else the whole unit would have been killed. A soldier who takes a stand like Major Hoepner knows that his or her efforts may well lead to no effect, but the principle demands that they not remain silent.

We know at least part of the outcome of this affair. Major Hoepner's email did not stop the military from abusing detainees. Some enhanced interrogation techniques were approved, and most significantly for the mission in Iraq, our abuse of detainees stained our involvement there. Only a few months later there were images displayed across the world of abuse

---

39 Douglas A. Pryer "The Fight for the High Ground: The U.S. Army and Interrogation During Operation Iraqi Freedom, May 2003 – April 2004" (Command and General Staff College Foundation Press, Kindle Edition), 2.

40 Pryer, "The Fight for the High Ground," 1.

previously unimaginable. The photos, taken by military police assigned to the Abu Ghraib Prison west of Baghdad, showed nude Iraqi males piled on top of one another into human pyramids. They showed a hooded and wired prisoner standing on a box and a smiling female Army specialist pointing at the genitalia of nude Iraqi males.

The catastrophic damage done by our mistreatment of detainees is obvious today, but the reasons we ultimately found ourselves abusing them is not as apparent. This path was not an inevitable one. In fact, it was preventable, the fundamental reason it occurred was a leadership failure. It is impossible to know whether there were others who displayed Major Hoepner's same courage, but we do know that ultimately most chose to remain in the comfort of the group. And we are a morally diminished country because of our participation in torture.

The vast majority of military leaders will never be faced with a situation as clear-cut as those faced by Hugh Thompson or Nathan Hoepner, but there will likely be situations when one will be faced with a situation like that of Staff Sergeant W. It could be a sexist remark that everyone laughs at; or a weak, mediocre member of a team who is the object of a cruel leader's ridicule; rules that are not followed, which leads to a breakdown of good order and discipline; a cruel and mean-spirited chief or non-commissioned officer who bullies his or her way through the days, insisting 'that's how we've always done it;' the sarcastic and well-liked colleague who demonizes and dehumanizes Muslims or other races or religions; a charismatic but flawed commander who cuts corners and breeds a culture of cheating and short-cuts that can lead to catastrophic failures.

It is only when those moments come, when young military leaders experience that twinge of discomfort, wondering if they will be able to recount the episode to their spouse or best friend and say with clarity that they did the right thing, that they will know if they are willing to stand up to the test. Standing apart is not easy, and moral courage, more than physical courage, defines soldierly virtue. In his own reflections at a speech in 1966, Robert Kennedy summarized:

> Few men are willing to brave the disapproval of their fellows, the censure of their colleagues, the wrath of their society. Moral courage is a rarer commodity than bravery in battle or great intelligence.[41]

---

41 Goldstein, "Hugh Thompson, 62, Who Saved Civilians at My Lai, Dies"; "Robert F. Kennedy Speeches," John F. Kennedy Presidential Library and Museum. https://www.jfklibrary.org/Research/Research-Aids/Ready-Reference/RFK-Speeches/Day-of-Affirmation-Address-as-delivered.aspx, accessed May 28, 2018.

References

Augustine, "Letter 189 to Boniface," in *Political Writings*, ed. Margaret Atkins and Robert Dodaro, Cambridge Texts in the History of Political Thought. Cambridge, U.K.; New York: Cambridge University Press, 2001), 217.

Bonadonna, R. R. *Soldiers and Civilization: How the Profession of Arms Thought and Fought the Modern World into Existence*. Annapolis, MD: Naval Institute Press, 2017.

Burns, K. and Novick, L. (dirs.) *The Vietnam War*. 1,035 min. Washington, DC: Florentine Films, 2017.

Cohen, E. "America's Crisis of Courage," November 8, 2017. https://www.theatlantic.com/politics/archive/2017/11/americas-crisis-of-courage/545063/.

Goldstein, R. "Hugh Thompson, 62, Who Saved Civilians at My Lai, Dies," *The New York Times*, January 7, 2006, https://www.nytimes.com/2006/01/07/us/hugh-thompson-62-who-saved-civilians-at-my-lai-dies.html?mtrref=en.wikipedia.org.

Homer, *The Iliad of Homer*, trans. Alexander Pope, 1899th edn. Project Gutenberg, 2006, 636.

Kaurin, P. *The Warrior, Military Ethics and Contemporary Warfare: Achilles Goes Asymmetric*. Farnham: Ashgate, 2014.

Lee, P. *Reaper: The Inside Story of Britain's Drone Wars*. London: John Blake Publishing, 2018.

Miller, W. I. *The Mystery of Courage*. Cambridge, MA: Harvard University Press, 2000.

O'Brien, T. *If I Die in a Combat Zone*. New York: Dell Publishing, 1977.

O Brien, T. *The Things They Carried*. New York: Broadway Books, 1990.

Pryer, D. A. "The Fight for the High Ground: The U.S. Army and Interrogation During Operation Iraqi Freedom, May 2003 – April 2004," 2. Command and General Staff College Foundation Press. Kindle Edition.

Royal Air Force, "Ethos, Core Values and Standards," *Air Publication* 1, January 2008.

Sparrow, R. "Drones, Courage and Military Culture," *Routledge Handbook of Military Ethics*, edited by George Lucas. New York: Routledge, 2015.

Tillich, P. *The Courage to Be*. Binghampton, NY: Yale University Press, 1952.

U.S. Department of Defense, Office of the Assistant Secretary of Defense (Public Affairs), News Briefing with Secretary of Defense Donald Rumsfeld and Gen. Peter Pace, November 29, 2005, transcript, https://www.globalsecurity.org/military/library/news/2005/11/mil-051129-dod01.htm.

U.S. Marine Corps, "Marine Corps Values," *What Are the Marine Corps Values?* http://www.hqmc.marines.mil/hrom/New-Employees/About-the-Marine-Corps/Values/, accessed June 9, 2018.

von Clausewitz, C. *On War.* Book I, Chapter 3, https://www.clausewitz. com/readings/OnWar1873/BK1ch03.html, accessed June 9, 2018.

Walsh, C. *Cowardice.* Princeton, NJ: Princeton University Press, 2014.

5

WISDOM

Overview

Rick Rubel

In this overview, I will discuss the virtue of wisdom and apply this virtue to the ethics of military decision-making using a military case study. For the purpose of this discussion, I define *wisdom* as the quality of having experience, knowledge and *good judgment* to make the best decision in a given situation. However, looking deeper into the components of wisdom, Aristotle provides the relationship between wisdom and reasoning. Aristotle believed we must acquire, from our upbringing, habitation and practice, the ability to use reason in order to make the best decision in a specific situation. This reason is developed through both the practice of good habits and the understanding of what a good life and a good person looks like.

He believed that the key to wisdom and good decision-making was 'Practical Wisdom' or 'phronesis.' Phronesis is a virtue rooted in a natural and human capacity "to do the right thing in the right place, at the right time in the right way."[1] The Greek word 'Phronesis' translates literally as 'prudence' or 'practical wisdom.' As a working definition, phronesis *means: the habit of making the right decisions and taking the right actions in the context of relentless pursuit of excellence for the common good*. Once practical wisdom is attained, it would allow the decision-maker to have a general sense of knowing the proper behavior in all situations."[2]

Phronesis is an intellectual virtue rather than a moral virtue because we learn it through instruction rather than through practice. However,

---

1 "Phronesis as Practical Wisdom," Pradeep Bhatta, https://gaurabgurung.wordpress.com/2013/11/09/what-is-phronesis/, accessed December 13, 2018.
2 Bhatta, "Phronesis as Practical Wisdom."

without *phronesis,* it would be impossible to practice the moral virtues properly. A person who has all the right moral virtues knows what ends to pursue. However, without *phronesis,* that person will not know how to set about pursuing the right ends.[3]

To develop moral virtues, one must stay within the mean between the extremes on each virtue. A person's character is made up of dispositions to act in a variety of situations; one may be disposed to over-react, under-react, or react in a way that is in the mean between the extremes. For example, in moments of danger, one may be disposed to under-reacting, which produces the deficient vice of cowardice; the person who is prone to over-react, on the other hand, will manifest the excessive vice of recklessness. The person disposed to react in the appropriate way will be courageous. A person with excessive pride may be arrogant. A person with deficiency of perseverance may be a quitter. These dispositions greatly influence our action: courageous people do courageous things, cowards do cowardly things, and arrogant people make arrogant decisions.

There is also a developmental aspect to this, as we know from Aristotle that we become honest by doing honest actions (habituation). But we can also become dishonest by doing dishonest things. There is a continuous loop between our actions and our character. Our character drives our actions, but our actions come back and shape our character.

Wisdom and Decision-making Models

While utilizing the wisdom, judgment, and experience, there are *several military models* that can be used to frame this decision-making process. I would argue that the military has a unique process of decision-making that distinguishes it from other professions. We have many constraints on us that other professors do not have, such as:

- Our oath to a constitution
- Our orders that we are compelled to follow
- Our mission that we have a *duty* to complete successfully
- Our solemn responsibility to protect the lives of our people
- Our own personal morals to make sure we can carry out the orders
- The uniqueness of having to intentionally take human life in a war
- The responsibility to protect the innocent.

---

3 Bhatta, "Phronesis as Practical Wisdom."

Decision-making and Giving Orders

As military officers, if we can attain experience, knowledge and judgment, we can then make important decisions. Once we make a decision, we then give an order to our troops. Once we give that order, we expect that order to be followed. So we need to make the right decision, because the order will result in an action for which we are accountable. Not to over-dramatize the stakes, but the orders we give often risk the life of a member, or result in killing the enemy in war.

Given an Order from a Superior

When given an order by a superior, the follow-on decision for subordinate officers or senior enlisted is equally as important.

When given an order, we have three options available to us:

1. Follow the order – if the order is legal and within our moral sphere, the order should be followed. The order is "presumed to be legal … and is disobeyed at the peril of the subordinate."[4] If the order is determined to be illegal or a serious moral injustice – we are required to disobey (willful refusal)
2. Dissent – If the order is legal, but perceived to be immoral by our own moral judgment, we may feel that we have to dissent – an expression of opposition. Dissent is encouraged in the military. We want our people to tell us when they think we have made a mistake in judgment. For example, in the U.S. Navy Submarine Force, there is a program called 'Forceful backup.' This program requires a sailor to speak up when given an order that may be flawed (not just recommended, but required)[5]
3. Disobey – Disobedience in the military is a serious action and should be done rarely (it may occur only once in our career).

The 'constitutional paradigm' is an unofficial process to guide a service member in this rare disobedience of an order. The paradigm suggests that the service member try to have the order changed (dissent), disobey in public (openly tell the person who gave you the order that you will disobey), and then be prepared to accept the consequences of disobedience (Courts-Martial). These steps have been taken from Dr Martin Luther King's "Letters from Birmingham Jail" where Dr King was literally sitting

---

4   *Manual for Courts Martial*, United States, 2016.
5   Commander Surface Force Instruction 3540.3A.

in jail, protesting an immoral law. The steps are not meant to encourage service members to disobey, but instead to try to help them think through the very serious option of disobedience.

Multi-dimensional Decision-making

When making a decision, and then giving an order or trying to decide whether to follow or obey an order, we need to do some serious thinking and examine the problem from many dimensions.

We need to consider, what is the right thing to do:

- Legally (what does the law say?)
- Ethically (is it right from a moral view?)
- Tactically
- Strategically (the larger context of winning the war)
- For our people (bring our people home alive)
- For ourselves (our career however, should be a low priority, yet playing in the background).

These are all *considerations* for judgment. The problem is, of course, that we may get a different answer from each dimension. What is legal is not necessarily moral. What is tactical may not be right strategically (we may have to lose a battle to win a war). To complete the mission, we may lose some people.

So when we get a different answer from each dimension, we are faced with a very difficult decision: which dimension trumps the others? This is where military ethics becomes particularly difficult.

Critical Thinking and Judgment

While these dimensions are particular to military operations, another way of viewing decision-making is to take the critical thinking approach applicable to decision-making in all walks of life. This involves challenging the assumptions and viewing the problem from a different perspective.

In any decision-making situation, we often make decisions without all the necessary information. This is due to partial or inaccurate reporting, and most often, a limited time to make the decision. In the absence of perfect information, we have to fill in the unknowns with *assumptions*. We often do this subconsciously in the flash of a decision. However, to make a better decision, our judgment should force us to explicitly think about (and even list) the assumptions we have made. This should help us realize that some assumptions are actually pivotal (the way we make that assumption may actually change our final decision). There is great value in identifying these pivotal assumptions in our decision-making process. This critical understanding may require us to get more information on that particular point so that we can make a better decision. I will demonstrate that with the short case study that follows.

Emotions and Decision-making

Because military members often deal with the loss of human life, emotions can play an important part in decision-making. If we have strong emotions (particularly, revenge, hatred, anger) these emotions can completely cloud our judgment. We may be acting on irrational responses that circumvent our experience, knowledge, and judgment.

To counteract the effects of emotion and the irrationality that may result, we need to think about the attributes of the Stoic philosophy. The Stoics trained themselves to accept what had happened; control their response and keep their character intact.

Organization Moral Traps

Organizational forces may also play a large role in our judgment and decision-making. We can fall into organizational moral traps such as:

- Groupthink and peer pressure – like-minded group
- Unethical command climate – standards set by the boss
- Excess loyalty – do whatever you are told
- Ends justify the means (if the ends are really important, the means do not matter. This activates the 'slippery slope effect')
- Self-preservation and self-promotion – concern for our own career, don't 'rock the boat'
- Lack of moral courage (everyone sees something wrong, but no one speaks up).

Dr Phillip Zimbardo, in his famous Stanford prison experiment, showed that anyone of us (good people) may turn bad if placed within certain organization situations or cultures. He demonstrated that his 'role-play' guards quickly became sadistic and even brutish, given a small amount of role-play power. Further, he goes on to say that good apples, if put in a bad barrel can become bad. People work that way also. A good person put in bad 'barrel' can demonstrate bad actions. As military leaders, we are the 'barrel-makers' – we make a good barrel or bad barrel.[6] We have to create command climates that foster good moral decisions on the part of our subordinates.

Moral Conscience

The final moral decision-making model to be discussed here is the test of moral conscience – 'Can I live with my decision?' This is most often a positive (forward-looking) moral test, because it forces us to look at the consequences of our decision and the effect that decision will have on our psychology and moral character.

The Loneliness of Command

It needs to be pointed out that a Commanding Officer may often make a decision based on her or his singular judgment, usually without being able to consult with anyone else. This is particularly true with Command-at-Sea. In the situation of shipboard command, the Commanding Officer (CO) is literally in the middle of the ocean with no boss around. In these situations, the CO must decide the best course of action, using any of the approaches or models described above, and there is little question that however they decide, and however it turns out, they are accountable.

---

6 Saul McLeod, "Stanford Prison experiment," https://www.simplypsychology.org/zimbardo.html, 2008, updated 2018.

Case Study 1:
Wisdom and Judgment

Rick Rubel

In the case study below, we examine the decision required of the decision-maker, the CO, in the context of the various decision-making models discussed previously.

Rescuing the Boat People[7]

The U.S. Navy has a history of sending COs 'over the horizon' with general guidance and asking them to use their best judgment. Often this judgment is used to decide between two competing obligations – completing the mission versus saving innocent lives. There are times when a CO cannot completely meet both obligations.

U.S. Navy Lt David Soleski moved his sunglasses out of the way so he could look through his binoculars. As he looked at 'skunk Charlie-Delta' (surface contact-D), he mumbled out loud to Ensign Davis, his junior officer of the deck: "Looks like another junk going nowhere fast." Soleski was the officer of the deck (OOD) of the *USS Dubuque*, an Austin-class amphibious transport dock. As OOD, he was the captain's watch officer on the bridge

---

7 Capt. Rick Rubel, USN-Ret. This case is based on the story of Capt. Al Balian, USN, commanding officer of the *USS Dubuque* (LPD-8). The sources used for this case are "Rescuing the Boat People," a case by Paul E. Roush; the CBS 60 Minutes interview of Capt. Balian by Diane Sawyer; and NROTC Holy Cross University case "The BOLINAO Affair: A Case Study of *USS Dubuque* (LPD-8)." The storyline in the case is added for narrative purposes.

responsible for the operation and safety of the ship. At this moment, they were transiting the South China Sea, near Singapore, one of the busiest seaways in the world. The Navy indexes its surface contacts by starting with 'A' each morning and going through the alphabet, they already were up to 'D,' and it was only 2:20 p.m. Soleski was doing his best to weave in and out of the surface traffic, trying to keep all shipping more that 4,000 yards away from his warship.

Davis answered Soleski: "Sir, CIC [combat information center] has this guy, skunk Charlie-Delta, with zero speed, currently at 6,000 yards."

"Very well," said Soleski, and he continued to watch.

As the contact got closer, the two officers observed a large number of people in the boat, standing and waving at the ship. They were not waving greetings but were quite frantic and appeared to be waving pieces of white cloth. Soleski was hoping he could keep skunk Charlie-Delta more that 4,000 yards away from the ship, so he would not have to notify the captain, who was in his cabin. "It'll be close to 4,000 yards CPA [closest point of approach]," he told Davis. Both officers were looking through their binoculars as the boat approached 4,500 yards. Soleski and Davis both were startled and said at the same time, "Did you see that? It looked like one of them jumped in the water!"

Soleski reached for his phone to call the CO. "Captain, this is Lieutenant Soleski, officer of the deck. I have a contact off the port bow, bearing 220 degrees true, at 4,500 yards, with zero speed. It appears to be a junk with a lot of people waving." The captain didn't see a problem with that description and said, "OK, proceed on your course and speed." Soleski then quickly added, "Sir, they are waving frantically at us, and we think we just saw one of the people jump into the water." After a short pause, the captain, said, "I'll be right up to the bridge."

As Captain Balian walked from his cabin to the bridge, a trip he could make with his eyes closed, he huffed under his breath, "We don't have time for this." The ship was transiting from its homeport of Sasebo, Japan, to Bahrain to assume the flagship for minesweeping operations in the Persian Gulf. Just two months earlier, USS Roberts had been struck with a mine, so minesweeping operations were high priority. The Dubuque also was carrying 900 Marines to the Gulf, including a force reconnaissance team and was slightly behind planned intended motion.

"The captain's on the bridge!" announced the quartermaster of the watch as the CO arrived. The captain wore several Vietnam campaign ribbons on his chest, a Silver Star, and a Purple Heart. He was familiar with this situation, because he had rescued refugees twice before.

"What do you have, Dave?" he asked Soleski.

"Sir, we have this Chinese-type junk at about 3,800 yards, and we think we saw someone jump into the water."

The messenger of the watch handed the CO his binoculars without being asked. "Let's get closer to them and slow down."

"Aye, sir. Left standard rudder, make turns for 10 knots," Soleski ordered the helmsmen and lee helm.

As the ship pulled within 500 yards of the junk and stopped, the waving became more frantic and about a dozen more people jumped into the water. As the swimming refugees slowly worked their way toward the ship, the sailors grabbed life jackets to prepare to throw to the swimmers. As they watched the swimmers get tired and flounder, it was hard to tell if any of them went under the waves. When the swimmers reached about 100 yards from the ship, the sailors began throwing the life jackets into the water.

"Who said to throw life jackets in the water? That'll just encourage more of them to jump in the water," the captain said.

Soleski took that to mean crewmembers should stop throwing life jackets, and he put the word out.

The captain got on the ship's loudspeaker and ordered, "Don't let the refugees aboard the ship." The crew began pulling any lines that were in the water to prevent any of the refugees from boarding the ship.

The captain said, "They look Vietnamese. Have seaman Phan come to the bridge." Phan spoke Vietnamese, so when he arrived on the bridge, the captain gave him the microphone and said, "Tell them not to board our ship and to go back to their own boat." Phan translated the captain's orders, but it came out very choppy as he struggled to remember the words from his childhood.

The captain told Soleski to have the executive officer (XO) and the operations officer come to the bridge. He told the XO to put a small team together in the ship's motor whaleboat, including Phan, and go check out the junk. "Do not board the junk, we don't know what's going on there, and I don't want to put anyone at risk. Take a grunt with you for small arms protection," the captain said.

The operations officer reported to the captain and was asked to summarize the standing orders from higher authority that govern this situation. The operations officer ran below and came back within a few minutes with a summary of the operation orders and regulations:

1. U.S. Navy Regulation 0925. 'A commanding officer must render assistance to any person found at sea in danger of being lost.'
2. COMSEVENTHFLT OPORDER 201. 'The natural inclination of mariners, the customs and traditions of the sea, and reference (a)

[Navy Regulations] require U.S. Navy ships to render aid to vessels and persons found in distress. In those instances wherein relief of persons in life endangering circumstances cannot be accomplished; by repair to boats, reprovisioning or navigational assistance, rescue is normally by means of embarkation.'

3.   CINCPACFLT OPORDER 201. 'If refugees encountered at sea are experiencing, or are apt to experience undue hardship or if circumstances (e.g. adverse weather, pirates in vicinity, unseaworthy vessel, etc.) are such that death may ensue, refugees may be embarked.'

Although events were moving slowly, things were becoming rather chaotic. It took about 20 minutes to get the team together and launch the motor whaleboat. A few minutes after it left the side of the ship, the XO reported back on the radio: "Captain, it looks like they have a makeshift sail about 5 feet by 6 feet, and we have asked them several times, and they say they don't have an engine. The boat seems seaworthy; it only has a slight list to starboard. And I think that's because all the refugees are on the same side and it's trimmed (fore and aft) about right. There are about 60 people on the boat, including women and children. The people look a bit emaciated and are pretty desperate-looking. To be honest, sir, seaman Phan is struggling with their dialect, and we have to ask everything several times and may get a different answer each time we ask the same question. They left Vietnam seven days ago, heading for the Philippines. Also, about 20 people have died so far on the trip. Over."

The captain asked through his radio, "Do you see any bodies in the water?"

" I don't see any, sir," the XO said as he looked around.

The captain had seen this before: refugees risking everything to leave their country.

He thought about what he should do. The operation orders were not completely definitive, and because the boat seemed seaworthy, maybe he was not required to embark them. He had orders to transit for an important mission in Bahrain. If he spent much more time with this junk, he would be endangering his mission. If he picked up the refugees and embarked them, he could be endangering his crew with unknown diseases and security concerns. And with the Marines on board, there was no extra space. Also, if he picked them up, he would have to find a country to accept them – that is not an easy diplomatic problem to solve without a lot of time.

On the other hand, he was concerned about the report that 20 of the refugees had already died. He reasoned that they had traveled more than 250 miles in seven days, so they should be able to go the remaining 200 miles in about the same amount of time. So maybe if he gave them provisions, they would be fine.

Case Analysis

So as we examine the options available to the Captain:

The options in this case are to (1) Do nothing and pass by, (2) Embark the refugees aboard the *Dubuque*, (3) Provide assistance, but not embark the refugees.

Option 1 *(Do nothing)*

Option 1 is clearly prohibited by the governing instructions, regulations and orders. However, the distinctions between options 2 and 3 are not quite as clear cut. The governing instructions and operational orders provide broad guidance but do not clearly require a CO to embark refugees. With wording such as 'normally by means of embarkation' and 'refugees may be embarked,' one could interpret that embarkation is not a requirement.

Option 2 *(Embark)*

Cons to option 2:

- If the refugees are embarked, the ship will have to find another country willing to accept them. This might take several weeks, and cause a delay in their arrival for the critical mission
- Embarking the refugees seems to have the most negative impact to the mission – getting the ship to its location on time in order to begin minesweeping operations to protect U.S. ships. A ship has already been hit by a mine, and the USS *Dubuque* needs to deploy the mine counter-measure vessels to prevent a reoccurrence
- Embarking the refugees could cause widespread disease to the crew, seriously compromising the mission
- There might be refugees among the group who harbor anti-American sentiments.

Pros to option 2:

- This option provides the most benefit to the health and survival of the refugees. They could be quarantined, fed, and be given medical help by the ship's corpsman.

Option 3 (*Providing assistance*)

Cons to option 3:

- Without exactly understanding their condition and needs, the ship may not provide enough assistance
- Without knowing the exact status of their propulsion, the CO may not know how to calculate the amount of supplies (Did the sail get them here or did they have an Engine?)
- If the CO miscalculates, more may die.

Pros to option 3:

- Helping the refugees in their journey might not cause significant impact to the ship's mission (Orders are to get the ship to its destination on time).

In many situations, we have to make important decisions based on partial – or even inaccurate – information. That is what happened in this case. The CO gathered visual and verbal information, including inspection of the boat, but had to make his final decision based on inaccurate information due to translation problems and misunderstandings.

What the Captain Did: The Captain chose option 3 (assist with provisions)

- He provided provisions to the refugees on the vessel.
- He gave them 300 pounds of fresh fruit.
- 107 pounds of canned food.
- 60 pounds of uncooked rice.
- 50 gallons of fresh water, and navigational charts.

What Happened?

After the ship departed:

- Food only lasted a few days
- The boat drifted in the current for a further 19 days
- Thirty refugees died before they reached land; and their bodies were eaten by other refugees in order to survive.

In the confusion of the situation, and with poor translation, the captain did not know:

- The boat had a working engine for the first few days of the trip. The translator got this wrong when he reported the boat had no engine
- The boat had actually been adrift for 17 days, not 7 days. Because of this, the captain miscalculated that the boat traveled 250 miles under sail, thus miscalculating how long it would take them to get to land and not giving them enough food
- One of the swimmers trying to get to the ship drowned away from the ship
- There were almost 80 people on the junk, and not 60 as reported.

We can examine this decision from the various decision-making models:

- From the view of giving orders: his crew did as they were commanded
- From the superior order: should someone on the ship have dissented? Should someone have pointed out that this decision to supply provisions might cause more deaths?
- From the multidimensional model, looking at it from each dimension:
    - Legally – his directives require him to do something, but they are vague about how to actually help them. He did not violate any laws or regulations by assisting the refugees without embarking them
    - Ethically – with people jumping into the sea in desperation, he clearly had a moral responsibility to save as many lives as possible. That is the moral obligation of anyone in charge of a rescue scene
    - Tactically – At the local scene, the CO commands from the U.S Navy perspective. Largely, the decision of what to do is his
    - Strategically – From the larger world view, when news of this decision was publicized through the media, it provided negative publicity for the U.S. since an American Captain had allowed people to die
    - People – we should demonstrate humanity in our treatment of our fellow human beings
    - Ourselves – The CO received non-judicial punishment and was reprimanded for his decision.

Each of these dimensions gives a bit of a different answer and some of these views actually contradict some others.

- **Critical thinking** –There is clearly an advantage here in listing the unknowns in the case, then *explicitly* replacing those unknowns with an assumption. We should note that the assumption of the refugee boat propulsion (sail or engine?) is pivotal. If we assume the boat had an engine, we might make one set of decisions; if we assume the sail got them here, that is another set of decisions.

- **Organizational ethics** – In looking at this from the organizational model, it appears to be that the primary influences here are due to loyalty. The service member's training is to follow orders, they are instilled in us from our first day in military service. There is no other way to get people to do things that are objectionable (deploying for 12 months, risking their lives, and killing other human beings) without training them to follow orders.

There is further evidence that this CO was somewhat autocratic; he did not ask for anyone else's input. Still further, there appeared to be a general lack of moral courage among the crew in that no one spoke up or dissented, when it must have been anticipated that more people could die.

- **Moral conscience** – Probably one of the most relevant decision-making models had to be the conscience of the CO. It would seem that the simple test of moral conscience might have provided a different decision, 'Can I live with this if more people die?'
- **Judgment in Command** – finally, there is the model of command-at-sea. In this model, the CO is the lonely person that is clearly accountable for every decision, however it turns out. This is unique from other positions of leadership decision-making.

This case points out the difficulty of military ethics and the life and death decisions we deal with. The CO's official obligations are clear – his mission to safely transit his ship to its destination on time.

The moral obligations of the CO are also clear – to save refugees' lives. In this situation, and in many military situations, it does not seem that both obligations can be met completely and simultaneously.

My analysis of the decision: As we look at this case, we have the advantage of hindsight. It is far too easy, knowing the outcome, to then look backwards and identify errors in judgment. Like all situations in life, we have to make decisions on partial (or erroneous) information. This misinformation can easily become the source of faulty assumptions. Capt. Balian told me himself, that "You get what you INSPECT not what you EXPECT." I interpret that to mean the he thinks he did the best he could with partial information, but perhaps he should have looked deeper for more truths.

I am not prepared to condemn his decision. Military ethics is hard.

Case Study 2:
Operationalizing Wisdom: Aggressive Restraint in the Global War on Terror

Steven M. Kleinman

Knowing others is intelligence;
Knowing yourself is true wisdom.
Mastering others is strength;
Mastering yourself is true power.

– Tao Te Ching, Chapter 33

One of the foremost challenges facing the United States military and intelligence communities at the dawn of the American-led Global War on Terrorism was to conceive a strategy for effectively defeating a network-centered terrorist organization, one that was structurally ambiguous and a vast conceptual departure from the conventional military forces for which the Pentagon had decades of planning. An idea emerged within the special operations community that the key center-of-gravity for any organization – including network-centered extremist organizations that were supported by communications and financial transfer systems dating back to antiquity – was its leadership. The emerging paradigm suggested that, without the vision of a charismatic leader and absent a compelling figure who served as the animating force around which the members could form themselves and recruit others, the organization itself would rapidly decay into irrelevance.

This approach was swiftly translated into an overarching and enduring operational principle that became widely (and artfully) known as 'cutting off the head of the snake.' This strategy – which soon became accepted as common wisdom – carried the perceived certainty that the elimination of the leader of a terrorist organization would have cascading effects that would leave the group fundamentally incapable of persisting as a meaningful threat.[8]

This analogy-cum-strategy can be accurately described as a subset or specialized counter-terror application of the longstanding operational concept of find, fix, and finish. Dating back at least to the Korean War (although there are arguably examples in the writings of Civil War generals), this maxim informed military planning and operations throughout the Cold War. In the context of military action, *find* refers to locating the enemy (a task made progressively easier with the proliferation of highly sensitive – and accurate – technical surveillance and reconnaissance assets). *Fix* describes the need to ensure the target remains reliably in place long enough to apply kinetic energy (bullets, bombs, or missiles). Finally, *finish* graphically captures the 'defeat' (i.e., death, incapacitation, or isolation) of the targeted individual.[9]

There is, however, an alternative archetype that presents a far more accurate reflection of the world in which military forces currently operate. This model suggests that violent extremist groups organize and make decisions in a manner more comparable to a biological virus than a reptile. If so, a radically different response is in order, one driven less by force and intelligence than by restraint and wisdom. Primed by force and intelligence, a military commander with reliable ground truth would act (or react) aggressively when an occasion arose whereby a terrorist leader or cell might be eliminated. Informed by restraint and wisdom, however, the same commander might, through a combination of reflective thinking, context-related experience, and applied knowledge (i.e., wisdom) might act with *strategic non-action*.

In the chaos that is warfare, the application of precision kinetic energy has a high probability of success in achieving a tactical outcome while also potentially setting into motion a cascade of unanticipated and potentially costly effects. These effects can range from the euphemistic 'collateral damage,' where innocents near the target are severely injured or killed, to creating significant friction and animosities with the nation's allies and coalition partners, to generating even deeper and more problematic resistance within a local population. The employment of wisdom, in

---

8   Sean Naylor, *Relentless Strike: The Secret History of the Joint Special Operations Command* (New York: St. Martin's Griffin, 2016); A. Peritz and E. Rosenbach, *Find, Fix, Finish: Inside the Counterterrorism Campaigns that Killed Bin Laden and Devastated Al-Qaeda* (New York: Public Affairs, 2012).

9   Peritz and Rosenbach, *Find, Fix, Finish*.

contrast, can theoretically achieve a far more important strategic outcome simply by avoiding the potential consequences of an ill-planned attack when the pieces are in place that present an alternative – and possibly wiser – course of action. This is not to suggest that all attacks are unwise, but rather that wisdom encourages commanders to consider the possibility of 1) non-action as a meaningful response in the moment, 2) leveraging the potential strategic dividends of a situation where there is a possibility of achieving information dominance, and 3) foregoing the certainty of a tactical strike in favor of avoiding the vexing uncertainty that can emerge from the elimination of a known leader. This reflects a coherent and accessible understanding of the essential nature of wisdom noted previously: the application of knowledge.[10]

Another argument against the relentless embrace of find, fix, and finish emerges from the work of twentieth-century strategist J. F. C. Fuller, who viewed war as an integration of three separate spheres: the physical (decimation of the adversary's forces, which had long been the centerpiece of conflict), the mental (employing rapid maneuver and other tactics to confuse the adversary), and the moral (taking actions that weaken the adversary's will to continue the fight). Adding the mental and moral spheres formed a fairly radical departure from conventional strategic thought, and Fuller added to this innovation by suggesting that these two dimensions of war were ultimately more important – and potentially more decisive – than the physical. Paralysis of the mind and the spirit, Fuller argued, through shocks of doubt and ambiguity delivered to the psyche and the soul should be the fundamental objective of war and is far more useful – especially in the long-term – than targeted physical destruction. A final yet crucial aspect of this strategy was Fuller's belief that any advance in physical weaponry will, at some point, be offset and largely nullified by some means of effective counter in the form of an innovative new strategy or defensive posture.[11] The organic human mind simply does not evolve as quickly as technology; as a result, for thousands of generations to come the psyche will likely remain vulnerable to circumstances that generate confusion, fear, uncertainty, and the desire to escape.

The focus of this case study will be the 2006 killing of Abu Musab al-Zarqawi, then the bellicose and intractably independent leader of al-Qaeda in Iraq. While the airstrike that led to his death was driven by brilliant intelligence work, the events surrounding the attack – including

---

10 Noel Hendrickson, *Reasoning for Intelligence Analysts: A Multidimensional Approach of Traits, Techniques, and Target* (Lanham, MD: Rowman & Littlefield, 2018).

11 Frans P. B. Osinga, *Science, Strategy, and War: The Strategic Theory of John Boyd* (London: Routledge, 2007).

the 'collateral damage' (i.e., the death of others near Zarqawi, including a child), the moral consequences of that outcome, and the subsequent escalation of terror in Iraq – support an alternative view that cutting off the head of this snake in this instance ultimately created more and even deadlier serpents. Operating with exceptional intelligence but uninformed by wisdom, little consideration was given to alternatives that might have had even greater tactical and strategic significance.

By the spring of 2006, Zarqawi had transformed al-Qaeda in Iraq into what was undeniably the deadliest insurgent group in the country. It was at this same time that he had moved past Osama bin Laden, who by then had been effectively isolated, to the top of the Joint Special Operations Command, or JSOC, target list.[12] After several years of steadfastly maintaining his independence from bin Laden and al-Qaeda during his time in Afghanistan (in large measure due to his insistence that the primary targets should not be the Americans, but rather the corrupt leaders in the region and Shiites), Zarqawi had finally paid *bayat* – an oath of allegiance – to bin Laden.[13] Questions remained, however, as to just how much direction Zarqawi accepted from bin Laden and whether this act was largely a means of building the credibility of Zarqawi while defending the credibility of bin Laden. Questions also abound as to Zarqawi's role in the Iraqi insurgency. According to a Jordanian intelligence officer, Zarqawi was never the leader of the Iraqi insurgency, although he did become something akin to a symbol of the resistance, in large measure the result of the continuous references to Zarqawi that emanated from American officials.[14] What is certain, however, is that under Zarqawi's leadership al-Qaeda in Iraq had carried out a number of provocative attacks, including the bombing of several of the holiest Shia sites in Iraq. In one particular attack on a Shiite mosque, over 100 Muslim worshipers were killed. Among the dead was Ayatollah Mohammed Bakr al-Hakim, a popular politician many believe would have been the first Iraqi president in the post-Saddam era.[15] This quickly led to an escalating series of violent clashes between the Sunni and Shia.

A Jordanian by birth who spent time learning to fight in Afghanistan, Zarqawi was an insidious threat to trigger a nation-wide sectarian civil war that would instantaneously up-end the Coalition's progress toward

---

12 Naylor, *Relentless Strike*.

13 Lawrence Wright, *The Terror Years: From Al-Qaeda to the Islamic State* (New York: Vintage Books, 2016).

14 Mary Anne Weaver, "The Short, Violent Life of Abu Musab al-Zarqawi," *The Atlantic*, 8 June 2006, available at https://www.theatlantic.com/magazine/archive/2006/07/the-short-violent-life-of-abu-musab-al-zarqawi/304983/.

15 Wright, *The Terror Years*.

establishing a stable, democratic society. His brutal methods – including videotaped decapitations and the sadistic torture of prisoners – left wide swaths of the Iraqi populace living in terror. Zarqawi's most lethal legacy, however, reaches far beyond the Iraqi insurgency. In the view of former FBI agent Ali Soufan, Zarqawi was a major influence on the evolution of al-Qaeda in Iraq into the cadre of violent extremists known as the Islamic State of Iraq and Syria, or ISIS.[16]

Through meticulous intelligence collection – with the interrogation of high-value detainees as a centerpiece – JSOC (The Joint Special Operations Command) was able to identify Abd al Rahman as Zarqawi's spiritual advisor. Employing the considerable reconnaissance and surveillance capabilities of drones continuously deployed in the skies over Baghdad, JSOC intelligence analysts closely tracked Rahman's movements with the expectation that he would lead them to Zarqawi. This is precisely what unfolded on June 7, 2006. Having "found" the location of Zarqawi's safehouse and 'fixed' the insurgent as present at that location, two U.S. Air Force F-16 aircraft 'finished' the target with 500-pound, laser-guided bombs (JDAM or Joint Direct Attack Munitions). A standby unit of JSOC's Delta forces immediately deployed to the scene and were able to make a positive identification of Zarqawi (who actually survived the bombing but died of his wounds shortly afterward). There were several others in the house at the time, including two women and a young girl.[17]

The expected decline in violence in Baghdad – something that was believed, according to the strategic construct, to be a near certainty once the head of the snake was severed – did not unfold as predicted. Abu Ayyub al-Masri, an Egyptian who had served as Zarqawi's deputy, was quickly installed as the new leader of al-Qaeda in Iraq and the attacks resumed unabated. In the short term, violence continued to rise in Iraq and the hopes of an end to the American occupation of Iraq were greatly diminished.[18] In the long term, al-Masri would also become an instrumental figure in founding the Islamic State of Iraq (which subsequently evolved into what is now ISIS).

The JSOC commander, Gen. Stanley McChrystal, went on record with his belief that the targeted killing of Zarqawi took place too late.[19] Or, perhaps, the leader of one of most aggressive and intractable insurgent groups in Iraq was killed too soon.

---

16 Ali H. Soufan, *Anatomy of Terror: From the Death of Bin Laden to the Rise of the Islamic State* (New York: W. W. Norton & Co., 2017).

17 Naylor, *Relentless Strike.*

18 Naylor, *Relentless Strike.*

19 Naylor, *Relentless Strike.*

There can be no doubt that Zarqawi was a major threat, and his forceful hand in shaping al-Qaeda in Iraq into a lethal force is undeniable. What is in question, however, is whether the successful effort to find, fix, and finish the extremist leader was, in real terms, a success given the circumstances at the time and, of course, with the benefit of hindsight. The targeted killing was well executed by any relevant standard. Was it, however, a wise choice from a strategic perspective?

What is incontrovertible are the following points:

1. The work of JSOC and national intelligence personnel had not only found Zarqawi, they had identified the various rings of the network that surrounded him. While there was always the risk that he might fall off the radar again, the probability of rediscovering his location and, more importantly, monitoring his movements, communications, and contacts was exceptionally high given the richer understanding of the people who surrounded him and his unique patterns of life

2. The strategy of 'cutting off the head of the snake' proved once again to be an ineffective (arguably counter-productive) means of neutralizing a violent extremist group. As described previously, Zarqawi was quickly and nearly seamlessly replaced by al-Masri. And contrary to expectations driven by the metaphor-based strategy – one with scant empirical support – violence accelerated after the killing of Zarqawi.

Psychologist Karl Weick, whose research has explored collective sense-making under pressure, offers a most useful and relevant definition of how wisdom might be applied in an operational setting. Fundamental to this definition is the idea that, when making sense of a chaotic environment, it is not necessary that the sensemaking process should result in taking definitive action. Rather, it is just as likely to lead to an assessment that one should not take action or that a deeper understanding of the circumstances is required. In place of a targeting operation, an organization might be better served by the time and energy invested in gaining greater clarity about an ambiguous situation.[20]

Wisdom, according to Weick, is truly a combination of both knowledge and ignorance. His research strongly suggests that the essence of wisdom is not the product of what is known at any given moment; rather, it is a process of managing what is known (while being acutely aware of what is not yet known) and how that knowledge is expertly applied to the situation at

---

20 Karl E. Weick and Kathleen M. Sutcliffe, *Managing the Unexpected: Sustained Performance in a Complex World* (Hoboken, NJ: John Wiley & Sons, 2015).

hand. Moreover, he warns against an overconfidence in embracing what is thought to be true about a given situation since, at its core, wisdom involves the adept balancing of both knowing and doubting.[21] While literally cutting off the head of a snake will kill the animal, for example, killing the leader of a terrorist organization may not be an analogous – nor reliably effective – means of defeating that organization. This is especially true given the decentralized command and control of violent extremist networks, a feature that might make them far less vulnerable to 'counter-leadership targeting' than conventional, hierarchical military organizations.[22]

In the first chapter of his timeless treatise on strategy, Sun Tzu describes the five constant factors that govern the art of war. Among these are the commander, to which he ascribed the virtues of courage, benevolence, and wisdom. This case study puts forward the hypothesis that the acme of strategic wisdom for the commander is not necessarily to avoid all conflict, but rather to circumvent, wherever possible, all manner of conflict where there are few sound opportunities for constructive adaptation or the possibility of selecting among several expedient alternatives.[23]

To effectively sort out the best option in an environment shaped by volatility, uncertainty, complexity, and ambiguity, one can adopt an approach to understanding modeled after the philosopher Seneca, who spent much of his time in deep reflection upon the experiences that came to pass. Following this approach, commanders – and intelligence officers – will find the door open to the study of wisdom.[24]

References

Bhatta, P. "Phronesis as Practical Wisdom," https://gaurabgurung.word press.com/2013/11/09/what-is-phronesis/.

Cantrell, R. L. *Understanding Sun Tzu on the Art of War.* Arlington, VA: Center for Advantage, 2003.

Commander Surface Force Instruction 3540.3A.

Federal Register. *Manual for Courts Martial* (MCM) United States 2016.

Greene, R. *The 33 Strategies of War.* New York: Penguin Group, 2007.

Hendrickson, N. *Reasoning for Intelligence Analysts: A Multidimensional Approach of Traits, Techniques, and Targets.* Lanham, MD: Rowman & Littlefield, 2018.

---

21 Weick and Sutcliffe, *Managing the Unexpected.*

22 Ian O. Lesser, et al., *Countering the New Terrorism* (Santa Monica, CA: RAND, 1999).

23 Robert Greene, *The 33 Strategies of War* (New York: Penguin Group, 2007).

24 James Miller, *Examined Lives: From Socrates to Nietzsche* (New York: Farrar, Straus, and Giroux, 2011).

Lesser, I. O., B. Hoffman, J. Arquilla, D. Ronfeldt, M. Zanini, and B. M. Jenkins. *Countering the New Terrorism*. Santa Monica, CA: RAND, 1999.

McLeod, S. "Stanford Prison Experiment," 2008, https://www.simply psychology.org/zimbardo.html, updated 2018.

Mary Anne Weaver, "The Short, Violent Life of Abu Musab al-Zarqawi," *The Atlantic*, June 8, 2006, https://www.theatlantic.com/ magazine/archive/2006/07/the-short-violent-life-of-abu-musab-al-zarqawi/304983/.

Miller, J. *Examined Lives: From Socrates to Nietzsche*. New York: Farrar, Straus and Giroux, 2011.

Naylor, S. *Relentless Strike: The Secret History of the Joint Special Operations Command*. New York: St. Martin's Griffin, 2016.

Osinga, F. P. B. *Science, Strategy, and War: The Strategic Theory of John Boyd*. London: Routledge, 2007.

Peritz, A. and E. Rosenbach, *Find, Fix, Finish: Inside the Counterterrorism Campaigns that Killed Bin Laden and Devastated Al-Qaeda*. New York: Public Affairs, 2012.

Roush, P. E. "Rescuing the Boat People," CBS 60 Minutes: interview of Captain Balian by Diane Sawyer; and NROTC Holy Cross University case "The BOLINAO Affair: A Case Study of *USS Dubuque*" (LPD-8).

Soufan, A. H. *Anatomy of Terror: From the Death of Bin Laden to the Rise of the Islamic State*. New York: W. W. Norton & Co., 2017.

Suellentrop, C. "The Tie Between Zarqawi and bin Laden," June 8, 2006. *NYTimes.com*. June 7, 2018, https://opinionator.blogs.nytimes. com/2006/06/08/the-tie-between-zarqawi-and-bin-laden/.

Weick, K. E. and K. M. Sutcliffe. *Managing the Unexpected: Sustained Performance in a Complex World*. Hoboken, NJ: John Wiley & Sons, 2015.

Wright, L. *The Terror Years: From Al-Qaeda to the Islamic State*. New York: Vintage Books, 2016.

6

HONESTY

Overview

James L. Cook[1]

A standing joke in the American air force has it that the two biggest lies in the universe occur when the inspector general (IG) arrives to evaluate an air base and its operations.

"We're glad to see you," says the base commander.

"We're here to help," says the IG.

The joke's irony reflects a sense that workplace dishonesty is commonplace throughout the military. After all, an IG visit can spell rapid doom for a commander and sometimes subordinates too. Who in their right mind is glad to see the grim reaper arrive with the inspector general badge pinned to its hollow, merciless chest? Adding insult to injury, the arrival of the inspection team caps what many a busy unit considers to be an enormous distraction because preparations for an IG visit can last more than a year. Similarly, while the purpose of the inspection system is indeed to help units maintain peak performance in garrison as well as readiness for war or another kind of contingency, 'to help' strikes many a military member as a euphemism for 'to terrorize.'

Too often military members approach the subject of honesty with the joke's sense of irony. Though they may pay full-throated lip service to truthfulness, there's a lingering suspicion that only a fool or a saint would be consistently honest in the military. Even when honesty isn't outright self-destructive, from this perspective it still causes pain for no gain. By the same reasoning, a degree of strategic dishonesty is thought

---

1 Disclaimer: The views expressed in this overview are the author's opinions. They do not represent official positions of the United States Air Force or Defense Department.

necessary and even praiseworthy, demonstrating one's good judgment and professional skill just as a competent doctor might when she uses precisely the right amount of some otherwise poisonous substance in just the right circumstance to heal rather than kill. Fool the inspection team in any way possible – for instance, by pencil-whipping checklists, embellishing performance reviews, and neglecting to document sundry failures – and the unit wins. Similarly deceive one's chain of command when it comes to training, the amount of equipment on hand, and so on: the unit wins again! And isn't the nation as a whole better off when its military units fend off unnecessary interference?

What's So Great About Honesty?

To answer, we must investigate what honesty is, especially in military contexts. It won't be easy to define. If we know anything from the aporetic dialogues of Plato that try to define specific virtues, it's that doing so may be impossible. Think of *Euthyphro* on piety, *Laches* on courage, *Republic* on justice, and so on. Definitions elude the interlocutors in part because human interactions exhibit more layers of complexity than a usable definition can capture. But these same aporetic dialogues show us what we gain from the attempt: We recognize our own ignorance, the very definition of wisdom in Plato's *Apology*,[2] and appreciate relationships among the virtues that otherwise would have remained hidden.[3]

The ancient Greek word for virtue, *areté* (ἀρετή), can also be translated as excellence. As a virtue, then, honesty is supposed to make life itself excellent, or at least contribute to that end. The Roman sense of virtue is somewhat similar, which shouldn't surprise us given that the word's root is *vir*, man, in a culture that idolized masculine strength and embodied it in the god Virtus.[4]

Truth-telling forms the heart of honesty in antique ethical frameworks. Consider the Roman goddess Veritas. She embodies truthfulness and is the mother – the source – of all virtues, including Virtus and Honestas. So

---

2 Plato, *Apology* 23b, trans. Hugh Tredennick and Harold Tarrant, in *The Last Days of Socrates* (London: Penguin, 1993), 44.

3 *Republic*, Book IV (419a – 445e) provides Plato's best-known account of how the four cardinal virtues interrelate. *The Republic of Plato*, 2nd edn, trans. Allan Bloom (New York: Basic Books, 1968), 97–125.

4 Some derivative words in Romance languages and their usages in several well-known works diverge sharply from the ancient Greek and Roman senses. Machiavelli's *virtú* is an obvious case in point because it signals human excellence from a perspective that considers carefully calculated dishonesty to be a high and admirable art. For present purposes, we can bracket such later, pejorative senses of virtue.

we shouldn't be surprised at military honor codes that link truth-telling to many other senses of honesty, including the minimum standards of behavior expected of military members.[5] The honest person tells the truth, certainly, but also refrains from stealing and cheating, from committing adultery, from self-aggrandizement at the expense of subordinates, and from committing any number of other transgressions that would detract from the unit's effectiveness and bring dishonor to the military as a whole. How do we know these things are dishonest? First, we deduce they're wrong because they contradict established principles and traditions. Experience too shows how corrosive they can be. Finally, most military members think at least partly in aesthetic terms about how one should behave, and this way of thinking finds dishonesty to be viscerally off-putting. All of this makes sense if we so much as glance at the *Oxford English Dictionary*, which tells us that the word honesty has been used in many different if often overlapping ways. Moral connotations are most frequent, but the aesthetic sense sometimes creeps in too when honesty is used as a synonym for something like the 'proper degree of elegance,' as in the notion of 'honest clothing' that marked a renaissance woman's social status at the same time it exemplified her moral character. This variability is not surprising considering the weight of ancient Greek thought in Western ethics and education, with concepts such as *kalos* (καλός), beautiful, bridging to ideas that our era finds more obviously moral, including the honest. Later koine usage of words such as *semnos* (σεμνός) linked the honest (as the King James Version sometimes translates the word; cf. Philippians 4:8) to the noble, sublime, and holy. Depending upon the era and the context, synonyms for honesty have also included integrity, forthrightness, truthfulness, justice, righteousness, honorableness, candidness, and many more.

An especially telling synonym is probity, from the Latin *probare*, which can mean not just to judge as being honest but also to prove. Someone deemed to be honest would have proved their worth. This is where Plato's Cephalus seems to have erred in *Republic* I. When Socrates asks the rich old man about his state of mind on death's threshold, Cephalus replies that his conscience is clean because his wealth has allowed him to avoid pitfalls of poverty such as theft, cheating, and failing to offer sacrifices.[6] Despite his comforting belief, we know Cephalus cannot accurately appraise his own character until it's been severely tested. No one can. A prisoner locked in solitary confinement may not be able to cheat or steal, but that does not mean the prisoner is honest. Two generations later, Aristotle insists that

---

5 For instance, the U.S. Air Force Academy's Honor Code, established in 1954, states: "We will not lie, cheat, or steal, nor tolerate among us anyone who does."

6 Plato, *Republic* 331b, *The Republic of Plato*, 2nd edn, trans. Allan Bloom (1968), 7.

the rarefied happiness that accompanies virtue is not a passive state but an *activity* of the soul.[7] This ancient Greek attitude buttresses the military sense of honesty, probity, as something one must continually prove in word and deed. Lying and other dishonest actions signal holistic moral rot and an inability to accomplish assigned missions.

Or at least that's true much of the time. Oddly, sometimes well-known military figures appear dishonest or at best morally ambiguous and yet are not universally condemned. American Marine Lieutenant Colonel Oliver North admitted lying under oath about the Iran-Contra affair and was found to have intentionally shredded and altered documents relevant to the official investigation. Eventually he was convicted on three felony counts, but the convictions were vacated for reasons related to an earlier grant of partial immunity for cooperation with investigators. Despite admitting he had lied to Congress and obstructed an official investigation, North prospered from his notoriety, becoming a radio and television personality as well as a bestselling author.[8]

No doubt it is easier to stomach dishonesty in the face of real, potential, or imagined enemies than it is to tolerate it within one's own ranks. One reason the American military policy often called simply 'Don't Ask, Don't Tell,' or DADT, was so damaging was that it required dishonesty on the part of many who wanted to serve in the U.S. military but had to conceal their sexual orientations on pain of expulsion from the service. Some argue the U.S. administration's present policy sets up a variation of the same problem by not whole-heartedly welcoming otherwise qualified transgender military members. Just as DADT failed to discourage patriotic lesbian, gay, and bisexual service members from entering and serving in the military, but did force them to conceal certain facets of their identities, the present struggles with open transgender service would seem to discourage the total honesty that the military touts and does in fact need if it is to thrive.

America's struggles with the lesbian, gay, bisexual and transgender (LGBT) military members indicates what may be the hallmark of honesty in the military. At an individual and service-wide level, perhaps it is the willingness to reevaluate and if necessary reject previous convictions, especially a civilian's uninformed and untested views about war and military life. Philosopher Friedrich Nietzsche provides an object lesson. In

---

7   Aristotle, *Nicomachean Ethics*, 2nd edn, 1102a, trans. Terence Irwin (Indianapolis: Hackett Publishing Co., 1999), 16.

8   Julian E. Zelizer, "Why the Russia Investigation Could Be More like Iran-Contra than Watergate," *The Atlantic*, February 27, 2018, https://www.theatlantic.com/politics/archive/2018/02/why-the-russia-investigation-could-end-more-like-iran-contra-than-watergate/554345/.

the run-up to the Franco-Prussian War he was caught up in a ubiquitous web of cultural myths about Teutonic destiny and war's glories. Small wonder that he fairly pined to get into the fight, even composing patriotic songs extolling German dutifulness and military prowess. Because he was employed at the University of Basel, however, his livelihood required that he obey Swiss law, which then as now favored neutrality. At length the Swiss authorities decided to allow him to serve with his native Prussia, but only in the role of medic. The militant young philosopher ended up on the long train ride from the Prussian victory at Sedan back to Karlsruhe, tending to the war's castoffs, the maimed and dying and sick. No doubt his experience with battle's ugly aftermath did as much as his philosophical reflections and correspondence with less militant colleagues to cure him of his uninformed militarism. His honesty could not accommodate the facts he had encountered, especially the horror of what he thought would be a glorious experience in the wake of Prussia's single battlefield victory.[9]

This points us to something important about the nature of honesty in the military, both what it is and how one can develop and maintain it. The most obvious obstacles are self-serving desires that track with Hobbesian motivations for war: competition, diffidence, and glory.[10] Military members tend to hold onto lies that help them survive their training, falsehoods that are comforting and coherent, that their superiors embrace, and that burnish their own self-perceptions, especially when new truths seem disorienting, embarrassing, or heretical. Each of us lives within systems of convictions that try to inoculate us against contrary facts. Can any reflective, honest person in uniform avoid facing what Nietzsche did, namely, a crisis of conscience when old ways of thinking tremble in the face of brutal experience? It seems unlikely. Nietzsche captured this insight in an aphorism that has surely occurred to many in active military service even if they wouldn't have chosen the same vocabulary: "I mistrust all systematizers and get out of their way. The will to system shows a lack of honesty [Rechtschaffenheit]."[11]

Nietzsche's point is that when we try but fail to reconcile apparently opposing things, yet persist in denying their opposition and even insist they are mutually consistent, we have 'systematized' against all reason and thereby demonstrated dishonesty. Military rhetoric praising honesty is inconsistent with the lies we tell ourselves – for example, that we

9   Julian Young, *Nietzsche: A Philosophical Biography* (Cambridge: Cambridge University Press, 2010), 135–47.

10 Thomas Hobbes, *Leviathan*, ed. C.B. Macpherson (New York: Penguin, 1978), Part I, chapter 13, 185.

11 *Götzen-Dämmerung* [*Twilight of the Idols*]. Sprüche und Pfeile 26. Kritische Studienausgabe [Collected Works] vol. 6, ed. Giorgio Colli and Mazzino Montinari (Munich: Deutsche Taschenbuch Verlag, 1988), 63.

complete much more military training than is even temporally possible. At a minimum, we must stop countenancing blatant dishonesty. That is the message of retired U.S. Army officer Lenny Wong, now a faculty member at the U.S. Army War College in Pennsylvania, who co-authored an influential study entitled 'Lying to Ourselves: Dishonesty in the Army Profession.'[12]

Systemic failure to tell the truth, especially to the powerful in our military organizations and in the halls of civilian policy-makers, sooner or later destroys the reputations of individual military members and of the military as a whole. H. R. McMaster's *Dereliction of Duty* chronicles this failure on the parts of senior officers in the Vietnam era.[13] Shortly before that book appeared, one of the most tragic figures of the period, former U.S. defense secretary to two presidents Robert S. McNamara, had offered his *mea culpa* for (among other transgressions) publicly declaring the success of the ongoing Vietnam war even though he knew the U.S. and its allies would not prevail.[14] More recently, General David Petraeus survived what might have been a longer fall after providing classified information to his biographer-lover.[15] Sadly, some observers suggest the general had also corrupted certain subordinates who allegedly lied on his behalf. (Under military law in the U.S., codified in the Uniform Code of Military Justice (UCMJ), adultery is a punishable offense). While this may seem to some national military cultures an unwarranted intrusion into private lives, legitimate operational concerns ground the rule, among them worries about unit morale if the offense involves colleagues' spouses and the possibility of blackmail that could compromise classified information. In any case, observers did not fail to notice the temporal coincidence: Loyal subordinates insisted that despite the biographer's ubiquity while the general was still on active duty, the affair began only after his retirement from the army, when he led the Central Intelligence Agency (CIA) and could no longer be prosecuted under the UCMJ. Why would anyone take such risks? To quote the widely-read article 'The Bathsheba Syndrome,' success can cause one 'to lose touch with reality.'[16]

---

12 Leonard Wong and Stephen J. Gerras, "Lying to Ourselves: Dishonesty in the Army Profession" (Carlisle, PA: Strategic Studies Institute and U.S. Army War College Press, 2015), https://ssi.armywarcollege.edu/pdffiles/pub1250.pdf.

13 H. R. McMaster, *Dereliction of Duty* (New York: HarperPerennial, 1997).

14 Robert S. McNamara, *In Retrospect: The Tragedy and Lessons of Vietnam* (New York: Times Books, 1995).

15 Jessica Bennett, "Paula Broadwell, David Petraeus and the Afterlife of a Scandal," *The New York Times*, May 28, 2016, https://www.nytimes.com/2016/05/29/fashion/david-petraeus-paula-broadwell-scandal-affair.html.

16 Dean C. Ludwig, and Clinton O. Longenecker, "The Bathsheba Syndrome: The Ethical Failure of Successful Leaders," *Journal of Business Ethics* 12, no. 4 (1993): 272.

One hears the Latin *honestas* in the English word honesty, and that should remind us of another important sense of the word. Honesty is not just being virtuous but also enjoying the respect that derives from a reputation for consistently ethical behavior. Words such as honor, respectability, and reputation capture this sense of honesty. We might at first shy away from this side of honesty, thinking rightly that it is better to strive to develop the virtue itself than the reputation for having it. But to think that way would be to ignore why the ancients put so much stock in virtue generally. Virtue in the sense of *areté* is not solely about being virtuous; it's about living the life most worth living in the here and now. If Aristotle is correct that each of us is a *zoon politikon* – a social animal[17] – the excellent life is a thriving existence within human society that depends partly on the fruits of good reputation. Of course it's conceivable that the normal, healthy tether between virtue and the reputation for virtue could be severed: It's possible that a genuinely good person could have the undeserved reputation of being bad, and vice versa, a bad person could enjoy a great reputation. In *Republic* II Socrates explains that the former would still live more excellently than the latter despite suffering the slings and arrows that accompany a bad reputation. However, Socrates indicates that such a person would be far better off with that respectability that the Romans would later call *honestas*.[18]

This sense of honesty as reputation is more crucial in the military than in many other walks of life because of the stakes that military members face as well as the breakneck pace of battle, other field operations, and even, at times, training. The stakes and tempo of military life require trust of one's fellows in the field, and in turn that trust depends on everyone's but especially the leaders' reputation for honesty. These facts make one of literature's most famous soldiers, Shakespeare's Iago, especially sinister. Iago first arranges for Cassio, a competent and loyal captain, to lose his good reputation, a kind of honesty that an ancient Roman might have called *honestas*, then pretends the matter is trivial.[19] Iago might deceive

---

17 Aristotle, *Politics* 1253a, trans. H. Rackham (Cambridge, MA: Harvard University Press, 1990), http://www.perseus.tufts.edu/hopper/text?doc=Perseus:abo:tlg,0086,035:1:1253a.

18 Plato, *Republic* 361b – 368a, *The Republic of Plato*, 2nd edn, trans. Allan Bloom (1968), 39–44.

19 CASSIO: Reputation, reputation, reputation! O, I have lost / my reputation! I have lost the immortal part of / myself, and what remains is bestial. My reputation, / Iago, my reputation! / IAGO: As I am an honest man, I thought you had received / some bodily wound; there is more sense in that than / in reputation. Reputation is an idle and most false / imposition: oft got without merit, and lost without / deserving: you have lost no reputation at all, / unless you repute yourself such a loser. What, man! / there are ways to recover the general [Othello] again: you / are but now cast in his mood, a punishment more in / policy than in malice, even so as one would beat his / offenceless dog to affright an imperious lion: sue / to him again, and he's yours. (*Othello*, Act 2, scene 3)

the desperate Cassio, but he speaks quite differently – and, as any military member can attest, more accurately – when he talks to the general himself, Othello, later in the play.[20]

Iago's interactions with Cassio and Othello indicate another interesting aspect of honesty in its robust sense of general virtue, including a reputation for being good, that is somewhat surprising: The reputation for honesty is fragile. One might think it would be otherwise because a reputation for honesty emerges so slowly, accreting one sensible act and wise statement after another over many years; surely such a painstakingly-built edifice could not crumble quickly. But then there's the old truism: 'One "Oh, shit!" erases a hundred "Attaboys"' – in American military jargon a piquant way of saying that a reputation for honesty or any other virtue can take years to develop but can be destroyed virtually overnight. Perhaps one reason for this surprising fact hearkens back to the often-ironic view of honesty in the military we saw at the beginning of this overview. If one can wax so cynical about honesty in certain contexts, how honest is one deep down despite having a fine reputation? Another possible reason why honesty sometimes seems so fragile is that expectations of the honesty of military members can be very high, depending on the nation and the era. At present, for example, polls show that the U.S. military enjoys a towering reputation for moral probity compared with other walks of life in the U.S., especially the roles of, say, politicians or lawyers.[21] One often hears the figure 'one percent' in the U.S., meaning that only about one out of one hundred U.S. citizens serves in the military, so perhaps there is also a mystique about service that makes people outside the military and sometimes even within think of the uniformed service members as a societal elite. And how could members of a respected elite who are willing to put themselves in mortal danger for the sake of their nation be anything but honest? The logic is flawed, of course, but flawed logic often accompanies high expectations that can be easily disappointed.

This short overview has left much undone and has not even tried to answer what may be the two most important questions of all, questions that go back at least as far as Plato's *Meno*: Can honesty, or for that matter

---

20   Good name in man and woman, dear my lord, / Is the immediate jewel of their souls: / Who steals my purse steals trash; 'tis something, nothing; / 'Twas mine, 'tis his, and has been slave to thousands: / But he that filches from me my good name / Robs me of that which not enriches him / And makes me poor indeed. (*Othello*, Act 3, Scene 3)

21   Brian Kennedy, "Most Americans Trust the Military and Scientists to Act in the Public's Interest," Pew Research Center, October 18, 2016, http://www.pewresearch.org/fact-tank/2016/10/18/most-americans-trust-the-military-and-scientists-to-act-in-the-publics-interest/.

any virtue, be taught? If so, how? Those questions must wait for another essay. For now it's enough to admire the embodiments of military honesty, such as a revered French marshal in the Thirty Years' War:

> The deputies of a great metropolis in German ... once offered the great Turenne ... one hundred thousand crowns not to pass with his army through the city. 'Gentlemen,' said he, 'I can't in conscience accept your money, as I had no intention to pass that way.'[22]

---

22 Excerpted from the *Percy Anecdotes* (London, 1823) in *The Oxford Book of Military Anecdotes*, ed. Max Hastings (Oxford: Oxford University Press, 1985), 110.

Case Study 1:
Honesty and Deceit in War

Ian Fishback

There is a tendency to think that war is morally problematic because it involves ubiquitous killing and killing is ordinarily forbidden. Most killing outside of war is murder; most killing between adversaries in the context of war is not murder. If (1) there is no distinction between killing and murder or (2) if there is no morally relevant difference between war and non-war contexts, it might follow straightforwardly that all war is unjustified (i.e. pacifism is correct) and being a military professional is deeply immoral. Therefore, distinctions between killing and murder are believed to be central to understanding the ethics of war. To be clear, I believe that pacifism is incorrect and being a military professional is morally admirable. However, the distinction between killing in war and murder is foundational for understanding why. Furthermore, although it is less frequently discussed, it seems that ubiquitous deceit in warfare is also morally problematic. Consider the following analog to questions regarding killing in war. Deceit, like killing, is ordinarily forbidden. When deceit is forbidden it is dishonesty. Some forms of deceit are not dishonest though. Most deceit outside of war is dishonesty; most deceit between adversaries in war is not dishonesty. If (1) there is no distinction between deceit and dishonesty or (2) if there is no morally relevant difference between war and non-war contexts, it might follow straightforwardly that all war is unjustified (i.e. pacifism is correct) and being a military professional is deeply immoral. Therefore, distinctions between deceit and dishonesty are also central to understanding the ethics of war, even though they are less frequently discussed than distinctions between killing and murder. Furthermore, one might think it appropriate to treat killing in war and deceit in war as a unified concept. Consider the paradigmatic example of a conflux of deceit and killing in war: the ambush. There are many means of conducting an ambush, all of which involve empathizing with an enemy to dupe him. The essence of the tactic is manipulating an enemy's senses in order to lull him into a false sense of security prior to destroying him. This kind of deceitful killing excites strong moral disapprobation in ordinary domestic life. Nonetheless, an overwhelming number of people believe that such deceitful killing is morally acceptable, even admirable, in war. This may be an indication that our moral judgments about war are mistaken and ought to be revised in order to be more like our moral judgments in contexts other than war. There is, however, another possibility. What appear to be categorical prohibitions in contexts other than war are instead *prima facie* prohibitions that almost never admit of exceptions outside of war. However, in the context of war the exceptions are so common that it seems as if there are no *prima facie* prohibitions. What does this phenomenon tell us about the virtue of being an honest military professional?

Aristotle believed that virtue is a matter of being a certain kind of person who is capable of being motivated to act in an appropriate manner. Since the kind of act one ought to perform varies with context, an important aspect of virtue is the ability to discern the moral relevance of context. Virtues are acquired by habit; the more one practices virtue, the better one becomes at discerning the right thing to do in different contexts and performing the act that is the best fit within a given context. Since context matters, it matters whether one is in war or not. Furthermore, with respect to deceitful killing, it is much easier to behave virtuously outside of war in ordinary domestic life. There, so long as a person learns to abstain from deceitful violence absolutely, that person will most likely do the right thing all of the time. However, the same is not true of war. In war, a person who abstains from deceitful killing in all circumstances will frequently behave wrongly. This is not to say that military professionals ought to deceive their enemies all of the time or that all manner of deception are morally permissible in war. It is not true that any kind of deceit is acceptable in war, just as it is not true that any kind of killing is acceptable in war. One reason is that there is a difference between deceit and dishonesty, just as there is a difference between killing and murder. This is because it is possible for a combatant to be open about attempting to deceive an adversary. Opposing belligerents know that they are attempting to ambush each other. When an ambush occurs, the targets are surprised that an ambush is occurring at a specific place and time, but they are not surprised that they are ambushed within the context of war. An analogy can be made with a trick play in American football. When a team successfully surprises an opponent with a flea-flicker, the opponent feels deceived and may even praise their opponent for achieving the deception. There is no sense that dishonesty occurred though, for both teams know that they are trying to deceive each other. Certain kinds of deception are permitted within the normative framework of football, just as many kinds of deception are permitted within the normative framework of war.

Military professionals tend to separate killing from deceit in war and focus on acquiring virtue with respect to the former while neglecting the latter. Consider the amount of time and effort that military professionals spend thinking about and preparing for scenarios in which one might be required to kill. Rules of engagement are written, vehicle checkpoint escalation of force procedures are practiced, and close quarters battle drills are executed. If a lethal target is developed during operations, considerable time and energy are spent deliberating over the ethics and laws that regulate killing. This can be held in contrast with the small amount of time and effort military professionals spend thinking about and preparing for scenarios in which one might be required to deceive. There is a simple explanation for this asymmetry. Military professionals embrace killing as a part of their *raison d'être*. However, military professionals tend to self-identify as extraordinarily honest persons who never deceive. Counterinsurgents in particular tend to view their role as honest liberators whose primary task is overcoming a deceitful adversary, rather than persons who practice deceit on a regular basis. As a result, they tend to be more honest with themselves about the amount of killing inherent in their craft and more dishonest with themselves about the amount of deceit inherent in their craft. For the remainder of this case study, I will discuss two phenomena, wearing distinguishable insignia and negotiating with a key leader during an insurgency. Both phenomena require significant degrees of the military virtue of honesty. Rather than explaining how best to acquire this virtue, it is my intent to highlight the nuance involved in assessing these types of situations and motivate the reader to think about how best to prepare for them.

Acceptable deception is bounded by norms, even during armed conflict. One such norm is the moral and legal requirement for combatants to distinguish themselves with easily recognizable insignia. These expectations are often strained during contemporary urban guerrilla warfare, where insurgents do not have natural concealment, such as mountains or forests. In such circumstance, insurgents often do not wear prescribed insignia to escape detection by their enemies.[23] By doing so,

---

23 Michael Walzer, *Just and Unjust Wars: A Moral Argument with Historical Illustrations: Fifth Edition* (New York: Basic Books, 2015), chapter 11 "Guerilla War."

insurgents hope to hide among the civilian population. Counterinsurgents predictably criticize this behavior. The U.S., for example, once cited such tactics as the basis for claiming that some insurgent organizations ought not be recognized as lawful combatants. It is not my aim to analyze these claims in great detail here. Rather, I will note some features of the debate as they relate to the matters of deception in honesty.

One point is political. Civil war is often a contest for legitimacy. Therefore, counterinsurgents have incentives to argue they follow the law and insurgent organizations do not. Therefore, they frequently employ hypocritical standards, such as defining terrorism in a biased manner that exclusively applies to non-state actors. Furthermore, counterinsurgents frequently don civilian clothes and claim that they wear identifying insignia because they carry a driver's-license-like military identification card stowed in a breast pocket. This behavior is not considerably different than insurgent behavior. To the degree it is different, it is probably the case that insurgents would adhere to the same standard of carrying an identification card in a pocket on offensive operations if they were informed of such a standard. However, counterinsurgents usually are not trying to build and maintain mutually agreed upon standards of conduct with insurgents. Instead, their aim is to achieve a politically advantageous position of plausibly claiming insurgents violate the laws of war. In short, counterinsurgents deliberately control context in order to portray insurgents as dishonest. Instead, counterinsurgents could deliberately control context in order to incentivize insurgents to honestly adhere to norms that maximally protect civilians. I submit that counterinsurgents behave dishonestly when they do this, for they are portraying themselves as doing everything they can to respect civilian immunity and portraying their enemies as flagrantly disrespecting the same norms. Counterinsurgents often have the power to instantiate rules that would be respected by insurgents. Instead of exercising this power, they deliberately choose not to. Their goal is not insurgent compliance with the morality and law of war. Rather, it is to manipulate the law and insurgent behavior so that the two come apart. An excellent example of this is the U.S.' use of the term 'terrorist' to describe improved explosive device attacks on combatants during Operation Iraqi Freedom and Operation Enduring Freedom. These attacks were not terrorist attacks. They were attacks on enemy combatants. By treating such attacks and vehicle borne improved explosive device attacks on civilians as relevantly similar morally and legally, the U.S. counterinsurgents did not provide incentives for insurgents to limit targeting to enemy combatants.

Furthermore, insurgents disguise themselves as civilians and often claim they have a moral right to do so. This hardly seems like deception, let alone dishonesty. At worst, it is brazen violation of existing norms by openly renouncing the rule, for insurgents rarely claim to be wearing uniforms. In that sense, they are being honest. Counterinsurgents often behave hypocritically in another way too. They also frequently assume the guise of civilians, driving civilian vehicles and wearing civilian clothes and carrying a driver's license like identification card in a breast pocket. The identification card is supposedly insignia that identifies the combatancy status of the bearer, yet it is not visible. Therefore, how could it be identifiable? The explicit purpose of this behavior is to blend in with the civilian population during non-offensive operations, such as intelligence collection. Counterinsurgents do not wear civilian clothes during raids and similar missions targeting suspected enemy combatants, such as raids. Such behavior is clearly deceit. However, it is unclear whether it is dishonest. If it is honest deceit, then what grounds to counterinsurgents have for claiming that insurgents who blend in with the civilian population also practice honest deceit?

There is another domain of counterinsurgency that is fraught with deceit: key leader engagements and non-kinetic (i.e. politically influencing, rather than killing or capturing) targeting. Key leaders are often neither friends nor enemies; they occupy a gray area between ally and adversary. Indeed, the whole point of non-kinetic targeting is to nudge such persons to become more ally-like and less adversary-like in their behavior. However, almost all non-kinetic targeting occurs with the background knowledge that it is possible to shift from non-kinetic means to kinetic means if the situation changes. Thus, a Sunni sheik who cooperates with insurgents might be viewed as an important non-kinetic target for purposes of reconciliation. However, should the Sunni sheik prove to be irreconcilable and an obstacle to peaceful transition, a counterinsurgent commander may later elect to target the sheik with kinetic means. Likewise, the non-kinetic target often views the counterinsurgent commander through a similar lens. The target may seek reconciliation with the counterinsurgent. However, if the counterinsurgent is unwilling or unable to satisfy the target's demands, then the target may elect to revert to open warfare.

The virtue of honesty in counterinsurgency is dependent upon the combatant's ability to be sensitive to subtle instances of context and act accordingly. It is not my aim to outline all of the contextual clues that such a commander must be sensitive to. Rather, it is to highlight the need to be cognizant of the moral demands of honesty in non-kinetic targeting. Consider a straightforward key leader engagement with a sheik suspected of cooperating with insurgents. The sheik might use the meeting itself as a pretext for putting the counterinsurgent in time and space for an ambush along the route to the meeting. Within the context of a broader civil war, the sheik could maintain plausible deniability for providing targeting information to the ambushing force. Meanwhile, the counterinsurgent could suffer catastrophic casualties from such an attack. The counterinsurgent is thus vulnerable to the sheik. Likewise, the sheik is vulnerable to the counterinsurgent, because the counterinsurgent often has the overwhelming combat power to kill or capture the sheik at the key leader engagement. Indeed, during the Iraq and Afghanistan wars, it was common for counterinsurgents to do so. Did such activity cross the line from deceit to dishonesty? This is a complicated question and the answer is sensitive to context. However, such behavior is strikingly similar to killing one's enemies during surrender negotiations, which is generally believed to be morally reprehensible. Most men and women find such behavior unacceptable during war. If so, perhaps it is dishonest to arrest sheiks at key leader engagements and for sheiks to target counterinsurgents in route to key leader engagements. I will discuss the contours of such a discussion in other writing. Here my aim is merely to motivate the reader to have such a discussion with his or her brothers and sisters in arms.

Case Study 2:
Cannibals, Gun-deckers, and Good Idea Fairies: Structural Incentives to Deceive in the Military

Michael Skerker

A recent study reported that U.S. Army officers think of themselves as being persons of integrity while also reporting systematic dishonesty in the execution of their professional duties.[24] The authors conclude that the structure of the modern U.S. Army tacitly encourages and effectively necessitates falsifications of some reports, non-compliance with some training requirements, and exaggerations of readiness postures. A less comprehensive set of interviews I conducted with U.S. Navy officers reveals some of the same problems as well as some forms of deception peculiar to the Naval Service. To be clear, these problems are not universal, with different warfare communities apparently having more rule-compliant cultures (or more generous funding streams) than others and different commands enjoying better or worse ethical cultures due to better or worse leadership.

The behavioral vectors of compulsion and compliance characterizing a hierarchical organization like the military creates morally hazardous conditions for organization members. Personnel expect their subordinates to comply with directives without negotiation or resistance while subordinates know they are professionally, if not legally, bound to obey

---

24 Wong and Gerras, "Lying to Ourselves."

their lawful orders. The larger the organization and 'steeper' the hierarchy, the greater the chance that high-echelon order-givers will be ignorant of the facts on the ground as well as the existing workload for subordinates (who may be getting demand signals from several layers of management). By contrast, in an egalitarian or less hierarchical organization, bad ideas or unreasonable demands can be more readily challenged, vetted, and reformulated among peers.

Current exigencies in the U.S. military related to funding and the promotion process mean this potential for moral hazards is too often realized. Officers routinely report that there is insufficient time to perform mandated trainings and insufficient funding to perform necessary maintenance of materiel. Added to this structural problem created by a mismatch between the demands placed on the military by politicians and the relative dearth of funding politicians provide is a perverse incentive structure for personnel promotion. Many commands have a zero defect mentality: officers are expected to meet 100 percent of the objectives set for them by superiors. Concurrently, promotion boards are increasingly rigorous, looking for any blemish to exclude one highly qualified candidate from another. Given that higher echelon officers typically depend on computerized reports rather than on-site inspections to judge compliance, harried subordinates might falsify, exaggerate, and fudge records of compliance with a reasonable hope of successful deception.

There may be a further temptation to do these things because of their apparent triviality. There is a sense in some commands, at least with respect to falsifying certain reports or short-changing certain requirements, that 'everyone is doing it and everyone *knows* everyone is doing it.' It is like a community of worshippers who have lost faith and yet persist in their mantras. Finally, it is noted by the personnel in certain commands that the service members who truthfully report their failure to meet (unreasonable) demands are reprimanded and/or fail to promote.

When personnel are told that all trainings and safety checks are mandatory but there is not enough time or manning to accomplish them, even conscientious personnel will engage in a kind of triage to determine which duties are truly important. Now common sense and bureaucracy are age-old enemies; a well-designed system will permit professionals to engage in a certain amount of discretion while still deferring to a common set of rules and experience-based hierarchy. Yet an obvious danger lies in group members relying on their common sense rather than rules. As one retired commander put it to me 'I think I'm smart enough to know which requirements are really important, yet I expect *my* subordinates to follow my instructions with 100 percent fidelity. The problem is *everyone thinks this way* (and not everyone is as smart as me).' Since command expects 100 percent compliance, but this is impossible, leaders are then put in the position of ordering subordinates to do what is actually important while at the same time doctoring reports to show full compliance. This doctoring can range from 'pencil-whipping' training requirements (falsely indicating in writing that everyone in the command completed a training), to cannibalizing equipment, to 'gun-decking,' (falsely indicating in logs that required maintenance is complete).

A 2002 U.S. Army War College monograph showed that Army units had 297 days of annual mandatory training to pack into 256 available training days.[25] Given this impossible math, individuals and units throughout the military ignore; rush through; or pencil-whip trainings that seem unimportant. Stultifying, didactic PowerPoint-based trainings on subjects seemingly collateral to one's primary mission like sexual harassment, proper record keeping, and recreational safety are prime candidates for pencil-whipping. As a Department of the Navy civilian employee, I can attest to feeling tempted to ignore or click as fast as possible through some computer-based trainings with no relevance to my job as a professor (safe load-carrying postures? wilderness survival training?). I feel the same frustration that officers report to me: some higher power decrees that I must find a spot in my already overloaded schedule to urgently complete a non-urgent and extraneous training probably assigned in a wholesale, non-reflective fashion by a person selecting the 'all Naval employees' tab on a dropdown menu in order to inoculate the government against lawsuits or bad press. If the subordinate fakes compliance, she or he would close a circle of deception and cynicism in which non-pedagogues create pedagogically inadequate trainings to placate a demand signal or to create a talking point in the future regarding comprehensive training without regard to existing workloads and in abdication of managerial responsibility to prioritize subordinates' tasks, thus nearly ensuring that compliance will be inadequate.

More serious is the widespread practice of cannibalization in some sectors of the Navy. Whereas readiness can be faked or fudged on computerized readiness reports – exaggerating the number of 'green' (fully operational) or 'yellow' (could be operational provided some maintenance) systems on superiors' computerized dashboards – more aggressive actions are required to inflate readiness postures when it comes to physical inspections. The U.S. Congress has for some time

---

25 Leonard Wong, *Stifling Innovation: Developing Tomorrow's Leaders Today* (Carlisle, PA: Strategic Studies Institute, U.S. Army War College Press, 2002).

mandated comprehensive inspections of Fleet readiness every five years in a process called INSURV. Experts working for defense contractors inspect Navy equipment to ensure that every widget and valve is set according to blueprint specifications. The difficulty is that post-Cold War defense department budget cuts have reduced the availability of spare parts and the number of available personnel to the point that several officers told me that no ship has every piece of equipment nor the manning it is supposed to have. So officers play a shell game during INSURV inspections, often with the full knowledge and coordination of port commanders, borrowing needed equipment from various ships to temporarily put on the ship being inspected. Officers tell me that the inspectors know what is going on, as does Navy leadership; it is unclear if some Congressmen know as well.

A field grade officer told me he served under a captain who told his Commodore he was going to have his crew do their best, but show inspectors the ship's shortcomings without any cannibalization. The Commodore told him to 'pound sand' and to engage in cannibalization.

The most dangerous form of deception is gun-decking, including falsifying reports to indicate non-functioning pieces of equipment are operational or that unfulfilled maintenance requirements have been fulfilled. An infamous case of the gun-decking in the Naval Service involved a Marine air wing's gun-decking of maintenance logs of MV-22 Osprey aircraft, to make a sufficient number of the crash-prone vehicles appear operational ahead of a Congressional funding vote.[26] In a less well-reported case, a cruiser could not deploy to conduct humanitarian assistance in its area of operations because department heads in five mission areas had falsified their equipment readiness in a Navy-wide database. This deception was only revealed when the ship had to go do its job following an earthquake.

The challenging environment occasioned by limited time and budgets can be exacerbated by toxic leaders and 'good idea fairies.' The toxic leader 'leads through fear.' He or she cannot be told bad news without losing composure and attacking the messenger. Cowed subordinates learn it is better to give the skipper whatever he or she wants, regardless of whether it is true. For example, a commodore read the riot act to his subordinate admirals and captains over the fact that a balky new communications system was non-functional on several aircraft in his fleet. During the next meeting, every subordinate reported

---

26 Lt Col. Gary Slyman (USMC), Patricia Jacubec, and Jonathan Cox, "Falsification of the MV-22 Readiness Records," in *Case Studies for Ethics for Military Leaders*, 5th edn, ed. Capt. Rick Rubel (USN-Ret.) and George A. Lucas (Boston: Pearson, 2014), 141–47.

to the commodore that the system on their crafts were 'green.' Great success, except that on some craft 'green' meant that communications could only be maintained for four minutes. In another case, an admiral saw first-hand how department heads of an amphibious assault ship had been systematically falsifying readiness reports to inflate the number of 'yellow' aircraft. The admiral saw what the captain of the ship did not: fist-sized rust holes in some craft and other evidence that the crew had been lying to the captain about the number of non-operational craft out of fear of his temper.

The tyrant is one type of bad officer. Another source of stress for subordinates is the 'good idea fairy.' One field grade officer told me "the most dangerous person in the military is an O-6 without a staff." A senior officer in a new billet has a short time to make an impact given that his or her rotation may only last two years. New initiatives may be directly assigned to junior officers who already have a full suite of duties or merely suggested to juniors in the *optimistic impersonal* tone: 'wouldn't it be *great* if someone did X?' Junior officers are well familiar with the sensation of being 'voluntold' to do something: being recruited for an ostensibly optional endeavor that is only optional in the sense that continued employment in the military is optional.

What is frustrating with all these scenarios is that everyone involved seems to know that games are being played. The entities sending training and maintenance requirements downrange know that subordinates do not have the time and funding to accomplish these tasks and so will half-heartedly comply with them, if at all. Order-givers can hardly trust their dashboards full of green lights. Some training requirements themselves seem like half-hearted efforts to react to some scandal or placate a member of Congress without any attention paid to the training's efficacy or utility. Obviously, there is a real concern for safety when it comes to gun-decking and cannibalization. There is also a subtle degradation of ethical culture when even good people feel they need to systematically falsify, fudge, and exaggerate in order to make the system work properly. There is the risk that people accustomed to making common sense exceptions to create good outcomes start making lazy or corrupt exceptions to facilitate bad outcomes. Further, such a corrosive environment risks creating cynicism about the moral universe. Is all life just a game? Do you have to put your thumb on the scale in every instance? Polls consistently show that many Americans see the military as a kind of school of virtue, especially for young people. Something has to change in order to fully live up to this ideal.

References

Aristotle, *Nicomachean Ethics*, 2nd edn, 1102a, translated by Terence Irwin. Indianapolis: Hackett Publishing Co., 1999, 16.

Aristotle, *Politics* 1253a, translated by H. Rackham. Cambridge, MA: Harvard University Press, 1990, http://www.perseus.tufts.edu/hopper/text?doc=Perseus:abo:tlg,0086,035:1:1253a.

Bennett, J. "Paula Broadwell, David Petraeus and the Afterlife of a Scandal," *The New York Times*, May 28, 2016, https://www.nytimes.com/2016/05/29/fashion/david-petraeus-paula-broadwell-scandal-affair.html.

Hastings, M. ed., *The Oxford Book of Military Anecdotes*. Oxford: Oxford University Press, 1985.

Hobbes T., *Leviathan*, edited by C.B. Macpherson. New York: Penguin, 1978, Part I, chapter 13.

Kennedy, Brian. "Most Americans Trust the Military and Scientists to Act in the Public's Interest," Pew Research Center, October 18, 2016, http://www.pewresearch.org/fact-tank/2016/10/18/most-americans-trust-the-military-and-scientists-to-act-in-the-publics-interest/.

Levene, M. and P. Roberts, *The Massacre in History*. New York: Berghahn Books, 1999.

Ludwig, D. C. and C. O. Longenecker, "The Bathsheba Syndrome: The Ethical Failure of Successful Leaders," *Journal of Business Ethics* 12, 1993: 265–273.

McMaster, H. R. *Dereliction of Duty*. New York: HarperPerennial, 1997.

McNamara, R. S. *In Retrospect: The Tragedy and Lessons of Vietnam*. New York: Times Books, 1995.

Mearsheimer, J. J. *Why Leaders Lie*. New York: Oxford University Press, 2011.

Nietzsche, F. *Götzen-Dämmerung* [Twilight of the Idols]. Sprüche und Pfeile 26. *Kritische Studienausgabe* [Collected Works] vol. 6, edited by Giorgio Colli and Mazzino Montinari. Munich: Deutsche Taschenbuch Verlag, 1988, 63.

Plato, *The Republic of Plato*, translated and edited by Allan Bloom. New York: Basic Books, 1968.

Plato, *Apology* 23b, translated by Hugh Tredennick and Harold Tarrant, in *The Last Days of Socrates*. London: Penguin, 1993, 32–67.

Slyman G. Lt Col. (USMC), Patricia Jacubec, and Jonathan Cox, "Falsification of the MV-22 Readiness Records," in Capt. Rick Rubel, USN-Ret. and George Lucas, *Case Studies for Ethics for Military Leaders*, 5th edn. Boston: Pearson, 2014, 141–47.

Walzer, M. *Just and Unjust Wars: A Moral Argument with Historical Illustrations: Fifth Edition*. New York: Basic Books, 2015.

Wong L. *Stifling Innovation: Developing Tomorrow's Leaders Today*. Carlisle, PA: Strategic Studies Institute, U.S. Army War College Press, 2002.

Wong, L. and S. J. Gerras, "Lying to Ourselves: Dishonesty in the Army Profession," Carlisle, PA: Strategic Studies Institute, U.S. Army War College Press, 2015, https://ssi.armywarcollege.edu/pdffiles/pub1250.pdf.

Young, J. *Nietzsche: A Philosophical Biography*. Cambridge: Cambridge University Press, 2010, 135–47.

Zelizer, J. E. "Why the Russia Investigation Could Be More like Iran-Contra than Watergate," *The Atlantic*, February 27, 2018, https://www.theatlantic.com/politics/archive/2018/02/why-the-russia-investigation-could-end-more-like-iran-contra-than-watergate/554345/.

7

INTEGRITY

Overview

Don Carrick

Background and Rationale

It will already be clear to any reader who has got this far in this book that possession of the so-called cardinal virtues (courage, temperance, prudence and justice) may no longer be sufficient to enable the modern-day soldier[1] to deal successfully with the myriad moral and legal challenges of twenty-first-century warfare, and to 'do the right thing' on a particularly difficult day. One central reason for extending the list of virtues from the original four to the fourteen specified in this volume is that we are no longer living in an age when wars typically comprised a series of battles between the massed armies of the two (or more) nations that were involved in the conflict: in such wars, possessing the cardinal virtues was taken to be all that the soldier needed to adequately perform their role defined function of helping to win the war by (in Carl von Clausewitz's classic words) 'destroying the enemy's army, occupying his cities and breaking his will to resist.' Modern wars are very rarely undertaken to defend the realm against an aggressive invader: much more commonly, a state's forces are required these days to be deployed on 'operations other than war' such as counter-insurgency, peace-keeping, peace enforcement and missions, as well as on humanitarian interventions. Conflicts like these typically involve encounters between small units of regular troops on the one side and similar sized units of irregular forces (insurgents, terrorists, guerrillas or whatever)

---

1 For the sake of brevity, I will throughout this overview use the term 'soldier' to cover all members, male and female, of all branches of the armed forces, land-based, sea-based and air-based.

on the other, but in an environment in which the enemy – legitimate targets – are increasingly difficult to identify as such and who, in many cases, are indistinguishable from the civilian population that the regular forces are supposedly there to protect. Abiding by this distinction between legitimate and illegitimate targets is a fundamental tenet of the rules and precepts of *jus in bello*: what it is and is not permissible for soldiers to do in wartime.

This principle of non-combatant immunity (henceforth the PNCI, for short) is now incorporated into the Laws of Armed Conflict (the LOAC) and the various Conventions, and is thus morally and legally binding on the armed forces of the nations who (unlike many of their opponents) subscribe to the LOAC and the Conventions. Modern soldiers therefore now carry a great responsibility, not just because they are morally and legally obliged to abide by the PNCI on pain of punishment and disgrace (which adversely affects them), but also because any deliberate breach of the PNCI that becomes public knowledge can have a hugely disproportionate, adverse effect on the attempt to win the 'hearts and minds' of the host population of the country in which the conflict in question is taking place by lowering their trust in their 'liberators': this correspondingly reduces the chances of success for the 'good' side, and increases those for the 'bad.'

In this overview section I argue that respecting and abiding by the PNCI, no matter how great the pressures or temptations to act in breach of it, exemplifies possession of the virtue of *integrity* which is, as a result, another essential addition to the list of virtues that must be possessed by the twenty-first-century professional soldier.

Personal Integrity

The virtue of integrity, the dictionary reminds us, is "1. The quality of having strong moral principles or 2. The state of being whole/the condition of being unified."[2] The key words here are 'strong' applied to moral principles, and 'whole/unified,' applied to the agent. Possessing integrity requires that such strong moral principles must be ingrained into the agent, as it were: they must be part of her character – of her whole being – and not just instilled into her by rote at a superficial level, but without any real internal commitment to live by them at all times and in all circumstances. Integrity accordingly provides a link between reason and action: a person with integrity will intuitively know (or will have quickly worked out) what is 'the right thing to do' in a particular situation and will carry on and do it without any hesitation. So to say that someone does possess the strong

---

2   The definition quoted comes from the *Concise Oxford English Dictionary 11th Edition*.

moral principles required for them to be regarded as a person of integrity, is to make a value judgement about them as a human being, although having complete integrity also necessitates possession of a *strong will*; strong enough to resist the situational and emotional influences that can put extreme pressure on an agent's ability to 'keep going regardless' and achieve the morally right end of the action question.

Thus far, the conclusion of such a line of reasoning seems to be fairly obvious: in our context, the strong-willed soldier with integrity, as decision-maker, can deal with the pressures of being in the middle of a scene of wholesale death and destruction and still act coolly, calmly, rationally and objectively, making the right decisions at all time. But this analysis fails to take into account the fact that there is more than one type of integrity relevant to the role of soldiering.

Professional Integrity

Soldiers must also faithfully comply with the rules and precepts of ordinary morality (so displaying personal integrity). Soldiers are required to abide by the code of conduct of conduct appropriate to their profession, as well as the LOAC and Conventions, and such code will expressly or implicitly contain a requirement to obey all orders (or, at least, legal ones) and to abide by the rules and precepts of the professional role they have taken on. The soldier is thus required to display *professional* integrity as well as personal.

But the central difficulty with this notion of the professional integrity of the soldier is that, as well as mandating that he or she acts like a properly virtuous human being (i.e. maintains their personal integrity) the soldier is in a chain of command, and will, sometimes receive an order from above that can lead to a tension – or direct conflict – between the need to abide by abiding by the fundamental demands of ordinary morality (particularly, in the soldier's case, the fundamental prohibition against the deliberate killing of the innocent) and achieving the objective of the mission in question. Admittedly, when the goal of soldiers' actions in a 'total war' was simply to defeat the enemy and help his nation to win the war in question, the demands of 'ordinary' morality could and would sometimes be ignored in favour of achieving the supposedly greater good,[3] but in modern conflicts 'amongst the people,' respecting the immunity of non-combatants has a very high priority which must be maintained: any deliberate – or even

---

3   The use in the closing stages of World War II of 'area bombing' against civilians with the stated purpose of to reducing their morale being one of the most egregious examples of morally very dubious actions.

accidental – breach of the human rights of the civilian population of the country in which the conflict in question is taking place can have decidedly detrimental knock-on effects. Winning, and keeping, the hearts and minds of the people now has tactical and even strategic importance in most such conflicts. Accomplishment of a particular mission may certainly maintain personal integrity, but not as an end in itself if it causes the agent to lose sight of the overall goal.

The tension between maintaining personal integrity and maintaining professional integrity can therefore put an enormous strain on the soldier in question. Soldiers must try their best to maintain a balance between the possibly conflicting demands of personal and professional integrity, but sometimes this ideal will be well-nigh beyond reach. The recent case of a mission by a U.S. Special Forces team in the Afghan conflict vividly illustrates the problems and the terrible dilemmas that can afflict the soldiers involved. The facts of the case were these:

In June 2005, four members of SEAL Team 10 were inserted in the Hindu Kush mountains of Afghanistan's Kunar province. The objective of the operation (code name 'Red Wings') was to reconnoitre and 'get eyes on' Ahmad Shah, a close associate of Osama bin Laden, whose attacks had been taking a heavy toll on U.S. Marines operating in eastern Afghanistan. After setting up their observation post on a mountainside overlooking a village near the Pakistani border in which this key Taliban leader was believed to be encamped with a small army, the four-man SEAL team was approached at midday by two Afghan men and a 14-year-old boy, herding their flock of goats. The SEALs debated over whether to kill the men to protect their cover, or try to hold them prisoner, or simply turn them loose and abandon the mission. After arguing among themselves as to what was the right thing to do, the four SEALS decided to let the Afghans go, and to attempt to re-position.

A little later, however, nearly one hundred Taliban fighters materialized, coming across the same ridge over which the goatherds themselves had fled. The SEAL team fought for several hours, killing an estimated 35 of the enemy, but eventually they were overwhelmed. Their commanding officer, Navy Lieutenant Michael Murphy, was shot and killed as he called for backup. Two of the three enlisted members of the Team were also killed in the relentless gunfire. Petty Officer Marcus Luttrell, the lone survivor,[4] was badly wounded, and escaped by jumping down steep cliffs, falling hundreds of feet at a time. He was found and rescued by local Pashtun

---

4 P. O. Luttrell's story of the events was published under the title *Lone Survivor* (Marcus Luttrell with Paul Robinson. New York: Little Brown, 2007), and subsequently filmed, again as *Lone Survivor* in 2013.

tribesmen, who, for several days, extended him extraordinary hospitality and protection. When finally located and rescued by Army Rangers, Luttrell learned that Lieutenant Murphy's original call for assistance had resulted in an even greater tragedy. An MH-47 Chinook, with seven Army Rangers and seven Navy SEALS aboard, had volunteered to rescue their comrades, but a Taliban rocket-propelled grenade hit the rescue helicopter as it was landing, killing the two pilots and all fourteen Special Forces volunteers on board: the worst single incident of battlefield fatalities sustained by U.S. forces in the Afghan conflict.[5]

So why did the SEALs decide against killing and in favour of releasing their captives, knowing full well that this could put their own lives in jeopardy and put their whole mission at risk? The short answer is that the action of killing the shepherds would have been, quite simply, an act of *murder* (commonly as the unlawful premeditated killing of another human being without justification or valid excuse).

So from the personal integrity point of view, the Team's decision to spare the lives of the shepherds was obviously, morally and ethically, the correct one. Nevertheless, it was by no means an easy one to make. The Team members deliberated carefully about their dilemma for some time and eventually took a vote which came down in favour of letting the shepherds go, albeit only narrowly, with two votes cast in favour, one against, and one abstention. The mental agonising involved was tremendous. Marcus Luttrell (who voted in favour of release of the shepherds) says in his autobiography "It was the stupidest, most southern-fried, lamebrained decision I ever made in my life. I must have been out of my mind. I actually cast a vote which I knew could sign our death warrant. I'd turned into a fucking liberal, a half-assed, no-logic nitwit, all heart, no brain, and the judgment of a jackrabbit" and then, "No night passes when I don't wake in a cold sweat thinking of those moments on that mountain. I'll never get over it. The deciding vote was mine, and it will haunt me till they rest me in an East Texas Grave."[6]

But although I have argued in support of prioritizing personal integrity over professional integrity, and maintain that it is never justifiable to deliberately kill innocent non-combatants it remains the case that counter-arguments can, and have been, raised in support of the view that if the commander of SEAL Team 10, Lieutenant Murphy, had been

---

5   This synopsis of the events in 'Operation Red Wings' is reproduced (with slight amendments to the wording) by kind permission of its author, George R. Lucas Jr. and Ashgate Publishing Ltd, from the Foreword to *Ethics Education for Irregular Warfare* (D. Carrick, J. Connelly and P. Robinson, eds., Aldershot: Ashgate, 2009).

6   Luttrell, *Lone Survivor*, 294.

more concerned with mission accomplishment (and thus prioritizing professional over personal integrity) then he might have been more open to consider killing the shepherds. Such lines of argument are typical of those used by absolute realists, that is, those who maintain that ethics and morality have no place in wartime decision-making, and that the only question to be answered when finding the justification for going to war and making war is 'What is in the best interests of the state?' Realist wartime decision-makers at all levels of command are on the face of it being guided by the original utilitarian principle of acting with the goal of promoting the greatest happiness of the greatest number. At first sight, this looks like an admirable principle to follow, but following it to its logical conclusion can lead all too easily to justifying the unjustifiable action of sacrificing the innocent few as part of the process of defeating the guilty many. In our scenario, therefore, the actual act of killing the shepherds would have been a relatively straightforward task – they were unarmed and defenceless, and the SEALs were heavily armed with any number of lethal weapons: a decision to kill could have been translated in to the action of killing with little or no (physical) trouble to the soldiers. Following the elimination of the shepherds, the SEALs could have continued with their mission and, let us assume, successfully completed their mission with no loss to themselves or their compatriots. An air strike could then have been called down on the Taliban commander (an obviously high-value target) and he would have been eliminated, thus achieving both the short- and long-term objectives of the mission. The greatest happiness of the greatest number could have been achieved, but the human cost, even if it was 'only' three dead shepherds, was too high.

So a final question for you: what would *you* have done if you had been the decision-maker of SEAL Team 10 on that fateful day in 2005? Would you – *could* you – have adopted the absolute realist position, given priority to mission completion, compromised your personal integrity, and ordered the killing of the shepherds? And if you had done so, could you have lived with your conscience afterwards?

Case Study 1: Integrity, Institutions, and the Banality of Complicity

Michael Robillard

Introduction

When I was a young cadet at West Point, I had an officer mentor who gave me some professional words of wisdom. He said, 'as an officer, you can only really fall on your sword once, so make sure that when you do, it's for a big enough reason.' At the time, this sounded to me like perfectly good advice. Certainly, I thought, there would be moments within one's military career where one would likely witness instances and decisions within the larger institutional body that he or she did not agree with or found morally questionable; commanders making ethically dubious statements, peers letting certain things slide, sister units failing to report certain transgressions up the chain of command and instead handling matters 'in house,' or perhaps just a general attitude of soldiers turning a blind eye to the myriad day-to-day instances of institutional hypocrisy and the shirking of standards. Despite their moral unsavoriness, none of these things, at least in my mind at that time, seemed to rise to the level of the type of thing that would warrant an officer ending his entire career over. Indeed, choosing to take a vocal stand on *every* rule broken, corner cut, or standard shirked by one's peers seemed to me not only highly hypocritical and highly exhausting but also deeply injurious to the fostering of any degree of long-term trust or credibility among one's peers. Put simply, no one wants to be 'that guy.' Hence, my mentor's general advice of 'pick your battles' seemed entirely appropriate.

Looking back now, I believe that my mentor's well-intentioned advice was flawed in one very important way. The flaw, I believe, is most clearly captured by Hannah Arendt in her work *Eichmann in Jerusalem* and her description of evil as being something fundamentally *banal*. Indeed, when we typically think of evil, we oftentimes envision instances like Auschwitz, the My Lai massacre, and the Rwandan genocide. And while these instances are clearly and undoubtedly manifestations of evil, what we often fail to recognize is that these instances are fundamentally *culminations* of evil arising from a long causal chain of individual instances of attitudes, sentiments, actions, and omissions within an entire network of institutional and individual actors that are, for the most part, commonplace and unnoteworthy. Oftentimes a general institutional climate will be the predecessor to a particular culminating evil or immoral event. And prior to the manifestation of a general institutional climate, will be the slow, day-to-day, banal accumulation of words said or unsaid, orders questioned or unquestioned, acts performed or not performed, and minor moral transgressions called out or ignored until each of these individual moments aggregate into something far more morally pernicious than any of their constituent parts.

Seldom if ever does one open a door or around a corner to suddenly, discover "A ha! There it is. Pure evil, right there!" Rather, like the frog slowly cooked to death in the bathtub or individual grains of sand eventually aggregating into an entire heap of sand, immoral acts, at least within a large institutional body like the military, often admit of a character and origin that is much more subtle, mundane, and creeping in nature. This description of how particular, pronounced immoral actions eventuate from little, banal, day-to-day acts, omissions, and attitudes within the larger military institution generates a significant problem for my mentor's professional advice to 'pick your battles.'

We can articulate the tension as follows. If each, singular, one-off instance of a witnessed minor moral transgression within a military unit fails to ever rise to the level of a *severe* evil or manifestly immoral act, then challenging one's peers or superiors, disobeying orders, whistleblowing, or falling on one's sword will almost always seem like a disproportionate response or radical overreaction to the singular, one-off minor immoral act one has witnessed and is attempting to respond to. The consequence of this phenomenon can then be one of the well-intentioned officer, earnestly committed to falling on his or her sword when manifest evil or heinous immorality rears its head, but perpetually waiting for a clear and definitive moment that never truly arrives. With each moment of waiting in silence, of remaining complicit, and of not voicing one's moral opinion or disapproval over minor moral transgressions, a particular social and institutional precedent is necessarily set, often making it that much harder for the military leader to respond to the same or similar minor transgressions the next time around. Consequently, a subtle climate can begin to emerge around the military leader where more severe immoral acts might be more likely to eventuate before he or she has adequate time to jump in and stop them.

Baghdad, Iraq 2003

I can remember a time in Baghdad when this phenomenon affected me most. About two months into the deployment, our platoon inherited a soldier who had been a reject from a more 'high-speed' unit within the brigade. From the individual soldier's perspective, the move was a clear demotion, one which he was not at all happy with. From the perspective of our platoon however, the move was seen as a clear and obvious gain. In a combat environment, the sudden acquisition of more experience and more technical competence is a hard thing to shake a stick at. I initially shared this same optimism about our new arrival.

As the weeks went by, however, I began to have my doubts about just how positive an acquisition this really was. Given that he came from a more high-speed and respected unit, there was an immediate halo effect that this soldier garnered among his peers, subordinates, and even superiors. And given that he had all the right credentials, at least on paper, I too oftentimes found myself instinctively deferring to his judgement either because I gave him too much respect too easily or because I didn't want to start a pissing match within the platoon that I would surely lose. As a new, 22-year-old, wet-behind-the-ears, 2nd Lieutenant, one who took over his platoon mid-deployment after all his men had already bonded over the initial invasion of Iraq without him, I had to be wise about saving face and preserving the little bit of street cred that I had.

In any event, as the weeks went on, I began witnessing this soldier saying and doing little things here and there that suggested that he might have been a bit too trigger-happy and a bit too covetous of 'seeing some action.' Our company's time in Baghdad up until that point had consisted largely of what I would describe as 'aggressive policing.' Presence patrols, cordon and searches, raiding homes, with the occasional RPG (rocket-propelled grenade), mortar, IED (improvised explosive device) (or failed IED), or AK-47 fire. Enough to keep us on our toes, but nothing ever amounting to or warranting a conventional, manoeuver fire-fight; the very thing our light infantry unit had trained for and had essentially been built for. I imagine this unclimactic state of affairs had something to do with this particular soldier's over-aggressive posturing and his desire to get into something more exciting.

This overly bellicose posturing was most clearly evidenced in this soldier's particular aesthetic and in the additional gear that he had personally shipped over from civilian manufacturers to add to his standardly issued U.S. Army kit; things like a form-fitted ammo vest, hands-free audio earpiece and microphone, custom form-fitted adjustable chin-strap for his helmet, a 'gangster grip' for his M-4 carbine, and growing his sideburns intentionally long. In essence, he was emulating the aesthetic found within many Special Forces units at that time. Importantly though, he wasn't Special Forces, nor Delta, nor was our unit. Despite this, several of the other soldiers within the company and the platoon also began to emulate this same aesthetic. In retrospect, I probably should have seen this as a warning sign of a potential climate problem. At the time, however, it didn't strike me as something that was all that bad. Likewise, when it came to his frequent retellings of how high-speed his old unit was and how he planned to soon get back to them or the derogatory way in which he sometimes referred to Iraqi civilians. None of these things struck me as severely morally problematic. At best they were banal.

Fast-forward another month or so and we are driving back from our daily company meeting at one of Saddam Hussein's palaces to our platoon headquarters located at the power plant a few miles away, when over the radio comes the report of shots fired on our headquarters from the adjacent neighbourhood. Up until that point in the deployment, we had experienced perhaps one instance of harassment fire from that particular neighbourhood, but really nothing else. Otherwise, the civilians in that region had been quiet and agreeable, so the report of an attack coming from that particular area seemed somewhat surprising to me. We had a constant two-man team on the roof of our main building providing security overwatch for the side of the powerplant facing that particular neighbourhood. Sure enough, on that particular day, the main soldier on the rooftop who called in the attack was the very same soldier previously described.

According to him, the story went as follows. He and his subordinate were pulling a standard security shift just as they had done dozens of times before, when all of a sudden, an Iraqi man came out the door of his house and fired a burst of celebratory fire into the air in the general direction of our main building. In all likelihood, the man was firing his AK-47 to celebrate his team winning a soccer match. While this is clearly an exceptionally dangerous and negligent practice, it is nonetheless a common practice within Iraqi culture, and one we were all too familiar with and all too annoyed with by that point in the deployment. As a result of the shots coming too close to our building, my soldier reportedly fired a warning shot next to the man, causing him to retreat back into his home. My soldier then maintained overwatch of the doorway through his optics, waiting for the man's next move. According to his official report, the man then emerged from his door about 30 seconds later and levelled his AK-47 directly at my soldier. Feeling imminently threatened, my soldier then shot and killed the man. Immediately thereafter, a second man emerged from the doorway and scrambled to grab his friend's body along with the weapon. Having been imminently threatened by the first man, my soldier didn't want to take any chances, and saw the second man's grabbing of the weapon as a hostile act and so opened fire on killing him as well.

All of this was corroborated by the young subordinate who was also pulling guard on the roof that day. All of my soldier's actions were consistent with the parameters of our brigade's official rules of engagement at the time. The gathering of civilian testimonies from members of the neighbourhood the very next day were ambiguous at best. People heard gunshots but didn't see anything. People didn't think that either man who had been killed held any ill will towards Americans or would ever intentionally shoot at us. We logged the reports and sent everything up the chain of command. For several days thereafter there were murmurs among some of the other soldiers in the platoon about what actually took place. Some quietly voiced their doubts about the legitimacy of the official report. I had my doubts as well especially after hearing my soldier boast with a smile on his face about him finally getting his first two 'confirmed kills.' I obliquely questioned him a bit more about what happened, but his story was the same. I questioned his subordinate who was with him on the rooftop that day but I wasn't able to gain much else from him nor did I expect to. At that point I decided to stop digging any further. My credibility and legitimacy in the platoon was already tenuous at best. I was already a black sheep within the platoon and among the officers within the company and I didn't want to cause further detriment to my legitimacy by tacitly suggesting that the darling of the platoon had just committed a war crime all without sufficient evidence to back it up. I bit my tongue, didn't kick up any dirt, and we moved onto the next mission.

Synopsis and Conclusion

To this day, I regret a lot of things about my actions and inactions in Iraq, this particular case being one of them. Put simply, I wish I had followed my gut more. By that, I mean, I wish I followed my gut more and had the integrity to allow that inarticulate, perceived feeling inside to rise up and take the form of actual, articulated speech however clumsily. I clearly had a gut instinct, both before and after the particular morally weighty event, about a subtle trend I was perceiving within my platoon and within one of my soldiers. However, I doubted that instinct for several reasons and didn't act on it. One of those reasons was for fear of damaging my social status and legitimacy within the platoon. Another reason was because I too easily and readily deferred to the symbols of institutional authority and status within the unit that this particular soldier had. A final reason I remained complicit and silent was because I was waiting for a moment of unquestionable, discernible immorality to clearly manifest itself before taking decisive action.

In aggregate, I consider these things to constitute a lack of integrity on my part. Not a profound lack of integrity mind you, but rather a series of banal, day-to-day moments of complicity in response to a series of banal, day-to-day transgressions that eventually led to the deaths of two civilians (most likely in my opinion) and a setback to our overall strategic aims. This, I believe, is generally how immoral acts arise within large-scale institutions like the military as opposed to some easily recognizable, cartoonish manifestation of evil just suddenly appearing *ex nihilo*. Looking forward, I believe future military leaders can at least arm themselves better against these kinds of events by pre-emptively being on the lookout for similar pernicious creeps in unit climate as well as recognizing just how much complicity can create preconditions for much more severe moral wrongs. Additionally, I believe leaders can better prevent such instances by being able to clearly and precisely articulate the unit's mission and purpose and the moral and prudential reasons informing that purpose. Lastly, in order to prevent such events from occurring in the future, I would remind future military leaders that they are just that, *leaders*, and that at some point they must be the first ones to exercise initiative and take the lead on changing attitudes, climates, and institutional cultures. For whether we are talking about institutions or animals, when it comes to leadership, the same adage holds true; "either you're training the dog, or the dog is training you."

Case Study 2: Getting Away with Murder? The Limits of Integrity

Don Carrick

Being true to oneself (i.e. maintaining one's integrity) is a fundamental part of one's identity as a whole person, so if someone is not true to themselves, and their integrity is ruptured, the consequences can be devastating. The agent in question can lose all sense of self – of who they essentially are – when they act in a way that is directly contrary to their core beliefs and feelings. Sustaining such a deep moral injury can have a devastating effect. In our context, the Vietnam War was the first modern conflict to bring the consequences of sustaining moral injury into the public domain, with the realisation that mental health issues like Post-traumatic stress disorder (PTSD) were disturbingly common among veterans. The integrity of the U.S. Army personnel had been compromised by their inability to adjust to and accept the effects of committing or witnessing actions that went total against their deeply held moral beliefs, the most egregious being the notorious incidents of the rape, torture and murder of some 400 defenceless civilians (mostly women, children and babies) at My Lai. One soldier who took part in that massacre (and who personally admitted to killing two small children) said "Why? Why did I do that? *That is not me.* Something happened to me. You reach a point where you snap, that is the easiest way to put it, you finally snap. Somebody flicks a switch and *you are a completely different person.*"[7]

---

7 Quoted in Jonathan Glover, *Humanity: A Moral History of the Twentieth Century* (London: Pimlico Press, 2001), 61.

It is perhaps not surprising, then, that there is a marked reluctance among Courts Martial to find soldiers guilty of serious crimes committed during wartime, if conviction for such crimes results in the irreversible loss of a soldier's identity. Yet this is exactly what has happened in several cases in recent times creating, I suggest, a dangerous precedent by conflating and confusing the distinction between *excusing* a seriously wrong action (i.e. the action remains wrong, but the actor is excused from blame and punishment because of their 'diminished responsibility') and *justifying* a putatively seriously wrong action (i.e. the putatively wrong action is turned into a right one).

Consider in this regard the recent case of British Royal Marine Sergeant Alexander Blackman. The facts were these: Sgt Blackman (initially referred to as 'Marine A' in media reports, having been granted anonymity and usually called Marine A after that) was on patrol on September 15, 2011 in Helmand province in Afghanistan in command of a Marines unit. Following a fierce firefight with a group of Taliban fighters, Blackman and his patrol came upon a grievously wounded Taliban fighter, lying helpless on the ground (the fighter had been injured by fire from a helicopter gunship that the patrol had called in to help them). Seeing that the Taliban fighter was still alive but not knowing (or perhaps not caring) that one of the patrol members was videoing the encounter with his helmet camera, Blackman raised his rifle and deliberately shot and killed the fighter, saying as he did so "Shuffle off this mortal coil, you c**t – it's nothing you wouldn't do to us" and then "Obviously this doesn't go anywhere fellas – I just broke the Geneva Convention."

Blackman's own words therefore show his clear awareness that what he did was morally and legally very wrong indeed, but he still committed the act in full knowledge of this. He was originally convicted at a court martial on a charge of murder and sentenced to life imprisonment, but when the result of the trial became known to the media, there was a huge outcry of support for Blackman, fuelled by a campaign sustained and funded by a populist right-wing U.K. newspaper, the *Daily Mail*, which led to the creation of an online petition supporting Blackman that attracted about 100,000 signatures. There was also considerable support for him obtained from high ranking Royal Marine and Army officers. Buoyed by such support, Blackman's lawyers first appealed against the length of his sentence and succeeded in getting it reduced from life to seven years. Then, on a second appeal, the conviction itself was reduced from murder to manslaughter.

Shortly after the conclusion of the second appeal, Blackman was released from prison, having by that time served the appropriate proportion of the original sentence.[8]

This was a classic example of what the Utilitarian philosopher John Stuart Mill cautioned against when he referred to "the tyranny of the majority": whipped up by the media, the cool, calm voice of reason becomes overwhelmed and emotion takes over – a not untypical response at a time when the 'soldier as hero' is the predominant stereotype.[9]

However, the Marine A case should not be treated as a one-off aberration. It is not unique. In 2016 during a violent confrontation in Israel in the city of Hebron between stone-throwing Palestinian protesters and Israeli Defense Force soldiers, one of the protesters fell to the ground, severely wounded. In a sequence of actions remarkably similar to the Blackman case, IDF Sergeant Elor Azaria walked up to the wounded protester and deliberately shot him in the head, killing him. Azaria was subsequently charged with manslaughter and convicted of this offence at a court martial.[10] He was given an 18-month custodial sentence. As in the Blackman case, there was an immediate public outcry about the alleged unfairness of the verdict and sentence followed by a campaign for his release, supported in this case by the Israeli Prime Minister Benyamin Netanyahu. Giving in to the pressure, the length of sentence was reduced at the instigation of the IDF Chief of Staff Gadi Eisenkot to 14 months, with Azaria eventually being released after serving less than a year in custody, although his request for a formal pardon was refused by the Israeli President Reuven Rivlin.[11]

To my mind (and I speak as a one-time practising lawyer), the killing of the Taliban fighter and the Palestinian protester were indeed clear-cut cases of unjustifiable and unlawful killing, amounting to murder, as Blackman himself impliedly admitted at the time ("I just broke the Geneva Convention"). The fighter clearly did not pose a threat to the patrol because the gravity of his wounds had rendered him semi-conscious and unable to move, and he was not armed, so there was no possibility that Blackman

---

8 Under English law, convicted criminals who behave themselves whilst in prison can be released after serving approximately one half of the custodial part of their sentence, although they remain 'on licence' for the reminder of the term.

9 This view is especially prominent in the U.S., although in that country and elsewhere they can be affected by whether the war that is being fought at the time is seen as a 'good' or 'bad' war: for instance there was a time late in the Vietnam War when soldiers returning home from a tour were treated as villains rather than heroes, and they were reviled and spat on by those opposed to the war.

10 The following account of the Azaria case is based on a report in *The Guardian* newspaper dated January 4, 2017.

11 Reported in *The Independent*, November 20, 2017.

was shooting him in self-defence – the action of killing could not be *justified* on that ground (similarly in the case of the seriously wounded Palestinian protester who posed no threat to Sgt Azaria).

What the Blackman and Azaria cases therefore reveal is that the well-meaning wish to remove the stigma of disgrace from the soldiers in question, and thus preserve their integrity, can have counter-productive results. Firstly, and as I have argued, the distinction between justification and excuse becomes dangerously blurred in such situations.

Secondly, the perceived obsession with finding reasons to excuse the behaviour of perpetrators of heinous crimes might show humanity and compassion towards the soldiers in question, but it shows none whatsoever towards the (innocent, non-combatant) victim: it does not do justice to them. The great majority of media reports on the Blackman case (and those in the extensive literature on the My Lai massacre) do not even mention the names of the (innocent, non-combatant) victims[12] who were killed.

Thirdly, this over-emphasis on protecting the reputation and integrity of the perpetrators, as opposed to the victims, of crimes in wartime may have the opposite effect to that intended. Soldiers of otherwise good character and with an exemplary military record prior to the incident in question, like Blackman and, I believe, Azaria, may well become confused by the fact that insisting on regarding them as still being heroes who had 'done nothing really wrong' can cause considerable and possibly damaging mental turmoil for them in the future. Their memory of their actions may be suppressed by the feelings of relief engendered by the misguided flood of public sympathy created by the media, but it cannot be removed. Sooner or later their consciences are likely to remind them of the grave wrongness of what they did, and negative affective responses may well follow: it was reported in 2017 that Blackman did feel shame and guilt about his killing of the Taliban fighter. A documentary film-maker called Chris Terrill who was apparently considering making a film about the affair, was quoted as saying "[Blackman's] guilty of an illegal killing. He says, 'If I could turn back time and undo what I did, I would'."[13]

Finally, we should remind ourselves that it is now, and will continue to be, of central importance during the continuance of 'wars amongst the people' that we do not lose sight of the need to win the hearts and minds of the local civilian population. Media publicity of the killings at My Lai and those by Blackman and Azaria, and numerous others, reported and

---

12   The Palestinian killed by Azaria was named as Abdel Fattah al-Sharif.

13   Stephen Morris, "Marine A, who killed wounded Taliban fighter, released from prison," *The Guardian*, April 28, 2017, https://www.theguardian.com/uk-news2017/apr/28/marine-a-alexander-blackman-released-from-prison.

unreported, can and do have grossly disproportionate adverse effects on the 'winning hearts and minds' aspect. Justice must be done, and seen to be done, in the eyes of the locals, and well-meaning but misguided attempts to absolve the perpetrators of serious crimes do no favours to anyone involved, least of all the soldiers in question. Letting Blackman and Azaria and the rest off the moral and legal hook sends out the wrong signals, not just to them and the local population but also to their fellow soldiers. It should never, ever be the case that soldiers should be allowed to think that they can get away, literally as well as metaphorically, with murder. Reverting to the Vietnam War cases, Lieutenant William Calley, the perpetrator of the My Lai massacre, was quite clearly guilty of that dreadful crime, yet he was let off with a very light sentence and received very little public criticism. On the other hand, Warrant Officer Hugh Thompson [see also the chapter on Courage] who, observing the slaughter taking place, landed his helicopter between the rampaging troops at My Lai and a group of their intended victims, ordered his door gunner to shoot any of the soldiers who attempted to continue with their killing spree, was generally reviled for his actions. It was only some years later that he was rewarded with a medal for the courage he had displayed. So which one of them was the *real* hero and the *real* man of integrity?

We can only hope that when the education of soldiers of all ranks involves choosing role models to emulate, they will look to soldiers like Warrant Officer Thompson or Petty Officer Marcus Luttrell of SEAL Team 10 as true exemplars of men of integrity.

References

Arendt, H. *Eichmann in Jerusalem: A Report on the Banality of Evil*. London: Penguin, 1977.

Beaumont, P. "Netanyahu backs call for convicted Israeli soldier to be pardoned," *The Guardian*, January 4, 2017, https://www.theguardian.com/world/2017/jan/04/israeli-soldier-guilty-manslaughter-shooting-palestinian-elor-azaria-fattah-al-sharif.

Berg, Peter, dir. *Lone Survivor*, 2013. Universal City, CA: Universal Pictures, 2013. Film, 121 mins.

Carrick, D., J. Connelly, and P. Robinson, *Ethics Education for Irregular Warfare*. Aldershot: Ashgate Publishing, 2009.

Glover, J. *Humanity: A Moral History of the Twentieth Century*. London: Pimlico Press, 2001.

Luttrell, M. with P. Robinson, *Lone Survivor*. New York: Little, Brown and Company, 2007.

McKernan, B. "Elor Azaria: Israeli president refuses to pardon soldier who shot and killed unarmed Palestinian," *The Independent*, November 20, 2017, https://www.independent.co.uk/news/world/middle-east/israel-elor-azaria-idf-pardon-request-rejected-ruevin-rivlin-palestinian-shooting-a8065006.html.

Morris, S. "Marine A, who killed wounded Taliban fighter, released from prison," *The Guardian*, April 28, 2017, https://www.theguardian.com/uk-news2017/apr/28/marine-a-alexander-blackman-released-from-prison.

8

PERSEVERANCE

Overview

Alan T. Baker

"If you're going through hell, keep going."

– Attributed to Winston Churchill

The story of Louis Zamperini captured the attention of the Allies in the 1940s and again in recent years thanks to the biography by Laura Hillenbrand, *Unbroken: A World War II Story of Survival, Resilience, and Redemption*. We discover a troubled youth who took up running and became a star athlete competing in the 1936 Olympics in Berlin. After World War II broke out, Zamperini became a bombardier on a B-24 bomber that eventually crashed and sank in the Pacific Ocean. Louis and another airman survived a milestone 47 days adrift at sea. They floated on a flimsy life raft in shark-plagued waters before being found. Their celebration was quickly dampened by the stiff realization that their rescuers were also their enemy. Louis became a prisoner of war and endured constant brutality at the hands of one particular guard who regarded this former Olympic athlete as his 'number one prisoner.' This guard was so notoriously abusive that he was listed as 23rd on General MacArthur's 40 most wanted war criminals following the war.

Louis Zamperini exemplifies the military virtue of perseverance. As Laura Hillenbrand describes, "Confident that he was clever, resourceful, and bold enough to escape any predicament, he was almost incapable of discouragement. When history carried him into war, this resilient optimism would define him."[1] His persistence and endurance serves as a beacon

---

1 Laura Hillenbrand, *Unbroken: A World War II Story of Survival, Resilience, and Redemption* (New York: Random House, 2010), 7.

calling us to embrace and emulate his strength. Zamperini exemplifies how perseverance earned him admiration from his colleagues. It also gained him deep respect from his adversaries.

That was World War II. But what about today? The virtue of perseverance collides with our over stimulated, dopamine enriched, instant gratification culture. Within this highly saturated 'one click payment' society, could it be possible to retrieve perseverance as a deeply desirable virtue for military commanders and leaders seeking to serve ethically within the military system? Is it reasonable to expect officers and enlisted personnel to practice and embody the personal virtue of perseverance? As Louis Zamperini exemplified perseverance, can our current generation of military leaders maintain the admiration of their colleagues and gain respect from their potential adversaries by practicing perseverance?

Perseverance is a conditional virtue. Unlike other virtues discussed throughout these surrounding chapters, perseverance has prerequisites that separate it from other laudable virtues such as justice, obedience, loyalty, and courage. In other words, perseverance is contingent upon two preexisting conditions: time and suffering.

The first prerequisite for perseverance concerns our concept of time. Although the notion of time will be addressed later within this chapter, perseverance is a process and increases in value over a duration of time. It cannot best be described by a moment in time. We cannot point to perseverance and define its value by a single episode such as we can by telling the truth, taking an oath of loyalty, or dispensing justice. Each of these other virtues have specific and singular examples for us to reflect upon and say, 'Yes, that was a virtuous act.' However, perseverance has no particular event to highlight because it encompasses a process of time and not a single event or sequence of events within time. There is a *pattern* of perseverance whereas there is a *practice* of loyalty or justice or courage or humility. The longer the duration of time, the greater one grows in perseverance.

The second prerequisite for perseverance is that it grows deeper as a consequence of trials and suffering. Those who are not suffering have neither the awareness or need to persevere. Their comfortable lifestyle and living conditions are such that they do not see themselves as persevering. Nor would they likely be aware of other people who, through their suffering, are persevering. No one would say the wealthy, beautiful, and privileged practice perseverance. They may be committed to speaking truthfully, honoring their commitments, and being socially responsible, but they are not developing perseverance. Those who are free from suffering have little incentive to grow the virtue of perseverance. Instead, they would isolate themselves from activities or occasions that might stimulate this virtue. Is it possible that insurance companies tap into our avoidance of suffering by allowing us to pay premiums to reduce risk? Although avoidance of trials seems like a very reasonable ambition, it is simply not possible. We cannot isolate ourselves no matter how high the insurance premiums. There will come seasons of suffering and conflict in which we are given an opportunity to either cave in to despair or grow deep in the virtue of perseverance. As a writer of ancient wisdom once remarked, 'To everything there is a season … A time to love, and a time to hate; a time of war, and a time of peace.' No one seeks suffering. We attempt to flee from suffering but it always finds us. Yet it is only within the crucible of suffering we discover and grow the virtue of perseverance.

As a military chaplain, I spent the first Gulf War living in a small tent next to an unnamed airstrip in the Arabian Desert along with 4,500 U.S. Marines. The U.S. Marine Corps motto is 'Semper Fidelis,' which means 'always faithful.' The Marines often abbreviate their motto to 'Semper Fi.' It must be their recruit training experience that instills their love for writing, speaking, or shouting 'Semper Fi' whenever the opportunity arises. Of course, the motto offers me wonderful cannon fodder for extemporaneous sermons to Marines regarding God's faithfulness.

Yet even chaplains suffer from despair. At one discouraging point during combat, I sat in my lonely tent wondering why God had placed me here. Why would God want me in the desert, surrounded by all the noise of jets and frequent Scud missile alerts?

Ingeniously resourceful, the Marines repurposed a large dry erase marker board for outlining and hopefully shortening my sermons. I mounted this board inside my tent. As I considered my discouragement and sought remedy, the word came to me – 'clarify.' Maybe I was stuck in the desert to clarify my purpose and life's vision. Maybe God wanted my aspirations distilled down to serving others willingly with a whole heart. So, I wrote 'clarify' at the top of this blank whiteboard.

I reflected a while longer, and after some time I sensed another word – 'purify.' I thought to myself that God frequently took people away from society's distractions in order to purify them for higher purposes. I wrote the word 'purify' on the board immediately below 'clarify.'

Finally, I sensed one more word – 'mortify.'

I remembered that in the early centuries of church history, anchorite monks suffered and persevered in the desert for extended periods of time. Some of them built isolation platforms for the express purpose of mortifying their flesh and thereby increasing their faith.

In the desert, far from home and family and comfort, I saw I had become a reluctant follower of their early path. So, I wrote the word 'mortify' under the first two.

Before the ink dried, I could hear several aircraft on final approach after a combat mission. I left my lonely tent and ran to the flight line in order to welcome the pilots back.

My fog lifted as I experienced first-hand the pilots' relief at successfully and safely completing their mission, as I witnessed the esprit-de-corps of the ground crew as they quickly turned around the aircraft for another take-off. My discouragement was washed away as I found myself smiling at the optimism of those Marines. I was encouraged. I had renewed vision and a sense of purpose here in the desert. I had hope.

As I returned to my empty tent, I saw a Marine had dropped by while I was away. Maybe he wanted to talk. He left me a message. To the three words on my board, the Marine had added a fourth: Clarify, Purify, Mortify, *Semper Fi.*

He had given me a valuable and much needed message that transcended the three earlier words. These two Latin words, *Semper Fidelis,* allowed me to grow in perseverance within my own crucible of suffering. God, who is *always faithful,* reminded me to be faithful as their chaplain.

Simply because trials are universal does not mean they are always present. This opportunity to practice the virtue of perseverance was unique to my time in combat. We gain perseverance in response to current suffering and we grow in perseverance as we accept the possibility of future trials. Our character is shaped by practicing perseverance in the ordeal of suffering. Character does not produce perseverance. It is the other way around: perseverance produces character.

Two truly heroic leaders who exemplify the warfighting virtue of perseverance are George Washington and Winston Churchill.

Pulitzer Prize-winning biographer, David McCullough, in his graphic description of the battles of the War of American Independence of 1776, describes George Washington as someone who, in the face of overwhelming odds, would simply not give up. He realized his soldiers lacked sufficient weapons, proper training, and basic supplies. Disease plagued the soldiers frequently. Washington suffered from arrogant subordinates who sought to displace him.

> He was not a brilliant strategist or tactician, not a gifted orator, nor an intellectual. At several crucial moments he had shown marked indecisiveness. He had made serious mistakes in judgment. But experience had been his great teacher from boyhood, and in this, his greatest test, he

learned steadily from experience. Above all, Washington never forgot what was at stake and he never gave up.

Again and again, in letters to Congress and to his officers, and in his general orders, he called for perseverance – 'for perseverance and spirit,' for 'patience and perseverance,' for 'unremitting courage and perseverance.'[2]

Winston Churchill was not only one of the greatest twentieth-century leaders, he also exemplified perseverance. Throughout his life, he suffered numerous disappointments. Whether enduring frustrating years in school, leading his nation through the hardships of World War I, when he departed from government following the disastrous Gallipoli Campaign or struggling with his own unpredictable emotions and speech impediment, Winston Churchill persevered. One of his greatest gifts as a warrior turned Prime Minister was his ability to inspire others who faced obstacles they feared they could not overcome.

On a visit to his old school, Harrow, in 1941, Churchill addressed the young men: "Never give in, never give in, never, never, never – in nothing, great or small, large or petty – never give in except to convictions of honour and good sense. Never yield to force; never yield to the apparently overwhelming might of the enemy." This speech is often quoted but what is less known is that immediately after that phrase he added, "We now find ourselves in a position where I say that we can be sure that we have only to persevere to conquer."

Both Churchill and Washington exemplify the professional military virtue of perseverance. They embody the two prerequisites of perseverance by living through experiences that were not simply episodes in time but processes of time that included suffering. Let us now seek to understand two specific attributes of perseverance: persistence and endurance.

Persistence

Examples of military service illustrating the virtue of perseverance abound. Angela Duckworth, professor of psychology and a 2013 MacArthur Fellow, published her first book, *Grit*, with an affirming subtitle, *The Power of Passion and Perseverance*.[3] The book's introductory sentence confirms the valued intersection of perseverance and military culture, "By the time you set foot on the campus of the United States

---

2   David McCullough, *1776* (New York: Simon & Schuster, 2005), 293.

3   Angela Duckworth, *Grit: The Power of Passion and Perseverance* (New York: Scribner, reprint edition, 2018).

Military Academy at West Point, you've earned it." Why would a civilian professor from a public university draw an example of perseverance from the military? It is because perseverance holds two core elements essential to military readiness. These are persistence and endurance.

The principle requirement needed for persistence is patience. While patience is frequently underappreciated within our hyperactive society, it achieves remarkable outcomes for those who intentionally practice this unique element of persistence. In a culture prone to action, patience seems counterintuitive. In warfare, where speed-to-decision may be critical to battlefield success, patience seems optional. After all, doesn't the practice of patience compete against immediate action? We see patience popularized in old Hollywood war movies with the order, 'Don't fire until you see the whites of their eyes.' How can patience be a virtue? Because patience is also an intentional activity that values resolve above immediacy. It must be exercised as a healthy antidote to impulsivity. Patience provides the human with generative time for reflection before action. Its application and habituation limits unintended or adverse consequences. This is why parents insist their children 'count to ten' when they become angry. It serves to diffuse and reframe their anger. Patience is also built into strategic national defense decision-making by requiring nuclear release authority to follow a chain-of-custody and not simply a quick press of a button. The greater the potential consequences, the higher the necessity for patience.

Persistence not only requires patience, it requires firmness coupled with resolve. You cannot persist without a foundation of patience. By slowing the process down, patience actually strengthens an organization as it unlocks time based capacity-building tools such as prioritizing, phasing, scaling, delegating, and experimenting. Without patience, these capacity-enriching tools are easily overlooked. I am reminded of Leo Tolstoy's line from *War and Peace*, "The strongest of all warriors are these two – Time and Patience."[4]

Persistence increases agility among military members by forcing them to focus on the strategic imperative as they habituate healthy responses to frequent change. To quote Stephen Covey, "The main thing is to keep the main thing the main thing." For example, Henry Ford's first two companies went out of business. His third had extremely low sales. Yet rather than abandoning his dreams, he maintained the strategic imperative of changing transportation. In the midst of collapsing businesses, his failures spurred him forward to find a better way to mass-produce affordable cars.

---

4 Leo Tolstoy, *War and Peace* (1869).

He wasn't in the car manufacturing business. He persisted in the strategic imperative of changing transportation.

Several years ago I spoke with Ron Johnson, then Senior Vice President of retail operations for Apple. Ron pioneered the concept of the Apple Retail Stores and the Genius Bar. He achieved a stunning level of growth by exceeding a billion dollars in annual sales within two years of their debut. I complemented him on the Genius Bar. I said, "I love the fact that I can now walk into a place to repair my computer." Ron simply answered, "The Genius Bar is not there to repair computers. It is there to repair relationships." Ron understood the value of persistence. He increased the agility of employees by having them retain the strategic imperative of valuing relationships over products. He prioritized the customer over the product. He scaled the Genius Bar to fit consumer demand. He, like Henry Ford, was in a strategic business. Whereas Ford persevered by changing transportation, Johnson persisted in strengthening relationships.

Complex organizations facing unfamiliar and potentially volatile situations have a high need for leaders who persevere. The longer you persist, the greater your resolve. The greater your resolve, the stronger your basis for decision-making. The stronger your foundation, the more successful your mission.

A military model for this dynamic can be developed based on an analysis of the United States Marine Corps recruiting model. Recruiters were incentivized and promoted based on the number of enlistments they achieved. Their goal was to cast a wide net. Yet the number of volunteers inducted did not correspond to the actual number of graduates from basic training. Attrition was high. Many inductees were simply not fit or were not prepared to meet the challenges faced during recruit training. The Marine Corps then changed the recruiting model by requiring their recruiters to adopt a new metric based on the virtue of perseverance. Recruiters were no longer incentivized and promoted by the number of enlistees they brought on the bus to recruit training. Their success was now based on the number of enlistees who actually graduated from basic training. The model was flipped from entrance to exit. Successful recruiters now had to exercise prudence while their recruits practiced perseverance to make it through recruit training. This military recruiting model required both persistence and endurance in order to produce flourishing outcomes.

Endurance

If the first requirement for perseverance is patience, the second ingredient of endurance follows closely behind. Endurance is frequently understood as both positive and long term. Whereas the duration of persistence is short term, the focus of endurance is the distant horizon. As mentioned earlier, persistence and patience grow capacity for an organization. The core element of endurance is different than that of persistence and patience. It enriches personal competencies by generating hope. Endurance contributes to members within the organization by accelerating growth of their individual competencies. Persistence keeps the focus on 'one day at a time.' Endurance seeks to 'keep the long look.'

My story of joining the military integrates these concepts of persistence and endurance. I was a product of the Southern California public school system. It did not discipline me to be academically rigorous. When I graduated from high school, I received an appointment to the United States Naval Academy. The news of my appointment was a surprise because it came very late. I was humbled to learn I was the alternate candidate. The primary appointee turned down his nomination at the last moment. If I accepted, three days remained as a civilian before shaving my head and reporting as a plebe.

I sought the counsel of my elders. My father loved me very much. He wanted me to succeed yet he also wanted to set realistic expectations for his son. Adolescence frequently highlights the generation gap and brings conflict between fathers and sons. Mark Twain recognized this: "When I was a boy of 14, my father was so ignorant I could hardly stand to have the old man around. But when I got to be 21, I was astonished at how much the old man had learned in seven years." Having this generational conflict with my own father while at the same time respecting his counsel, I accepted the appointment to the Naval Academy. My Dad's last words to me as I departed Southern California were, "Son, Annapolis is a tough place. Plebe Summer is incredibly difficult. You may not last. Don't cancel your local college plans for this fall."

I was hurt. How could he think that might be the case? He was right. The editor published the following in my Annapolis yearbook, "Al came, looked around, got a free haircut, saw that he didn't like the place, and stayed." Throughout plebe summer, I simply wanted to survive another miserable parade or uniform inspection. My goal was to avoid gaining special attention by upperclassmen and thereby risk becoming an attrition statistic. I needed patience and daily persistence not to quit. My short term goal was simply to survive another day.

I then received a letter from home. My Dad closed his letter with the sentence, "Keep the long look." As more letters arrived, I soon realized it was his signature line. Throughout my first year I may have eaten three meals per day but I lived off of those letters. My Dad was feeding me and developing me in a culture that required endurance. Out of nearly 1,600 freshmen less than 1,000 would graduate.

My short-term goal of meeting my parents on plebe-parent weekend grew to a long-term goal of saluting them at graduation. I realized that Dad's advice to me just before I left California had incited me to persevere. He took an immature teen and incentivized me toward my future not by *promising* but by *pushing* me toward hope. Struggling was no longer a signal for alarm but a sign of progress. As Brené Brown writes in *Daring Greatly*, "… hope is a combination of setting goals, having the tenacity and perseverance to pursue them, and believing in our own abilities … If we're always following our children into the arena, hushing the critics, and assuring their victory, they'll never learn that they have the ability to dare greatly on their own."[5]

In the military, it takes persistence to acquire the technical skills and physiological competencies necessary to pilot a fighter jet. These proficiencies must be learned and practiced daily in order to sustain them. When an aviator achieves these skills and responds to the flight controls reflexively, she can simultaneously maintain real-time tactical presence while retain the enduring confidence of eventually catching the carrier three-wire upon landing. In another example, a sailor on a moonless night must exercise persistence in identifying buoys and simultaneously hold enduring hope of reaching the pier in the morning.

Summary

When both persistence and endurance are aligned, perseverance is the outcome. The virtue of perseverance develops organizational capacity and personal competency. As with the example of Marine Corps recruiting, it decreases attrition while building greater accountability. Perseverance is fueled by both short-term persistence and enduring long-term hope. These two ingredients of perseverance, persistence and endurance, are time-focused. You might say, 'She persisted for months,' or, 'The nation endured this for years.' It might be helpful to consider that the ancient Greeks had two words for time, *chronos* and *kairos*. We still use the first in words like 'chronological' and 'anachronism.' It refers to our calendar and clock time, measured in seconds, minutes, hours, and years. *Kairos* is different. Whereas *chronos* is quantitative, *kairos* is qualitative. It measures moments, not seconds. It seeks the right moment, the opportune moment,

---

5 Brené Brown, *Daring Greatly: How the Courage to Be Vulnerable Transforms the Way We Live, Love, Parent, and Lead* (New York: Avery, Reprint edition, 2015).

the perfect moment. Perseverance couples both of these time-focused words in a balanced approach of persistence and endurance. Persistence lives in *chronos* time. Endurance lives in *kairos* time. Let me share a personal example.

Both my calf muscles were in knots. Yet they did not bother me as much as the blisters on my feet. My knees continued to grind away as I limped along the Chesapeake and Ohio tow path toward the finish line. Whatever was I thinking when my friend and running mate, Graham, first asked me to run with him in the John F. Kennedy 50 Mile Ultramarathon? All I now knew was pain. Although my body continued to limp forward, my spirit to finish the race was eight miles behind me in the muddied footprints of my New Balance shoes. I had nothing more inside of me to count on. The knots in my muscles and blisters on my feet robbed me of all joy. I was now three miles from the finish line. I was at the 47-mile-point of a 50-mile race. But I was in serious trouble. I 'hit the wall' at the 39th mile and simply couldn't break through. 'Hitting the wall' is an expression that means your feet become sandbags, your mind becomes jelly, and you give up all heart to stay running. These last eight miles were all I could endure. For these eight miles I rambled on, encouraged by my running mate, Graham, who tried to keep me going. I was now furiously angry at him for convincing me to attempt to do such a lame brained activity as run a 50-mile race. I had never run an ultramarathon. I hadn't even run a regular marathon. What was I thinking?

In this race, persistence was measured by keeping one foot ahead of the other. This was the only metric I needed. It was a simple short-term endeavor that required me to be accountable to Graham if I were to be successful. Accountability was measured by decreasing the distance to the finish line. I needed patience to fight off the desire to simply 'get it over with.'

I was living in *chronos* time feeling deeper pain at every step. Counterbalancing this commitment to persistence was a desire to endure. In order for me to endure, I needed hope. I needed to fix my mind on crossing the finish line. It was an impossible horizon that I seemed unable to reach. Yet there was hope. I wanted to endure. This is the experience of *kairos* time. *Its focus is not the minute but the moment.* I no longer focused on my race time. That was simply *chronos* time. I needed something more. I thirsted for *kairos* time. My goal was to simply cross the finish line.

Completing the race would bring me qualitative joy because its focus is on my development and not my attrition. Put another way, persistence frequently focuses on short term gains. Endurance reaches for long term goals. Both persistence and endurance require progress measured in *chronos* and *kairos*. You need both to persevere.

Who do you admire for their perseverance? Are there family members and friends that exude persistence, patience, perseverance, and hope? David Brooks, in *The Road to Character*,[6] suggests great people have great models, "Thomas Aquinas argued that in order to lead a good life, it is necessary to focus more on our exemplars than on ourselves, imitating their actions as much as possible." Find those exemplars of perseverance, whether from those you know or those you read about, and grow from them. Perhaps you will be able to reflect their strength of character in your life as you model and grow in this significant virtue.

---

6 David Brooks, *The Road to Character* (New York: Random House, 2015).

	PERSEVERANCE	
	Requirements (Qualities)	
PERSISTENCE		ENDURANCE
	Central Ingredient	
Patience		Hope
	Duration	
Short Term Gains		Long Term Goals
	Contribution	
Capacity Building		Competency Enriching
Organizational		Personal
	Goal	
Habituate		Completion
	Tense	
Present Tense		Future Focused
	Metrics	
Lagging (looking back)		Leading (looking forward)
	Motto	
One day at a time		Keep the long look
	Measures	
Quantitative		Qualitative
	Ultramarathon	
Keep one foot ahead of the other		Crossing the finish line
	Sailor	
Finding the buoy		Reaching the pier
	Marine	
Clarify, Purify, Mortify		'Semper Fi'
	Midshipman	
Surviving Chow Call		Graduating

Figure 8.1   Elements of Perseverance as a Leadership Virtue

Case Study 1:
Perseverance, Leadership, and the 'We'

Michael Robillard

"For the strength of the pack is the wolf, and the strength of
the wolf is the pack."

– Rudyard Kipling

Introduction

When people typically think of perseverance, they often have notions of
a person struggling against great odds and challenges, having moments
of doubt and a desire to give up, but forging ahead nonetheless. Too often
this picture of perseverance is understood in terms of *individual* willpower.
These case studies aim at suggesting an alternative notion of perseverance,
one which conceives of perseverance not as a hardened willing of the
individual 'I' but as a conscious individual surrender and subordination to
the ideals, values, and greater mission of the 'we.'

Perseverance as understood in this light has particular import for
questions of military leadership especially with respect to considerations
of self-narrative. When one consciously reconceives of one's self-narrative
as not being simply that of the atomic individual and lone wolf but that of
a member of a team and a leader of a pack, such a reframing of identity can
serve to bolster one's resolve and perseverance in times of adversity and
hardship. Somewhat counter-intuitively, in consciously choosing to bring

one's 'I' into greater overall alignment and subordination with the expressed reasons and values of the 'we,' such an alignment can often serve as a deep and newfound reservoir of strength, energy, and perseverance from which a leader can draw in times of adversity and struggle. Accordingly, perseverance in a military leadership context might hinge less so on the hardened willing of the leader's individual ego but more so a softening of that very same ego as he or she surrenders to the shared values of the group's highest ideal.

I can still remember the moment in Florida Phase of Ranger School in March of 2003 when perseverance and its specific relationship to the 'we' mattered most for me. We had begun in early January of that year with an original class of about 350 candidates. One night, early in Benning Phase, temperatures in Georgia actually dropped to a record low of 12°F causing a record number of 11 Ranger students to quit in a single evening. By the time we hit the swamps of the Everglades six weeks later, the original class had dwindled to just over 100 students due to a combination of people failing out, quitting, recycling, or being medically dropped. Additionally, by this time, everyone had lost at least 20lbs, was psychologically and physically drained, and was nursing one or several structural or medical maladies: a broken foot, chilblains on exposed skin from the Mountain phase, sinus and upper respiratory infections, severe tendonitis, sprained ankles, blisters and fissures on hands and feet, pulled muscles, rashes, infections, and in some cases, cellulitis in the little nicks and cuts that had accumulated over weeks of exposure in the field with minimal hygiene.

Shortly before our official graded patrols (the ones which would ultimately determine whether or not we would graduate or have to recycle and spend another six weeks of purgatory in the swamps), the instructors chose me to be the acting platoon leader of one of our practice patrols. 'Excellent!,' I thought. This would be my one shot to practice, to learn, and to get the mechanics of the patrol down tight with little to no consequences before the graded patrols began a few days later. Due to a comedy of errors as well as my own technical failings, I got the patrol severely lost, burnt a good deal of time wandering around in the dark when people could have been catching up on sleep, and, all around, failed the mission.

The following morning, at sunrise, the instructors handed over leadership of the platoon to another ranger student while I returned to my squad to quietly carry a machine gun, embarrassed, defeated, and above all, *certain* that I would not only fail my upcoming graded patrols and have to repeat Florida phase, but that I would *never* graduate from Ranger

School at all and would have to arrive at my follow-on unit tab-less and humiliated. Certainly, this was the only rational conclusion one could make from my failed practice patrol the night before. My career was over. My reputation was over. My life was over. Everything inevitably was going to go to sh*t.

"You've lost perspective."

These were the words that my friend Greg said to me, that same morning as we slogged through the swamps on our daytime patrol, knee-deep in greenish-black swamp water, lugging 80lbs of gear on our backs, weapons hanging to our front with near lifeless noodle arms.

"You've lost perspective. That's all."

"No, I haven't," I replied. "You don't understand. This is different. I *ruined* the patrol. I'm a failure. I'm not cut out for this. I'm never going to graduate. I'm going to be stuck here forever or they are going to kick me out and then I'm going to have to go to my platoon without a Ranger tab and my career will be over before it even has begun. I should just quit right now and save everyone the hassle."

"Well. What you say might be actually the case," Greg rebutted. "Or, it might not be. Why don't you just give it another 24 hours to gain some perspective and see how you are feeling then? Can you give it another 24 hours?"

"Yeah. I suppose," I replied. "I can give it another 24 hours."

To this day, at age 37, I can honestly say that those 24 hours had to have been some of the longest I've ever spent deep inside my own head, watching and observing the wrestling match between the deafening voice telling me to quit right then and there and the faint voice of a friend telling me to hang on until morning.

So wait I did. And, by morning, the emotional gravity of epically screwing up the night before had dissipated just a bit.

Now, 24 hours removed from my irredeemable failure, my fellow platoon members seemed to have, for the most part, forgiven me for having burnt the 60 minutes of sleep they could have otherwise caught the night before. I had gotten a good MRE (meal ready to eat) in me, had caught 60 good minutes of sleep, had shaved, brushed my teeth, changed my t-shirt and socks, and was now feeling a bit less defeated. I began considering that *maybe, just maybe* Greg's words had some wisdom to them and that things weren't as catastrophic and utterly hopeless as I originally thought.

Another 24 hours went by. I started paying attention and re-engaging the patrol, ambush, reconnaissance classes and decided to not totally mentally check out just yet.

Then another day passed.

And another.

Then time for graded patrols.

I began entertaining the radical idea that maybe my screw-up a few nights before wasn't as bad I thought, or, at the very least, that it was not a definitive predictor of an inevitable future. Maybe the encouraging words of a friend counted for something after all.

To my amazement, I passed my patrol.

A ray of hope miraculously punched through the clouds of despair in my own mind. From that point on, I knew that all I had to do was keep walking, humping the weight on my back, helping my platoon members, and not get injured. I did just that, and a week later or so, I ended up graduating Ranger School successfully. But, had it not been for the conscientious and thoughtful words of a friend and fellow teammate at a time when I was at my lowest, I'm sure I would not have.

Synopsis

The preceding anecdote might be summed up as follows.

Military leaders will inevitably make mistakes. They will likewise encounter moments of resistance, despair, and hardship over the course of their careers (in combat and in training). At the lowest of these times, leaders might feel a sincere desire to quit, to give up, or to hunt for excuses to extricate themselves from the demanding or overwhelming situation. This is only human. Operating by a narrative of 'I and I alone,' it is therefore exceptionally difficult, if not impossible, to imagine how individual perseverance during such trying times could always be ready at hand for one to access or able to be manufactured on the spot at will. Knowing this, it is therefore essential for military leaders to foster a 'we' and an ecosystem of shared values and practices such that both subordinates *and leaders themselves* can draw strength, perseverance, and perspective from one another during those inevitable dark and trying times.

However, when the self-narrative of a leader is something to the effect of, 'I and I alone am the sole recipient and benefactor of the failure or success of this given act,' then the capacity to persevere through difficult obstacles and trials becomes severely diminished. Pragmatically-speaking, if a leader perceives him or herself as having 'screwed up' and has no ecosystem of the 'we' whatsoever to fall back on, to gather differing perspectives, and to draw strength from, then the likelihood of the leader's self-doubting thoughts to spiral out of control becomes markedly increased. Like a microphone held too close to a speaker, the feedback loop of one's initially moderately negative thoughts can amplify into something radically distorted and out of sync with objective reality. The intersubjective agreement of group members who happen to have cooler heads at that moment, therefore provides a pragmatic mechanism and proxy whereby a leader can regather perspective on the objective world when it is has been lost or disrupted. This feature of intersubjective agreement helps to bolster individual perseverance not only in cases of clear and recognizable hardship, but also, and arguably more frequently, in cases of ambiguous data.

Much of the time, a military leader's perseverance under conditions of extreme uncertainty will largely hinge on answering the questions; 'What exactly am I looking at?' and 'What does this mean?' Without a we or team to pool their intersubjective perspectives in order to make better sense of the ambiguous data, an individual with a propensity for negative thinking will likely interpret otherwise neutral data in a negative light, therefore diminishing his or her overall capacity to persevere and to maintain an objective perspective on things.

The paradox of course, is that once one has lost perspective, then it is very hard if not impossible for one *to recognize that one has lost perspective*. Hence, pre-emptively building and fostering a strong ecosystem of the we can serve as an *ex ante* mechanism to help leaders regain perspective and maintain perseverance in the event that they become overwhelmed by the pressure of the moment and begin to spiral into a place of self-doubt. The likelihood that one of us in the group loses perspective at some point of hardship or radical uncertainty is probably rather high. The likelihood that *all of us at the same time* lose perspective however, is arguably very low. Hence, the intersubjective agreement of the group can function as a way for leaders to maintain a cool, distanced perspective and thereby maintain perseverance as well since the leader's thoughts will be more accurately representative of the objective world.

In addition to just maintaining objective perspective, a well-functioning 'we' which clearly understands its mission, purpose, and values can generate a benevolent ecosystem of peer-pressure and accountability whereby each member of the group is able to access new levels of commitment, drive, and perseverance as they work together towards a common goal that is otherwise impossible to achieve were each to act individually. During times of a well-functioning 'we,' persons hold one another to a higher standard, lean on one another in times of individual hardship, and motivate one another towards a shared, common goal. As a result, during times of hardship, individuals are able to dig deep and to tap into reserves of perseverance and determination otherwise inaccessible since quitting or giving up necessarily entails negative implications not just for the individual but for the entire group. That I quit and I and I alone will suffer the negative consequences is one kind of motivator. That I quit and now *my team* will suffer the negative consequences for my actions is a different kind of motivator entirely. Accordingly, a felt sense of obligation to the 'we' and a corresponding desire to not let the team down, can serve as yet another way in which individual perseverance can be found by way of the group.

Conclusion

In this case study, I have highlighted two different ways in which individual perseverance can be found, fostered, and enhanced in relation to the group. For one, individual perseverance can be made better by the group insofar as a group provides an ecosystem of intersubjective perspectives that can aid a military leader in maintaining a cool head and an objective view of things during times of actual or perceived hardship or in times of radical uncertainty. Secondly, individual perseverance can be bolstered in virtue of the group since the leader's failure to persevere carries negative implications that extend well beyond just his or her personal world. Both of these deep wellsprings of motivation are often readily available to the military leader provided he or she softens his or her individual ego and subordinates it, if only partially, to the higher mission of the team.

And while there is always a very real danger of groupthink, of excessive conformity and obedience, and of subordinating one's individual 'I' too much or too readily to the collective, military leaders should nonetheless recognize the importance of the 'we' and the higher set of shared ideals that brought that we together in the first place. And as much as I would like to say that I earned my Ranger tab through my own individual grit, heart, and perseverance, the fact of the matter is that earning it was very much a team effort. The thesis of this case is therefore the following; that individual perseverance is largely predicated upon group perseverance. Put another way, there is no such thing as a 'self-made man.'

Case Study 2:
Thinking Beyond the Past: Nudging the Pentagon toward the Twenty-first Century

Steven M. Kleinman

"To institute a new order of things, leaders need to be able to persevere against the naysayers and rise above obstacles. They need to be able to overlook the limits of today to build the business for tomorrow."[7]

The Pentagon, occupying more than six million square feet of floor space, is among the largest office buildings in the world. As the headquarters for the U.S. Department of Defense, it also established itself over the decades since World War II as one of the biggest bureaucracies in the world, with the static thinking and entrenched perspectives that go with such a label. Unfortunately, the nation's grand strategy has not been immune to the insidious effects of this mindset. Although the procedural practices that shape war plans, force configuration, and operational deployment planning are arguably unknowable given the size and scope of the American military enterprise, examples abound of an underlying thought process that is circular, conventional, and extraordinarily slow to adapt.

The deep-seated traditions and mirror imaging that underpin the Pentagon's approach to the global forces of volatility, uncertainty,

---

7   Yoram Wind and Colin Crook, *The Power of Impossible Thinking* (Upper Saddle River, NJ: Prentice Hall, 2006), 45.

complexity, and ambiguity create an organizational atmosphere that is nothing if not resistant to change. As a result, it is not enough for the visionary spirit who invests fully in the cause of transforming such a hidebound mentality to possess the ability to think lucidly, learn rapidly, and communicate persuasively. While these attributes are critically important, it is *perseverance* – the ability to endure in crafting the future under the relentless assaults of those who cling desperately to the past – that will ultimately make the difference between success and failure.

This case study focuses on the work of Air Force Colonel John Boyd (1927–1997), a Korean War-era fighter pilot and engineer who became one of the twentieth-century's most innovative and influential strategists.[8] But beyond his monumental contribution to strategic thought, it was his epic perseverance in bringing an innovative model of strategic decision-making to an organization renown for groupthink. Viewed by those in his own service as a stubborn iconoclast with maverick tendencies that ran counter to a system shaped by well-established orthodoxy and a rigid chain of command, his incomparable ideation and resilient cognitive constructs were, after years of headstrong tenacity, ultimately embraced by the senior leadership at the Pentagon.

His pioneering thinking about such concepts as energy maneuverability or *fast transients* – the ability to adapt and respond more quickly than the adversary – and his inventive synthesis of classical strategy (the maneuver theories of Sun Tzu and B. F. Liddell Hart), science (Werner Heisenberg's uncertainty principle and Kurt Gödel's theory on the limits of knowledge), and philosophy (Jean Piaget's thoughts on structuralism and Thomas Kuhn's alternative views on the progress of science) led to a wholly new approach not only to how airpower is deployed, but how conflict itself can be waged in the modern era. His radical rethinking about air combat pushed an obstinate Air Force leadership to let go of its obsession with the development of faster and heavier fighter aircraft to those, such as the F-16, that were far more agile. At the same time, the U.S. Army incorporated Boyd's ideas about rapid and adaptive movements into its groundbreaking AirLand Battle concept while the U.S. Marine Corps embraced Boyd's decision-making framework as the philosophical foundation for its emerging maneuver warfare doctrine.[9]

The intricate complexities of Boyd's strategic paradigm reflect the stunningly complex thinking of the man. To effectively integrate the critical ideas found in such a broad array of groundbreaking works

---

8   Colin Gray, *Modern Strategy* (Oxford: Oxford University Press, 1999), 90–91.

9   Frans P. B. Osinga, *Science, Strategy, and War: The Strategic Theory of John Boyd* (London: Routledge, 2007), 3–4.

required an uncommon ability to gather and assimilate incredible volumes of information. The totality of Boyd's work reflects a painstaking and relentless effort to make unique connections between seemingly disparate fields and schools of thought, resulting in strategic principles of maneuver that toppled centuries of military thinking tied to attrition warfare. For Boyd, understanding how humans think (i.e., observe their surroundings, draw sense from those observations, render decisions about various courses of action, and ultimately act creatively within their environment) was as vitally important as understanding the engineering and physics of flight. The emerging synergies between men and machines created systems informed by opportunities to adapt to circumstances, thoughtfully respond, and ultimately set the pace of conflict while leaving the adversary struggling to react and gripped by survival-oriented thinking.

The nascent form of Boyd's strategic concepts began to take shape in the skies over Korea when he began to explore the reasons behind the success of the American F-86 fighter against the Russian-made MiG-15. Despite the disadvantage of flying a slower aircraft with a wider turn radius and lower ceiling, the American pilots prevailed in aerial combat. His two primary conclusions – that the bubble canopy on the F-86 provided better situational awareness and the ability of that aircraft to more rapidly change speed and altitude (the aforementioned fast transients) – were central to the strategic paradigm he would one day champion. And these weren't simply theoretical constructs. During his assignment following the war at the U.S. Air Force Fighter Weapons School at Nellis Air Force Base, Nevada, Boyd soon earned the accolade "40 second Boyd" based on his ability to transition from the aerial equivalent of prey to predator in a remarkable brief period.[10] As a result, he was tasked with revising the Air Force manual on aerial combat tactics for fighter pilots.[11]

Unique to Boyd's approach to air combat was that it extended beyond the technical aspects of air and aircraft to the dimensions of mind and morale. Central to this psychological approach was the concept of disrupting the adversary's ability to meaningfully respond to circumstances by presenting circumstances that required adaptive decision-making at a pace beyond their cognitive capacity.[12] In a very real sense, Boyd's new approach to conflict focused less on what to do, than how to think.[13] Unlike the classic approach championed at the military's war colleges which focused on

10   Osinga, *Science, Strategy, and War*, 22.
11   Robert Greene, *The 33 Strategies of War* (New York: Penguin Group, 2007), 132–33.
12   Greene, *The 33 Strategies of War*, 132.
13   John Andreas Olsen, *Airpower: The Strategic Concepts of John Warden and John Boyd* (Annapolis, MD: Naval Institute Press, 2015), 3–4.

massing physical force against an enemy's physical center of mass, Boyd encouraged combatants to employ a decision-making cycle that was more rapid, novel, and adaptive than the enemy's decision cycle. In doing so, the adversary was left with fewer and more limited options and, in extreme cases, a reaction sequence that was nearly frozen in time and place.[14]

One of the inventive elements of Boyd's strategic construct was the attention given to the moral dimension of conflict. He promoted the notion that the effort to highlight the disconnect between an adversary's stated values and their actual behavior could be of equal or greater influence than kinetic energy in overwhelming their resolve to endure.[15] In several of his presentations, remarkable both for their original thinking as for their exhaustive length, Boyd described the fundamental intent of his grand strategy as building toward a national goal that would fortify the moral spirit and physical strength while diminishing these same resources among the adversary. At the same time, the nation's approach to conflict would positively influence the parties that have not yet committed to a side. This, he contended, was accomplished by adhering to a compelling overarching philosophy that appeals to both allies and potential adversaries in a fashion that leaves them able to understand and willing to support the intended end state.[16]

Introducing a fundamental shift in patterns of thinking and acting in organizations is rarely easy, and this is especially true in the realm of warfighters. The armed forces have long operated from a core of conservatism with traditions being held aloft as the standard not only of the past but as a path to the future. This would accurately describe the culture Boyd (then a major) encountered when he reported to the Pentagon for an assignment in 1966 that would involve the design of the next generation of fighter aircraft (referred to as F-X, or Fighter Experimental). What he found upon reporting for duty was an Air Force intent upon creating an aircraft in the image of the heavy and lumbering F-111 fighter-bomber, the polar opposite of the type of quick and extremely nimble fighter Boyd envisioned – and was committed to developing.[17]

Rather than a relentless focus on the mission of securing the nation through airpower, a number of the senior officers Boyd found himself working with were more concerned with angling for promotion and meeting the requirements set forth by the large and politically influential

---

14   Osinga, *Science, Strategy, and War*, 1.
15   Grant T. Hammond, *The Mind of War: John Boyd and American Security* (Washington, DC: Smithsonian Books, 2001), 186.
16   Osinga, *Science, Strategy, and War*, 238.
17   Hammond, *The Mind of War*, 68.

contracting companies that were increasingly shaping the military's weapons procurement system. Before Boyd could even think about introducing his radical new thinking on strategy – and begin designing the type of highly agile fighter aircraft that reflected this strategic paradigm – he would have to find a way to effectively operate within an intransient bureaucracy that held fast to the prosaic patterns of the past. In this regard, Air Force generals were in nearly unanimous agreement that the next generation of fighter aircraft must first and foremost be unquestionably faster than anything the adversary might produce. The Air Force fighter cabal viewed top-end velocities that reached multiples of the speed of sound was of such vital importance that they would readily accept the inherent limitations posed by a lack of responsiveness when pressed into combat against a post-Vietnam adversary (primarily the air force of the Soviet Union).

As noted above, there was another entity at play in this dynamic, one operating in alliance with the Air Force leadership: the commercial interests of the well-connected contracting companies that handsomely profited from Defense Department projects (especially those involving the development of new weapon systems – such as new generation combat aircraft – which routinely involved massive expenditures). As a result, designing a new fighter aircraft could be shaped as much by the potential profit as by the need for innovation to meet the challenges of the Cold War. In the end, the desires of the Air Force generals and the chief executive officers of the contractors were in alignment as the aircraft that were really, really fast were also really, really expensive. And neither of these factions were above taking whatever action was necessary to sabotage those – like Boyd – who might undermine their ambitions.

Such senior level opposition would understandably deter most military officers; John Boyd, however, simply viewed the conflict unfolding in the halls of the Pentagon as analogous to the conflict he had been studying at the Fighter Weapons School. To persevere and ultimately emerge victorious against this 'adversary' (i.e., the staid thinking among Air Force leaders), Boyd operated in the very same fashion he would have if engaged in combat with an enemy aircraft. He thus followed an insurgent strategy designed to "intimidate, discourage, and outsmart his opponents."[18]

To achieve these tactical objectives, Boyd embodied what is arguably the key element of perseverance: preparation. Despite his casual, even unkempt outward appearances (something he purposely affected to cause his opponents to underestimate his abilities), he was nothing if not

---

18 Greene, *The 33 Strategies of War*, 132.

meticulous in his preparation. Before any meeting of substance, Boyd diligently "mastered every detail [to ensure he] knew more than his opponents: he could quote statistics, studies, and engineering theories to support his own project and poke holes through theirs."[19] He feigned interest in the claims contractors would make when appearing before Air Force leaders before launching a blistering counterattack filled with detailed analysis and irrefutable technical assessments. Boyd was not only tenacious, he was also right. The contractors ended up ceding critical ground – and credibility – in front of the very audiences they needed to convince.

Boyd knew that a key to his overall strategy was to find and recruit like-minded individuals throughout the Pentagon who had grown weary of status quo. They shared a vision for the future that ran in stark contrast to that which prevailed within the military bureaucracy. This often placed their respective careers in great peril if their radical thinking were to become known to their supervisors, but it also made them very dangerous. They could clearly see the desperate need for innovation in both strategy and materiel and they were prepared to act upon the technical and philosophical imagination they shared. Boyd soon operated at the center of a Pentagon-wide network of small cells comprising people with subject matter expertise in an array of relevant areas (e.g., engineering, procurement, finance, etc.). And each also brought a number of important connections throughout the centers of power within the monolithic Defense Department. As Boyd would soon learn, there were several senior leaders who were looking beyond the traditional approach to national security and were therefore open to new ideas that could help move the nation beyond the bitter experience of the Vietnam War.

Seven years after arriving at the Pentagon and beginning his seemingly Quixotic pursuit of a fighter built in the image of his own strategic paradigm, Boyd found precisely the influential ally he desperately needed. As with any kingdom, there can be only one true sovereign. In the American Armed Forces this was the Secretary of Defense, the office James Schlesinger entered in 1973. Some believe it is incumbent upon the Defense Secretary to serve as the decisive defender of the military culture while others take office intent upon introducing disruptive reforms. Fortunately for Boyd, Schlesinger readily embraced the latter belief. He was deeply disillusioned by the state of affairs he found within the department and was thus eager to entertain alternative thinking. It did not take long for him to become Boyd's chief ally in what amounted to a coup in strategic thought

---

19   Greene, *The 33 Strategies of War*, 132.

(and weapons development). After receiving a series of detailed briefings, Schlesinger granted his unreserved support for the development of a generation of more agile fighter aircraft to replace the faster albeit clumsier planes of the previous generation. This approval actually occurred outside the knowledge of senior Air Force leaders. As a result, when assembled for what they anticipated would be a briefing on a proposed weapon system, they listened with dismay as Boyd launched into his presentation by informing them that the Secretary of Defense had already approved the proposal and that the purpose of the briefing was only to inform them of what was to come. On this occasion, Boyd – infamous for his exceedingly lengthy presentations – made sure he lived up to this contemptible reputation.[20]

In a 2005 paper, *Shared Virtue: The Convergence of Valued Human Strengths Across Culture and History*, Dahlsgaard et al.[21] sought to identify the core virtues that were common across the world's major philosophical and religious traditions. Included among these was a category they labeled as *strength*. Examples set forth in this category include the values of bravery, honesty and perseverance.

It is then an accurate depiction of events to refer to the uncommon bravery and enduring strength of Colonel John Boyd, whose perseverance in pioneering a new model of strategic thinking helped move a conventionalist military into a new era.

References

Brooks, D. *The Road to Character*. New York: Random House, 2015.

Brown, B. *Daring Greatly: How the Courage to Be Vulnerable Transforms the Way We Live, Love, Parent, and Lead*. New York: Avery, Reprint edition, 2015.

Collins, J. M. *Military Strategy: Principles, Practices, and Historical Perspectives*. Washington: Potomac Books, 2002.

Dahlsgaard, K. P., C. Peterson and M. Seligman. "Shared Virtue: The Convergence of Valued Human Strengths Across Culture and History," *Review of General Psychology* 9, no. 3 (2005): 203–13.

Duckworth, A. *Grit: The Power of Passion and Perseverance*. New York: Scribner, reprint edition, 2018.

Gray, C. *Modern Strategy*. Oxford: Oxford University Press, 1999.

---

20   Greene, *The 33 Strategies of War*, 133.
21   Katherine P. Dahlsgaard, Christopher Peterson and Martin Seligman. "Shared Virtue: The Convergence of Valued Human Strengths Across Culture and History," *Review of General Psychology* 9, no. 3 (2005): 203–13.

Greene, R. *The 33 Strategies of War*. New York: Penguin, 2007.

Hammond, G. T. *The Mind of War: John Boyd and American Security*. Washington, DC: Smithsonian Books, 2001.

Hillenbrand, L. *Unbroken: A World War II Story of Survival, Resilience, and Redemption*. New York: Random House, 2010.

McCullough, D. *1776*. New York: Simon & Schuster, 2005.

Miller, J. *Examined Lives: From Socrates to Nietzsche*. New York: Farrar, Straus and Giroux, 2011.

Olsen, J. A. *Airpower: The Strategic Concepts of John Warden and John Boyd*. Annapolis, MD: Naval Institute Press, 2015.

Osinga, F. P. *Science, Strategy, and War: The Strategic Theory of John Boyd*. London: Routledge, 2007.

Wind, Y. A. and C. Crook. *The Power of Impossible Thinking*. Upper Saddle River, NJ: Prentice Hall, 2006.

9

TEMPERANCE

Overview:
The Virtue of Temperance[1]

Stephen Deakin

"Abstemiousness is vital – in food, in smoking, in social activities. So is need for regular sleep."

– Field Marshal Montgomery[2]

"Be an example to your men, in your duty and in private life. Never spare yourself, and let the troops see that you don't in your endurance of fatigue and privation. Always be tactful and well-mannered and teach your subordinates to do the same. Avoid excessive sharpness or harshness of voice, which usually indicates the man who has shortcomings of his own to hide."

– Field Marshal Rommel[3]

Temperance

The virtue of temperance is traditionally viewed as one of moderation and self-control in the use of alcohol, food and sex, although it has a much wider application than this. It is associated with good judgement, a sound mind,

---

1 Nothing in the overview should be construed as necessarily being the views of the U.K. Ministry of Defence. I am grateful to Donald Carrick, Nigel de Lee, Charles Garraway and Dennis Vincent for their helpful comments. As ever, responsibility for the arguments herein rests with the author alone.

2 Field Marshal Bernard Law Montgomery, *The Path to Leadership* (London: Collins, 1961), 250.

3 Daniel Butler, *Field Marshal: The Life and Death of Erwin Rommel* (London: Casemate, 2015), 105.

practical intelligence, restraint, patience, self-discipline, balance, discretion and control of addictive and negative human passions, while being active and purposeful rather than passive. It relates to knowing what the good life is and to a commitment to work towards achieving this. Temperance is positive about human appetites; it is their inappropriate use, especially excessive, or insufficient use, which is its concern. Temperance is the virtue of 'enough.' A temperate person is a well-balanced person who works to control the excesses of their passions, faculties, appetites and desires because they want to be a good person and they want to contribute to the common good.

In the West, ideas about temperance emerge from an amalgam of the ancient Greek thinkers and Christianity, and these find expression in the Just War Tradition. For a millennium or more the chivalric tradition celebrated these virtues. Medieval knights were to use their strength for the good; with forbearance, self-control and moderation, to oppose evil. Showing temperance was a quality of a good knight. They were to be brave in battle, to be sacrificial, to serve others and to protect the Church. Such beliefs came to shape the virtues of military behaviour in the West. They find expression in the motto of the United States military academy at West Point – "Duty, Honour, Country" – and in the motto of the British military academy at Sandhurst, "Serve to Lead." They also find expression in the work of senior military leaders: Field Marshal Montgomery wrote, "The soldier is the enemy of the beast in man and none other."[4] MacArthur, the American World War II general, remarked, "The soldier, be he friend or foe, is charged with the protection of the weak and unarmed. It is the very essence and reason for his being."[5] Soldiers have a great need to develop temperance.

Temperate Leadership

Principles

Temperance is an essential part of leadership at all levels.[6] Temperance is an enabling virtue, for the other virtues each require self-control, discipline, sound judgement, personal mastery, a commitment to and a knowledge of what is good and a willingness to make sacrifices for the common good

---

4   Field Marshal Bernard Law Montgomery, *A History of Warfare* (London: Collins, 1968), 567.

5   William Manchester, *American Caesar: Douglas MacArthur 1880–1964* (New York: Black Bay, 2008), 488.

6   Karl Ingen Tangen, "The Need for Temperance: On Organisational Leadership and Temperance," *Scandinavian Journal for Leadership and Theology* 2 (2015).

to achieve them. Militaries rightly lay great emphasis on their soldiers[7] being leaders since their professional responsibilities especially require this. Every soldier is a leader: of themselves, of their peers and of their subordinates if they have any. Non-Commissioned Officers and Officers are particularly required to lead. This can be seen in military training: civilians are transformed into people who work sacrificially for others as part of a team, who are well presented, who are obedient to legitimate authority, and who fight legally in accordance with the Law of Armed Conflict. There are time-honoured ways to achieve this, such as a focus on the practice of the military virtues, marching drills, military etiquette, working as a team member and education in relevant military subjects. Many soldiers testify that such military training and education has changed them for the better.

Soldiers, like everyone else, struggle to be virtuous, and traditionally they have a mixed reputation for virtue. They may have soldierly virtues associated with the field of battle, such as courage, self-sacrifice and loyalty, but they are often fit, energetic, men (and women) who can behave in intemperate ways. Rather than being known for their moderation, good judgement and restraint they are sometimes known for their rowdiness, drunkenness and sexual excesses! Armies often find that the majority of their disciplinary cases involving soldiers are alcohol-related. Soldiers can be supported in this area by temperate leadership. Today, some Messes in the British military forbid soldiers to buy each other drinks. It is intended that this policy will reduce consumption of alcohol and the problems that can stem from this. In Burma in World War II, allied soldiers in the front line used Calcutta as a place for rest and recreation. Their leader, Field Marshal Slim, went to considerable trouble to provide in Calcutta, 'wholesome amusements' for his soldiers to protect them, their morale and their families.[8]

While there are well known examples of lack of temperate behaviour among military personnel it is noteworthy that, in the West, there is an expectation of temperate behaviour from soldiers, and when it is known that this has not occurred the military discipline system is used against offenders. Temperate military leaders will aim to create a work environment that supports this virtue.

Woven into the virtue of temperance is the recognition of a mean of moderate behaviour and a recognition that judgement is required about exactly what this is in each case. Temperate soldiers are not expected to

---

7 The words 'soldier' and 'armies' are used for the sake of simplicity throughout this overview to stand for all military personnel and organisations unless otherwise specified.

8 Field Marshal Viscount Slim, *Defeat Into Victory* (London: Pan, 2009), 153.

be perfect. In the West today militaries commonly describe themselves as adhering to *values*, although these often look much like the classical *virtues*. The British Army values are, Selfless Commitment, Respect for Others, Loyalty, Integrity, Discipline and Courage.[9] These values are therefore the ethical goals that a British soldier should aim at, by exercising the corresponding virtues. They are meant to enable soldiers to behave well and to be effective both on and off the field of battle. A practical way of presenting these British Army values/virtues is to show them with some of their excesses and deficiencies in an Aristotelian manner using a 'traffic light' metaphor.

Red	Green	Red
Cowardice	Courage	Recklessness
Careless Disorder Neglect	Discipline	Obsessive Pernickety Overcritical
Ignorance Disrespect	Respect for Others	Unthinking/Uncritical Acceptance
Deceit	Integrity	Unimpeachable Saintliness
Treachery	Loyalty	Blind Obedience Unthinking Obedience
Selfishness Narcissism	Selfless Commitment	Personal Indifference Martyr

Figure 9.1   Traffic Light Metaphor

Source: Adapted from McCormack.[10]

Soldiers should keep to the middle, the green, temperate column rather than allow themselves, or those they lead, to move to one of the red extremes. To do this they require temperate virtues of good judgement, moderation, balance, restraint, discipline and the like together with a knowledge of the other virtues to recognize where the mean is.

---

9   British Army, *Values and Standards of the British Army* (Official document), 2008.
10   Philip McCormack, "Ethics, Military Judgement Panel," in *Leadership*, ed. Stephen Deakin, Sandhurst Occasional Papers No. 18 (2014).

Temperate Leadership Challenges

Military leaders can be very task-focused. This is understandable, their task in battle is to overcome their fears and, as quickly as possible, to break the will of the enemy to fight. However, an over-strong focus on task can lead to toxic leadership whereby leaders achieve results by overworking and perhaps belittling their own staff. Such leaders may be so disliked that their subordinates think about killing them in battle, since it is often easy to do so unnoticed in such circumstances.[11] The temperate soldier-leader will recognize that while there are many times that a task focus is vital, there are also many times when the people whom she leads have a higher priority than the task. For example, temperate leaders will discourage 'workaholism' and set a good example in this regard. Many soldiers report that they feel under pressure to be at work before their boss and to leave only after him or her. Failure to do this is perceived as showing a lack of commitment and as being likely to harm promotion prospects. A temperate leader will cut through all this and promote on other performances, she will positively encourage her soldiers to lead balanced lives and to spend time with their families and on social activities.

Soldiers live and work in a strongly hierarchal rank structure and they are subject to military discipline that curtails their freedoms in ways that are alien to a civilian. Temperate leaders will not abuse this authority and they will resist temptations stemming from the 'power corrupts' phenomenon. They will not allow bullying, harassment and ill-treatment of anyone in their command and they will discipline anyone found doing so. They will share the hardships of those that they lead. This may mean not being first in the queue for food, or not complaining about the quality of the food, or not using rank to gain extra unreasonable privileges over subordinates. In World War II, Field Marshal Slim had a reputation among his soldiers for having temperate leadership qualities. One way in which he demonstrated this virtue was to put his own headquarters staff on half rations when his soldiers in the front line had to endure the same.[12]

Temperate military leaders will be fully proficient professionally, for in war their subordinates' lives depend on this. They will not sacrifice the lives of their men due to lazy or poor planning or their ambition for success and glory. Finding the mean here may be difficult and open to misunderstanding by others. When does the required determined aggression become arrogant, self-centred, 'win at any price' egotism? Stalin

---

11   George Reed, "Toxic Leadership," *Military Review* (July–August 2004): 67–71.

12   Slim, *Defeat into Victory*, 222–23.

deliberately encouraged rivalry among his Army leaders fighting the Nazi regime, leading them sometimes to take unwarranted risks and to act without the necessary planning. This probably resulted in the unnecessary deaths of many of his soldiers. Montgomery and American counterpart, General Patton, are understood to have thought of themselves as rivals and it may be that Montgomery's costly defeat at the battle of Arnhem in 1944 was at least partly a product of this: some think that Arnhem was an attempt by Montgomery to beat Patton to Germany and thereon to Berlin. Temperate soldier leaders will choose to keep their career ambitions in perspective. However ambitious they are for promotion, they will find the mean between such ambition and the high value they place on the other virtues. For temperate soldiers, leadership is not primarily about high military rank; it begins with dealing with even the small things in a trustworthy manner which then gives them the moral authority to lead.

Temperate Fighters

Great courage is required of soldiers on the battlefield since they face the possibility of losing their life or being badly wounded. It is often acknowledged that really brave soldiers are ones who are fearful, but who overcome this fear to continue to fight. The temperate soldier will control his, wholly understandable, impulses to flee the battlefield. He will look for ways to increase the probability of his survival where this is possible and this will require an assessment of other virtues such as courage and prudence and self-sacrifice.

Law and War

Temperate soldiers will obey the laws of war. Just war requires temperate fighters who will act with restraint and moderation. Just War thinking accepts that wars will occur, it seeks to limit war and its effects through the Law of Armed Conflict (LOAC). As the British *Manual of the Law* notes, "The LOAC is consistent with the economic and efficient use of force. It is intended to minimize the suffering caused by armed conflict rather than impede military efficiency."[13]

Obedience to LOAC requires self-control and moderation and sound judgement by soldiers and by political leaders. There will be many occasions in war when soldiers (and sometimes their political leaders) must use their

---

13   JSP 383. *The Joint Service Manual of the Law of Armed Conflict* (Shrivenham: Joint Doctrine and Concepts Centre, 2004), 22.

judgement about the application of LOAC principles. The British *Manual of the Law* bases itself on the principles of Military Necessity, Humanity, Distinction and Proportionality. LOAC cannot codify everything and cover every eventuality. It requires ethically and legally aware soldiers and their temperate judgement for it to succeed. Temperance is at the heart of the law of armed conflict.

When to surrender and when to accept a surrender in battle are often decisions taken in difficult circumstances that benefit from temperate judgement. An interesting case concerns the sinking by the British Royal Navy of the German battleship *Bismarck* in 1941. The *Bismarck* had earlier sunk the British battle cruiser HMS *Hood*, with the loss of over 1,400 lives – there were three survivors. Prime Minister Churchill ordered the Royal Navy to "Sink the Bismarck" and the ship was then attacked by Swordfish aircraft, carrying torpedoes, one of which hit the ship and damaged her steering, with the result that she could only move slowly in a large circle. She was now so vulnerable to attack that her sinking by the British Navy with great loss of her crew's lives was a foregone conclusion. Two British battleship and other ships attacked the *Bismarck* and they did not offer her the chance to surrender even though some of them fired at the ship from a close range and could clearly see the vessel and many of the crew that they were killing. There is evidence that some of *Bismarck*'s crew offered to surrender, by light signal, flag and semaphore during this attack and that this was ignored by the British.[14] A temperate judgement by her captain, Ernst Lindemann, would have been to abandon ship and to scuttle the *Bismarck* early in the battle to save the lives of her crew. Instead, Lindemann decided to fight until he could fire his guns no more, when the order may have been given for the crew to scuttle her and abandon ship (Lindemann, and also the fleet commander Admiral Lütjens, went down with the ship). Over 2,000 of the *Bismarck*'s crew perished in this battle, with around only a 100 survivors. The conclusion to be drawn from this incident is that both the German and British commanders could have acted with more temperance and thereby have likely saved many lives.

Restraint in war can be a difficult temperate judgement. The Just War principle is that minimum force should be used to achieve an end that is a military necessity. The great Prussian military strategist Clausewitz in his *On War*[15] is sometimes thought, perhaps erroneously, to believe that practising moderation in war operations will cause more suffering

---

14 Ian Ballantyne, *Killing the Bismarck* (Barnsley: Pen and Sword, 2011).
15 Michael Howard and Peter Paret (eds.) *On War* (Princeton, NJ: Princeton University Press, 1984).

in the long run. He famously wrote that, "to introduce the principle of moderation into the theory of war itself would always lead to a logical absurdity."[16] Meanwhile, his competitor, the eminent strategist Antoine-Henri Jomini in *Summary of the Art of War*[17] can be read as being more obviously aware than Clausewitz of the moral and political advantages of using minimum force and political strategies to achieve aims in war. The ethical mean here no doubt lies between the two strategist's arguments.

Courageous Restraint

The policy of courageous restraint was introduced in Afghanistan in 2009 due to concerns that too many innocent Afghan civilians were being killed by the international coalition as it fought the insurgents. In addition, these deaths were seen to be hindering the aim of winning the hearts and minds of Afghans: they were thought to be fuelling enemy activity and to be making the task of the coalition more difficult. The situation in Afghanistan at that time was an extremely complex one: soldiers were engaged in war, counter terrorism, counter insurgency and humanitarian and stabilization efforts often at much the same time. Many coalition soldiers were killed in the fighting: over 450 members of the British Army died between 2001 and 2015. The enemy was difficult to identify and distinguishing between combatants and non-combatants was often a great problem. The enemy used the Law of Armed Conflict against coalition forces; for example, by exploiting the protection of ambulances by the Red Cross (using the symbol of that organization as an aiming point), by deliberately ignoring the distinction between combatants and non-combatants and by taking advantage of the Coalition's reluctance to shoot civilians used by the insurgents to hide behind. The policy of courageous restraint required that soldiers use temperate judgement above the level set by the Law of Armed Conflict before they opened fire and possibly killed anyone.

Coalition soldiers were deployed to Afghanistan to support the government to help it bring stability to the country. They were now required by the policy of Courageous Restraint to put their lives at even more risk to do this, and it was not 'their' war. Soldiers claimed that the policy of courageous restraint was getting their comrades killed unnecessarily. A young British Army platoon commander leading his men in Afghanistan set the issues out succinctly,

16 Howard and Paret, *On War*, 76.
17 Charles Messenger (ed.) *The Art of War* (London: Greenhill, 1992).

... to make any progress in these wars among the people the infantry have to be exposed to more risk ... we have to get out into the communities, win over the people ... exactly when the risk is highest to us. And that is very hard to accept when you are the one taking the increased risks and when you are the one who has to keep smiling while you do it. Would you? Is it worth your face, your leg, your life?[18]

A British NCO gave his opinion about the policy of courageous restraint,

Our hands are tied the way we are asked to do courageous restraint. I agree with it to the extent that previously too many civilians were killed but we have got people shooting at us and we are not allowed to shoot back. Courageous restraint is a lot easier to say than to implement.[19]

Lt Gen. Sir Nick Parker Deputy Commander ISAF (International Security Assistance Force), recognized the problem and said that soldiers must be able to do their task, "but what we must do is not alienate the population."[20] As Bury notes, there is "a balance between operational effectiveness and morality." [21] Finding this middle ground may sometimes be difficult in war and thinking and practice should be guided by the virtue of temperance.

Conclusion

Most religions, philosophies, political ideals and self-help theorists offer goals that require self-control to achieve them. It is difficult to think of attempts that encourage virtuous living that do not require temperance in their followers – except perhaps for contemporary moral relativism with its misplaced emphasis on individual personal autonomy. An intemperate person allows their passions to rule them which in a soldier can lead to cruel and to inhumane behaviour or to passivity and to cowardice. Good leaders set an example; they balance competing ethical demands to find a virtuous result. It is often claimed that acts of self-restraint performed regularly will help people to become stronger in this virtue. Soldiers have many opportunities to practise these.

---

18   Patrick Bury, *Callsign Hades* (London: Simon & Schuster, 2010), 257.
19   Thomas Harding "'Courageous restraint' putting soldiers' lives at risk," *The Daily Telegraph*, July 6, 2010.
20   Thomas Harding, "Britain's top general in Afghanistan admits 'courageous restraint' must change," *The Daily Telegraph*, July 11, 2010.
21   Bury, *Callsign Hades*, 235.

Case Study 1:
Tempering Corruption

Michael D. Good[22]

Four nights in Manila with a prostitute. A designer handbag for his wife. Cash and other gifts totaling US$140,000. Meals and luxury hotel visits. One night with a prostitute at a karaoke club. Roundtrip airfare from Japan to the U.S. A monthly stipend of US$1,000.[23] The list continues. And then continues more. These are a few representative bribes discovered by investigations into Glenn Defense Marine Asia, a husbanding company operating primarily in Southeast Asia – the U.S. Navy's Seventh Fleet area of operations, headed by Leonard Glenn Francis, aka 'Fat Leonard.' In the last five years civilian authorities[24] have filed criminal charges against 30 individuals. Five others have been charged under the Uniformed Code of Military Justice. Over 550 military personnel, including 60 flag officers, have come under investigation. Though misconduct has been substantiated in only 70 cases, the onion continues to reveal more layers. To date, nearly half of the 550 military personnel have been cleared of wrongdoing, but new information continues to surface and there remain hundreds of personnel under investigation for corruption and bribery.[25]

---

22 The views expressed herein are solely those of the author in his private capacity and do not in any way represent the views of the U.S. Naval Academy, U.S. Navy, or the Department of Defense.

23 Craig Whitlock and Kevin Uhrmacher, "Prostitutes, vacations and cash: The Navy officials 'Fat Leonard' took down," *The Washington Post*, last modified March 26, 2018, https://www.washingtonpost.com/graphics/investigations/seducing-the-seventh-fleet/.

24 U.S. Federal Court and one person has been prosecuted by Singaporean authorities.

25 From November 2017 to March 2018, the total number under investigation rose from 420 to 550.

As a military officer, I am deeply saddened by this situation. Perhaps that's too weak – rather, I'm appalled, angry, and a little disgusted. You should be, too. My first question and probably yours is "How could they have does this?" Although, we cannot see completely through their eyes and understand every factor pulling on their wills, I think we nevertheless must attempt to answer that question. Not merely to gossip, but so that we might see where and how they mis-stepped. Then, we can examine ourselves and take appropriate actions in our own lives to build bulwarks which can protect us from becoming the kind of people who choose to do these things. We ought to be concerned with how we can become the kind of people who cannot fail to see the wrongness of their actions and the kind of people who have the will power and inner goodness to turn from wrongdoing.

In the many instances of bribery and corruption surrounding the scandal of the U.S. Seventh Fleet and Glenn Defense Marine Asia there seem to be multiple contributing forces. I intend to discuss a couple of them. First, I recount two stories from my own time in the U.S. Navy in order to illustrate how sometimes military cultural expectations can inappropriately inflate one's sense of self-honor and also to provide an example of how con men can groom others into developing a (misplaced) sense of loyalty. Then, I address malformed or misplaced desires and their role as major contributing forces to the choices of those who have committed wrongdoing. Finally, I discuss practical steps that military personnel (and anyone else) can take to change, replace, and build bulwarks against malformed desires.

Two Brief Stories

Lunchtime at the University of Southern California

As a young lieutenant (O3), I was stationed at the University of Southern California (USC) where I taught courses and trained midshipmen in the Naval Reserve Officer Training Corps (NROTC). As one of a few uniformed personnel on campus, I stood out. Walking among huge groups of students turned out to be especially frustrating for me. Not usually prone to anger, I made a point to reflect on just why I would get 'road rage' while walking among the crowds. Memories came to me of the two ships on which I had just spent nearly four years. Sailors got out of my way. When I walked through passageways, sailors hugged the bulkhead. It is an instinctive thing, I think, an unwritten norm. By the time I left my second ship, there were only 10 people or so on the ship who outranked me. That meant that the other 260–300 people got out of my way. It is a normal thing for military personnel to make way for officers, even very junior ones. I hadn't really thought about it – never noticed it. It is just the way that things are. I had grown to expect it, though, as my subconscious reaction to the student throng attested. But it was my position or rank on the ships that sailors responded to, not me. My frustration was due to others (in this case, the students of USC) not treating me in the way I had grown used to being treated. I had no recognizable authority or special authoritative role placing me over these university students. The privileges accorded to those of my rank on a ship or in other military contexts were not due to me there, outside of those contexts.

Liberty in Bali

My first tour as a young junior officer consisted of two deployments in two years. My major collateral duty during this tour was as MWR (Morale, Welfare, and Recreation) officer. In this role, I had the esteemed duty to arrange tours, book hotel rooms, and find ways to keep sailors (non-destructively) busy while in liberty ports. Ships in port spend money in two ways – for provisions and for liberty. So, next to the Supply Officer, I had the most amount of money to spend. Halfway through my second deployment, my ship anchored in Bali, Indonesia. At the port brief, which is held on the ship prior to any liberty, the local MWR contacts informed me that I had a car waiting for me at the landing. This offer was strange and surprising. I had coordinated nearly 20 port calls at this point and had never been offered a car. Usually, the CO had a car, the crew had a few vans, and the wardroom and CPO Mess might each have a dedicated van. When I arrived at the pier, I went into the building which functioned as an office for the husbanding agent. Waiting there for me was a car, a driver, and the husbanding agent, Fat Leonard himself. The whole situation felt wrong. I refused the car.

How Could They Do That?

Roles, Expectation, and Pride

Clearly, I was not important enough to rate a car when I was in Bali. And I wasn't even tempted to take it. It wasn't because I was a paragon of virtue – I wasn't. It wasn't because I knew the rules and didn't want to break them – I didn't really know the rules, though admittedly, it didn't feel right. It didn't feel right because I never expected to get a car. I had no reason to expect it. I did not rate one, and (because of my experience so far) I knew it. But there are built-in expectations concerning COs and some others. Rank and role in the military place those who hold them into positions of influence and social-political status that they otherwise wouldn't have. For instance, in my experience alone I've witnessed my COs meet with all sorts of dignitaries – mayors of major cities, governors of provinces, members of royal families, famous Hollywood actors and directors, Miss America, famous professional athletes, and industry and business executives. Most meetings include the XO (Executive Officer) and CMC (Command Master Chief), sometimes they even may include department heads and others. Upon completion of their tours, this same group of people – COs, XOs, CMCs, and Department Heads – go on to serve in higher staffs. It seems reasonable that some of the expectations formed in these positions carry-over into follow-on positions, just like it did to me on a smaller scale at USC. Many of the military personnel so far indicted in the Glenn Defense Marine Asia scandal are those who served previously in these higher-ranking positions on ships, squadrons, or within the Supply Corps (Logistics, contracting, etc.). What happened to me during my lunchtime walks at USC happens in one degree or another to every officer. We all come to expect being treated in a certain way, then switch roles. If we are not careful, the military structure itself – moving us from one role to another – can facilitate in us, the development of a malformed sense of importance, arrogant pride, which leads to having (at a minimum) inappropriate expectations about how we ought to be treated and to a false sense of entitlement.[26]

Loyalty, Bought and Paid For

Bribes offered by Glenn Defense Marine and its proxies include prostitution, fancy hotels, cash, concert tickets, elaborate meals, and more. Officers and other Naval and DoD (Department of Defense) personnel have admitted to divulging classified and proprietary information, to 'fixing' contracts helping to defraud the U.S. Navy, to manipulating ship schedules to benefit Glenn Defense Marine Asia, as well as other crimes and forms of professional misconduct.[27] How could they have done this? Well, perhaps they were provided a car in a liberty port. Perhaps they found their hotel bill mysteriously paid. They were asked to host a catered rug flop in exchange for discounts on rugs.[28] Maybe then, they

---

26   See Chapter 11 on "Humility" in this volume.
27   Whitlock and Uhrmacher, "Prostitutes, vacations and cash."
28   A rug flop is where a rug merchant peddles his wares at a catered party. There are usually discounts, or free leasing, offered to the host.

felt comfortable asking for a favor. Perhaps concert tickets. A prostitute. Reservations at a fancy restaurant. They got something for nothing, were made to feel special, and came to expect special treatment, special hook-ups. There are many ways to run a con and many ways to groom a mark.[29] If I had taken the car, I would be in debt to Fat Leonard. Even if he never asked me for anything afterward, I likely still would advocate for him out of a sense of good will and misplaced loyalty. If he did ask me for something, I could either give it or I could admit to accepting unauthorized gifts. In both cases, I would be compromised, just like he would have wanted.[30]

Malformed Desire and the Power of Moral Incontinence

In January 2016, the Commander of Carrier Strike Group (CSG) Fifteen, a one-star admiral, was relieved of command and issued a punitive letter of reprimand. The previous August, he was underway for six days on a ship. Later, in December, he was again underway, this time for five days on a different ship. In each of these incidents the ships' IT departments have record of him indulging in pornographic websites for over four hours.[31] The interesting question here is, of course, how could he have done this? Why couldn't he have waited a few short days before gratifying himself? He apparently was able to refrain while at his office on base (his office computers were searched and no pornographic sites were identified, although sites of women in bikinis were). The regulation is clear. It is also common knowledge that routine scans are done for security reasons – so the odds of getting found out are very high. I can only conclude that he just couldn't help himself. He must have formed a habit – or addiction – that was stronger than his willpower.[32] He was now in a situation such that he had to gratify his desires – he couldn't say no to them.

---

29 See Maria Konnikova, *The Confidence Game: Why We Fall For It ... Every Time* (New York: Viking Penguin, 2017).

30 See "Good Loyalty and Bad Loyalty" in Chapter 3 of this volume. Another case that I have personal knowledge of: a friend of mine had to advise his boss to return to pay a 'comp'd' hotel bill with a check, so that he could prove that he paid it. It turned out that he later had to produce the check to avoid charges of misconduct.

31 Jeanette Steele, "Admiral with Porn: Didn't know it was this much," *The San Diego Union-Tribune*, last modified March 8, 2016, http://www.sandiegouniontribune.com/military/sdut-navy-admiral-porn-investigation-2016mar08-story.html.

32 See Chapter 11 of this volume which discusses *hubris* – what I will call 'arrogant pride.' Very likely, hubris helped play a rationalizing role in the admiral's decision to break Navy regulations. I do not think that the whole situation can be attributed to hubris, however, as he took care in other professional environments to avoid explicit pornographic material.

Tempering One's Desires – A Quick Practical Look

The Road There

Pride, (false) loyalty, and malformed desires together worked within many of those caught up in the Glenn Defense Marine Asia scandal. It is impossible to say whether these three vices were present in each of the individual cases. However, in the few cases made public, it is not difficult to see at least two of them as obviously present. How did they become the kind of people who could do this? As with anyone, it starts in what she allows herself to think. By allowing herself to think about what she deserves, to what she is entitled, and how nice it would be to gratify that particular desire, she has started a journey down the road of vice – of permitting those thoughts to stain her emotional attitudes and so shape her desires. What she habitually puts, or allows, before her mind (thinks about) and the way that she habitually thinks about those things tempers her desires. It shapes them into either virtuous ones or vicious ones. Desires affect intentions – they inform what she wants to do, what she can't bring herself to do, and what she will do. We should assume (with possibly few exceptions) that those who took bribes did not join the U.S. Navy with the goal of defrauding it. They must have grown into the kind of people who were prepared to do vicious things in order to gratify their desires.

The Road Back (and the One Not Taken)

How do they come back – or better, how do we become the kind of people who are unwilling to do vicious things to gratify our desires? Well, we wouldn't be tempted to gratify vicious desires if we were to become the kind of people who had virtuous ones. So, we ought to develop the virtue of temperance and habitually and systematically reshape and strengthen virtuous desires. We do this first in our thought life – where we have great freedom of choice. We choose to have a proper understanding of what we are really owed. We choose to have appropriate expectations of how others ought to treat us in a professional capacity. We avoid envious thoughts about what other people in similar situations received. There are numerous ways to retrain one's mind and how it thinks and many safeguards that we can put into place to facilitate this retraining. Cultivating good relationships with our senior enlisted advisors, maintaining positive communications with a support system at home – including prearranging someone to hold us accountable and to periodically ask us previously-agreed-to tough questions throughout a tour or deployment (or life). We can systematically reflect on the type of person we want to be. Think of how we would like people to talk about us behind our backs. Are we desiring the things and acting on the things that will facilitate that kind of talk?

Case Study 2:
Unit Temperance and
the Haditha Case

David M. Barnes[33]

"To consciously kill a child or, in a rage, execute unarmed men and women, would be a criminal act meriting punishment and dishonor."

– Bing West (2006)

When we think of the virtue of temperance, we usually think of it in terms of one's appetites and how to moderate them. In a military context, one thinks of cases where individual service members have been intemperate; where a leader, for example, cannot regulate desires for alcohol or for sex.[34] Certainly, one could form military case studies around this conception of individual temperance; leaders at all levels must be temperate. However, what does it mean for a military unit to be temperate? Setting aside the ontological issues about collective agency, groups are often labeled and judged collectively;[35] a unit, for example,

---

33 The views expressed here are those of the author and do not necessarily reflect the official policy or position of the Department of the Army, the Department of Defense, or the U.S. Government.

34 For an excellent discussion of temperance in the military, see James H. Toner, "Temperance and the Profession of Arms," in *Morals Under the Gun* (Lexington: University of Kentucky Press, 2000), 125–42.

35 The concept of collective or group agency and corresponding responsibility, as List and Pettit note (2011), is controversial. Yet, there seems to be something at work when groups of individuals operate with a common or shared purpose. Consider the case outlined by Searle (1990, 402). A number of individuals are scattered about in a park. Suddenly it starts to rain, and each runs to a shelter. Although there may be some coordination, running to

might be a 'good unit' or a weak one. If, then, we were to judge a unit as temperate, what does that look like?

What is a Temperate Unit?

Perhaps it is fruitful to consider the virtues and vices of the units and soldiers who form them. We understand that claiming superior orders is not a defense for committing war crimes, for example, so we could begin by surmising that temperate units do not commit war crimes. As Robinson points out, "temperate units will not commit atrocities, even if ordered to do so by a superior …"[36] While this claim may be true, mere avoidance of war crimes seems insufficient for a complete description of a temperate unit. A unit may be intemperate and never commit an atrocity. What we seem to be looking for are the characteristics that demonstrate a unit's restraint in combat; for example, a temperate unit moderates its appetite for extreme battle lust when it is not needed. A temperate, military unit restrains from collective, wholly emotionally driven conduct. Reason and the habit of combat restraint in war help the unit, not only to comply with the Laws of Armed Conflict and International Humanitarian Law, but also to enable them to instantiate unit temperance.

An infamous case from Iraq helps illustrate this point: On November 19, 2005, a group of U.S. Marines from 3rd Battalion, 1st Marines (Battalion 3/1) killed 24 Iraqi civilians. Accounts "paint[ed] a picture of a devastatingly violent response by a group of U.S. troops who had lost one of their own to a deadly insurgent attack and believed they were under fire."[37] Labeled as a 'massacre' by some, the Haditha incident highlights more than the complexities of prosecuting crimes in war and concerns about violations of *in bello* discrimination. As Savage and Bumiller note, "Many cases involving civilian deaths arise during the chaos of combat or shortly afterward, when fighters' emotions are running high."[38] Might the Haditha case be one where grief over recent loss overcomes temperate restraint?

---

the shelter is not something they are doing together. Now imagine another scenario with the same individuals executing the same movements, but as members of a dance troop. In both cases, there is no difference in the collection of individual behavior: A is running to the shelter, and B is running to the shelter, etc. The dancers are engaged in collective action, whereas the park-goers are not. How should we explain the difference; would we parse moral responsibility for the group of individual dancers?

36 Jim Robinson, "Plato and the Virtues of Military Units," *Journal of Military Ethics* 13, no. 2, 2014): 190–202.

37 See Tim McGirk, "Collateral Damage or Civilian Massacre in Haditha?" *Time*, March 19, 2006, http://content.time.com/time/world/article/0,8599,1174649,00.html.

38 Charlie Savage and Elisabeth Bumiller. "An Iraqi Massacre, a Light Sentence and a Question of Military Justice," *The New York Times*, January 27, 2012, http://www.nytimes.

Were war crimes committed that day? Clearly, there was much public debate. Eight Marines were charged after months of investigation, and only one, Staff Sgt. Frank Wuterich, went to trial seven years later. On January 23, 2012, he pleaded to one count of negligent dereliction of duty; the counts of assault and manslaughter were dropped.[39] Much about that fateful event is contested. Did these Marines commit murder? As Bing West notes, "Iraqis claim that enraged Marines executed the civilians."[40] Alternatively, lawyers for the defense, West continues, "claim the deaths were accidents that occurred while the men were following the Rules of Engagement for clearing rooms when under fire." Were the civilian dead tragic causalities caught in the wrong place at the wrong time?

What is certain is that 24 Iraqi men, women, and children were killed that day. What remains in question is the how and why those deaths occurred. This case study is not meant to settle the legal argument. Rather, the tragic loss of life in Haditha allows us to consider the virtue of temperance of a military unit.

Put another way, what does it mean for a unit to be temperate or, alternatively, intemperate? Was that squad from Battalion 3/1 a unit instantiating the virtue of temperance, or is this an example of the vice of intemperance? Were they overcome by raw emotion and desire for revenge? If temperance is a virtue we believe units ought to have, then we need to understand what it means for units to be temperate. We then have to determine how to train units to habituate the virtue. Finally, if unit temperance, like other virtues, is the golden mean between two vices, what should we say about a unit with too much temperance?

What Happened

On the morning of November 19, 2005, a thirteen-man squad mounted in four Humvees turned a corner and—boom!—the fourth Humvee in the column disappeared in a red flash and a thick cloud of smoke and dust. A

com/2012/01/28/us/an-iraqi-massacre-a-light-sentence-and-a-question-of-military-justice.html.

39 See J. Joyner, "Why We Should Be Glad the Haditha Massacre Marine Got No Jail Time," *The Atlantic*, January 25, 2012, https://www.theatlantic.com/international/archive/2012/01/why-we-should-be-glad-the-haditha-massacre-marine-got-no-jail-time/251993/; C. Savage and E. Bumiller, "An Iraqi Massacre, a Light Sentence and a Question of Military Justice," *The New York Times*, January 27, 2012, http://www.nytimes.com/2012/01/28/us/an-iraqi-massacre-a-light-sentence-and-a-question-of-military-justice.html; N. Helms and H. Faraj, *No Time for Truth: The Haditha Incident and the Search for Justice* (New York: Arcade Publishing, 2016), 327–31.

40 Bing West, "The Road to Haditha," *The Atlantic*, October 2006. https://www.theatlantic.com/magazine/archive/2006/10/the-road-to-haditha/305230/.

popular lance corporal, Miguel "T.J." Terrazas, was killed—ripped apart—and two other Marines were badly burned. Back at battalion headquarters, streaming video from an Unmanned Aerial Vehicle circling overhead showed a confused situation, with Marines at various locations maneuvering amid radio chatter indicating incoming fire. The remaining ten men in Terrazas's squad approached a car that had stopped nearby. When the five men inside started to flee, the Marines shot and killed them. The platoon leader later reported that his men took fire from a nearby house. They assaulted first one house, and then a second. When the battle was over, fourteen Iraqi men, four women, and six children had been killed. [41]

No one in the unit had any idea that the world for so many that day would be shattered. The day began like so many others in Iraq: wake-up, PT, orders brief, rehearsals, pre-combat checks, etc. Each Marine knew that there could be enemy contact; intel had indicated as much. But, this mission was supposed to be more innocuous – resupply an outpost and return to the forward operating base (FOB).

Nevertheless, the background leading up to the affair is almost as complicated as the actual events on 19 November. The operating environment that Battalion 3/1 took over in Haditha in 2005 was hotly contested. The prior unit, Battalion 3/25, had lost many Marines during their tour. Furthermore, many of the 3/1 Marines were veterans of the Second Battle of Fallujah. During that prior fight, as West notes, "ten battalions fought block to block in a ferocious urban slugfest. The deeper the Marines penetrated into the city, the fewer civilians they encountered and the tougher the fighting became, with jihadists hiding among the 30,000 buildings, waiting to kill the first American to open the door."[42] For Battalion 3/1, the fighting in this second battle for Fallujah was so fierce and up close, that 'reporters referred to the ROE (rules of engagement) as "Enter every room with a boom."'

It would be too simple to blame the ROE. ROE is designed as a set of rules intended to clearly outline for soldiers and Marines guidance as to the amount of force and permitted targets to ensure that they can successfully accomplish the mission.[43] ROE helps contextually quantify *in bello* discrimination and proportionality for each mission. It is contextual, as there may by theatre specific ROE, unit ROE, or even ROE for a specific area or mission.

---

41 West, "The Road to Haditha." See also Joyner (2012); Savage and Bumiller (2012); McGirk (2006), Perry (2007), and Helms and Faraj (2016): 1–25.

42 West, "The Road to Haditha."

43 *Joint Pub. 1-02, Dictionary of Military and Associated Terms* defines ROE as "directives issued by competent military authority that delineate the circumstances and limitations under which U.S. [naval, ground, and air] forces will initiate and/or continue combat

In terms of tactical tasks, the ROE for house clearing, as was noted in Fallujah, is different, in this case less restrictive, than the ROE for a cordon and search. In any situation, it is never permitted to intentionally kill civilians, but in Fallujah, after the civilians had mostly fled, the unit's standard operating procedure (SOP) was to throw "in fragmentation grenades and [enter] with blasts of M-16 fire," according to the platoon commander, Lt Max Frank.[44]

Haditha, nevertheless, was not Fallujah. Normal operations in Haditha demanded more restraint – more temperate restraint. Entering a house in Haditha for a cordon and search meant that the Marines should expect civilians, and they developed tactics, techniques, and procedures for entering a house with civilians present, all the while prepared for a possible enemy attack.

Why it May Have Happened

So, which approach and which engagement rules were applicable on November 19? The legal debate certainly centered on this question. However, our task is to look deeper beyond the law to ask what ought to have been expected from a temperate unit in this situation.

If sorting which approach (and ROE?) was necessary and permitted sounds nearly impossible, especially when the same two approaches could be used in the same operating area, one could harken back to Krulak's 'Three Block War' for some insight. In his "The Strategic Corporal: Leadership in the Three Block War,"[45] General Krulak argued that Marines "may be confronted by the entire spectrum of tactical challenges in the span of a few hours and within the space of three contiguous city blocks." In other words, Marines might have to provide school supplies to children on one block, search a civilian home for contraband or intelligence on another, then assault a trained, entrenched

---

engagement with other forces encountered." As a practical matter, ROE serve three purposes: (1) provide guidance from the President and Secretary of Defense (SECDEF), as well as subordinate commanders, to deployed units on the use of force; (2) act as a control mechanism for the transition from peacetime to combat operations (war); and (3) provide a mechanism to facilitate planning. ROE provide a framework that encompasses national policy goals, mission requirements, and the law. (Chapter 5, "Rules of engagement," *Operational Law Handbook 2015*, International and Operational Law Department. The Judge Advocate General's Legal Center and School, Charlottesville, VA.)

44 Tony Perry, 2007. "Marine recalls scene of Haditha killings," *LA Times*, May 31, 2007, http://articles.latimes.com/2007/may/31/world/fg-abuse31.

45 Charles C. Krulak, "The Strategic Corporal: Leadership in the Three Block War," *Marines Magazine*, January 1999.

enemy, where the "fight will be increasingly hostile, lethal, and chaotic." Although Gen. Krulak did not discuss the Strategic Corporal in terms of temperance, he could have.

A unit should practice disciplined restraint in all operations, and this combat restraint will be exercised to different degrees depending on the mission, the threat, the presence of noncombatants, etc.[46] Even in the most extreme of circumstances, in close battle, temperate units must simultaneously and aggressively seek out and destroy the enemy, yet they must maintain control through disciplined initiative, discriminate targets, while judiciously and violently applying force.

Conceptually, the ideals of a temperate unit exercising combat restraint seems accurate and desirable. The presumption in the military is that well-trained, well-led units will be temperate. So, what happened in Haditha? Testifying under immunity during his videotaped deposition, "Lt. Max Frank, who had been ordered to take the bodies to the city morgue, said he assumed that the Marines had 'cleared' three houses of suspected insurgents according to their standing orders."[47] In addition, initial reports seemed to confirm this assumption of the events.[48] Brian Rooney, the battalion commander Lt. Col. Chessani's lawyer notes, "The myth of Haditha ... is that the men were hit by an IED, they went berserk, and because one of their brothers was killed they just decided to go into these homes and kill everybody they saw. The reality is that these men were hit by an IED, small-arms fire from both sides of the road ensued, and these men acted professionally, the way they were trained."[49]

"Even so," as associate professor James Joyner writes, "it's hard to write off the killing of a 76-year-old man in a wheelchair or the calm execution of six children huddled in a room as 'the fog of war.'"[50]

---

46 These are some of the mission variables unit commanders use to plan military operations. Army commanders "use the mission variables, in combination with the operational variables, to refine their understanding of the situation and to visualize, describe, and direct operations. The mission variables are mission, enemy, terrain and weather, troops and support available, time available, and civil considerations (METT-TC)." Department of the Army, *ADRP 5-0: The Operations Process*, Washington, DC, May 2012, paras 1–32, 1–7.

47 Tony Perry, "Marine recalls scene of Haditha killings," *LA Times*. May 31, 2007. http://articles.latimes.com/2007/may/31/world/fg-abuse31.

48 See Helms and Faraj (2016: x).

49 PBS.org. "Rules of Engagement: The Media Coverage of Haditha," Frontline, February 19, 2008. https://www.pbs.org/wgbh/pages/frontline/haditha/themes/media.html.

50 James Joyner, "Why We Should Be Glad the Haditha Massacre Marine Got No Jail Time." *The Atlantic*. January 25, 2012. https://www.theatlantic.com/international/

What Can We Learn?

What occurred that day in 2004 was certainly a tragedy. And, an enormous amount of effort was expended trying to ascertain what had happened and who was to blame. Just as important, nevertheless, is determining how to prevent incidents from this occurring or finding ways during the chaotic violence of war to minimize the harm suffered. Perhaps looking at the virtue of temperance, unpacking what it means for units to be temperate, for units to habituate temperance, and for units to exercise disciplined combat restraint may provide some answers or ways forward. A unit that acts from temperance, has habituated temperance, and acts in order to be temperate instantiates the virtue.

Much like the Strategic Corporal, the Marines on November 19 were trained to operate in the chaos that day. The Marine unit must be temperate and practice restraint when they have to provide school supplies to children on one block, search a civilian home for contraband or intelligence on another, then assault a trained, entrenched enemy. "The grunt must make instant," as Bing West reminds us, "difficult choices in the heat of battle. He must keep his honor clean and resist the sin of wrath when fighting an enemy who hides among compliant civilians."[51]

Further Questions to Consider

1. What does it mean to say that a unit is temperate? Was the Marine unit a temperate unit?
2. Were the actions of the squad intemperate? Were they overcome by raw emotion and desire for revenge?
3. If the 3/1 squad was by most accounts otherwise temperate, how should we account for the actions that day?
4. If temperance is a virtue we believe units ought to have, how should we train units to habituate the virtue?
5. In a way it seems clearer to point out examples of units being intemperate; they lack sufficient temperance. Nevertheless, if unit temperance, like other virtues, is the golden mean between two vices, what should we say about a unit with too much temperance?

---

archive/2012/01/why-we-should-be-glad-the-haditha-massacre-marine-got-no-jail-time/251993/.
51 West, "The Road to Haditha."

References

ADRP 5-0: The Operations Process. 2012. Department of the Army. Washington, DC. May 2012.

Ballantyne, I. *Killing the Bismarck.* Barnsley: Pen and Sword, 2011.

British Army. *The Values and Standards of the British Army.* Official Document, 2008.

Bury, P. *Callsign Hades.* London: Simon & Schuster, 2010.

Butler, D. *Field Marshal: The Life and Death of Erwin Rommel.* London: Casemate, 2015.

CBC News. "Evidence suggests Haditha killings deliberate: Pentagon source," August 2, 2006. http://www.cbc.ca/news/world/evidence-suggests-haditha-killings-deliberate-pentagon-source-1.576884.

Harding, T. "'Courageous restraint' putting troops lives at risk," *The Daily Telegraph,* July 6, 2010.

Harding, T. "Britain's top general in Afghanistan admits 'courageous restraint' must change," *The Daily Telegraph,* July 11, 2010.

Helms, N. R. and H. Faraj. *No Time for Truth: The Haditha Incident and the Search for Justice.* New York: Arcade Publishing, 2016.

Howard, M. and P. Paret (eds.) *On War.* Princeton, NJ: Princeton University Press, 1984.

JSP 383. Joint Service Manual of the Law of Armed Conflict. Shrivenham: Joint Doctrine and Concepts Centre, 2004.

Joyner, J. "Why We Should Be Glad the Haditha Massacre Marine Got No Jail Time." *The Atlantic.* January 25, 2012. https://www.theatlantic.com/international/archive/2012/01/why-we-should-be-glad-the-haditha-massacre-marine-got-no-jail-time/251993/.

Konnikova, M. *The Confidence Game: Why We Fall For It ... Every Time.* New York: Viking Penguin, 2017.

Krulak, C. C. "The Strategic Corporal: Leadership in the Three Block War," *Marines Magazine,* January 1999.

List, C. and P. Pettit. *Group Agency: The Possibility, Design, and Status of Corporate Agents.* New York: Oxford University Press, 2011.

Manchester, W. *American Caesar: Douglas MacArthur: 1880–1964.* New York: Black Bay, 2008.

McCormack, P. "Ethics: Military Judgement Panel," in *Leadership,* edited by Philip Deakin. Sandhurst Occasional Papers No 18. Sandhurst: The Royal Military Academy.

McGirk, T. "Collateral Damage or Civilian Massacre in Haditha?" *Time,* March 19, 2006, http://content.time.com/time/world/article/0,8599,1174649,00.html.

Messenger, C. (ed.) *The Art of War*. London: Greenhill, 1992.

Montgomery, Field Marshal. *The Path to Leadership*. London: Collins, 1961.

Montgomery, Field Marshal. *A History of Warfare*. London: Collins, 1968.

PBS.org. "Rules of Engagement: The Media Coverage of Haditha," Frontline, February 19, 2008. https://www.pbs.org/wgbh/pages/frontline/haditha/themes/media.html.

Perry, T. "Marine recalls scene of Haditha killings," *LA Times*. May 31, 2007. http://articles.latimes.com/2007/may/31/world/fg-abuse31.

Robinson, J. "Plato and the Virtues of Military Units," *Journal of Military Ethics* 13, no. 2 (2014): 190–202.

"Rules of Engagement," 2015. *Operational Law Handbook 2015*, International and Operational Law Department. The Judge Advocate General's Legal Center and School. Charlottesville, VA.

Savage, C. and E. Bumiller. "An Iraqi Massacre, a Light Sentence and a Question of Military Justice," *The New York Times*, January 27, 2012, http://www.nytimes.com/2012/01/28/us/an-iraqi-massacre-a-light-sentence-and-a-question-of-military-justice.html.

Searle, J. "Collective Intentions and Actions," in *Intentions in Communication*, edited by P. Cohen, J. Morgan, and M. E. Pollack. Cambridge, MA: Bradford Books, MIT Press, 1990.

Slim, Field Marshal Viscount, *Defeat into Victory*. London: Pan, 2009.

Steele, J. "Admiral with porn: Didn't know it was this much," *The San Diego Union-Tribune*. Last modified March 8, 2016, http://www.sandiegouniontribune.com/military/sdut-navy-admiral-porn-investigation-2016mar08-story.html.

Tangen, K. I. "The Need for Temperance: On Organizational Leadership and Temperance," *Scandinavian Journal for Leadership and Theology* 2, 2015.

Toner, J. H. "Temperance and the Profession of Arms," in *Morals Under the Gun*. Lexington: University of Kentucky Press, 2000, 125–42.

West, B. "The Road to Haditha," *The Atlantic*, October 2006. https://www.theatlantic.com/magazine/archive/2006/10/the-road-to-haditha/305230/.

Whitlock, C. and K. Uhrmacher. "Prostitutes, vacations and cash: The Navy officials 'Fat Leonard' took down," *The Washington Post*. Last modified March 26, 2018. https://www.washingtonpost.com/graphics/investigations/seducing-the-seventh-fleet/.

10

PATIENCE

Overview

Michael A. Flynn

As a professor of literature, my approach to philosophy is through philology, following the Continental school, to approach ideas as Nietzsche did, through language. So as I thought about writing an overview on the virtue of patience, to begin at the beginning for me was to turn to Aristotle's definition in his *Nicomachean Ethics*. As I looked over the book, I was a bit surprised when reminded that he classifies it as the moral virtue concerned with anger. J. A. K. Thomson translates Aristotle's original Greek πραότης[1] to 'patience,' the mean between 'what might be called a sort of irascibility, because the feeling is anger' and 'unirascibility,' one of the many words Aristotle invents to articulate an unnamed extreme on one end of the spectrum.[2] I remembered Aristotle's golden mean, of course

---

1   Aristotle, *Aristotelis Ethica Nicomachea*, edited by I. Bywater (Oxford: Oxford University Press, 1894), http://data.perseus.org/citations/urn:cts:greekLit:tlg0086.tlg010.perseus-grc1:1125b.30.

2   Aristotle, *The Nicomachean Ethics*, trans. J. A. K. Thomson, ed. Hugh Tredennick (New York: Penguin, 1986), 160. I should note that not all translators agree that πραότης translates to 'patience.' David Gross, for instance, translates the term to 'good temper' (96). But S. C. Woodhouse's authoritative *English-Greek* dictionary offers 'praotis' (πραότης), as one of the translations, along with 'gentleness' and 'meekness' (S. C. Woodhouse, *English-Greek Dictionary* (London: Routledge and Kegan Paul, 1971), 598), for 'patience.' Subsequent scant considering of patience as a virtue in moral philosophy from Augustine, Aquinas through Hume (see N. Bommarito, "Patience and Perspective," *Philosophy East and West*, 64, no. 2 (2014): 269 on this), calls to question whether this is exactly what Aristotle had in mind. However, most recent pedagogy and overviews of Aristotle's *Ethics* translates this mean to 'patience' (see M. Dimmock and A. Fisher, "Aristotelian Virtue Ethics," in *Ethics for A-Level* (Cambridge: Open Book Publishers, 2017), 53, for one example). So, on the authority of Woodhouse's translation and ethics texts of which that of Dimmock and Fisher is representative, and philosophic discussions such as that of Bommarito, and,

– that virtuous action lay in the middle of the two extremes – but my first thought was that he would have put patience in the middle of a different spectrum, one with 'rashness' on the one side, for instance, and 'lethargy' or 'apathy' on the other. But as I thought more about patience as a moral virtue in a military context, and as I read through the other contributions to this chapter, I began to see Aristotle's wisdom in considering patience in the context of anger.

In her case study for this chapter, Nikki Coleman praises Royal Australian Air Force (RAAF) pilots' patience for their refusal to drop bombs in air strikes when they judged that there was not a 'valid military reason,' but at the same time, in Aristotelian fashion, Coleman recognizes that too much patience in battle might be just as dangerous: "a fighting force which does not make a decision has its decision made for it by the opposing side." In Colonel James Cook's case study, the first anecdote tells of a British Royal Air Force Commander counseling patience to an ally whose anger had gotten the best of him and who suggested that the NATO Coalition in Kosovo consider targeting Milosevich's family, all civilians. Both cases show how crucial to one's dignity and humanity it is to check battlefield anger with the virtue of patience.

If anger then is the context for Aristotle's consideration of patience, Thomson's translation hits the mark: 'Irascible' stems from the Latin 'ira': "anger, wrath, rage."[3] The virtue of patience so conceived is the balance between two extremes; at one end is disproportionate wrath or rage when restraint is called for; at the other is failure to be angry when rightful indignation is called for. The patient man stands at the middle point between the enraged berserker and the docile coward.

I wonder whether Aristotle had in mind some of the foundational texts of Western literature that tell war stories of how their protagonists' troubles stem from failure to hold to the mean of patience between irascibility and unirascibility. I refer here to the *Iliad* and the *Odyssey*. In the *Iliad*, Achilles' character is undone when he fails to control his rage, and the Greeks suffer heavy losses when, to make sure that they feel more acutely his revenge, Achilles refuses to join them in battle against the Trojans. His rage brings disaster to both himself and to his comrades. In the *Odyssey*, most, if not all, of the scrapes Odysseus and his men get themselves into might have been avoided had they found the right balance of patience. But they never did. By the story's end, the entire fleet sinks, and every man except for Odysseus perishes.

---

finally, translators of such high standards for rigor such as Thomson and Tredennick, who revised Thomson's original, keeping "patience" as the translation for πραότης, I argue that "patience" approximates what Aristotle had in mind with this moral virtue.

3   "ire, n.," *Oxford English Dictionary*, Online. March 2018.

Now, by contrast, in my role as a naval officer, not as a professor of literature, I could write volumes on the virtue of patience – patience taken more broadly than I argue Aristotle takes it – in a contemporary military context. For instance, a conning officer when driving the ship must be patient for it to respond to a course change – over-correcting when it does not respond quickly enough can be disastrous. As an electronic intelligence collector, I waited hours for a searched-for emitter to light up, and sometimes waited almost half a day in vain. That tried my patience. 'Hurry up and wait' is a military cliché because it seems like sometimes that is all we do: hurry up to get somewhere and then wait interminably for orders on what to do next. And I have not yet met anyone who would prefer less hurrying and more waiting – the saying should probably be 'Hurry up and wait ... wait ... wait.' It also takes patience to wait for routine paperwork to get through the chain-of-command. No improvements in technology seem to speed that up. These days paperwork sits unnoticed or unheeded in someone's electronic inbox instead of sitting unnoticed or unheeded in his desk inbox, but it does not seem to make its way up and back down the chain any faster than it did before. Getting through a deployment, away from one's family for several months for over a year, again and again – that takes patience. Many said in Iraq that the days take forever, but the months fly by. For me, it all took forever. If any time flew by, it was the times that I missed watching my son grow from a one-year-old to a two-year-old. All those special moments flew right by, and it took patience to endure the loss. The quote from *Reef Points*, the book that the United States Naval Academy (USNA) plebes are supposed to memorize, the quote that everyone from my generation learned right away, and never forgot, is this one: "Just puttin' in time."[4] And that quote is not just easily memorized because it is the shortest one in the book, although that is why we all learn it first. It is memorable because it articulates a profound truth: stick it out; have the patience to endure; put in the time until your time comes; persevere, and you will get it done.

But all that is covering too much ground. Therefore, because an overview of this length cannot hope to do justice to the virtue of patience in war – the instances for its necessity too many, its importance impossible to overstate – I will consider the virtue in two of the most famous case studies in Western war literature: Homer's *Iliad* and *Odyssey*.

---

4   Clarence, qtd. in *Reef Points 1985–1986: The Annual Handbook of the Brigade of Midshipmen* (Annapolis: United States Naval Academy, 1985), 286. Attributed to someone named Clarence, although it is unclear if this is his first or last name.

The Virtue of Patience in the *Iliad*

One need look no farther than the first line of Peter Green's translation of the *Iliad* to see that irascibility is the main theme:

> Wrath, goddess, sing of Achilles Peleus's son's
> calamitous wrath, which hit the Achaians with countless ills –
> many the valiant souls it saw off down to Hades,
> souls of heroes, their selves left as carrion for dogs
> and all birds of prey, and the plan of Zeus fulfilled –
> from the first moment those two men parted in fury,
> Atreus's son, king of men, and the godlike Achilles.[5]

I choose Green's translation for this passage because his syntax matches Homer's, emphasizing 'wrath' twice, first by opening the poem with it, next as an enjambment onto the second line ('calamitous wrath'), and his wording conveys the ambiguity of the Greek original, suggesting that the wrath was both self-destructive and harmful to his comrades. Notice that, paradoxically, Homer does not mention any harm Achilles' wrath did to the Trojans, his enemies, the purported objects of his fury – rather, Homer only asks the muse to help him sing of how Achilles' rage hurts both his friends and himself.

That Achilles' irascibility hurts his friends is at the center of the plot, and easy to see. His anger at Agamemnon's robbing him of his war prize is out of all proportion with what is called for. If Aristotle's patient man is "unperturbed and not led by passion, but to be angry in the manner, at the things, and for the length of time, that the rule dictates,"[6] Achilles fails on all these counts. To begin, nothing less than divine intervention – Athena's descending from Olympus, holding "him back by his long red hair"[7] – keeps him from yielding to his temper, pushing through the crowd to murder Agamemnon, the Greek army's commander-in-chief. Not only does Achilles withdraw from the fighting, prophesying that he will be missed "while many are falling and dying before bloodthirsty Hector,"[8] but he also convinces his mother to beg Zeus to "help the Trojans drive the Achaians [Greeks] back to their ships with slaughter!"[9] Here his rage drives him to what many would consider treason – planning the death and injury of his own people.

---

5   Homer, *The Iliad*, trans. Peter Green (Oakland, CA: The University of California Press, 2015), 1:1–7.

6   Aristotle, *The Nicomachean Ethics*, trans. David Ross, eds. J. L. Ackrill and J. O. Urmson (New York: Oxford University Press, 1980), 97.

7   Homer, *The Iliad*, trans. W. H. D. Rouse (New York: Penguin Books, 1995), 15.

8   Homer, *The Iliad*.

9   Homer, *The Iliad*, 18.

Nor is his disproportionate rage assuaged with time. Phoinix, a Greek emissary sent to persuade Achilles to join the fight, points out that not even gods hold a grudge as long: "Come, Achilles, tame that awful temper! You must not let your heart be hard. Even the gods can be moved and they are greater than you in excellence and honour and might. They can be turned by the supplication of mankind ... ."[10] It is not until the Greek army is pushed back to their ships, the fleet almost burned by the Trojans, and Patrocles, Achilles' best friend, is killed by Hector, that Achilles is moved to join the fight again. Achilles is not moved, however, by loyalty or by duty to his fellow Achaeans. Only rage at his friend's death moved him to join the fight.

At this point in the epic it becomes more apparent how Achilles' irascibility hurts not only others but himself, damage that is not so easy to see perhaps on first reading. Here Jonathan Shay's interpretation enlightens.[11] Shay reads the *Iliad* as the tragedy of Achilles, as the story of a warrior who at the beginning was a paragon of moral virtue, but whose character and humanity deteriorated by the end due to moral injury and combat trauma. At the poem's opening, while still a paragon of virtue, Achilles has a reputation for showing mercy to defeated soldiers, granting quarter when asked, sparing their lives. By the end of the narrative, in contrast, he will not hear of it, as he states: "Before Patrocles met his doom, mercy was rather more to my mind; I took many Trojans alive and sold them. But now not one shall escape death of all that God puts into my hands."[12] Shay points out how Hector's wife Andromache, of all people, praised Achilles' past mercy and reverence for the dead, in that he followed all funeral decorum in rendering honors. Not so anymore. After defeating Hector, Achilles disgraces himself by dragging Hector's body around the city, then sequestering the cadaver, refusing burial or honors. Apollo's indictment of Achilles' debased character is unflinching: "That abominable Achilles ... has no sense of decency, no mercy in his mind! Savage as a lion, which is the slave of his strength and furious temper ... like him Achilles has lost all pity; he has in him none of that shame which does great good to men as well as harm."[13]

Achilles' rage persists until Hector's father, Priam, goes into the Greek camp to plead for Hector's body so that he might be properly interred; in one of the most moving scenes in the poem, in a supreme demonstration

---

10   Homer, *The Iliad*, 112.
11   Jonathan Shay, *Achilles in Vietnam: Combat Trauma and the Undoing of Character* (New York: Scribner, 1994).
12   Shay, *Achilles in Vietnam*, 246.
13   Shay, *Achilles in Vietnam*, 283.

of what Aristotle's conception of patience in his *Ethics* (control of anger and emotion when circumstances call for it), Priam "came near Achilles and clasped his knees, and kissed the terrible murderous hands which had killed so many of his sons."[14]

Wrath subsided, Achilles is brought back into the community, and decorum is restored to some extent with a funeral for Patrocles and a series of ceremonial games, and Achilles' restores balance in his exercise of the virtue. He will return to the fight when called upon, but not out of rage, and even in full knowledge that his fate decrees that he will perish there – he is a hero after all. But that return to battle and even the Greek victory in the end will not atone for the damage to the Greek army and to his own character that might have been prevented had Achilles exercised patience, had he found the golden mean between irascibility and 'unirascibility.'

The Virtue of Patience in the *Odyssey*

Throughout his story Odysseus vacillates between irascibility and unirascibility, the two extremes on either side of the virtue of patience, only perhaps finding a balance when he regains his footing on his return to Ithaca and victory over the suitors, after having made all his mistakes over a decade of wanderings and missteps. But before that almost every scrape he and his men get themselves into can be attributed to botched patience.

To begin, when Homer picks up the thread of Odysseus' return journey, we find Odysseus preparing to leave the divine seductress Calypso's remote island, where he has been dawdling a full seven years! To be fair, Calypso was reputedly worth a detour or two: she was divine, a 'looker,' insatiable, and a great cook to boot. Despite all that, Odysseus admits that she was nothing more than a dalliance: "But they [Calypso and Circe, another of his dalliances] never won the heart inside me, never / So nothing is as sweet as a man's own country, / his own parents, even though he's settled down in some luxurious house, off in a foreign land / and far from those who bore him."[15] By his own admission, Odysseus did not even have the excuse that he had fallen head-over-heels for Calypso. He had long since grown tired of her, and for many years longed fervently for his wife. When Hermes visits the island to tell Calypso that Zeus has ordered Odysseus' liberty, Hermes finds him thus: "Off he sat on a headland, weeping there as always, / wrenching his heart with sobs and groans and anguish, / gazing out over the barren sea through blinding tears."[16]

14 Shay, *Achilles in Vietnam*, 291.
15 Homer, *The Odyssey*, trans. Robert Fagles (New York: Penguin Classics, 1999), 9:37–40.
16 Homer, *The Odyssey*, 5:93–95.

While this yearning for home and wife partially acquits him of rank philandering, it does not acquit him of failing to muster enough justified indignation during his seven-year imprisonment to demand release. If he is, in fact, as he claims, "known to the world / for every kind of craft – my fame has reached the skies,"[17] and his claim is not pure bluster – Athena, the goddess of strategy, repeatedly praises him for his cunning and ingenuity – then he certainly would have had it in his power to dupe Calypso into sending him on his way. But he did not do it. With Calypso he found himself on the other, lethargic extreme of the patience spectrum.

His recount of his adventures from this point on reads like a list of failures in exercising the virtue of patience. One of his early stops was in the land of the Lotus-eaters, users of a narcotic or hallucinogenic plant. There, his men who ate the fruit fell into an excess of patience: "Any crewmen who ate the lotus, the honey-sweet fruit, / lost all desire to send a message back, much less return, / their only wish to linger there with the Lotus-eaters, / grazing on lotus, all memory of the journey home / dissolved forever."[18]

In the subsequent adventure with the Cyclops, Odysseus' behavior shows him on the other end of the patience spectrum, rash and irascible. First, he insists on exploring the Cyclops' island even though there was no material need to do it because a good hunt had already replenished their food stores. Next, he insists on staying in the lair to set eyes on the giant even as his men plead with him to immediately flee with the goods they have just stolen. Even the Cyclops sees the rashness, questioning whether Odysseus and his men are "wandering rogues, who cast your lives like dice, and ravage other folk by sea?"[19] Having through cunning escaped the death trap in the giant's lair, a trap that his rashness put them in the first place, Odysseus and his men are still under attack as they row away, the Cyclops hurling giant boulders at their boats. Yet still Odysseus cannot control his irascibility: "again I began to taunt the Cyclops — men around me / trying to check me, calm me, left and right: / 'So headstrong – why? Why rile the beast again?'."[20] Odysseus taunts more; his men try to stop him; the hurled rocks get closer to the boats; still he taunts: "So they begged / but they could not bring my fighting spirit round. / I called back with another burst of anger, 'Cyclops – / if any man on the face of the earth should ask you / who blinded you, shamed you so – say Odysseus, / raider of cities, he gouged out your eye.'"[21]

---

17 Homer, *The Odyssey*, 9:21–22.
18 Homer, *The Odyssey*, 9:106–10.
19 Homer, *The Odyssey*, trans. Robert Fitzgerald (New York: Vintage Classics, 1990), 9:272.
20 Homer, *The Odyssey*, trans. Robert Fagles (New York: Penguin Classics, 1999), 9:548–50.
21 Homer, *The Odyssey*, 9:556–60.

Odysseus' failure to suppress this last boast will cost them all dearly. Cyclops prays to his father, Poseidon, god of the sea, to punish Odysseus, and Poseidon assents, planning to forever prevent Odysseus' returning home. Poseidon is only forced to relent ten years later when the other gods intervene. Thus, due to his ill temper, his irascibility, Odysseus' homecoming will be delayed an entire decade, and his entire fleet of twelve ships, and every man except himself, will perish on the trip. In terms of lives lost and strategic delays (if one believes Odysseus' version of the events, but Homer offers no other account), his loss of patience at this moment is his most disastrous military blunder in the whole Trojan campaign!

He was not the only one to make others suffer because of loss of patience. At one point he and his men, borne by a west wind that master-of-all-winds Aeolus had made sure would exclusively blow because he gave Odysseus a magic bag that contained and thus suppressed the winds blowing from all the other directions, were so close to making it home that they had their own land of Ithaca in sight. But Odysseus' men, impatient, distrusting that the bag contained only winds and not some booty Odysseus had but was not yet sharing, opened the bag while Odysseus dozed. The winds were released and blew them all the way back to the Aeolian islands.

After 11 of his 12 ships are destroyed by the Laestrygonians' harbor ambush, all the men killed and eaten, Odysseus' own ship, which survived because it was moored outside the harbor, makes it to the island of Circe, the witch, who turns men into swine. Odysseus defeats her magic and avoids this fate, saving his men and becoming her lover, but tarries too long – far too long: "And there we sat at ease, / day in, day out, till a year had run its course, / feasting on side of meat and drafts of heady wine."[22] His men's pleading finally rouses him from his lethargy: "'Captain, this is madness! / High time you thought of your own home at last, / if it really is your fate to make it back alive / and reach your well-built house and native land.'"[23]

Overcoming the excess of patience that kept them on Circe's island, they set off, and make it through quite a few more perilous scrapes, but a deficiency of patience seals their fate. Tired and worn out, they would not brook his warnings follow Circe's advice ("for there she said was our greatest peril")[24] to steer clear of the Sun God's island to rest for the night. Once moored, they were kept there a month by a change in wind, and their ship's supplies ran out. Circe had warned them that eating the Sun God's sacred cattle was forbidden, but patience to forbear a hunt for the easy prey failed them, and they slaughtered the best of the herd, feasting for a week

22 Homer, *The Odyssey*, 10:514–16.
23 Homer, *The Odyssey*, 10:520–23.
24 Homer, *The Odyssey*, trans. Stanley Lombardo (London: Hackett Classics, 2000), 12:283.

until the winds changed. Zeus answered the Sun God's prayers to punish them by destroying their ship with a lightning bolt. All, save Odysseus, perish at sea.

When he arrives back home in Ithaca, one could argue that it is his final mastery of patience that saves his skin from the danger of over a hundred suitors who would all wish him dead, both because they want both his wife and his land, and because he failed to bring home any of their kinsmen under his command. He forebears revealing his identity even to his father and to his wife, endures countless indignities and insults from the suitors, who beat him and pelt him with objects in his own hall. Mastering himself to not fight back, to keep his temper in check and preserve his disguise, in the face of all these indignities, requires a great deal of patience. Only when he has laid careful plans for revenge does he reveal himself. But his mastery of patience here is only temporary. He soon yields to rage.

His slaughter of every last suitor is morally unjustified, even in his warrior culture, and out of all proportion. He killed over a hundred of Ithaca's best men. Morally indefensible too was his slaughter of the serving women who conspired with the suitors, especially after making them clean his hall floors of the suitors' gore. That the text indicts Odysseus on these counts is evident when it requires another act of divine intervention to assuage the suitors' families' desire for revenge. All of Ithaca shows up the next day, armed and ready to punish Odysseus for this slaughter, but Zeus intervenes, making Odysseus fulfill one more pilgrimage of atonement. Here, as with Achilles, just a little patience would have helped quite a bit.

Conclusion

Even in the Achaeans' ancient warrior culture, patience was a virtue.

If Homer's works can be read as imaginative renderings of real issues the soldiers struggle with in war, then these ancient epics are alive today in how they teach us that the virtue of patience is critical to both survival and well-being: in these works patience was not only critical for the preservation of dignity and character, which alone justifies cultivating patience, but for the preservation of life as well. Achilles' loss of patience almost cost the Greeks the war, and it certainly costs many of them their lives. His loss of patience cost him his moral character as well. Odysseus' and his crews' fluctuations from patient to impatient, from unirascible to irascible, never finding the mean until the end, cost each man, except for Odysseus, his life.

Case Study 1:
Patience

Nikki Coleman

In October 2014 it was reported in the Australian media that Royal Australian Air Force (RAAF) pilots had pulled out of the first RAAF air strikes on Islamic State militants in Iraq because of the risk to civilians.[25] The intended target of the attack had moved from an open position to an urban location, and the risk to civilians was deemed too high so the strike was aborted. At the time, the Australian Chief of Defence Forces, Air Marshal Mark Binskin argued that this was a part of a measured approach and a part of a long term strategy, stating "there shouldn't be a rush to get a weapon away just for the sake of getting a bomb away – that would be the wrong reason for doing this."[26]

Since World War II Australian pilots have demonstrated a wariness in the use of lethal force. One notable example was in the 2003 invasion of Iraq. The RAAF 75th Squadron was tasked with air operations as a part of Operation Falconer and Operation Iraqi Freedom. RAAF pilots were operating in a joint operating environment and were placed under U.S. field commanders, while still operating within the Australian chain of command. It was reported in the media that Australian RAAF pilots defied the orders of their American commanders on at least 40 occasions and refused to drop

---

25 Ian McPhedran, "RAAF mission against ISIS: Pilots did not drop bombs because of collateral damage risk," News.com.au, October 8, 2014, http://www.news.com.au/national/raaf-mission-against-isis-pilots-did-not-drop-bombs-because-of-collateral-damage-risk/news-story/01d32393c58d4b52a76dfd98a670e64f.

26 McPhedran, "RAAF mission against ISIS."

their bombs due to intelligence given at pre-flight briefings not concurring with the situation on site. Squadron Leader Daryl Pudney stated publicly that "pilots broke off many missions after they saw the target and decided there was not a valid military reason to drop their bombs."[27] Despite the potential to cause problems with the American commanders, the then Australian Chief of Defence Force, General Peter Cosgrove, "backed the pilots' action, and said there were no recriminations."[28]

These two cases highlight the virtue of patience in a military setting. Patience is by definition "the ability to wait, or to continue doing something despite difficulties, or to suffer without complaining or becoming annoyed."[29] There are many situations in the military where patience is required. At one end of the spectrum is the practice of waking new recruits in the middle of the night to prepare for some activity, only to leave them waiting for many hours; this practice is commonly known as 'hurry up and wait' and is sadly not only restricted to new recruit training. At the other end of the spectrum is the restraint needed so as to only target combatants in the battlespace. In fact, I would argue it is the patience required by the soldier, to only kill combatants, and to do so in a proportional manner, which is a central virtue of the honourable soldier.[30] Writers like Shannon French and Stephen Coleman have argued that "warriors are given a mandate by their society to take lives. But they must learn to take only certain lives in certain ways, at certain times, and for certain reasons" and that perhaps it is by examining "who they do *not* kill that we can most easily distinguish the warrior from the murderer."[31] I would argue that patience and the restraint that comes from that patience is what separates a soldier from a cold-blooded murderer. It is the patience and the restraint, much more than the uniform or the rank structure, which truly defines the soldier.

Similar to other virtues discussed in this book, there needs to be a balance struck between too much and too little of a virtue. With regard to patience, too much patience in the battlespace could be seen as being

---

27 F. Walker, "Our pilots refused to bomb 40 times," *Sydney Morning Herald*, March 14, 2004, https://www.smh.com.au/articles/2004/03/13/1078594618101.html.

28 Walker, "Our pilots refused to bomb 40 times."

29 *Cambridge Dictionary* online, https://dictionary.cambridge.org/. Accessed May 9, 2018.

30 For the purposes of this discussion I will be referring to all soldiers, sailors, airmen and women, enlisted as well as non-commissioned officers and also officers as soldiers. I do recognise that there are subtle differences between the different services and ranks in regards to this issue, but for the purposes of brevity and consistency I will be using the term soldiers to refer to all military personnel.

31 Shannon French, *The Code of the Warrior: Exploring Warrior Values Past and Present* (Lanham, MD: Rowman & Littlefield Publishers, 2003), 3; Stephen Coleman, *Military Ethics: An Introduction with Case Studies* (New York: Oxford University Press, 2013), 21.

indecisive or cowardly. A fighting force which does not make a decision has its decisions made for it by the opposing side. Soldiers from all levels, from the lowest Private to the highest General must make life and death decisions, and be willing to explain their actions should it be required. An indecisive commander can negatively impact not only the operational effectiveness of their soldiers, but also the cohesion and morale of the entire unit.

In the above case studies, imagine the unlikely situation where a target was not killed because a pilot decided at the last minute that they were not prepared to fire. While in this scenario it is clear that it was the right thing to not fire, there may have been a different situation where the target may have been the commander of enemy forces who later chose to bomb a school and hospital. The reluctance of the pilot to kill an enemy combatant may have had the unintended consequence of killing many thousands of civilians.

Just as having too much patience can have a negative impact on a situation, so too can too little patience. Too little patience with regard to pilots leads to reckless behaviour, putting not only their own soldiers' lives at risk, but also those of non-combatants, particularly civilians who can too easily become collateral damage in an urban fighting environment. Too little patience can also have a serious negative impact upon unit cohesion and morale, on the mental health of soldiers and can seriously damage the reputation of a nation's military. One such potential example is the RAAF bombing of a house in Mosul in May 2017 during the fight to liberate Mosul from IS.[32] Two internal RAAF investigations found that it is most likely that two adults were killed and two children injured in the attack. Although the civilians were not directly targeted, their deaths have had a negative impact on the Australian relationship with the Iraqi government, upon the reputation of the RAAF and their goal to achieve zero civilian casualties, and most likely a serious negative impact on the mental health of the pilot and those involved in the decision to drop the bomb on the house. I am not suggesting here that the death of the civilians was as a result of a lack of patience – it would be extremely difficult to tell if any airstrike is the result of impatience, but we can readily imagine how an impatient pilot might release a weapon in haste and can see the lamentable results that could occur. However, a lack of patience can result in these kinds of mistakes being made, with drastic consequences to the people killed, their families, the pilot, and those involved in the decision to target the house.

---

32 Andrew Greene, "Iraqi newlyweds feared killed by Australian airstrike on Mosul," *ABC News*, http://www.abc.net.au/news/2018-03-29/raaf-airstrike-likely-killed-newlywed-civilians-in-mosul-iraq/9598106, retrieved May 9, 2018.

It takes decades of training to become a jet pilot with the RAAF. After many months, sometimes years, of screening interviews, medicals and aptitude testing, a potential pilot must first pass through the rigorous 17-week officer training school course (or the three-to-four-year degree course at the Australian Defence Force Academy). After initial officer training pilots go on to train for many years, first in the basics of flying, progressively moving up to more advanced flying skills. The majority of this training is leading up to the moment when a pilot will be required to pull the trigger and drop a bomb on a target. There will always be pressure to 'go through with the mission,' partly because of the years of training leading to that point, but also because of the orders received from commanders as well as the impetus that pilots have to prove themselves worthy in battle. Given these pressures, it is remarkable that Australian pilots have, as mentioned earlier, on so many occasions chosen to not simply complete the mission, but to show restraint and patience instead. One thought is that the pilots were holding to the larger overall mission, that in order to defeat the Islamic State the goal of zero civilian casualties was essential, since it is virtually impossible to win the support, the 'hearts and minds' of the local civilian population if those who are attempting to liberate those civilians are killing them and their loved ones. This long-term view of the overall mission is again a demonstration of patience; using restraint and not hitting the target in front of the pilot is a part of the bigger strategic picture, needed in order to bring about an eventual end to the 'war on terror.'

There are many military virtues which help define the professional soldier, but I would argue that the virtue of patience is central to the culture of the honourable soldier; one who has fought valiantly, yet honourably, to allow us all to live with our enemies when the fighting is over.

Case Study 2: Patience

James L. Cook [33]

This case study might seem more like three case studies than just one because it plays out at three different times and with three different casts of characters. But linguistically it's a single study, a reflection on how military officers use the word patience and on the ways they freight the concept of patience with converging shades of meaning. I think of the three conversations below as being akin to three acts in the same play. The excellent overview on patience that introduces this chapter of the book offers us a comprehensive sense of what the virtue of patience can be in its many guises; I'll add only that for the purposes of this case study, patience has much to do with staying a course and awaiting the right time to act or change direction.

There is no way I can document the following unrecorded conversations except to say that I was a participant or listener in each.

Act 1: Acting Air Commodore B, British Royal Air Force, Counsels Patience

Scene: The Interim Deployable Combined Air Operations Center (IDCAOC), at Ramstein Airbase, Germany

In the run-up to the 78-day coalition air campaign over Kosovo in 1999,[34] optimists and pessimists vied with one another, but at least in airforce

---

33 Disclaimer: The views expressed in this case study are the author's opinions. They do not represent official positions of the United States' Air Force or Department of Defense.

34 For an overview, see Andrew J. Bacevich, and Eliot A. Cohen (eds.), *War over Kosovo: Politics and Strategy in a Global Age* (New York: Columbia University Press, 2002).

circles the optimists seemed to have had the upper hand. Coalition air operations against Saddam Hussein's Iraq eight years earlier had introduced high-tech weaponry that dazzled many an air planner's imagination. Fueled by complementary doctrine on centers of gravity and related ideas, air planners and operators waved away many a truism about the need for combined arms efforts to influence enemies and, more importantly, maintain an occupying presence in a situation such as Kosovo. That was the case in my unit at the time, the IDCAOC, which included British, Dutch, French, German, and U.S. members, not all of them airmen. A wonderful U.S. Army lieutenant colonel with a thick Boston accent constantly reminded us what boots on the ground could accomplish that overflights could not, and even among the airmen many years of professional education had bolstered that combined-arms orthodoxy. Still, optimism prevailed as air operations began.

The theory did make a kind of sense: Good intelligence and smart weapons could conceivably combine to convince Serbian president Slobodan Milošević that ongoing ethnic cleansing efforts victimizing primarily ethnic Albanians in Kosovo, who were almost all Muslim rather than Orthodox Christian like most Serbs, simply were not worth the pain that a committed coalition air force could inflict from an altitude that afforded almost complete immunity to Serbian countermeasures.

Days, then weeks went by, but Milošević did not yield. My little unit, still experimental as the first proto-NATO mobile CAOC (Combined Air Operations Centre), had thought it would run the air war but instead ended up deploying members to the existing CAOC at Vicenza, Italy, just across the Adriatic Sea from much of the fight. The senior officers back at Ramstein kept in close touch with the deployed members of our unit and the Vicenza CAOC leadership, often debating the course of operations.

Frustration mounted at Ramstein, no doubt a mirror of attitudes at Vicenza, until one day the senior officer from one of the European nations looked across the conference table and addressed the senior officer from the U.S., a colonel who had graduated from the U.S. Air Force Academy before flying A-10s and F-15s, and then working in important staff positions:

> You Americans can end this if you just make Milošević feel the pain of the air attacks. Right now he does not because he cares nothing at all for his people. You Americans should do exactly what you did to Saddam and his Baathists: Kill their families. Surely we can figure out where Milosevich's family members are hiding.

Without mentioning it, the officer was referring to the tragedy at Amiriyah, Iraq, where 408 non-combatants, some associated with high-ranking

Baathists, died in an air attack on the bunker where they were sheltering. The attacks were meant to destroy reported weapons caches.[35]

The pause in conversation was electric, with the senior officers looking slack-jawed at their European colleague, wondering if they had misheard. The European officer's earnest body language must have convinced them they had heard correctly, and they turned almost simultaneously to the American colonel. In his flight suit he resembled the stocky, self-confident intercollegiate wrestler he had been in his academy days.

The pause grew longer as the American waited a few beats to ensure the unit's leader, a British RAF group captain acting as an air commodore, didn't want to speak next. The RAF officer was peering so intently at his European colleague that it was natural to imagine he was about to intervene in the conversation. But the commodore held his peace and finally turned toward his American colleague. Satisfied the floor was his, the U.S. colonel said simply,

> That was an accident, my friend. The U.S. is like any other nation represented here: We never target civilians. Period. Of course we'll follow orders, whatever they are, but I think our national governments and military headquarters are unified in their position: We'll continue to service our targets while ensuring diplomatic lines stay open so Milošević can cave in without isolating himself. We don't need to change anything at our level; we just need to keep the faith.

At this point the air commodore turned back to the group at large. He echoed and then amplified the American's message in three words which, in my mind's ear, I still hear from time to time: "Patience, gentlemen. Patience." That was all he said during the entire meeting.

Sadly, the U.S. colonel's assertion that even high-tech air forces make mistakes was borne out a short time after the discussion at the IDCAOC. A U.S. B-2 took off from Whiteman air force base in Missouri, flew across the Atlantic, and dropped weapons with pinpoint accuracy … on the Chinese embassy in Belgrade. The U.S. apologized for the intelligence error, though scattered reports persisted that the attack had been intentional,[36] a way of signaling to the Chinese that their support of Milošević violated international norms. No one in my unit believed that, but our European colleagues justifiably criticized us Americans.

"This is a coalition operation," one of my Dutch friends reminded me, "so when anyone in the coalition makes a mistake it throws mud on

---

35 Scott Peterson, "'Smarter' Bombs Still Hit Civilians," *The Christian Science Monitor*, October 22, 2002. https://www.csmonitor.com/2002/1022/p01s01-wosc.html.

36 John Sweeney, Jens Holsoe, and Ed Vulliamy, "Nato Bombed Chinese Deliberately," *The Guardian*, October 16, 1999, https://www.theguardian.com/world/1999/oct/17/balkans.

all of us." He was frustrated not just because of the mistake but because he thought it had been avoidable. Throughout the operation, the CAOC at Vicenza had put out two air tasking orders (ATOs), the directives that choreograph daily air operations. One ATO governed almost all aircraft and was scrutinized by all the participating nations; the other ATO was a U.S.-only product that controlled stealth resources such as the F-117 and B-2, and did not get the same level of multinational scrutiny as the other ATO. My Dutch friend wasn't just criticizing the botched intelligence that had led to the attack on the Chinese embassy; he was criticizing what he saw as a cultural issue among his American colleagues. He didn't directly indict the U.S. decision to avoid possible leaks by shrinking the circle of stealth ATO reviewers. Rather, he renewed his focus on something he and I had already discussed on several occasions – what he perceived as a culturally-influenced desire for instant solutions on the part of Americans.

"Do you know why many in Europe think America is dangerous?" he asked me in one of these conversations. "It's because you have too much money, too many weapons, and too little patience. Strong nations are like strong people – they can get away with rushing. We've learned patience, and you need to do the same."

In the span of a few days I had heard eloquent appeals to patience from military officers serving Britain, the Netherlands, and the United States. It was easy to think that like other virtues, patience in the military thrives among the like-minded who keep themselves on the straight and narrow path of the just-war tradition and the Law of Armed Conflict in a way that one nation fighting alone might not manage.

Act 2: Major General N, Afghan National Army, Reflects on Artillery, Fighter Aircraft, Navies, and Patience

Scene: The headquarters of an ANA Post, May–December 2009

Major General N deserved a better interlocutor considering the important role he had played in the Northern Alliance as a fellow Tajik and intimate of Ahmad Shah Massoud. But somehow the general had ended up at this little post, far outside the august circle of officers at ANA headquarters. Perhaps he had never quite recovered from the Lion of Panjshir's tragic assassination just before September 11, 2001 and simply needed some time outside the fastest of lanes. In any case, as the most senior among his American advisors, I was the closest thing he had to Uncle Sam.

Major General N's backwater posting was my good fortune because it allowed me to hear this tried and tested warrior comment on any number of issues. A perennial lament in his repertoire: The NATO coalition was intent on holding back his beloved Afghanistan by relegating the ANA to the status of a large light infantry – 134,000 was the planning number at the time – with a few helicopters and perhaps some short airlift capability. He insisted that the ANA needed high-tech artillery, state-of-the-art fighter aircraft, and other items that would allow it to dominate the Taliban. He was at first hesitant to mention his worries about other regional powers, especially Pakistan, but these came more to the fore as his trust in me grew.

The general's views were not as extreme as they might have been. Some of his officers insisted privately that a unified Baluchistan, currently split between Afghanistan and Pakistan, was in fact a natural and therefore rightful part of Afghanistan; that all right-thinking Baluchis saw themselves as Afghans rather than Pakistanis; and that therefore the NATO coalition should work to unify Baluchistan and put it under the Kabul government's control. The final result would be that Afghanistan would have access to the Arabian Sea and would therefore need a navy, a very powerful navy.

The general was not willing to go that far, but he detested the idea of the ANA as a light infantry only.[37] His eyes would light up every time he recounted B-52 attacks at Tora Bora, which he had watched from a distance. "That is the kind of firepower we need," he'd say through his interpreter. "Otherwise, how will Afghanistan survive once you Americans and the others leave?" In these conversations, and as I reflected on them afterward, it was easy to recall David Lean's magnificent 1962 film *Lawrence of Arabia*, in which Peter O'Toole's Major T. E. Lawrence and Alec Guinness's Prince Faisal try in vain to convince colonialist Great Britain, embodied by General Allenby (Jack Hawkins) and Mr. Dryden (Claude Rains), to give the Arab irregulars the artillery that would help put them on a par with other armies of the era. In the film's telling, the overwhelmingly powerful British have no intention of sharing their best battlefield technologies. Britain's goal is to use the Arabs to help defeat the Ottoman Turks, and once that's done, well, the Arabs are on their own. That, I feared, was roughly Major General N's read of Afghanistan's relationship with the NATO-based coalition, though he never quite said as much.

---

37 In hindsight I wonder if such an experienced warrior foresaw the difference that simple technologies could make and therefore longed for the ANA to have a broader, more decisive edge. If both Taliban and ANA function as light infantry, perhaps something as simple as night-vision devices can prove decisive, q.v., Andrew E. Kramer, "Using Night-Vision Goggles, Taliban Stage Lethal Attack," *The New York Times*, February 20, 2018, https://www.nytimes.com/2018/02/20/world/asia/afghanistan-taliban-attack.html; Najim Rahim and Jawad Sukhanyar," Attacks in Afghanistan Leave Dozens Dead and 2 Schools Burned," *The New York Times*, April 15, 2018, https://www.nytimes.com/2018/04/15/world/asia/afghanistan-attacks-schools.html.

In this the general's thinking was perfectly consistent with that of his staff. Several months earlier one of his colonels had put it to me very succinctly in his own emphatic English: "Here we are everyone – Pashtuns like me, Tajiks, Hazaras, Uzbeks – everyone together! And if you leave, we kill each other tomorrow. Do you care enough to stay?"

In one of our last conversations shortly before I left Afghanistan, Major General N brought up the aircraft and artillery yet again, but then voiced his own coda: "I don't think it will happen. Even the Soviets gave us air conditioning, but not you." (He was referring to new, coalition-funded construction he and I had recently inspected several miles from his headquarters in the vicinity of an older building he proudly showed me. "Massoud would sneak down and sit right here, sometimes even stay overnight. The Taliban never figured it out." He couldn't show me more because the ordnance disposal teams had swept only a narrow walkway free of landmines, but it was clear the construction site visit amounted to a pilgrimage – to a holy place and to the general's prime as a warrior.) "No, I don't think we Afghans will be anything but men with rifles. But," and now he turned to me with fire in his eyes, "I have been in this situation before. The Taliban had everything, and we had nothing, but we waited. And we survived. And we won. The key is patience, always patience."

A few years later I was back at my academic post at a U.S. service academy, happily reading and teaching my usual fare, heavy on ancient and continental philosophy. "Discipline," writes French professor Frédéric Gros, "is the impossible conquered by the obstinate repetition of the possible."[38] If Gros is correct, I mused, then perhaps patience is obstinacy pure, always enduring whether it conquers or not. I thought of Major General N, now thousands of miles away.

Act 3: Lieutenant T touts an Afghan Suicide Bomber

Scene: Under Camouflage Netting on a Coalition Post, Mid-September 2009

"Can't no nine women have they selves no damn' baby in one damn' month. No way that sh*t's gonna happen!"

That's an approximation of the way Lieutenant MoMo T, U.S. Navy, really talked. A better visual impression would be to take out the spaces between words and add more emphatic, piquant qualifiers, since everything he said came out as one continuous, profanity-laced stream, as though it were a

---

38   Frédéric Gros, *A Philosophy of Walking*, tr. John Howe (London: Verso, 2014), 159.

single long word surfing along its own bayou diphthongs. It took a little practice to understand him, but it was worthwhile because the man was extremely smart and very experienced. He had started in the enlisted ranks and decided to become an officer only very late in his career. He was the only naval officer in our mixed unit comprising mostly U.S. Army but also some U.S. Air Force members. Together we spent most of our days with the Afghan National Army or on the roads.

When we REMFs[39] decided we deserved a Coke and a cigar after a sufficient number of convoys and other time outside the wire, we'd sit under the camouflage netting, drink Cokes and bottles of water from Qatar (because, we were told, there was no company in Afghanistan capable of bottling water in sanitary fashion in the volume we required), smoke what I'm told were Cuban cigars if we were smokers, and stare thoughtfully at the Chinese underwear tag taped to the pole of the umbrella hovering over our precious picnic table.

I was well out of the blast radius when the tag's owner blew up his vehicle and his underwear – I merely felt the tremor and heard the boom. But our sleeping area was next to the detonation site, and the ground near our picnic table was sprinkled with bits and pieces of vehicle and driver. Someone had decided to memorialize the event, and as it turned out the suicide bomber too, by scissoring off the underwear tag, which was somehow intact and visible, and taping it to the umbrella pole.

MoMo's pregnancy metaphor responded to an army colleague who'd insisted the suicide bomber had died for nothing. After all, the lieutenant colonel said, the U.S. was surging troops into Afghanistan to recoup progress lost following the March 2003 invasion of Iraq, when resources flowed out of Afghanistan and into the new theater. With now rapidly expanding resources, the coalition wouldn't be deterred by a few suicide bombers; the surge would roll over the Taliban and other opponents of the Afghan government in Kabul. It was 2009, and optimists such as the lieutenant colonel were buoyant.

MoMo disagreed. His point was that historical events have lives and timelines of their own; increasing resources – throwing money and manpower at a problem in the short term – won't always result in success. Human gestation usually requires a single pregnancy of nine months duration, so only a fool would think nine women could have a baby in a month. MoMo was convinced that his notoriously impatient homeland would lavish resources on the fight in Afghanistan for a year or maybe two. But could the U.S. stay the course for as long as it would take to change

---

39 An acronym Lieutenant T embraced with great enthusiasm. See http://www.oed.com/.

Afghan culture and end the ethnic rivalries at the war's heart? Could American culture stomach a long-term presence in a developing nation, especially with even sporadic U.S. casualties? He didn't think so. Therefore, he said, the previous owner of the underwear tag was a patriot and a hero who'd given his life for a future whose details we couldn't foresee. We could only know that it wouldn't be an American future, or a NATO future, or a future driven by Pakistan, India, Turkey, or any other country that seemed to be vying for influence; it would be some sort of Afghan future. The suicide bomber and his compatriots would inevitably win.

It was one of those units that gathers in smelly tents to watch movies every week or so, and as luck would have it, a couple weeks later *We Were Soldiers*, Mel Gibson's 2002 film. appeared hand-written with chalk on the nearest ersatz marquee, a HESCO barrier. I glanced over at MoMo during the final scene, when the North Vietnamese colonel, who had lost at Ia Drang, thoughtfully removes and then restores a tiny American flag left at the battlefield. The moral is clear: We've lost the battle but will win the war through our superior patience.

I glanced over to catch MoMo's eye, but he had fallen into what appeared to be a peaceful sleep.

Epilogue

The acting air commodore who had stilled an uncomfortable debate among his senior pilots-turned-campaign planners with just three words – "Patience, gentlemen. Patience" – retired to Surrey.

Last I knew, Major General N had returned to his native Badakhshan province, in which the Taliban and sundry jihadists have become more active than ever.

MoMo retired as a lieutenant from the U.S. Navy and went home to his native Louisiana, where he's raising children as a single father.

References

Aristotle. *Aristotelis Ethica Nicomachea*, edited by I. Bywater. Oxford: Oxford University Press, 1894. Available at http://data.perseus.org/citations/urn:cts:greekLit:tlg0086.tlg010.perseus-grc1:1125b.30. Accessed 24 May 24, 2018.

Aristotle. *The Nicomachean Ethics*, edited by J. L. Ackrill and J. O. Urmson, translated by David Ross, New York: Oxford University Press, 1980.

Aristotle. *Ethics*, edited by Hugh Tredennick, translated by J. A. K. Thomson. New York: Penguin Books, 1986.

Bacevich, A. J. and E. A. Cohen (eds.), *War over Kosovo: Politics and Strategy in a Global Age*. New York: Columbia University Press, 2002.

Bommarito, N. "Patience and Perspective," *Philosophy East and West*, 64, no. 2 (2014): 269–86.

Coleman, N. "Patience," in *Military Virtues*, Chapter 10, this volume.

Coleman S. *Military Ethics: An Introduction with Case Studies*. New York: Oxford University Press, 2013.

Cook, J. "Patience, " Chapter 10, this volume.

Dimmock, M. and Fisher, A. "Aristotelian Virtue Ethics," in *Ethics for A-Level*. Cambridge: Open Book Publishers, 2017.

French S. *The Code of the Warrior: Exploring Warrior Values Past and Present*. Lanham, MD: Rowman & Littlefield Publishers, 2003.

Greene, A. "Iraqi newlyweds feared killed by Australian airstrike on Mosul," *ABC News*. Retrieved May 9, 2018, http://www.abc.net.au/news/2018-03-29/raaf-airstrike-likely-killed-newlywed-civilians-in-mosul-iraq/9598106.

Gros, F. *A Philosophy of Walking*, trans. J. Howe. London: Verso, 2014, 159.

Homer. *The Odyssey*, translated by Robert Fitzgerald. New York: Vintage Classics, 1990.

Homer. *The Iliad*, translated by W. H. D. Rouse. Mentor. New York: Penguin Books, 1995.

Homer. *The Iliad*, translated by Stanley Lombardo. Indianapolis, IN: Hackett, 1997.

Homer. *The Odyssey*, translated by Robert Fagles. New York: Penguin Classics, 1999.

Homer. *The Odyssey*, translated by Stanley Lombardo. London: Hackett Classics, 2000.

Homer. *The Iliad*, translated by Peter Green. Oakland, CA: The University of California Press, 2015.

Kramer, A. E. "Using Night-Vision Goggles, Taliban Stage Lethal Attack," *The New York Times*, 20 February 2018, https://www.nytimes.com/2018/02/20/world/asia/afghanistan-taliban-attack.html.

McPhedran, I. "RAAF mission against ISIS: Pilots did not drop bombs because of collateral damage risk," *News.com.au*, October 8, 2014, http://www.news.com.au/national/raaf-mission-against-isis-pilots-did-not-drop-bombs-because-of-collateral-damage-risk/news-story/01d32393c58d4b52a76dfd98a670e64f.

Peterson, S. "'Smarter' Bombs Still Hit Civilians," *The Christian Science Monitor*, October 22, 2002, https://www.csmonitor.com/2002/1022/p01s01-wosc.html.

Rahim, N. and J. Sukhanyar, "Attacks in Afghanistan Leave Dozens Dead and 2 Schools Burned," *The New York Times*, April 15, 2018, https://www.nytimes.com/2018/04/15/world/asia/afghanistan-attacks-schools.html.

Shay, J. *Achilles in Vietnam: Combat Trauma and the Undoing of Character*. New York: Scribner, 1994.

Sweeney, J., J. Holsoe. and E. Vulliamy. "Nato Bombed Chinese Deliberately," *The Guardian*, October 16, 1999, https://www.theguardian.com/world/1999/oct/17/balkans.

Walker, F. "Our pilots refused to bomb 40 times," *Sydney Morning Herald*. Sydney: Fairfax Publishing. March 14, 2004, https://www.smh.com.au/articles/2004/03/13/1078594618101.html.

Woodhouse, S. C. "Patience." *English-Greek Dictionary*. London: Routledge and Kegan Paul, 1971.

11

HUMILITY

Overview

Michael Skerker

Scholars disagree about the precise definition and application of some virtues, but rarely disagree about whether a trait *is* a virtue. People differ regarding how much self-control is appropriate with respect to bodily pleasures or whether physical courage is as central a virtue as was once thought, but all agree that some self-control is necessary and that one sometimes has to face one's fears. No one advocates embracing folly or injustice. Yet humility has had to fight for a place on the standard list of virtues. It was commonly thought a vice in the ancient Greco-Roman world and among European scholars in the Enlightenment period, but is considered the 'mother of all virtues' by many Christians. It is only in recent decades that secular authors have tried to rehabilitate humility and challenge its negative characterizations. After considering what lessons military leaders can draw from critiques of humility, we will consider how humility can protect military leaders from the moral hazards of the military profession. The definition of humility used in this overview is a trait guarding against an over-estimation of what one is entitled to enjoy as a consequence of one's genuine virtues and accomplishments.

Humility was chiefly championed in the West by Jewish and Christian thinkers. They argued that it was necessary to view oneself as lowly in comparison to God, and – particularly for Christians – following consideration of the scope of one's sins. These sins were grave even for relatively pious people, who, according to St. Augustine and his intellectual heirs, inherited a moral disease from Adam and Eve, disposing all but those specially graced by God to love themselves inordinately and desire inwardly that they be regarded as gods. This pride is the original and persistent sin that turns even the relatively good person away from God, as she secretly does good deeds in order to magnify her own reputation or earn salvation without divine assistance. By contrast, humility is a product of the proper realignment of the will toward God. Seeing the gulf between herself and God, the humble person grasps the folly of her insubordinate instincts.

Yet a good person who was meek, subservient, highly self-critical, and disinclined to accept moderate praise would seem like a bizarre model of praise to an ancient thinker like Aristotle. Arrogance was a vice, but *megalopsychia*, variously translated as magnanimity or pride, was considered the crown of the virtues. The arrogant man irrationally demands respect in excess of his achievements and virtues. By contrast, the proud man has the full complement of virtues he needs to lead a flourishing life in a well-ordered city and, as a wise person, has a rationally-appropriate assessment of his own character. One aspect of being a great person is self-knowledge of one's stature and the expectation of appropriate social recognition from one's peers. There would be something deficient about a person who did not appreciate his own worth – what else might he be capable of misjudging? Further, there would be something unseemly about a great person who did not see himself worthy of honors. Is he too shy to withstand such attention? While modern readers tend to dismiss this part of Aristotle's prescription of the moral life as being a cultural blindspot – we would think ill of a good person who demands constant applause – we can agree that there is something 'off' about the good person who constantly denigrates himself. We might wonder if he has low self-esteem as a result of a tough childhood or if he is slyly arrogant, fishing for compliments by bemoaning his minor flaws.

A sufficiently-modified, healthy Aristotelian pride would seem particularly important for military leaders. First, it would simply seem bizarre to express uncertainty about one's technical competence and military responsibilities given that service personnel are constantly ranked according to objective metrics and the responsibilities of rank and specialization are clearly delineated. Second, officers and senior enlisted must insist on military courtesies appropriate to their rank in order to ensure good order and discipline. Third, a leader who issues an order but then engages in self-flagellation detailing his short-comings and uncertainties will erode his subordinates' confidence in his orders. Fourth, and relatedly, a leader with the better moral or tactical idea needs to have self-confidence in order to express and defend their views against counter-proposals. It will not do to fold in the face of criticism, especially if that criticism is fueled by disrespect. Fifth, as in ancient Athens, the proud military leader's demand for appropriate recognition for his accomplishments plays a socially beneficial role. In any kind of social group, people will seek to emulate those who are praised and glorified. It is therefore vital that genuinely good people be praised rather than incompetent poseurs. Finally, a leader unable to recognize their own strengths may not to be able to accurately judge subordinates' strengths and weaknesses.

It was in part the re-discovery of Greco-Roman authors that led thinkers during the Enlightenment to write about human nature in more positive terms. Scholars in this period often criticized humility as a 'monkish' legacy of the Dark Ages, ill-suited to democracies. The subservience and self-abnegation that some religious forms of humility seemed to require was at odds with the confident, autonomous, mercantile, liberty-loving populace needed to support those continents' potential democracies.

This critique of humility offers more mixed lessons for military leaders. Military leaders need to be obedient to their military and civilian superiors and must temporarily waive some of the rights the full enjoyment of which would make military service impossible. Service personnel cannot publicly criticize civilian politicians for instance, and must accept restrictions on their religious liberty, freedom of association, privacy, and so on. Yet they ought not to be subservient in the sense of abandoning their own moral sense. Rather, they must always critically evaluate their orders, assessing whether the orders must be refused because of their illegal nature, or should be respectfully challenged when they seem immoral, foolish, or wasteful. Again, leaders need self-confidence and self-respect to fight unjust practices or proposals.

Recently, humility has received renewed attention and praise from moral philosophers who construe it somewhat differently than medieval theologians. Some scholars suggest that humility is not a low opinion of one's self but a virtue that guards against an over-estimation of what one is entitled to enjoy as a consequence of one's genuine virtues and accomplishments. I will now turn to this contemporary construal of humility.

Current events suggest that military leaders may need this sort of humility to balance their healthy pride. Every year in the U.S., dozens of senior officers and enlisted personnel are dismissed, generally for one of four reasons: professional incompetence, alcoholism, financial misdeeds, or sexual indiscretions/crimes. These reasons are, presumably, afoot in senior leader terminations in other countries too. Mishaps with equipment can perhaps be expected to sometimes happen even under competent leadership, given the complexity and inherent danger of military operations, but personal indiscretions are surprising. Military leaders are usually smart and well-disciplined; they must have these traits in order to make it to the upper ranks. The social prestige and healthy salary they enjoy is an external indication of the value most leaders surely bestow on their own rank, having worked so hard to attain it. Finally, leaders know they are under a microscope, scrutinized both by their subordinates and the superiors who must assess their potential for promotion. That a senior leader would risk a hard-won career and social prestige in an environment of strict discipline and social surveillance for a $10,000 bribe, an hour with a prostitute, or a lewd proposition made to a subordinate, seems to reflect a flaw that runs right through self-control, judgment, and reasoning.

Hubris seems a reasonable diagnosis of the common flaw exposing leaders to obviously bad decisions. The hubristic person feels he deserves that exceptions be made for him and that he be granted special privileges. Aristotle's arrogant man thinks he deserves honors even though he is not morally worthy. The hubristic person might have many virtues and correctly judge that he deserves recognition for those virtues, but then also, that as a kind of reward, he need not observe the same moral or legal rules that apply to everyone else.

Poor military leaders may be incompetent, while others are cowardly, stupid, lazy, or cruel. Yet another could be a fine person, possibly expert at his operational specialization, an inspiring speaker, a friendly comrade, but wrong in thinking that he is therefore, morally special. He might reason that he does not need to fill out the expense reports like everyone else; it's OK if he enjoys the luxurious banquet the defense contractor holds for him. After all, in private industry, he would be making ten times what he is now. Why not pursue an affair with a subordinate? The military has sent him to the other side of the world for 15 months. What can they expect? Sure, he grasps the rationale for prohibitions on fraternization, but this relationship won't cloud *his* judgment. This hubristic leader might also not be such a nice person. Maybe he is the kind of toxic leader who 'eats his young,' seeing subordinates as merely existing to serve and magnify him, rather than identifying himself as the one to lead, protect, and promote them. Maybe he's the officer who drives his people to the limit, belittling and threatening them, and then blaming them for his own poor decisions. Maybe the hubristic leader is so arrogant that they refuse to listen to advice or countervailing information, or is so ferocious, that their subordinates fear to bring bad news until it is too late.

The more modern version of humility mentioned above is the corrective to this defective kind of pride. Theologians remind us that even the genuinely accomplished and relatively virtuous person will fall well short of the glory of the Lord and deserve no special treatment according to *that* exacting standard. Readers more comfortable in a human rights framework can consider that all people are of equal moral value. Everyone is still bound by the same moral rules demanding equal respect for all even if some are more virtuous or more accomplished than others. Winning a medal, achieving Admiral, or being good in some moral respect does not release us from one's duties to another. One might be due a higher salary, a commendation, a salute, but not worship, and there are never any moral 'holidays.' A leader may not treat subordinates cruelly or indifferently. A leader may not help himself to more money than the state *that has trained and promoted him* to that rank determined he should receive. A leader may not sexually exploit subordinates or their spouses.

How then to cultivate a kind of humility that allows for honest self-appraisal, a reasonable demand that one's opinions be heard and one's rank respected, yet avoids an over-estimation of what one's excellences deserve? First, one must recognize that one's traits and accomplishments are largely the accumulation of forces originating from outside oneself. Second, one must recall the sole purpose of one's power and expertise is to serve others.

Let us consider what makes people special. We call people special when they are able to do things their peers are unable to do. Whereas the average person's skills and traits can readily be traced to environment, parentage, and training, the special person seems to come from nowhere, to be 'uncreated' in a sense. After all, they markedly exceed the abilities or traits of their peers with the same school or training environment. Yet in reality, there are no magic people; everyone is a product of their upbringing, training, and opportunities. The special person looks ordinary in a different context.

The leader who wishes to guard against hubris should consider all those things which have led to the attainment of their current (perhaps genuinely) excellent standing. Let us start with the often neglected basics that anyone needs to acquire in order to prosper in a demanding career. First, the fact that the excellent leader is alive means that they have received inoculations from childhood diseases and have grown up in a safe and sufficiently prosperous area to make it to adulthood. Consider how many *billions* of people in the world lack those building blocks. The excellent leader either benefited from taxpayer-funded public education or parentally-funded private education, and their parents or guardians have provided sufficiently good moral examples to follow.

Second, consider what it takes to become an excellent military leader. Every one of a service member's excellent military-specific skills was instilled at taxpayer expense by instructors who evidently cared for their trainees. If one made it to leadership, then that individual probably avoided roadblocks set up by corrupt or harassing superiors. They were not passed over for chauvinistic, political, or nepotistic reasons, they probably lucked out by having a few great mentors who took the time to create contacts with the right people and who were advocates, giving that person the benefit of the doubt when things went wrong; and endowing all the intangible things necessary for promotion upon this fortunate person.

Contributing factors might also be a combat tour at the right time or indeed, the lack of a combat tour in a chaotic area of operations, in which a mishap might have derailed a promising career; a missed assignment into a hopelessly dysfunctional department that wrecked others' reputations; leave of absence on a night when everything went wrong.

Reflecting on these sorts of factors can remind one that her current accomplishments are not that person's alone. Who one is, is partly a result of one's own conscious efforts and partly the effect of other's actions and raw luck. Even if we focus on the part of one's personality that really seems one's own – the part that is not a reflection of a parent's or mentor's similar trait – it is still hard to say *that* is one's own. If one has really 'just always been this way,' one can hardly then take credit for the trait. It would be like a rich child taking credit for his inheritance.

The second ingredient for humility can be adapted from a line in the Talmud: "If you know much Torah, do not be proud, for you were made for this purpose. Go and teach." One should consider that the reason taxpayers paid for one's education and training, the reason mentors offered guidance, the reason the power and perquisites associated with rank accrued, is solely and strictly for the benefit of one's subordinates, and through them, the state for whom the military serves. If you are a great leader, this is not for your benefit, but wholly and completely for the people you lead.

Case Study 1: Humility

Rick Rubel

After serving in the U.S. Navy for 30 years, having two Commands, and teaching Ethical Leadership for 19 years, I firmly believe that humility is the most important virtue of a leader. I have seen too many leaders who are arrogant and self-righteous, and they are not just annoying, they are dangerous. They are dangerous because they think they know everything when clearly they don't. They make decisions based on the (false) assumption that they know everything and therefore do not need to ask for input from others.

To define *humility*, in this context, I would first like to profile the opposite of humility:

- Humility is the lack (or opposite) of arrogance and pridefulness
- Pridefulness does not mean lack of pride in our own achievements, our subordinates or children. I refer to C. S. Lewis in *Mere Christianity* (Chapter 7, "The Great Sin").[1] Lewis defines pridefulness as "Pride or Self-Conceit." This is when we look down on people because we think we are superior to them or because you may have advantages over them. Lewis suggests that if we are looking down on someone, we cannot look up
- Lewis also describes pridefulness as the root of greed and selfishness (note: selflessness is an importantly related virtue, to be discussed later)

---

1   C. S. Lewis, *Mere Christianity*, Chapter 7, "The Great Sin."

- The more we dislike pridefulness in others, the more we have it in ourselves.

I would profile humility then, as,

- Someone who is *selfless* – who puts their needs and desires after others
- Someone with a modest opinion of themselves, their rank, or position
- Someone who recognizes the probability that they do not have all the answers
- Someone who would admit that there are things they don't know.

But humility is not binary; in which you either have it or you don't. In Aristotelian terms, one can have the right amount of humility, or an excess or deficiency. One should aim for the 'mean' of this virtue. A deficiency of humility could come across as arrogance, but an excess of humility might appear to look like low self-esteem, timidity, or shyness. So, the mean would be to aim for 'the right amount.'

With those profiles of humility and arrogance, we can begin to see why humility is such an important virtue for a leader.

Humility and Selflessness

The connection between humility and *selflessness* is crucial when talking about the virtues of a leader. By the nature of military leadership, we have to serve. The term 'service' implies the act of helping or doing work for someone. Most research in moral development, including that conducted by Kohlberg,[2] holds that at the most basic, lowest level of moral decision-making is in fact, egocentric consideration ("What is best for me?"). These developmental models suggest that we have to learn a higher level of moral decision-making such as 'carrot and stick,' reward and punishment, then respect for rules. And then, at higher levels, moral decision-making based on social order, and respect for others and their rights. If this is true, we have to recognize that egoism is basically natural, and selflessness must be learned from our environment, and then practiced.

To help change this paradigm from our (egocentric) upbringing to our (selfless) military service, Col. Paul Rousch, USMC Ret., created a "Constitutional Paradigm."[3] This paradigm starts with the idea that,

---

2 Lawrence Kohlberg, "Stages of Moral Development," 1971.

3 Col. Paul Roush, USMC Ret., in *The Constitutional Paradigm: Ethics in the Military Profession*, ed. George Lucas and Rick Rubel (Upper Saddle River, NJ: Pearson Custom Publishing, 2014).

as military members, there are many entities to which we must be simultaneously loyal. In his 'priorities of loyalties' he suggests that we pre-prioritize these loyalties, so if we come into conflict between two of these, we have previously agreed to their prioritization and will follow the highest loyalty.

These loyalties are (from the top down):

CONSTITUTION – The oath we all take
MISSION – Our current orders
SERVICE – Our branch of the military
UNIT – Our command
SHIPMATE – Our comrades in arms
SELF- Our own interests.

The obvious problem with this priority of loyalties is putting ourselves at the bottom. As discussed, this is hard for most of us to really do. As humans, we are basically self-regarding, self-preserving, self-promoting. This is where humility becomes essential. Clearly, self has to be at the bottom, so our own desires and self-interest are subordinated to the Oath, the mission, the command above us. If we put ourselves first, we cannot serve our nation and we may not chose to follow orders that are objectionable or risky. Does this mean we have to give up some of our individuality? Yes, it actually does. We have to be prepared to wear the same uniform and march together (literally and figuratively).

Lack of Humility and Moral Failure

When we cannot employ the virtue of humility to offset our natural state of egoism, we can get into trouble. As a military ethicist, I constantly read about Commanding Officers getting fired for wrong-doing. As I research these cases, I find that there is a common ingredient in most all of these cases. That common ingredient is – arrogance. After being in command, these Commanding Officers start to believe that they are above the rules and that they are much too important and can break the regulations or higher moral standards of behavior – for their own benefit. And, because they are not asking for any input from their subordinates, they begin to think that they are never wrong.

(Personal note: when I was in command, I felt that sensation happening to me. Suddenly people were laughing at my jokes (I must have gotten funnier?). People were telling me how good I was (I must have gotten better?). And women were smiling at me (I must have gotten better looking?). With the help of my wife, I realized that it wasn't me that had changed, it was my position of command.)

My dose of humility came from outside. If my wife had not been there (on an extended deployment) I would have had to find a way to self-impose humility to offset this false sense of pridefulness.

Arrogance Leading to Failure – Captain Graf, USN

What can happen when a CO fails to employ humility and gives into their arrogance and pridefulness can be seen in the case of Captain Graf, USN Ret.

A Navy admiral stripped Graf of her command of the Japan-based guided missile cruiser *USS Cowpens* in January 2010. The Inspector General (IG) report concludes that Graf "repeatedly verbally abused her crew and committed assault" and accuses her of *using her position as commander of the Cowpens 'for personal gain.'* Old Navy hands tell TIME (magazine) that those charges, substantiated in the IG report, came about because of the poisonous atmosphere she created aboard her ship.

The case has attracted wide notice inside the Navy and on Navy blogs, where her removal has generated cheers from those who had served with her since she graduated from the U.S. Naval Academy in 1985. While many denounced Graf, even greater anger seems directed at the Navy brass for promoting such an officer to positions of ever-increasing responsibility. Graf declined an interview request.

While in command at sea – where a captain's word is law and she or he has the power to make or break careers – Graf swore like, well, a sailor. She "creates an environment of fear and hostility [and] frequently humiliates and belittles watch standers by screaming at them with profanities in front of the Combat Information Center and bridge-watch teams," a crew member told the IG. According to 29 of the 36 crew members who were questioned for the Navy's report, Graf repeatedly dropped F bombs on them. "Take your goddam attitude and shove it up your f_____ ass and leave it there," she allegedly told an officer during a stressful maneuver aboard the 567-ft., 10,000-ton vessel.

Junior officers seeking her guidance were rebuffed. "This is one of the reasons I hate you," she allegedly told one who was seeking her help. When another officer visited her quarters to discuss an earlier heated discussion, her response was terse: "Get the f___ out of my stateroom." She allegedly told a male officer, "The only words I want to hear out of your mouth are 'Yes ma'am' or 'You're correct, ma'am.'" She also allegedly put a 'well-respected master chief' in 'time out' – standing in the ship's key control room doing nothing – 'in front of other watch standers of all ranks.'

While most of the witness statements contained in the IG report didn't specify whether the person testifying was male or female, the IG asked at least two female officers whether they viewed Graf as a role model. A younger woman recalled going to Graf to seek her help. "Don't come to me with your problems," she said, quoting Graf. "You're a f_____ department head." The officer also said that Graf once told her, "I can't express how mad you make me without getting violent."

A second female officer told the IG that Graf was a "terrible role model for women in the Navy," alleging that Graf once told her and a fellow officer on the bridge, "You two are f_____ unbelievable. I would fire you if I could, but I can't."[4]

Clearly Capt. Graf was competent as a naval officer and shiphandler, and she had been to the tactical schools to learn how to fight her ship. So her failing as a Commanding Officer and a naval officer had to be her character.

We know our character in many ways drives our actions. So, when one's character causes them to act in a manner such as Capt. Graf, we can easily look at their actions and 'map' them back to their character. We can assume that she had:

- Deficiency in Self-control
- Deficiency in Judgment
- Deficiency in Compassion
- Excess in Pride (arrogance)
- Deficiency in humility.

She apparently thought being in command was about her – it's always about your people. To be an effective leader, we also have an important responsibility to develop our people. That means make them better. They should respect, trust and desire to emulate you – you should be their role model. With a true leader, their people are better the day they left the job than the day they arrived. Clearly, Capt. Graf did not do that. She lacked the humility to realize that her style was not only ineffective, but abusive, immoral, and actually illegal. As C. S. Lewis says, this kind of pridefulness can blind us to see our faults in order to make the appropriate self-corrections.

A Case of Selflessness and Humility

The next case is presented as a demonstration of humility. In this true story, CDR Frank Holley, USN, CHC, decided to perform some actions that one

---

4 Mark Thompson, "The Rise and Fall of a Female Captain Bligh," *Time*, March 3, 2010. http://content.time.com/time/nation/article/0,8599,1969602,00.html.

could argue put his whole career on the line. I would further argue that he did this selflessly, for no benefit to himself, solely to help others while risking his career and possible a Courts Martial.

CDR Holley was sent to Haiti during the contingency operation in December 1996. The first democratically elected President of Haiti, President Jean-Bertrand Aristide, was overthrown by a military coup led by General Raoul Cédras. The U.S. negotiated the exile of General Cédras and the return of President Aristide, but a U.S. Joint Task Force was sent in to stabilize the situation until Aristide could return.

CDR Holley was part of that joint task force as the Force Chaplain. Once CDR Holley became situated in Haiti, he went to visit some religiously affiliated orphanages. He was told by the Sisters that several children each week were dying of malnutrition. He asked where all the food was that had been sent down by the NGOs. He was told that more than 34 shipping containers containing 2,000,000lbs of supplies was held at the dock of Port-au-Prince but authorities would not release the food. (Clearly, black market forces were at work hoping to sell food at inflated prices).

CDR Holley went to the dock, but the dock authorities would not release it without documentation signed by the Ministry of Interior. CDR Holley took the papers to the Minister of Interior's office but was told by his Assistant that he would have to make an appointment. CDR Holley told her, "We're doing this now," and pushed into the minister's office. On confronting him he was told, "This isn't the way we do things here." The CDR said, "I'm not leaving until you sign the papers now, so we can feed the kids."

The Minister signed the papers.

The next day, CDR Holley arrived at the pier with 20 tractor trailer trucks and hauled the shipping containers away. He arranged distribution of the food, and was told by several orphanages that the food would feed over 1,300 children for 7 months.

After this, CDR Holley went to see his CO and said, "I think I need to tell what I just did."

The CO was glad to hear it went okay, but remarked that CDR Holley could have been thrown into a Haitian jail. Shortly after that the CO began to receive calls from the U.S. Embassy complaining of CDR Holley's actions, as he had circumvented the State Department.[5]

CDR Holley had take a huge chance here, risking his career to feed starving children. No naval regulations or international laws were broken but it could have caused a diplomatic incident. Although Haiti was a corrupt

---

5   Rick Rubel and George R. Lucas, *Case Studies in Ethics for Military Leaders, 5th Edition* (Upper Saddle River, NJ: Pearson Custom Publishing, 2014).

and inept state, it was still a sovereign country and clearly CDR Holley had trampled on it. Although his methods were arguably questionable, his intentions were selfless – acting for the benefit of the children and not himself.

Obstacles to Humility

If humility is so important for a leader, what are the obstacles of humility? Why is it so hard to be humble?

- We want to present a strong appearance to our people to convince them that we have all the answers.
- Asking, "What do you think?" might at first appear to be a sign of weakness. But, shortly after that question, they will think, "He/she thinks enough about me to ask me my opinion." You are still leader and decision-maker, but with a simple question, you might be able to make a better result with more information, and, most importantly, you will achieve 'buy-in' from your people.
- We are competitive and don't want people to see our mistakes.
- Humility is often mistaken for weakness.

Confidence without Arrogance

While humility is often mistaken for weakness, confidence is often mistaken for arrogance. There is a very fine line between confidence and arrogance. Particularly, when we realize we cannot control how others perceive us. We want military leaders to be confident in their skills and abilities. But we do not want our troops to perceive that as arrogance.

I believe the key to that delicate equation is *compassion*. The virtue of compassion can easily be faked, but our people know sincere compassion when they see it. If we can be compassionate (truly care about our people) then they may realize that our confidence is not arrogance.

The *combination of compassion and humility* is a powerful, but all too rare combination for a leader. I have only see it a few times in my whole career. But when I see it – I will follow that leader anywhere. I will follow them anywhere, because they have the humility to know they don't have all the answers, and they have the compassion to truly care about me.

I was told a story a few years ago about the final examination for a graduate level leadership course. The students were furious with the professor for putting 30 points on one short answer question on a final exam. The professor defended himself by saying, "If you have listened to anything I have said all semester, you should know the answer to this question. The question was: "What is the name of the janitor who cleans this room?" (Humility and Compassion).

Do you know the name of the janitor who cleans your room?

Case Study 2:
Humility: Lessons from the Context of Interrogation

Erik Phillips

In the high-stakes professions of the military (globally speaking), effective communication is of course vital. While there exist many means of communicating more effectively, this case study will focus on an underlying virtue which, if fostered, can enhance the likelihood of success of each such strategy. This virtue – humility – has been identified by researchers as a character strength and has been shown to have positive motivational effects on employees in the workplace, to enhance organizational trust, and to facilitate social interaction more broadly.[6]

Despite its clear benefits, humility is often misunderstood. In this case, I reduce the concept into three components and provide examples of these various facets in action. Demonstrated in turn is humility as: a) a realistic perception of oneself, b) in a global (social) context while, c) remaining openminded to new information. I use as my vehicle research findings and real-world accounts from the field of interrogation, a particular assemblage chosen for its variability in time and context and which serves as a means of underscoring the universality of humility. In so doing, the humble

---

6 Annette Peters, Wade Rowat and Megan Johnson, "Associations Between Dispositional Humility and Social Relationship Quality," *Psychology* 2, no. 3 (2011): 155–61; James Collins, *Good to Great: Why Some Companies Make the Leap ... and Others Don't* (New York: HarperBusiness, 2001); Reinout de Vries and Jean-Louise van Gelder, "Explaining Workplace Delinquency: The Role of Honesty – Humility, Ethical Culture, and Employee Surveillance," *Personality and Individual Differences* 86 (2015): 112–16.

perspective will be shown to underlie myriad communication strategies and to promote favorable outcomes.

Realistic Perception of Oneself

During initial training as an interrogator in the U. S. Army, my class was inculcated with two core, and dangerous, notions. First, any admission or confession made by a detainee in response to our interrogation tactics was to be considered a truthful one.[7] Second, while in the interrogation booth, we were God. We were in total control, we were infallible, and we shaped the detainee's reality, leaving them at our mercy. And while the strictures of the Geneva Convention were taught, this was accomplished alongside practical lessons on how to push those boundaries to their very limits.[8]

Unsurprisingly, the truth of the matter is that interrogators are certainly not always God-like in their capabilities. Shortly after the establishment of the American prison at Guantanamo Bay, Cuba (GTMO), the Army stood up Joint Task Force 170 (JTF-170), charged with the collection of intelligence from the detainees housed therein.[9] In a typical session, the interrogator would proceed inflexibly down a list of questions with little concern for establishing rapport and would subsequently meet with little to no cooperation from the detainee.[10] JTF-170 explained their general lack of success as resulting directly from (unconfirmed) interrogation resistance training that all the detainees ostensibly received prior to their incarceration.[11] In so doing, the task force, at an organizational level, exemplified the actions of one lacking an accurate sense of self. Instead of

---

7   Richard A. Leo, "False Confessions: Causes, Consequences, and Implications," *Journal of the American Academy of Psychiatry and the Law* 37, no. 3 (2009): 332–43. Due to concerns of space and relevance, this issue is not discussed at length here. Briefly, these two beliefs in the hands of mostly 20-year-olds proved a dangerous cocktail for some of us, leading to wholehearted application of subtly coercive tactics, the likes of which have been shown to increase the prevalence of false confessions, not to mention ethical standards.

8   Chris Mackey and Greg Miller, *The Interrogators: Inside the Secret War Against Al Qaeda* (London: John Murray, 2005). This reflects only my own experience and, it should be said, differs sharply from others who underwent the same training; see example here.

9   John Pike, "Military: Joint Task Force 170," https://www.globalsecurity.org/military/agency/dod/jtf-170.htm. Accessed May 1, 2018.

10   Mark Fallon, *Unjustifiable Means: The Inside Story of How the CIA, Pentagon, and US Government Conspired to Torture* (New York: Regan Arts, 2017).

11   Indeed, an al-Qaeda manual was found later that year in which counter-interrogations strategies were laid out. Despite this fact, evidence in support of their claim is clearly lacking. Of the nearly 800 detainees ever imprisoned at Guantanamo Bay detention camp, all but 41 have been released, with the overwhelming majority of those released having no discernible ties to any terrorist organization. Regardless, the oblivious hubris of the organization, and 'extreme swagger' with which some of its individuals carried itself, is

a thorough, revealing scrutiny of their own competencies and limitations when faced with resistance, JTF-170 shifted the blame. And thus, instead of identifying weaknesses for the sake of correcting them, they persisted in a state of oblivion, subjecting themselves to the potential of overlooking future dangers. Hubris can, in this way, be blinding.

Many understand this aspect of humility: a downward correcting of arrogance, a tamping down of overconfidence. But humility is not the opposite of arrogance; in fact, a socially diminutive interrogator quashed under the weight of an overbearing detainee would in equal measure not be considered humble. On a continuum, humility sits squarely between the extremes of arrogance on one end and an ill-founded sense of inferiority on the other; it is a sober understanding of oneself that is neither overinflated nor underinflated. In fact, research supports the notion that a certain amount of pride can be healthy, given that it is based on an honest and accurate assessment of oneself, abilities, or accomplishments, as the case may be.[12]

Following from this honest, realistic self-appraisal is the ability to see more precisely where one fits within a given context at both the micro and macro levels; the humble individual appreciates their current actions and self-worth within the universe at large. It is the big fish in the pond realizing they may or may not be considered equally big if put in the ocean. Further, this perspective may lead to feelings of connection with forces larger than oneself, such as God, nature, or humanity. It is the latter which is of particular relevance and use in our discussion of humility in a social context. And it is exemplified well in an anecdote shared by Grant Hirabayashi, a second-generation Japanese-American who served as an interrogator during World War II.[13]

Hirabayashi was attached to Merrill's Marauders, an elite special operations unit charged with liberating North Burma. During the particularly messy siege of Myitkyina in May 1944, a Japanese POW tried to escape, was captured (and bayonetted three times in the process), and promptly returned to the American camp, specifically to Hirabayashi for questioning. Hirabayashi made sure the would-be escapee was first sent to the medic for treatment before returning the following day for interrogation. When the Japanese officer was asked if he had received adequate medical treatment, he sized up his interrogator and disdainfully spurned him, "You're a traitor." To which Hirabayashi observed, "If we were to cut our

---

apparent. To wit, instead of recognizing and admitting deficiencies in its own program or people, JTF-170 deflected responsibility.

12 Craig Malkin, *Rethinking Narcissism: The Secret to Recognizing and Coping with Narcissist* (New York: Harper Perennial, 2016); C. Peterson and M. Seligman, *Character Strengths and Virtues: A Handbook and Classification* (Oxford: Oxford University Press, 2004).

13 James Stone, David Shoemaker and Nicholas Dotti, *Interrogation: World War II, Vietnam, and Iraq* (Washington, DC: National Defense Intelligence College, 2008).

veins, the same blood would flow ... I am an American soldier. I'm an American fighting for my country, and you are fighting for your country." By this statement, Hirabayashi succinctly captured not only their respective positions within the context of the ongoing war, but also their commonality within the human condition, thus revealing an even vaster perspective – that of the self, accurately seen, within a frame of reference transcending their current state of affairs. And when an individual sees the finitude of their presence in a global social network, they consequently tend to shift their focus from themselves to others.

Other-focused

C. S. Lewis noted: "Humility is not thinking less of yourself; it's thinking of yourself less."[14] From the comprehensive point of view just discussed, the need to protect or repair or prove one's own image becomes less important, allowing the well-being of others to well up into salience. A humble person therefore turns most of their attention outwards to consider others. And it is this consideration of others that almost all interrogators cite as a fundamental principle for successful interrogations.

During the Vietnam War, Orrin DeForest, a CIA agent, estimates he conducted roughly 4,000 interrogations between 1968 and 1975. While there, he initiated a project in which he set up some homes on the eastern outskirts of Ho Chi Minh City to accommodate – and question – prisoners and intelligence sources. Prior to commencing operations, DeForest trained a small group of interpreters newly assigned to him on the proper means of conducting an interrogation. To this group he distilled the reason behind his success to two primary principles: rapport and what he termed a sympathetic approach to questioning. "You have to have some compassion for your subject ... You have to be in the frame of mind where you're saying to yourself, 'I want to talk to this fella. I want to understand why he was a guerrilla. He's got a story to tell, and I want to hear it.'" He continues: "This approach was something I felt especially strongly about, partly because I really was sympathetic."[15] He was, in other words, training his team to be humble in the sense of being other-focused – putting the other person's needs in front of their own, something which came naturally to DeForest.

While in Vietnam, DeForest briefly mentored Stuart Herrington, a U.S. Army officer who had joined the military intelligence field several years prior.[16] With interrogations eventually numbering in the thousands,

---

14   C. S. Lewis, *Mere Christianity*.
15   Orrin DeForest and David Chanoff, *Slow Burn* (New York: Pocket Books, 1991).
16   Stuart Herrington, *Stalking the Vietcong: Inside Operation Phoenix: A Personal Account* (New York: Ballantine, 2004).

spanning decades and ranging from Vietnam to Panama to Iraq (Desert Storm), Herrington in later years reflected on his career and described an effective interrogation as "extending decent, humane treatment to [the interrogatee], showing concern for himself, his needs ..."[17] This general approach is echoed in findings from systematic interviews conducted in 2014 of 42 then active and highly experienced American military and federal law enforcement interrogators: 88 percent reported most frequently using techniques considered to be relationship-building tactics.[18] And numerous other surveys of interrogators from around the world replicate this finding. This recurring theme of prioritizing a detainee's needs in order to build a relationship with them is no happy accident: a rapport-based approach to interrogation has been shown to increase information yield as well as admissions and confessions.[19] Stated differently, putting the concerns of others before your own facilitates a relationship marked by cooperation, and it is a hallmark of humility.

Open-mindedness

As we have seen so far, the humble person has a realistic perception of what their capabilities are, what they do and do not know. And the humble person can show a tendency to put another's needs before their own, what may be considered deference. It is perhaps not surprising, then, that the third element of humility is open-mindedness, which can be understood as a willingness to accept new information in the place of previously held (but mistaken) information; in short, to accept criticism and to admit when one is wrong.

Matthew Alexander knew when he was wrong and did not hesitate to acknowledge such errors in front of his detainees. Alexander led the team in charge of tracking down the whereabouts of then al-Qaeda in

---

17 "Effective Interrogation without Torture," The Hugh Hewitt Show, February 28, 2014. http://www.hughhewitt.com/effective-interrogation-without-torture-101-from-retired-army-colonel-stuart-herrington/.

18 Melissa Russano, Fadia Narchet, Steven Kleinman and Christian Meissner, "Structured Interviews of Experienced HUMINT Interrogators," Applied Cognitive Psychology 28, no. 6 (2014): 847–59.

19 Jane Goodman-Delahunty, Natalie Martschuk and Mandeep Dhami, "Interviewing High Value Detainees: Securing Cooperation and Disclosures," Applied Cognitive Psychology 28, no. 6 (2014): 883–97; Ulf Holmberg and Sven-Ake Christianson, "Murderers' and Sexual Offenders' Experiences of Police Interviews and Their Inclination to Admit or Deny Crimes," Behavioral Sciences & the Law 20, nos 1–2 (2002): 31–45; Taeko Wachi, Kazumi Watanabe, Kaeko Yokata, Yusuke Otsuka and Michael Lamb, "Japanese Suspect Interviews, Confessions, and Related Factors," Journal of Police and Criminal Psychology 31, no. 3 (2015): 217–27.

Iraq (AQI) leader Abu Musab al-Zarqawi, a fundamentalist known for his extremely brutal tactics. Understanding that detainees tend to view the interrogator as an ambassador for their own side, Alexander conceded what he saw to be strategic errors made on the part of the U.S. military. "Almost every detainee that I admitted those mistakes to, they were all surprised that I was willing to admit that…it was very appealing [to them]."[20] Such open-mindedness played a role in leading Alexander's team to their intended objective. Based on the interrogation team's reporting, on June 8, 2006, U.S. F-16 jets dropped two 500-pound bombs on a building just northeast of Baghdad, successfully killing al-Zarqawi and other members of AQI who were inside at the time.[21] Alexander thus proved simultaneously honest and strategic – he intentionally leveraged what he considered legitimate errors to his advantage in the interrogation booth.

Relatedly, a comprehensive examination of a group of U.K.-based counter-terrorism interrogation experts revealed that primarily focusing on the relationship within an interrogation enhanced cooperative behavior by suspects. Of particular importance here, one of the means by which an interrogator could reduce suspect resistance was by allowing the suspect to correct any mistakes the interrogator had made (for example, getting a name wrong) or proactively amending their own errors themselves (for example, "I don't think I've worded that right – let me try again.").

Putting the Pieces Together

The story of U.S. Marine Corps Major Sherwood Moran serves as a fundamentally sound example of an approach to interrogation steeped in humility. Moran found himself in the middle of a war, faced with a fanatical enemy unlike any the U.S. military had seen before, operating amidst the widespread belief that traditional questioning tactics would work not against such an ideologically alien enemy.[22] Moran was part of the Pacific forces of World War II, island-hopping their way

---

20 Matthew Alexander, "One Man Says No To Harsh Interrogation Techniques," NPR, February 14, 2011, https://www.npr.org/2011/02/14/133497869/one-man-says-no-to-harsh-interrogation-techniques.

21 "Al-Qaida in Iraq's Al-Zarqawi 'terminated'," NBCNews.com. June 8, 2006, http://www.nbcnews.com/id/13195017/ns/world_news-mideast_n_africa/t/al-qaida-iraqs-al-zarqawi-terminated/#.

22 Stephen Budiansky, "Truth Extraction," *The Atlantic*, June 1, 2005, https://www.theatlantic.com/magazine/archive/2005/06/truth-extraction/303973/.

towards Japan. After meeting with considerable success in his front-line battlefield interrogations, he captured some of his most important ideas in a letter-as-manual submitted in 1943 to the First Marine Division's Intelligence Section.[23]

Moran advocated a relationship-first approach to interviewing, suggesting that interrogators find common ground with their detainees by talking about things they knew and had in common. And he stressed as absolutely important the quality of being sincere. In other words, it was Moran's recommendation that interrogators stay within the limits of what they knew, and by implication, avoid extending beyond those lines – a feat only achievable if one knows their own capabilities and limitations.

He further admonished interrogators to forget the status of each detainee as enemy combatant or as POW, advising that they treat detainees "as a human being to a human being." And further, "make [the POW] and his troubles the center of the stage, not you [the interrogator] and your questions of war problems." In short, Moran advised taking an outward-facing focus by shifting away from the interrogator's own emotions, information requirements, and biases, instead concentrating on the human being in front of them as if on equal footing – not antagonizing them by having a "'superiority' standpoint."

The simple yet profound way in which Moran supports the stance of staying openminded to potentially new information (and which may displace one's previous notions as erroneous) was in his warning interrogators away from presumptive, leading questions. Thus, by extension, the interrogator understands to ask open-ended questions – ones that invite thought and discussion, that preclude one-word responses, and that, importantly, allow for unforeseen responses.

In Application

Humility is a way of being, and it can manifest in some of the ways discussed in this chapter, though its application and benefits are assuredly not limited to a military interrogation context. Researchers in various fields continue to understand this virtue in finer granularity as they test its components in diverse contexts and across a range of power dynamics between interactants (e.g., boss to employee, teacher to student, partners

---

23   "Sherwood F. Moran Letter," IAT / VAT. December 14, 2015, http://interrogators-against-torture.org/sherwood-f-moran/.

in a romantic relationship).[24] As such, the medic who confidently asserts how many combat troops they are reasonably capable of supporting while not hesitating to call for backup when that number is exceeded; the company commander who prioritizes her subordinates' autonomy by creating space for their contributions in an inclusive manner; and the supply sergeant who admits his own forecasting error as the cause for the unit's current shortage of supplies are all examples of those expressing aspects of humility in their respective professions.

It is important to note one final but common thread – mentioned by each of the interrogators listed above though not yet mentioned here – is that humility does not equate with a necessarily soft or resigned approach. Humility does not impede one's ability to be doggedly systematic in exploring all options for an upcoming mission or to ruthlessly pursue an objective. One can still be resolute in their bottom line even when admitting a personal error or placing another's welfare in front of their own. Such an approach is what Moran called "enlightened hard-boiledness," and across time, cultures, and contexts, a humility-based approach to social interactions has been shown to lead to improved results.

References

"Al-Qaida in Iraq's Al-Zarqawi 'terminated'." NBCNews.com, June 8, 2006. http://www.nbcnews.com/id/13195017/ns/world_news-mideast_n_africa/t/al-qaida-iraqs-al-zarqawi-terminated/#.WuUodJch1ph.

Alexander, M. "One Man Says No To Harsh Interrogation Techniques." NPR, February 14, 2011, https://www.npr.org/2011/02/14/133497869/one-man-says-no-to-harsh-interrogation-techniques.

Budiansky, S. "Truth Extraction." *The Atlantic*, June 1, 2005, https://www.theatlantic.com/magazine/archive/2005/06/truth-extraction/303973/.

Collins, J. C. *Good to Great: Why Some Companies Make the Leap ... and Others Don't*. New York: HarperBusiness, 2001.

Davis, D., E. Worthington and J. Hook. "Humility: Review of Measurement Strategies and Conceptualization as Personality Judgment." *The Journal of Positive Psychology* 5, no. 4 (2010): 243–52.

DeForest, O. and D. Chanoff. *Slow Burn*. New York: Pocket Books, 1991.

"Effective Interrogation without Torture 101 from Retired Army Colonel Stuart Herrington." The Hugh Hewitt Show, February 28, 2014, http://

---

24 Don Davis, Everett Worthington and Joshua Hook, "Humility: Review of Measurement Strategies and Conceptualization as Personality Judgment," *The Journal of Positive Psychology* 5, no. 4 (2010): 243–52.

www.hughhewitt.com/effective-interrogation-without-torture-101-from-retired-army-colonel-stuart-herrington/.

Fallon, M. *Unjustifiable Means: The Inside Story of How the CIA, Pentagon, and US Government Conspired to Torture*. New York: Regan Arts, 2017.

Goodman-Delahunty, J., N. Martschuk, and M. D. Dhami. "Interviewing High Value Detainees: Securing Cooperation and Disclosures." *Applied Cognitive Psychology* 28, no. 6 (2014): 883–97.

Herrington, S. A. *Stalking the Vietcong: Inside Operation Phoenix: A Personal Account*. New York: Ballantine, 2004.

Holmberg, U. and S. Christianson. "Murderers and Sexual Offenders Experiences of Police Interviews and Their Inclination to Admit or Deny Crimes." *Behavioral Sciences & the Law* 20, nos. 1–2 (2002): 31–45.

Kohlberg, L. "Stages of Moral Development," https://en.wikipedia.org/wiki/Lawrence_Kohlberg%27s_stages_of_moral_development, 1971.

Leo, R. A. "False Confessions: Causes, Consequences, and Implications." *Journal of the American Academy of Psychiatry and the Law* 37, no. 3 (2009): 332–43.

Lewis, C. S. *Mere Christianity*. London: HarperCollins, 2015.

Mackey, C. and G. Miller. *The Interrogators: Inside the Secret War Against Al Qaeda*. London: John Murray, 2005.

Malkin, C. *Rethinking Narcissism: The Secret to Recognizing and Coping with Narcissists*. New York: Harper Perennial, 2016.

Peters, A.S., W. C. Rowat and M. K. Johnson. "Associations Between Dispositional Humility and Social Relationship Quality." *Psychology* 2, no. 3 (2011): 155–61.

Peterson, C. and M. E. P. Seligman, *Character Strengths and Virtues: A Handbook and Classification*. Oxford: Oxford University Press, 2004.

Pike, J. "Military Joint Task Force 170," https://www.globalsecurity.org/military/agency/dod/jtf-170.htm. Accessed May 1, 2018.

Roush, P. "The Constitutional Paradigm," in *Ethics in the Military Profession: The Moral Foundations of Leadership*, edited by G. R. Lucas and R. Rubel. Upper Saddle River, NJ: Pearson Custom Publishing, 2014.

Rubel, R. and G. R. Lucas. *Case Studies in Ethics for Military Leaders, 5th Edition*, Upper Saddle River, NJ: Pearson Publishing 2014.

Russano, M. B., F. M. Narchet, S. Kleinman and C. A. Meissner. "Structured Interviews of Experienced HUMINT Interrogators." *Applied Cognitive Psychology* 28, no. 6 (2014): 847–59.

"Sherwood F. Moran, S.F. Letter." IAT/VAT. December 14, 2015, http://interrogators-against-torture.org/sherwood-f-moran/. Accessed May 1, 2018.

Stone, J. A., D. P. Shoemaker and N. R. Dotti, *Interrogation: World War II, Vietnam, and Iraq*. Washington, DC: National Defense Intelligence College, 2008.

"'Suggestions for Japanese Interpreters." Axis History Forum, July 15, 2006. https://forum.axishistory.com/viewtopic.php?t=104610.

Thompson, M. "The Rise and Fall of a Female Captain Bligh," *Time*, March 3, 2010. http://content.time.com/time/nation/article/0,8599, 1969602,00.html.

De Vries, R. E. and J. van Gelder. "Explaining Workplace Delinquency: The Role of Honesty – Humility, Ethical Culture, and Employee Surveillance." *Personality and Individual Differences* 86 (2015): 112–16.

Wachi, T., K. Watanabe, Yokota, Y. Otsuka and M. E. Lamb, "Japanese Suspect Interviews, Confessions, and Related Factors." *Journal of Police and Criminal Psychology* 31, no. 3 (2015): 217–27.

12

COMPASSION

Overview

Philip McCormack

In the 2011 Theos Annual Lecture, General Lord Richard Dannatt, former professional head of the British Army, articulated his understanding of the contemporary operational context within which British soldiers must serve:

> Our young soldiers ... must be able to kill and show compassion at the same time; they must be loyal to their country, their Regiment and their friends without compromising their own integrity.[1]

The key phrase from Richard Dannatt's lecture, for our purpose in this overview, is that soldiers "must be able to kill and show compassion at the same time." Responding to this lecture, Frank Jackson, Vice-resident of Uniting for Peace, wrote to the *Guardian* newspaper claiming that "'kill and show compassion at the same time' is the oxymoron to end all oxymorons (possibly exceeded only by 'the war to end all war')."[2] Jackson's response to Dannatt is not in the form of a careful scholarly treatise; it is a letter to a national newspaper. These two positions will be explored from differing perspectives in this overview. We will begin by seeking to offer a definition of the word compassion, locating it within Greek philosophy, Enlightenment tradition and Christian theology. It

---

1 Richard Dannatt, "The Battle for Hearts and Minds: Morality and Warfare Today," November 8, 2011 Theos Annual Lecture. https://www.theosthinktank.co.uk/research/2011/11/08/the-battle-for-hearts-and-minds-morality-and-warfare-today.

2 Frank Jackson, "Soldiers cannot kill and show compassion at the same time," *The Guardian* November 14, 2011. https://www.theguardian.com/uk/2011/nov/14/soldiers-cannot-kill-and-show-compassion.

will briefly consider a recent challenge to the concept of character that maintains that describing compassion as a virtue says little of empirical substance. The overview will conclude by offering a framework to view compassion and the soldier on the battlefield.

Compassion is defined in the *Oxford English Dictionary* as: 1) suffering together with another; fellow feeling; 2) the feeling or emotion, when a person is moved by the suffering or distress of another and by the desire to relieve it; 3) sorrowful emotion, sorrow or grief. Compassion is often confused with empathy, which is defined in the *Chambers English Dictionary* as, the "power of entering into another's personality and imaginatively experiencing his experiences: the power of entering into the feeling or spirit of something and so appreciating it fully." Empathy, therefore, is the ability to imagine oneself in another's place, and compassion is the emotional response to relieve the other's suffering or distress. Nancy Snow argued that "pity, sympathy and grief are all parts of the emotional landscape of our lives."[3] Compassion, she noted, contains an altruistic concern for the other's good and an urgency that grief lacks. In contrast empathy is more like a spectator, where one can remain at a safe emotional distance.

Debates about the moral worth of compassion are as old as ethical theory itself.[4] Aristotle considered compassion as a social virtue. In the *Art of Rhetoric*, Aristotle analyses the idea of pity:[5]

> Let us now consider Pity, asking ourselves what things excite pity, and for what persons, and in what states of our mind pity is felt. Pity may be defined as a feeling of pain caused by the sight of some evil, destructive or painful, which befalls one who does not deserve it, and which we might expect to befall ourselves or some friend of ours, and moreover to befall us soon. In order to feel pity, we must obviously be capable of supposing that some evil may happen to us or some friend of ours, and moreover some such evil as is stated in our definition or is more or less of that kind. It is therefore not felt by those completely ruined ...

---

3 Nancy E. Snow, "Compassion," *American Philosophical Quarterly* 28, no. 3 (1991): 195.

4 Natan Sznaider, "The Sociology of Compassion: A Study in the Sociology of Morals," *Cultural Values* 2, no. 1 (1998): 132.

5 The word Aristotle uses in the passage for pity is *eleousin* (ἐλεουσιν) from the verb form *eleeō* (ἐλεεω) which can be translated as to have pity on, show mercy to or have compassion on. The noun form *eleos* (ἐλεος) can be translated as pity, mercy or compassion. Martha Nussbaum, "Compassion: The Basic Social Emotion," *Social Philosophy and Policy* 13, no. 1 (1996): 29, states that the word pity and compassion speak about the same emotion. It was, she maintains, only from the Victorian period that pity "acquired nuances of condescension and superiority to the sufferer that it did not have formerly."

Robert Roberts referrers to Aristotle's approach as tragic compassion.[6] Roberts notes that it involves three propositions: 1) what has happened is evil, destructive or painful; 2) the suffering was undeserved; 3) one might imagine it happening to oneself. In contrast, Socratic and Stoic thought adopted a distinctly different approach; one that understood pity or compassion "as a moral sentiment unworthy of the dignity of both pitier and recipient."[7] In the *Apology of Socrates*, after sentence has been passed, Socrates says "I had not the intention of speaking to you as you would have liked me to address you, weeping and wailing and lamenting ... and which, as I say, are unworthy of me."[8] Socrates continues, "and in other dangers there are other ways of escaping death if a man is willing to say and do anything. The difficulty, my friends, is not in avoiding death, but in avoiding unrighteousness." Whether Socrates actually said this, or Plato used the reputation of the great philosopher to make his point is uncertain. What is abundantly clear, is the beginning of a tradition that holds that pity or compassion insults the dignity of the person who gives or receives such pity.

In *The Republic*, Plato maintains that,

> the good man is sufficient for himself and his own happiness ... and for this reason the loss of a son or brother, or the deprivation of fortune, is to him of all men least terrible ... And therefore he will be least likely to lament, and will bear with the greatest equanimity any misfortune of this sort which may befall him.[9]

The vitreous person, in this tradition, is morally sufficient in themselves to render compassion or pity an unworthy response from others. Strong echoes of the contrast between the Platonic/Stoic and the Aristotelian approach to compassion can be seen in key figures in Enlightenment philosophy. Immanuel Kant in his *Groundwork for the Metaphysics*, when considering the objective principle for a universal law of nature comments:

> Yet a *fourth* – for whom it is going well, while he sees that others have to struggle with great hardships (with which he could well help them) – thinks:

6   Robert Roberts, "Emotions in the Christian Tradition," in *The Stanford Encyclopaedia of Philosophy*, ed. Edward Zalta (Winter 2016 Edition). https://plato.stanford.edu/entries/emotion-Christian-tradition/.

7   Nussbaum, "Compassion," 41.

8   Plato, *The Apology of Socrates*, trans. Benjamin Jowett, ed., Jeffrey D. Breshears. Accessed November 2018.

9   Plato, *The Republic*, May 18, 2001. http://www.idph.net/conteudos/ebooks/republic.pdf, 241.

'What has it to do with me? Let each be as happy as heaven wills, or as he can make himself, I will not take anything from him or even envy him; only I do not want to contribute to his welfare or to his assistance in distress!' Now to be sure, if such a way of thinking were to become a universal law of nature, then the human race could well subsist, and without doubt still better than when everyone chatters about sympathetic participation and benevolence, and even on occasion exerts himself to practice them, but, on the contrary also deceives wherever he can, sells out, or otherwise infringes on the right of human beings.[10]

Later in the same work Kant would say "benevolence from basic principles (not from instinct) have an inner worth."[11] The idea of compassion as fellow-feeling is a form of human instinct, whereas Kant was prepared to accommodate a form of 'benevolence from principles.' Adam Smith in his *The Theory of Moral Sentiments* states that "my thesis is that our fellow-feeling for the misery of others comes from our imaginatively changing places with the sufferer, thereby coming to conceive what he feels or even to feel what he feels."[12] Smith then contends that "the spectator's compassion must arise purely from the thought of what he himself would feel if he were reduced to that same unhappy condition while also (this may well be impossible) regarding it with his present reason and judgment."[13]

A theology of compassion has an important role within the Christian tradition and Christian ethics. In the Gospels, Jesus is presented as being moved with compassion because he saw people who were "harassed and helpless, like sheep without a shepherd" (Mt 9:36; 14:14; Mk 1:41). In the parable of the Prodigal Son (Lk 15:11–32) the younger of two sons acts in a culturally inappropriate manner and demands his share of his future inheritance. In the parable the young son squanders his wealth, which results in personal hunger and deprivation. Realising his foolishness, the son returns to his father's house. The biblical story says that when "he was still a long way off, his father saw him and was filled with compassion for him; he ran to his son, threw his arms around him and kissed him." The Greek word translated as compassion in this passage is splagchnizomai (σπλαγχνιζομαι) which means to be moved in the depths of one's being, hence to be moved with compassion for another's plight.

---

10   Immanuel Kant, *Groundwork for the Metaphysics of Morals*, ed. and trans. A. W. Wood (New Haven, CT and London: Yale University Press, 2002), 40.

11   Kant, *Groundwork for the Metaphysics of Morals*, 53.

12   Adam Smith, *The Theory of Moral Sentiments*, ed. Jonathan Bennett, 2017. http://www.earlymoderntexts.com/assets/pdfs/smith1759.pdf, 1.

13   Smith, *The Theory of Moral Sentiments*, 3.

What is significant about this biblical story is that the father is aware that the plight of his son was deserved. He acted foolishly and suffered as a consequence and yet he was moved with compassion. This runs contrary to the second premise in the Aristotelian analysis of compassion.

The Parable of the Good Samaritan (Lk 10:25–37) is told in response to the question "who is my neighbour?" (Lk 10:29). In the story nothing is known of the man attacked by robbers, other than he is badly hurt. Those in the story who should show compassion to the injured person do not and "pass by on the other side." In stark contrast it was a Samaritan who took pity (σπλαγχνον).[14] The importance and significance of this biblical story is hard to overstate. Numerous countries around the world have introduced Good Samaritan Laws that both require an individual to come to the aid of another "who is exposed to grave physical harm, if there is no danger of risk of injury to the rescuer"[15] and provides protection to "the rescuer" from unintended consequences from their assistance. The existence of these Good Samaritan Laws continues to be deeply contentious.[16]

The twentieth century saw a "renaissance of virtue"[17] with many philosophers contributing to its revival. Will Durant in his work *The Story of Philosophy* coined the well-known phrase "we are what we repeatedly do. Excellence, then, is not an act but a habit."[18] Durant was reflecting on the *Nicomachean Ethics* and Aristotle's statement "the virtues we acquire by first exercising them."[19] We can see the same intellectual argument in Lord Moran's influential book *Anatomy of Courage*. Drawing from his experiences in World War I, Moran maintains "that a man of character in peace becomes a man of courage in war. He cannot be selfish in peace and unselfish in war. Character as Aristotle taught is a habit, the daily choice of right instead of wrong."[20] Recent advances in neuroplasticity[21] have demonstrated that the human brain remains remarkably plastic, throughout life, and that as we develop new skills our brains change to

---

14 This is the noun form of the verb σπλαγχνιζομαι.

15 John T. Pardum, "Good Samaritan Laws: A Global Perspective," *20 Loy. L.A. Int'l & Comp. L. Rev.* 591 (May 1, 1998) http://digitalcommons.lmu.edu/ilr/vol20/iss3/8.

16 See Kathleen M. Ridolfi, "Law, Ethics, and the Good Samaritan: Should There Be a Duty to Rescue?" *Santa Clara Law Review* 40, no. 4 (2000): 957–70.

17 John M. Doris, *Lack of Character: Personality and Moral Behaviour* (Cambridge: Cambridge University Press, 2002), 2.

18 Will Durant, *The Story of Philosophy* (New York: Garden City, 1926), 87. This particular quote is one of the most misattributed quotes on the internet.

19 Aristotle, *The Nicomachean Ethics*, trans. James A. K. Thomson (London: Penguin, 1953), 32.

20 Lord Moran, *The Anatomy of Courage* (London: Constable, 1945), 170.

21 See, Erik Smith, *Neuroplasticity: Old Brain Meets New Tricks* (independently published, 2017), 2, who states that "neuroplasticity is the brain's ability to change through experience."

accommodate the new activity.[22] Durant's succinct phrase "we are what we repeatedly do" appears to have even greater depth.

Increased interest in character and personality traits also lead to greater empirical scrutiny into human behaviour. Scholars such as John Doris[23] and Gilbert Harman[24] have questioned the empirical basis for the concept of character as presented within virtue ethics. Doris and Harman are content to accept that virtue or character can exist as a fleeting feature but this, according to Harman this "must be distinguished from virtue or character as an enduring characteristic of a person."[25] One virtue that both focus upon is compassion; for Doris compassion is used "as a sort of test case."[26] Doris accepts that his strategy is "opportunistic" because of the quantities of empirical work on compassion-relevant behaviour.[27] Studies cited that focused upon morally relevant behaviour were: Dime in the Phone Booth;[28] Lady in Distress;[29] Obedience to Authority;[30] Good Samaritan Experiment;[31] and The Stanford Prison Experiment.[32] What is striking about some of these experiments (Dime in the Phone Booth and the Good Samaritan Experiment) is how insignificant the situational factors were in altering moral behaviour. For example, in the Darley and Daniel experiment at Princeton Theological Seminary, only 10 per cent of theological students placed under significant time pressure stopped to help the 'victim' in need of help; some literally stepped over the 'victim' on their way to speak on the parable of the Good Samaritan. Those who did not

---

22 The implications for stroke victims are significant. For example, see Cameron S. Mang, et al., "Promoting Neuroplasticity for Motor Rehabilitation After Stroke: Considering the Effects of Aerobic Exercise and Genetic Variation on Brain-Derived Neurotrophic Factor," *Physical Therapy* 93, no. 12 (2013): 1707–16.

23 For example, see Doris, *Lack of Character*, "Heated agreement: Lack of Character as Being for the Good," *Philosophical Studies* 148, no. 1 (2010): 135–46.

24 For example, see Gilbert Harman, "No Character or Personality," *Business Ethics Quarterly* 13, no. 1, (2003): 87–94; and "Skepticism about Character Traits," *The Journal of Ethics* 13, Nos. 2/3 (2009): 235–42.

25 Harman, "Skepticism about Character Traits," 242.

26 For example, see Doris, *Lack of Character*, 29.

27 Doris, *Lack of Character*, 29.

28 See A. M. Isen and S. F. Simmonds, "The Effect of Feeling Good on a Helping Task that is incompatible with Good Mood," *Social Psychology* 41, No 4 (1978): 346–49.

29 See Bibb Latané and Judith Rodin, "A lady in distress: Inhibiting effects of friends and strangers on bystander intervention," *Journal of Experimental Social Psychology* 5, no. 2 (1969): 189–202.

30 See, Stanley Milgram, *Obedience to Authority: An Experimental View* (New York: HarperCollins, 2009).

31 See John M. Darley and Daniel Batson, "'From Jerusalem to Jericho': A Study of Situational and Dispositional Variables in Helping Behavior," *Journal of Personality and Social Psychology* 27, no. 1 (1973): 100–108.

32 See Philip Zimbardo, *The Lucifer Effect: How Good People Turn Evil* (London: Rider, 2007).

stop to help, however, did arrive in an anxious state to deliver their talk. Nevertheless, and this is the challenge that Doris and Harman make, there is a large body of empirical evidence that suggests moral behaviour can be effected by surprisingly small situational factors.

If character is as fragile or non-existent as Doris and Harman maintain, then Frank Jackson's assertion that the very notion of soldiers being able to kill and show compassion at the same time "is the oxymoron to end all oxymorons." General Dannatt is, therefore, terribly mistaken. In her book, *An Intimate History of Killing: Face to Face Killing in 20th Century Warfare*, Joanna Bourke documents how soldiers have killed their fellow humans in frequently brutal and degrading ways.[33] War is and most likely will continue to be brutal; however, there is more to this landscape than just depressing carnage. A central feature of compassion is 'fellow-feeling.' I contend that there is a very specific expression of 'fellow feeling' that professional soldiers intuitively identify with, at least in one regard: combatants "stand in a relationship of mutual risk."[34] Michael Ignatieff observes that "the tacit contract of combat throughout the ages has always assumed a basic equality of moral risk: kill or be killed. Accordingly, violence in war avails itself of the legitimacy of self-defence."[35] Soldiers have always lived, as Christopher Coker phrases it, "in the same community of fate" as their enemies.[36]

The striking thing is not that war crimes have been committed. Humanity has a capacity for atrocity. Rather the striking thing, for me, is that in the midst of war, there are innumerable examples where basic humanity has shone through despite the character of war. In his book *Acts of War: The Behaviour of Men in Battle*, Richard Holmes notes that in the Spring Offensive of 1918 the remarkable thing "was not how many British soldiers were killed trying to surrender, but how few. The Germans were remarkably scrupulous about accepting surrender in circumstances when, in hot blood, they might have killed easily out of hand."[37] Imagine the scene, the defenders have put up a robust defence of their position but now the attackers have the upper hand and a clear opportunity to exact a form of retribution on those who perhaps only minutes before have killed their friends and comrades. In the heat of war and close quarter fighting, how

33 Joanna Bourke, *An Intimate History of Killing: Face to Face Killing in the 20th Century* (London: Granta, 1999).

34 Paul Kahn, "The Paradox of Riskless War," *Philosophy and Public Policy Quarterly* 22 (Summer 2001): 3.

35 Michael Ignatieff, *Virtual War: Kosovo and Beyond* (New York: Picador, 2000), 161.

36 Christopher Coker, *Ethics and War in the 21st Century* (Abingdon: Routledge, 2008), 150.

37 Richard Holmes, *Acts of War: The Behaviour of Men in Battle* (London: Weidenfeld & Nicolson, 2003), 382.

might the attackers be expected to respond? Dan Grossman[38] and Richard Holmes have made the point that remarkably, many soldiers in most conflicts respond in a humane manner, as though adhering to a simple moral code. In the heat of battle there is a simple 'kill or be killed' reality that exists among those within this specific 'community of fate.' It is the ability to see in the 'other' elements of 'oneself' that can enable the human emotion of 'fellow feeling' particularly when there is no immediacy of 'kill or be killed.'

One of the weaknesses of Doris and Harman's criticism of character is that it does not give sufficient explanatory weight to the idea that the creation of character in the Socratic and Aristotelian traditions took time and was the consequence of deliberate intention and repeated action. It was a lifelong pursuit within the context of a community that espoused the cultivation of virtue (ἀρετη/aretē). Character was something to be cultivated through deliberate and conscious choice; it was not the 'fleeting feature' frequently manifested in the social psychology experiments. In his book *After Virtue*, Alasdair MacIntyre uses an allegory to describe how moral language had been detached from its Aristotelian source, with its teleological idea about human life. He states that "the language and the appearances of morality persist even though the integral substance of morality has to a large degree been fragmented and then in part destroyed."[39] The language was retained but the substance from which it was drawn was progressively eroded. Compassion like any virtue must be grown from the daily habits a person develops. If one had asked Aristotle how to become a carpenter, I suspect he would have replied "do woodwork." The ability to put up a bookshelf does not make one a professional carpenter. The skill of the tradesperson is honed over thousands of hours of repeated actions and behaviours. Compassion like any virtue must be honed by repeated habit.

Martin Buber's fascinating notion of *I and Thou* is an excellent example of how the virtue of compassion ('fellow-feeling') may be honed.[40] Buber described our potential relationship with others as following one of two traits: I and It; and I and You. If when we encounter another we see ourselves in them, the relationship is 'I-Thou.' If, however, we do not see ourselves the other takes on the characteristic of an object that is separate from us and the relationship becomes, I-It. 'Fellow-feeling'/compassion is based upon the capacity to see ourselves in the other as one who in basic nature

---

38 David Grossman, *On Killing: The Psychological Cost of Learning to Kill in War and Society* (New York: Back Bay, 1995).

39 Alasdair MacIntyre, *After Virtue* (Notre Dame, IN: University of Notre Dame Press).

40 Martin Buber, *I and Thou*, trans. W. Kaufmann. 'Thou' is the old English manner of distinguishing 'you,' singular from 'you,' plural.

is like us: a human being. The former Archbishop of Canterbury, Rowan Williams, argues that our human bodies are a means of profound moral communication. By this he does not simply mean, what someone verbally says. Rather, it is the body itself, regardless of the ability of the individual to physically speak or express thought that communicates in a profound manner to another, who themselves possess a human body.[41] Perhaps the social psychology experiments (referred to earlier) have only demonstrated the profound difference between virtue honed over prolonged time and the frequently fleeting and transient nature of modern relationships?

Compassion or 'fellow-feeling' is an important virtue for soldiers to hone deliberately because those who survive their combat/service tours usually wish to return home to their families and their lives. In his often painfully honest book *What It Is Like To Go To War*, Karl Marlantes comments that "too many veterans, from Vietnam but also from Afghanistan and Iraq, are still waiting to come home."[42] The desire to go home is hugely powerful for many soldiers and to do so 'in good order.' In some modern operational environments, however, the notion can arise for some soldiers that the 'norms' they have lived by do not apply in that context. The soldier's ability to locate their humanity even in the context of battle is vital; they must always understand themselves in terms not simply of what they do but who they are: a son, a brother, a husband, a father, a daughter, a sister, a wife and a mother. In the context of powerful situational forces, over which they may have no control,[43] soldiers who allow themselves to become agentic, become tools or instruments of another's will.[44] In this situation they lose agency and potentially act in opposition to the societal norms that had shaped their lives up to that point. The soldier's ability to deal with that narrative part of their evolving life story will be difficult, if there were occasions when there was no immediacy of 'kill or be killed' the absence of the virtue of compassion or 'fellow feeling' resulted in an immoral or illegal action / behaviour. One aspect of the process of coming home and continuing with one's on-going life story is the ability to incorporate the narratives of our experience in war within the overarching story we not only tell ourselves but also those whose relationship helps define who we are. It is the retention of a conscience that can look honestly at the past and know that our humanity, though tested, survived its encounter with the other and in that encounter not only saw itself but had compassion on the other.

---

41 Rowan Williams, "Religious Faith and Human Rights," May 1, 2008. http://www.lse.ac.uk/humanRights/events/rowanWilliams.aspx.

42 Karl Marlantes, *What It Is Like To Go To War* (London: Corvus, 2012), 192.

43 This one of Zimbardo's main points.

44 Milgram, *Obedience to Authority*, 83. Milgram always maintained that each has a choice; we chose to become agentic.

Case Study 1:
Compassion toward Enemies

John F. Sattler and Michael Skerker

I.

In 2004, I was commanding general of the First Marine Expeditionary Force (I MEF) in Iraq, the senior Marine in theater, with 50,000 service members (Army/Navy/Air Force/Marine) in the command. One of my responsibilities was giving approval to all deliberate, i.e. no troops in contact, air strikes. One night in November, days before we would enter Fallujah for a heavy combat, 'clear and hold' operation, I was woken by our Operations Officer and informed I was needed in the Operations Center to clear a potential deliberate target.

I was briefed by the night watch team and told several insurgent leaders were meeting on a rooftop in our area of operations. I glanced at the overhead view of a group of men on a rooftop in Fallujah illuminated on the large screen in the Operations Center.

"Sir, based on the activities of the men on the rooftop, we have determined them to be hostile. We have done the weaponeering to limit the CDE (collateral damage estimate) and the bug splat shows a CDE of 15. We have an aircraft on station ready to take down the target with your approval."

I had this same sort of 0200 conversation many nights before, and the Watch Officer's brief this night reflected many lessons learned from our team's months of conducting deliberate strikes. First, there was the issue of numbers. On previous nights, I had expressed my disappointment in some of my staff for looking at the 'magic number' 29 as a license for, rather than a check on, violence. The Secretary of Defense had authorized the Combatant Commander to clear deliberate targets with a CDE up to 29. This authority had been passed down to me as the MEF Commander, but could not be passed any lower. We have computer programs that can estimate the 'bug splat,' the blast effects of any kind of munition fired from a particular angle at a particular point against a particular building. If the bug splat generated a CDE of 30 or higher, I had to pass the request up the chain of command requesting approval from the Secretary of Defense.[45] This would have to be a High Value Target (HVT) or extremely important group of enemy for me to request to exceed a CDE of 29 (I never confronted this situation).

This night in November, I was confident that our weaponeers and targeteers had worked all the possibilities and 15 was the 'best' number they could give me. They would have anticipated my questions: "What if you change the angle of attack; delay the fuse; change the munition?" These questions were meant to see if a different method of attack would lower the CDE.

I was also confident they would not have gotten me out of bed on mere suspicion of militant activity. Once I had been called into the Command Center; shown imagery of the rooftop meeting of bearded men; and urged to say the two words that would permit a pilot in a circling F-16 or FA-18 to release his weapon: 'clear hot.'

"Who are these guys?" I asked.

"Well, we don't know for sure sir. But a group of military-aged men on a rooftop in Fallujah at 0200 cannot be up to anything good."

I denied permission, and forcefully reviewed the criteria for targeting: either 'Known Hostile' (we knew them by name/association as being members of the insurgency) or 'hostile intent' (based on their clear, military-style behavior). I told my team I expected more from them. They were acting somewhat like a lynch mob and compromising the targeting criteria. "That's not how we as Americans/Marines are going to fight this war," I said. "Hostile intent is not: wrong gender, wrong age, wrong place, wrong time!" I know my team was pressing to 'shape' the upcoming battle space by eliminating as many of the enemy leaders as possible before our warriors would engage them, but that did not give us the right to stretch the definition of 'hostile intent.'

After my critique, someone in the Operations Center responded, "we are well below 29." I responded with: "Roger that, if these knuckleheads are enemy combatants, prove it through analysis and we will eliminate them."

---

45 Note that troops in contact *did not follow this process*; every warrior has the inherent right to self-defense.

As I was walking out of the Operations Center, some lone voice stated "now we will have to fight them mano a mano." I clenched my jaw, but did not turn around and walked back to my room. If they were insurgents, he was right ... the decision not to engage and eliminate them could result in one or more of our warriors being killed or wounded in the fight to come. I had a sick feeling in my stomach ... had I made the right decision?

So this night in November, my staff gave me a solid target package defining the enemy leadership group meeting on the rooftop – a thorough briefing that clearly met the criteria of hostile intent. I listened intently and read the target folder. Then our intelligence officer added greater detail and answered a few questions. The men on the roof were the equivalent of mid-grade officers, significant leaders who would be critical to the enemy's execution in the upcoming battle.

We had good intelligence and we had done everything we could to lower the CDE. Still, the targeteers estimated 15 Iraqi noncombatants would be killed or wounded. These were 15 people who didn't go to bed expecting to die, and didn't ask to live in a building visited by insurgents. Compassion for foreign noncombatants led us to take every precaution to ensure that the strike was necessary, proportionate, and that the risk to noncombatants was minimized. Unfortunately, circumstances prevented us from reducing the risk to noncombatants to zero. This time, based on the value of the target, and the positive impact on our frontline fighters eliminating these enemy leaders would have, I granted permission, and in a matter of minutes, they were eliminated.

II.

Throughout my career, my philosophy has always been 'don't kill anyone who does not need to die.' I am not alone in this philosophy; I believe it is the default of every good combat leader. Every time I gave an order to take a life, whether directly by approving an airstrike or indirectly, by setting policies for the use of deadly force at vehicle check-points, I asked myself "what would the American people say?" I asked myself what my family – including my eight brothers and sisters – would think of my decision. When it came to deliberate targeting, any number 29 or below was legal (by the ROE), but was the military value of the target worth the (potential) number of noncombatants generated by the CDE? The moral/ethical will sometimes trump the legal!

I made a lot of unpopular decisions. No doubt I had peers and subordinates – probably Americans back home – who thought "None of those Iraqis is worth one Marine's life."

If I had heard any of my people say something like that, I would have fired him on the spot. As soon as we start seeing foreign combatants or noncombatants as less than human, as less than us, we have lost. I do not mean this only in a moral sense of having lost touch with our own decency, but lost in a strategic sense. Our mission in 2004 was clear: to pacify Fallujah, clear it of militants, and then turn it over to Iraqi government control. I looked at every fighting age male in Fallujah and saw a potential recruit: either for the insurgents or for the new Iraqi government.

III.

My concern, that every Iraqi be treated with dignity, led me to make regular personal inspections of the detention facility the MEF ran in our area of operations. Either myself or one of my three immediate deputies inspected the facility every day. I wanted to personally ensure that no one was being mistreated. I was concerned that mere instructions to treat detainees humanely would be inadequate; maybe some Marines would think I was just saying the politically correct thing because I had to. Further, while the Marines with whom I served are some of the finest human beings on the planet, none of them were trained to be prison guards. Everyone understands how the conditions of detention can lead people in authority to over time dehumanize detainees. These unannounced 'visits' to our detention facility multiple times a day by different leaders made clear our policy.

I knew, also, in this particular case, that the pace of operations meant we were sweeping up innocent people along with terrorists and insurgents. My team actually requested permission from the International Committee of the Red Cross (ICRC) to extend the initial detention period permitted under international law from 14 to 21 days, so we could better screen the huge number of detainees we were receiving. At first the ICRC refused, suspecting that we wanted the extra time to potentially abuse detainees. Rather, as we explained to ICRC representatives, the exact opposite concern was in play.

After the initial 14-day detention period, detainees would be formally entered into the detention process and moved from our temporary holding facility. Once this happened, it would be six months before their case would be reviewed again (based on sheer numbers). We wanted more time so we could screen locally and hopefully return those who were truly 'wrong gender, wrong age, wrong place, wrong time' to their families to be part of the security/rebuilding process. There was no way you could look into the frightened, sunken eyes of a young man behind bars desperately protesting his innocence – "please, mister, there was some mistake," – and not feel compassion. We wanted to ensure those we knew or had strong suspicion were enemy were entered into the formal detention process, but did not want to detain those young men collected on the battlefield out of necessity, but determined to be noncombatants one day longer than necessary.

Again, compassion has strategic significance here. We figured if an innocent Iraqi did not support the insurgency when we detained him, he certainly would support the insurgency after being imprisoned without trial for six months.

Case Study 2:
Compassion

Rafford M. Coleman

"It is, in part, that by being compassionate and kind rather than malicious or vengeful, a leader will make fewer enemies for himself and his organization and will thereby create more supporters, more dedicated 'soldiers' to aid in the overall corporate mission."[46]

– Donald T. Phillips

Institutional culture develops from core beliefs and character that are molded throughout the organization's lifespan. The values and virtues that build an ethos of professionalism, excellence, and winning are established not just by the words of leaders and supervisors but also by their actions. The skills, attitudes, and behaviors necessary to make any cooperative endeavor prosperous and triumphant starts with how the subordinates view their leader and his or her vision. Success hinges on if the leader knows and believes in the dreams of those in his or her charge. The duration of organizational success depends on the leader's ability to understand and, at times, commiserate with those he or she is managing, guiding, and leading. How these men and women consistently arrive at appropriate moral and ethical decisions beneficial to not only the individual, but also the institution in which they lead requires a four-part discussion on the importance of the virtue of compassion.

---

46 Donald Phillips, *Lincoln On Leadership: Executive Strategies for Tough Times* (New York: Warner Books, 1992), 60.

I. Definitions and Problems

Most definitions of the word 'compassion' involve the use of descriptors such as sympathy and sorrow. There is a general belief that compassion must possess an effort by someone to alleviate distress. Merriam-Webster's definition of compassion is the "sympathetic consciousness of others' distress together with a desire to alleviate it."[47] Should leaders leverage the virtue of compassion to persuade, inspire, and motivate subordinates when Merriam-Webster's definition can be inefficient and time consuming? Compassion cannot be fake. For compassion to be an effective tool, the leader must truly believe in using kindness to produce beneficial attitudes and behaviors from subordinates. Should compassion be an essential virtue for leaders? These are two very difficult questions to answer. If a leader were to focus too much on compassion it could interfere, slow or even undermine advancement toward the organizational or institutional goals. Leaders who exhibit no compassion will eventually fail. Their success rides on the backs of subordinates who will not trust leadership. Loyalty to the leader or organization will falter and subordinates' enthusiasm, motivation and drive will wane. Leaders must execute their responsibilities in ways that balance loyalties, priorities and the simple idea of 'sympathy.' This balance between mission priorities and the care for the subordinate is a skill taught and nurtured.

Part II: Leaders are not Born, They are Made

The easiest way to develop compassion within leaders is to have burgeoning leaders be both a student and a 'follower,' concurrently, early in their career. This experience will inform men and women about the hardships of being on the 'bottom' and almost immediately provide insight into various leadership-styles both positive and negative. More importantly, this aspect of development instills discipline and teaches institutional values to the 'follower' laying the desired foundation for the construction of a leader. If done properly, they should learn not only the organizational culture but also 'what right looks like.' The 'follower' focuses on learning their craft. Job proficiency increases credibility and reliability while also building a subordinate's trust in their leaders actions and intentions. As months turn to years, the 'follower' gains indispensable experience, technical acumen, and self-confidence. Consistent positive interactions between leader and

---

47 "Compassion," https://www.merriam-webster.com/dictionary/compassion. Accessed May 23, 2018.

led instills confidence in both and informs decision-makers about the developing leader's character and personality. The apprentice learns through observation and education how role models leverage compassion for effective leadership of subordinates. Given small opportunities to experiment with leadership, the apprentice ultimately applies various leadership traits to inspire, motivate and persuade others to get a job completed. Through these stages, the developing leadership pupil develops his or her own definition of compassion. While the study of leadership is never final, there is a point in which the basic tenets or objectives are understood or learned to such a degree that a new leader must be allowed to go to the 'lead.' The final objective, prior to unleashing a new leader, is honing the 'softer-side' of leadership. When a leader understands how and when he or she leverages compassion it better assists them in building trust and confidence and ultimately enabling accomplishment of any task regardless of risks or even dangers.

Part III: Leading with Love in Your Heart

There is a leadership principle known simply as, 'Lead with Love.' The premise is that leaders must care enough to build positive and influential relationships with subordinates and employees that generate trust, are respectful and productive. Disciples of the 'Lead with Love' philosophy are also devoted to General John A. Lejeune's comments in the *Marine Corps Manual* which states that the "relation between officers [leader] and enlisted [led] should in no sense be that of superior and inferior nor that of master and servant, but rather that of teacher and scholar. In fact, it should partake of the nature of the relation between father and son."[48] Leaders should reject notorious management-styles that rule with the 'iron fist' or apply draconian methods with money or production goals as the singular aim. Instead, a paternal or maternal interest for subordinates propagates a style of leadership in which the success of the subordinate equals and contributes to the success of the team or organization.

Compassionate leaders care about their people first and always. If danger is a part of the occupation, leaders care enough to ensure they prepare their people. Leaders ensure they don't waste life or limb when unnecessary. This mindset accelerates trust and loyalty as well as respect. Compassion's virtuous assets of patience, loyalty, honesty and reliability

---

48 Department of the Navy, United States Marines Corps. *Marine Corps Manual* W/CH 1-3 (Washington, DC: 1980). https://www.marines.mil/Portals/59/Publications/MARINE%20CORPS%20MANUAL%20W%20CH%201-3.pdf.

enhances the mentor and mentee relationship. If the true nature of the relationship between leader and subordinate is a healthy, kindred one, in which the leader's intentions and actions always consider the subordinates' development, welfare, and future, then compassion is clearly present. 'Lead with love' does not espouse the treatment of subordinates as children. It adds to the 'golden rule' of lead and treat others the way you would want to be treated. It requires that leaders make decisions based on personal connections. This level of seriousness helps leaders make ethical and moral decisions that keeps their power in check, benefits the individual and team, and prevents knee-jerk decisions that ruin careers and lives.

Compassion can be small gestures or second chances. As a servant leader, compassion is seen as caring enough for simple respect and acts of kindness. A leader has the ability to reinforce the idea of a person's value or worth. Leaders can make employees feel important and part of the success. Leaders can use their positions to cultivate potential and build character. When compassion of the leader intersects with the passion and enthusiasm of a subordinate, futures are positively impacted.

Part IV: Case Study: Tough Love

In August 1990, the invasion of Kuwait by Iraqi forces posed an immediate threat to global economies. President George H. W. Bush ordered U.S. intervention to halt Iraqi aggression and protect Saudi Arabia. The United States Marine Corps deployed most of its operating forces and activated thousands of Marine Reservists.

Corporal Shannon Clay[49] USMCR (United States Marine Corps Reserve), was a young black man raised in a loving working-class household in Prince George's County, Maryland. By the summer of 1990, he was not only a successful rising junior at the University of Maryland, but also high mobility multipurpose-wheeled vehicle (HMMWV) driver in his SMCR (Selected Marine Corps Reserve) unit. Cpl Clay's unit was based in Baltimore, Maryland and was commanded by a Vietnam veteran named Colonel Robert Early, a lawyer in Washington D.C.

One day, Cpl Clay sat in his vehicle gazing out over the dunes that were being sun-kissed by the rising sun. As he sat there listening to music on his Sony Walkman, he wondered what his family was doing. What were his friends doing? Did his girlfriend miss him? Corporal Clay's

---

49   This case study is based on true events and witnessed by the author. All names and some places have been changed to protect those involved and are pseudonyms based on actual people from a small USMCR unit that was activated and deployed.

homesickness was exceedingly bad this day. All military members grapple with homesickness regardless of age or rank. You never get used to it, you just learn how to cope with it. On this day however, it was really troubling him. Maybe it was the fact they were closer to Kuwait or the realization that war was inevitable. No matter the reason, Corporal Clay was desperate for any piece of comfort, any piece of home.

"Clay," said Corporal Sanchez. "Come on, we have to get the morning brief," he said. Corporal Clay reluctantly took off his headphones and followed Sanchez to a circle of other Marines awaiting the day's tasking. Gunnery Sergeant (GySgt) Liston began with a basic tactical and force protection update and then barked out assignments. "With only days until the deadline we have to get the rest of our unit up here but we also have to help out other units within Headquarters Battalion. Corporal Johnson … Lance Corporal Richards, you two hit the lotto. Y'all are leading two other hi-backs (M1038 Cargo variant HMMWV vehicles) back to Jubail. You got the Log Run (short for Logistics) to Camps 15 and 3," he said. "Staff Sergeant Palmer is waiting for all of you guys at Camp 15 but feel free to hit the PX, get some ice cream or make a call home to the states. Any questions?" Jubail was the initial staging area for all of 2nd Marine Division. For almost a month it was home to tens of thousands of Marines, sailors, and U.S. Army soldiers. With air-conditioned trailers, dining halls, video games, stores, and an abundance of phones, the former 2nd Marine Division 'temporary' bases in Al Jubail were heaven compared to the tent city carved out of the Saudi Arabian desert. GySgt Liston handed out the remaining local assignments. "Clay, you and Sanchez go help Communications platoon with laying wire and setting up antennas. They need help tying in communications with 10th Marines and the Division combat Operations Center," GySgt Adams said. Needless to say, laying wires in the desert heat was not as appealing as a road trip to Jubail. After glumly acknowledging the orders, Corporals Clay and Sanchez walked toward their GP Tents to get their gear and drive over to the Communications Platoon area. It was at that moment that the jealous and dejected Cpl Clay remembered. "Oh shit, I forgot to pick up the Commanding Officer's (CO) laundry yesterday." Cpl Clay, had been sent to the port the day before to pick up radios and had been told to check in at the laundry facility to see if Colonel Early's laundry was ready. Cpl Clay had forgotten. He ran to catch Cpl Johnson and LCPL Richards to see if they could pick up the CO's laundry but they were gone. Cpl Clay ran to the dispatcher to see how far ahead they were. The LCPL stated they had called outbound 10 minutes ago. Clay looked at Sanchez and said, "come on." "What are we doing man," Sanchez asked as Clay strapped into his HMMWV. "We are going to catch those Hummers," Clay said. He added, "And if we don't catch them, we'll go to Jubail and get the boss's gear and be back before dark." Sanchez did not agree with the plan. With a war about to start, driving 120 miles alone and without permission was crazy and in violation of the Commanding General's Order #1 for force protection. Sanchez knew that one of the things Clay wanted to do was get some ice cream and make a phone call to his girlfriend. Cpl Sanchez knew they were wrong but lacked the moral courage to speak up. He thought to himself, "hell I could use a shower and some ice cream too."

One might not think of warriors, who live a life of discipline and honor, as compassionate. Col Early never showed much emotion or caring for his sailors and Marines. He was always very serious, lacked a dynamic personality, and rarely talked to junior enlisted other than to say "Good Morning or Have a Great Day." As a former Infantry Officer now turned civilian lawyer, Col. Early was methodical and focused. Col. Early demanded excellence and always argued his points in a way that few could disagree with. He was not much of a motivator but his Marines could always tell he was motivated and enthusiastic. They just never knew why. Now, Cpl Clay's entire future was in Col. Early's hands. The Commanding General's office relayed that they wanted their 'pound of flesh' from the belligerent Marine who 'stole' an HMMWV six days ago. The investigating officer's report was damning. The young Marine had violated several general orders and Uniform Code of Military Justice articles. Any future the young Cpl had of continuing his career as a Marine seemed over. Col. Early mulled it over. He examined Cpl Clay's service records and consulted with his executive officer, Sergeant Major Mollohan, and SSgt Palmer. The time had come.

Cpl Clay was called into Col. Early's tent. Col Early had started the conversation with the young Marine (Cpl Clay) braced at attention but the yelling lasted only for a few minutes. Now they were all sitting. They would sit there for over an hour, a conversation between Cpl Clay, SgtMaj Mollahan, and the CO. While this 49-year-old white man from an affluent neighborhood of Montgomery County, Maryland had little in common with a 20-year-old young black man, both Early and Clay were Marines. Early was a father and a son. He viewed his Marines, regardless of gender or race, as 'his' Marines. Col. Early asked Cpl Clay why he had done what he did. The young Corporal, although nervous felt at ease and free to speak. He told the older and wiser veteran that he truly saw two positives that would come from his unauthorized drive to Al Jubail. Clay stated that not only would he get the much needed clothes for the CO but also improve his personal morale. In the end, both the service and the unit would benefit. Then Cpl Clay ended with, "But sir. I broke the rules. And there must be consequences. Marines don't break rules, unless they are not right or legal. That was not the case. I was selfish and immature. I apologize for embarrassing our unit sir. I am sorry for wasting your precious time. I deserve whatever punishment you see fit," said Cpl Clay. Col. Early paused and looked at the young man to gauge his sincerity and his contrition. He reflected on his years as a spoiled youth, and then as a young college man at Georgetown University in the late 1960s and his early years making bone-headed decisions as a young Marine 2nd Lieutenant. The three talked about women, children, life, the Corps and the future. Cpl Clay did not recognize this as mentorship, he had rarely heard the term but it did remind him of his own father and former coaches. His current coach from Maryland had sent him letters and the tone was similar. As the counseling and teaching ended, Cpl Clay was no longer fearful. He felt enlightened and inspired. He was ready to go to court martial and atone for his sins.

Sgt Maj Mollahan yelled out the tent and immediately thereafter Cpl Clay was joined by a Private First Class, a fellow Corporal, his squad leader, SSgt Palmer and two other Officers. "Cpl Clay, there are many that want you out of the Marine Corps. Others just want you to pay for the crime with some sort of painful time spent being punished. I don't think any of that is appropriate for you. I have watched you for the better part of two years. I called your coach back at Maryland. I even talked to both a Professor at College Park and one of your teachers from high school. Your peers think highly of you and the NCOs and SNCOs say you are lazy and not living up to your full potential. As intelligent as you are, you clearly make some very bad decisions. I am not sure if you were focused on helping me or just helping yourself. I think it was probably both. But I do know if you or Cpl Sanchez had been hurt or killed neither my laundry nor your girlfriend would have had been that important. You have a bright future. I think that one day you would make a fine Marine Corps SNCO or even a Naval Officer. I hope you will consider that. You committed an Offense but it was not egregious. In my heart, I believe you will make a difference one day and if I were to adjudicate you it may de-rail or prevent the positive you will do from happening. Therefore, here's my decision (all the Marines snapped to attention). Your promotion to Sergeant is on hold indefinitely. Sgt Maj, make sure Cpl Clay gets every crappy leadership detail that comes along." Col. Early turns back to Clay and said, " And finally, you are to apply for Marine OCS (Officer Candidate School) between now and when we go home. Do you understand?" he said. Everyone present yelled, "Yes Sir." Col Early looked at Cpl Clay and softly concluded with the following, "We will be at war within days. I need all my best people ready to go. You are one of my best people. Don't Let Me down!"

Cpl Clay would fight with his unit in securing the liberation of Kuwait earning a Combat Action Ribbon and two Certificates of Commendation for actions against the enemy. Two years later, he would later go on to graduate from the University of Maryland and commission as an Officer. At his commissioning in the audience that day was Colonel Early, USMC Retired. Compassionate leadership is born from a servant leader's commitment to building relationships similar to that of parent and an offspring. The leader must lead, loving both the job and those that he or she is leading. All leaders actions to or for subordinates must have a purpose. The stress and pressure that leaders put on their men and women should be in order to make them more resilient, to make them better and to help them reach shared goals. Effective leaders in winning organizations will always have some component of caring and compassion as a part of who they are. Leadership should not focus inward or simply on the institution. Leaders cannot be distant, emotionless, or aloof from subordinates. Leaders must generate inspiration and innovativeness. Leaders should strive to influence others as transformational teachers. And finally, leaders must care enough about their people's success to let compassion rule the day. When they do these things, everything else normally works out.

References

Aristotle, *The Nicomachean Ethics*, translated by J. A. K. Thomson. London: Penguin, 1953, 32.

Bourke, J. *An Intimate History of Killing: Face to Face Killing in the 20th Century.* London: Granta, 1999.

Buber, M. *I and Thou.* Translation with Prologue 'I and You' and Notes by Walter Kaufmann. New York: Charles Scribner's Sons, 1970.

Coker, C. *Ethics and War in the 21st Century.* London and New York: Routledge, 2008.

Dannatt, R. "The Battle for Hearts and Minds: Morality and Warfare Today," November 8, 2011 Theos Annual Lecture, https://www.theosthinktank.co.uk/research/2011/11/08/the-battle-for-hearts-and-minds-morality-and-warfare-today.

Darley, J. M. and D. Batson, "'From Jerusalem to Jericho': A study of Situational and Dispositional Variables in Helping Behavior," *Journal of Personality and Social Psychology* 27, no. 1 (1973): 100–108.

Department of the Navy, United States Marines Corps. *Marine Corps Manual W/CH 1-3.* Washington, D.C., 1980, https://www.marines.mil/Portals/59/Publications/MARINE%20CORPS%20MANUAL%20W%20CH%201-3.pdf.

Doris, J. M. *Lack of Character: Personality and Moral Behaviour*. Cambridge: Cambridge University Press, 2002.

Durant, W. *The Story of Philosophy*. New York: Garden City, 1926.

Grossman, D. *On Killing: The Psychological Cost of Learning to Kill in War and Society* New York: Back Bay, 1995.

Harman, G. "No Character or Personality," *Business Ethics Quarterly* 13, no. 1 (2003): 87–94.

Harman, G. "Skepticism about Character Traits," *The Journal of Ethics* 13, Nos. 2/3 (2009): 235–42.

Holmes, R. *Acts of War: The Behaviour of Men in Battle*. London: Weidenfeld & Nicolson, 2003.

Jackson F. "Soldiers cannot kill and show compassion at the same time," *The Guardian* November 14, 2011. https://www.theguardian.com/uk/2011/nov/14/soldiers-cannot-kill-and-show-compassion.

Ignatieff, M. *Virtual War: Kosovo and Beyond*. New York: Picador, 2000.

Isen, A. M. and S. F. Simmonds. "The Effect of Feeling Good on a Helping Task that is incompatible with Good Mood," *Social Psychology* 41, no. 4 (1978): 346–49.

Kahn, P. "The Paradox of Riskless War," *Philosophy and Public Policy Quarterly* 22 (Summer 2002): 3.

Kant, I. *Groundwork for the Metaphysics of Morals*, edited and translated by A. W. Wood New Haven and London: Yale University Press, 2002.

Latané, B. and J. Rodin. "A lady in distress: Inhibiting effects of friends and strangers on bystander intervention," *Journal of Experimental Social Psychology* 5, no. 2 (1969): 189–202.

Lord Moran, *The Anatomy of Courage*. London: Constable, 1945.

Mang, C. S., K. L. Campbell, C. J. D. Ross and L. Boyd. "Promoting Neuroplasticity for Motor Rehabilitation After Stroke: Considering the Effects of Aerobic Exercise and Genetic Variation on Brain-Derived Neurotrophic Factor," in *Physical Therapy* 93, no. 12 (2013): 1707–16.

Marlantes, K. *What It Is Like To Go To War*. London: Corvus, 2012.

Merriam-Webster. "Compassion." https://www.merriam-webster.com/dictionary/compassion, accessed May 23, 2018.

Milgram, S. *Obedience to Authority: An Experimental View*. New York: Harper Collins, 2009.

Nussbaum, M. "Compassion: The Basic Social Emotion," *Social Philosophy and Policy* 13, no. 1 (1996): 27–58.

Pardum, J. T. "Good Samaritan Laws: A Global Perspective," 20 *Loy. L.A. Int'l & Comp. L. Rev.* (1998): 591. March 1. http://digitalcommons.lmu.edu/ilr/vol20/iss3/8.

Phillips, D. T. *Lincoln On Leadership: Executive Strategies for Tough Times*. New York: Warner Books, 1992.

Plato, *The Apology of Socrates,* translated by B. Jowett, edited by J. Breshears, http://www.theareopagus.org/blog/wp-content/uploads/2014/09/Plato-The-Apolology-of-Socrates.pdf, accessed November 2018.

Plato, *The Republic.* May 18, 2002. http://www.idph.net/conteudos/ebooks/republic.pdf.

Ridolfi, K. M. "Law, Ethics, and the Good Samaritan: Should There Be a Duty to Rescue?" *Santa Clara Law Review* 40, no. 4, (2000): 957–70.

Roberts, R. "Emotions in the Christian Tradition," *The Stanford Encyclopedia of Philosophy,* Winter 2016 Edition, edited by Edward Zalta. https://plato.stanford.edu/entries/emotion-Christian-tradition/.

Smith, A. *The Theory of Moral Sentiments,* edited by Jonathan Bennett, 2017. http://www.earlymoderntexts.com/assets/pdfs/smith1759.pdf.

Smith, E. *Neuroplasticity: Old Brain Meets New Tricks* (independently published, 2017).

Snow, N. E. "Compassion," *American Philosophical Quarterly* 28, no. 3 (1991): 195.

Sznaider, N. "The Sociology of Compassion: A Study in the Sociology of Morals," in *Cultural Values* 2, no. 1 (1998): 132.

Williams, R. "Religious Faith and Human Rights," May 1, 2008. http://www.lse.ac.uk/humanRights/events/rowanWilliams.aspx.

Zimbardo, P. *The Lucifer Effect: How Good People Turn Evil.* London: Rider, 2007.

13

DISCIPLINE

Overview

Paul Robinson

In November 1920, the Bolshevik Red Army burst through the defences of the counter-revolutionary White Russian Army in Crimea. To avoid destruction, the Whites fled across the Black Sea to Turkey. Several days later, after a harrowing journey in overcrowded ships short of food and water, troops of the First Army Corps disembarked at Gallipoli. Walking down the quay, one White officer was startled to find himself confronted by the Corps commander, General A.P. Kutepov, who demanded to know why his coat was torn. When the officer failed to provide an adequate answer, Kutepov ordered his arrest and confinement in the Corps guardroom.

The arrest typified Kutepov's approach as commander of the First Army Corps at Gallipoli. When the White troops disembarked, they were utterly dejected. Kutepov put them to work, drilled them repeatedly, and imposed harsh discipline punishing slightest infraction. When Kutepov met the arrested officer again several months after their confrontation, he asked him if he understood why he had been arrested. "For having a torn coat," the officer replied. "No," said Kutepov, "I arrested you because you were dejected and apathetic. By making you indignant at your treatment, I revived your sense of self-respect." The officer agreed that it had worked.[1]

In this he was not alone. At first the soldiers at Gallipoli hated their general for his harshness. What was the point, they complained, of enforcing discipline on a defeated army? Why arrest an officer for a torn coat when he had just escaped from a war zone, and spent several days on

---

1 For the story of Kutepov and the officer with the torn coat, see V. Sukhanev, "Gallipoli," State Archive of the Russian Federation, fond 5881, opis 2, delo 612.

a barely seaworthy ship? It seemed unreasonable. But bit by bit, the morale of the troops improved. Their sense of purpose was restored, and so was their self-confidence. By the time they left, about a year after their arrival, many believed that the moral change which they had experienced was little short of a miracle.

The story of the 'Gallipoli miracle' reveals the importance of discipline as a moral force. Years later, White soldiers admiringly quoted Kutepov as saying: "If there's discipline, there's an army. If there's an army, there's Russia." Discipline, in other words, was the very foundation on which an army and a nation are built.[2]

The Roman author Vegetius made this point in a paragraph much quoted by European military thinkers:

> Victory in war depends not absolutely on numbers or sheer courage. Conduct and discipline only will ensure it. The Romans, we find, owed the conquest of the world to no other cause than a continual exercise of arms, an exact observance of discipline in their camps, and an unwearied cultivation of the other arts of war … A handful of men, inured to war, proceed, as it were, to certain victory, while, on the contrary, numerous armies of raw and undisciplined troops are but multitudes of men dragged to slaughter.[3]

The importance of discipline can be seen by contrasting war as fought by disciplined armies with war as fought by charismatic heroes.[4] Homeric warfare might be seen as an archetype of the charismatic version. Homeric warriors fight for their own glory; they break ranks when it suits them; they seek out opponents for one-on-one combat; they stop in the midst of battle to loot. The greatest hero of all, Achilles, even refused to fight after he felt that he had been insulted. Charismatic warriors pursue their own objectives, such as fame and plunder. Disciplined soldiers, by contrast, pursue the army's objectives. As the famous sociologist Max Weber pointed out, discipline ensures that soldiers act in a way which is "rationally uniform."[5] This provides predictability amid the chaotic conditions of war. Told to fight the enemy, disciplined soldiers don't refuse or stop to loot; they turn up when and where they are meant to; they maintain their

---

2   For a discussion of the 'Gallipoli miracle,' see Paul Robinson, *The White Russian Army in Exile, 1920–1941* (Oxford: Clarendon Press, 2002), 31–50.

3   Flavius Vegetius Renatus, *Military Institutions of Vegetius, in Five Books, Translated from the Original Latin. With a Preface and Notes. By Lieutenant John Clarke* (London: W. Griffin, 1767), 4–6.

4   I draw the distinction between charisma and discipline from Max Weber, "The Meaning of Discipline," in *From Max Weber: Essays in Sociology*, ed. Hans Heinrich Gerth and C. Wright Mills (New York: Oxford University Press, 1967), 253–65.

5   Weber, "The Meaning of Discipline," 253.

equipment so that it doesn't break; and they abide by the laws of war. As a result, they are likely to prevail over fighters who don't.

Charismatic warfare of the Homeric type eventually gave way to the discipline of the Greek phalanx and the Roman legion, just as later the honour-seeking of chivalric knights gave way to the discipline of Swiss mercenaries, Spanish *tercios*, and the infantry of the seventeenth-century 'military revolution.' Today's military leaders cherish discipline for a simple reason – historical experience has shown that it is essential to victory.

What, then, is discipline? Given its centrality in military life, one might imagine that it would have been repeatedly defined and discussed. However, descriptions of discipline in official military publications tend to be quite cursory, while scholarly examinations of military virtues generally only mention discipline in passing.[6] A survey of scholarly databases reveals just two articles devoted to defining military discipline, both written by a retired Russian officer, Colonel I. N. Volkov.[7] Discipline is taken for granted, and intuitively understood, but rarely analyzed.

As Volkov points out, discipline has two related but separate meanings, both of which can be seen in the story of Kutepov and the torn coat. The first meaning is shown by the general's punishment of the officer; the second by Kutepov's insistence that the punishment had a moral purpose. On the one hand, discipline refers to the actions taken by those in authority to ensure desirable behaviour by those under their command. This includes, but is not limited to, punishment for infractions of military regulations. On the other hand, discipline refers to what Volkov calls a "phenomenon of individual self-consciousness." Discipline of this sort is often called 'self-discipline' and may be seen as a moral or spiritual characteristic, which manifests itself in behaviour.[8] Discipline of this second sort overlaps to some degree with various other virtues, such as obedience, self-control, restraint, and promptness. It also involves attention to detail.

Most often, discipline, both as a system imposed from above and as self-discipline, is associated with obedience. Max Weber, for instance, wrote that,

---

6 For instance, in his discussion of military virtues, Richard A. Gabriel devotes only a single paragraph to the subject of discipline: Richard A. Gabriel, *The Warrior's Way: A Treatise on Military Ethics* (Kingston, Ontario: Canadian Defence Academy Press, 2007), 150. Peter Olsthoorn's *Military Ethics and Virtues: An Interdisciplinary Approach for the 21st Century* (Abingdon: Routledge, 2011) mentions the word 'discipline' just once in its index.

7 Col. I. N. Volkov (Ret.), "What is the Essence of Military Discipline?" *Military Thought* 11, no. 2 (2002): 118–22; Col. I. N. Volkov (Ret.), "Relationship Between Military Discipline and Self-Discipline," *Military Thought* 14, no. 4 (2005): 148–54.

8 Volkov, "Relationship," 148–49.

> The content of discipline is nothing but the consistently rationalized, methodically trained and exact execution of the received order, in which all personal criticism is unconditionally suspended and the actor is unswervingly and exclusively set for carrying out the command.[9]

Various military documents take a similar line. A 1960 U.S. Army report defined discipline as "a state of mind which leads to willingness to obey an order no matter how unpleasant or dangerous."[10] Another American report, published in 1978, stated that, "self-discipline can be defined in terms of an absolute *motivation to obey*."[11] More recently, *The Values and Standards of the British Army* notes that, "To be effective on ... operations, the Army must ... act as a disciplined force. Commanders must be certain that their orders will be carried out."[12] And, *Duty with Honour: The Profession of Arms in Canada* states that, "Discipline ... allows compliance with the interests and goals of the military institution ... Discipline among professionals is fundamentally self-discipline that facilitates immediate and willing obedience to lawful orders and directives."[13]

This narrow focus on obedience is insufficient for a proper definition of discipline, however. Discipline goes beyond meeting the minimal requirements of orders, instructions, or regulations. It is as concerned with how things are done as with what is done. Richard Gabriel defines discipline in terms of intellect. He writes:

> A good soldier must be able to improvise as circumstances demand, and that requires that he or she think about those circumstances in a disciplined manner ... True discipline is the steady application of a course of action carefully thought out.[14]

Gabriel's definition draws attention to the fact that discipline implies an ability to function in the absence of orders, and so cannot be defined purely in terms of obedience. War often involves extremely chaotic circumstances. Communications may not work. Nobody may be around to tell the soldier what to do. Discipline involves doing what has to be done, regardless. As another British Army document, entitled *The Army Leadership Guide*, says,

---

9   Weber, "The Meaning of Discipline," 253.

10 Mark J. Osiel, *Obeying Orders: Atrocity, Military Discipline and the Law of War* (New Brunswick, NJ: Transaction, 1999), 26.

11 Policy Sciences Division, *Military Self-Discipline: A Motivational Analysis* (Arlington, VA: CACI, 1978), 4.

12 *The Values and Standards of the British Army* (no publication details provided), 8.

13 *Duty with Honour: The Profession of Arms in Canada* (Kingston, Ontario: Canadian Defence Academy – Canadian Forces Leadership Institute, 2003), 27.

14 Gabriel, *The Warrior's Way*, 149.

"Good discipline means soldiers will do the right thing even under the most difficult of circumstances."[15] An article about military psychiatry published during the Second World War similarly noted that,

> Proper discipline should in no sense be based upon the fear of disciplinary correction, since in this instance we merely have schoolroom discipline. The discipline upon which a successful army must be built is a different kind – a kind that endures when every semblance of authority has vanished.[16]

Discipline, it is believed, enables soldiers to succeed in such conditions by habituating them to pay attention to detail and to understand the importance of precision, exactitude, and timeliness. For this reason, it is often associated with drills of various sorts. Parade ground drill, for instance, teaches soldiers to move together exactly and precisely. Kutepov supposedly always turned up early for any meeting he was due to attend, and then walked around outside the building before entering at the precise moment when he was scheduled to appear. In combat one cannot have soldiers turn up late (or early, for that matter). The disciplined soldier is one who abides by such precision at all times.

To act in such a way, the soldier needs to put aside his or her own personal preferences. Discipline is thus commonly associated with self-restraint and self-control. For the Romans, the model was that of the consul Manlius Torquatus who awarded his son a laurel crown for "an act of the utmost gallantry" involving single combat against an enemy before a battle, and then ordered his son's execution for disobeying orders not to do such a thing.[17] The son had not merely been disobedient; he had failed to exhibit self-control, putting his own desire for glory above the collective good. Self-control may be seen as an Aristotelian mean, lying between rashness on the one hand and cowardice on the other. It is also often connected with an ascetic outlook; excessive luxury is felt to undermine self-control. The disciplined person is one who foregoes pleasures to get the job done. Discipline is thereby connected to many of the other virtues discussed in this book – obedience, courage, temperance, and patience.

The instillation of these virtues requires a multi-faceted approach. Discipline has often been associated primarily with coercive methods. Roman discipline was notoriously harsh by the standards of the time and

---

15 *The Army Leadership Guide: An Introductory Guide*, First Edition, 8, accessed April 13, 2018, https://www.army.mod.uk/media/2698/ac72021_the_army_leadership_code_an_introductory_guide.pdf.

16 P. S. Madigan, "Military Neuro Psychiatry, Discipline, and Morale," *Journal of Criminal Law and Criminology* 32, no. 5 (1942): 491–92.

17 Plutarch, *The Makers of Rome*, trans. Ian Scott-Kilvert (London: Penguin, 1965), 64.

caught the attention of non-Romans who observed the Roman army at work. Greek historian Polybius, for instance, reported that officers had "the power to inflict fines, distrain on goods, and to order a flogging," and that "The punishment of beating to death is also inflicted upon those who give false evidence, those who in full manhood commit homosexual offences, and finally upon anyone who has been punished three times for the same offence."[18] Referring to himself in the third person, the Jewish general Josephus who led an army against the Romans in 67AD, recorded how:

> Josephus knew that the invincible might of Rome was chiefly due to unhesitating obedience and to practice in arms ... he now reorganized his army on the Roman model ... Above all he trained them [his soldiers] by stressing Roman discipline at every turn; they would be facing men who had conquered the entire world by physical prowess and unshakable determination. He would feel certain of their soldierly qualities even before they went into action, if they refrained from their besetting sins of theft, banditry, and looting.[19]

In this passage, Josephus links discipline to both obedience and self-control. From the time of the Renaissance onwards, military leaders in the West consciously followed this Roman model, often citing Vegetius's comments on discipline. Early modern and modern armies took matters far beyond the Romans, however, in imposing forms of drill and uniformity which had never been part of the Roman military experience. This gave discipline some negative connotations, associating it with mindless conformity, inflexibility, and excessive concern with trivialities. In the conditions of modern war, in which authority is often delegated to the lowest level, and soldiers need to be able to demonstrate autonomy and initiative, many feel that discipline needs to take a different form.[20]

History indicates that this is quite possible. In their study of Greek and Roman warfare, Philip Sabin, Hans van Wees and Michael Whitby write of "a striking feature of ancient Greek as opposed to Persian or Roman warfare: the marked lack of physical discipline and the laxness of any other sort of discipline."[21] This should not be misunderstood. Greek phalanx warfare relied on discipline; it was a team effort. Self-discipline was essential. What was lacking was the other type of discipline – the coercive type. Punishment

---

18 Polybius, *The Rise of the Roman Empire*, trans. Ian Scott-Kilvert (London: Penguin, 1979), 333.

19 Josephus, *The Jewish War*, trans. G. A. Williamson (London: Penguin, 1959), 180–81.

20 Osiel, *Obeying Orders*, 207. See also Policy Sciences Division, *Military Self-Discipline*, 2–3.

21 Philip Sabin, Hans van Wees and Michael Whitby, *The Cambridge History of Greek and Roman Warfare*, vol. 1 (Cambridge: Cambridge University Press, 2007), 34.

for cowardice, insubordination, and the like was very rare. Yet phalanxes were still able to operate successfully as disciplined bodies. Similarly, V. Sukhanev, the Russian officer who recorded the story of Kutepov and the torn coat, noted that his own unit did not need Kutepov's harsh discipline. It disciplined itself, he wrote. The unit contained a large number of highly educated personnel who wanted to stick together.[22] Their education and cohesion enabled them to be disciplined without the threat of punishment.

A study of Roman discipline by Sara Phang reveals that, despite the observations of Polybius and Josephus, the Roman army did not rely solely on drills and harsh punishment. It also kept soldiers busy while in camp, surrounded them with symbols, uniforms, and etiquette which built a sense of military identity, encouraged austerity and discouraged luxury.[23] In his book *Discipline and Punish*, Michel Foucault theorized that discipline is achieved by what he called the "micro-physics of power." This operates "at a quite different level" to that of legal punishment. It "is not exercised simply as an obligation or a prohibition on those who 'do not have it' [but] invests them, is transmitted by them and through them,"[24] in effect ensuring that people internalize the need for discipline and enforce it themselves. According to Foucault, one of the most important of these "micro-physics" is controlling soldiers' bodies: they are expected to stand in a certain way, cut their hair in a certain way, and walk in a certain way; they are expected to dress in a certain way; and they are expected to endure physical hardship to develop fit, healthy bodies.[25] Other methods of internalizing discipline identified by Foucault include "the constant surveillance of troops," and "drills, physical training, organized group recreation, mental testing, medical measurement, examination, and classification."[26] Also important are leadership and small group cohesion – as in the case of Sukhanev's unit, the desire to remain a part of the group may be as important in maintaining discipline as any external coercion.

The objective of discipline, ultimately, is not mindless automata drilled to parade ground perfection. As Gabriel says, "It is simply not true that discipline is the enemy of thought." Rather, "Only when the mind is properly disciplined can it think and make choices."[27]

---

22 Sukhanev, "Gallipoli."
23 Sara Elise Phang, *Roman Military Service: Ideologies of Discipline in the Late Republic and Early Principate* (Cambridge: Cambridge University Press, 2008).
24 Michel Foucault, *Discipline and Punish: The Birth of the Prison* (New York: Vintage, 1979), 26–27.
25 For a discussion of the cult of the body in the military, see Nancy Sherman, *Stoic Warriors: The Ancient Philosophy Behind the Military Mind* (Oxford: Oxford University Press, 2005), 18–41.
26 Osiel, *Obeying Orders*, 211.
27 Gabriel, *The Warrior's Way*, 149, 156.

To conclude, discipline has a twofold meaning. On the one hand, it consists of measures, including, but not limited to, coercion, used by those in authority in order to ensure desirable behaviour among subordinates. On the other hand, it is a state of mind manifested in certain forms of behaviour. This second form of discipline might alternatively be referred to as self-discipline. The ideal is soldiers who can be relied upon to exercise self-control and self-restraint, and to act with precision, exactitude, and timeliness. The ideal of discipline, therefore, is not soldiers who merely obey out of fear of punishment, but soldiers with the spirit to discipline themselves even when authority is weak or absent.

Case Study 1:
The Necessity of Self Control
and The Perils of Anger[28]

Benoit Royal

Some men freely choose to follow dangerous professions or to pursue risky passions. The profession of soldier is one such, but not the only one. The level of mortal risk, which the individual decides to accept in such cases, is the result of a very personal commitment which has its roots in the depths of his conscience and which implicates only himself. On the other hand, the power to inflict death has moral consequences well in excess simply of the possibility of suffering it oneself. It is in here that one of the primary specificities of the military profession is to be found: to accept the responsibility for killing and to risk being wounded or killed oneself. But this responsibility acquires an additional dimension once it no longer concerns only one's own person, but all those in the unit one commands. A further decision-making burden lies within this dimension, for the military commander alone bears responsibility for the act of collective death, whether of suffering it or inflicting it.

This responsibility is inherent in war and conflict. The success of the mission may lead to sacrificing lives on both sides and exercising such responsibility presents painful dilemmas. What level of risk to take? What level of force to apply? When does the use of force cease to be an acceptable norm and become unacceptable violence? Finally, do the ends justify the

---

28 Extracts from Benoit Royal, *The Ethical Challenges of the Soldier: The French Experience* (Paris: Economica, 2012).

use of any means to complete a mission, which must in every case be central to the commander's concerns?

The urgency and the time pressure when faced with the dilemma of a choice that might go as far as putting life on the line, demands that those in authority prepare themselves during peacetime. Faced with such eventualities, people need something very strong and clear to hold on to, recognised as reference points by everyone. In war, soldiers need meaning to guide their actions. They need pillars of consciousness that are called ethical virtues. Faced with situations that are humanly and morally unacceptable, often at the limit of what is bearable, only sound and well-grounded ethical principles will allow soldiers and leaders to find appropriate responses in the field.

The Discipline of Self-Control

Concerning the value of discipline, let me quote Sun Tzu, who, two-and-a-half millennia ago, wrote in *The Art of War*: "Order or disorder depends on organization and direction, courage or cowardice, strength or weakness of tactical dispositions."

Strength of character, discipline and self-control are clearly among the indispensable characteristics of everyone with the responsibility to lead in combat. Although, like all intrinsic qualities, these are unequally distributed between individuals they can, however, be easily enhanced: bravery and withstanding danger can be taught. Armies have long implemented such training and have further developed it in the form of 'battle hardening.'

The need to train potential combatants – to harden them to make them able to withstand all the vicissitudes of war – is as ancient as war itself. But the most effective method of achieving this has changed over the centuries, in parallel with the way that the character of warfare has changed. These days, battle preparation is undertaken in specialist army training centres. The process involves bringing units of soldiers face to face with the greatest possible range of the physical or psychological conditions encountered when undertaking missions in a modern, hostile environment. Becoming battle hardened allows one to undergo physical and psychological preparation for combat, thereby increasing hardiness, endurance, and resistance to fatigue.

This type of training concurrently helps develop new social links between those who go into battle together, thus tending to reinforce the feeling of duty towards the group. Moral obligation increases with mutual knowledge: there are very few people who are not sensitive to what others think of them. In a military unit, two feelings often arise through people interacting with each other: on the one hand, the fear of being seen weak, fearful, and incompetent and, on the other, the desire to prove oneself and be admired.

Placed in situations like those likely to occur in real conflicts, the combatant thereby develops his strength of character, strengthens his team spirit, and increases his ability to resist stress and to respect self-discipline. Able to control his feelings of fear, he learns how to remain master of himself in all circumstances as shown by the following personal accounts:

Côte d'Ivoire – Abidjan, October 2008

In October 2008, a low-level human intelligence gathering patrol of the Unicorn battalion's armoured squadron is engaged in a mission in the Abobo Centre neighbourhood, to the north of the city of Abidjan. The unit comprises two P4 jeeps, an NCO and five men, some of them on their first overseas operation.

The patrol stops regularly to contact the local population and various individuals – priests, shopkeepers, members of the neighbourhood councils and leaders of voluntary groups – with whom the French forces have been establishing links. At this stage relations are normal and the exchanges cordial. The atmosphere is calm, as it has been since the start of the tour over three months ago. Unconcerned, the patrol completes its work near a gendarme-commando base, then works its way around the perimeter, and finally leaves the area to head back to the Port-Bouët camp, where the French forces based in the Ivorian capital are stationed.

While going through a market, clearing a way through the crowd, the patrol is stopped at a crossroads by two pick-ups containing gendarme-commandos. Two Ivorian soldiers get out of the first vehicle, weapons in hand. One of them, seemingly the commander of this small detachment, menacingly points his pistol at the patrol leader. The second gendarme, armed with an AK47, threatens the other P4, carrying the deputy patrol leader.

The unexpected aggression petrifies the patrol leader. The muzzle of the pistol is inches away from his eye. He sees that the weapon is cocked and ready for use. Throughout, the commander of the Ivorian detachment keeps up barrage of shouts and threats. Although it can have lasted only a few seconds, to the patrol leader it seems like an eternity.

The deputy patrol leader, an experienced solider, analyses the situation coolly. To his eyes, the Ivorian soldier threatening him seems to be afraid. He orders the other men in the vehicle to discreetly cock their FAMAS [French assault rifles], but not to show their weapons and not to make any sudden movements. He is ready to authorise the use of deadly force if the situation deteriorates. The patrol leader recovers his wits. The danger is real, and the anger of the Ivorians could easily escalate into armed confrontation. He is worried about the lives of his men, as well as the hundreds of civilians wandering around near the vehicles. One shot and it will be a bloodbath. He sees that the crowd is beginning to move. Conscious of the danger, people are lowering their heads and running from the area. The tension needs be lowered. That is now the patrol leader's priority.

He waits until the Ivorian detachment commander completes his harangue and falls silent. Taking advantage of this pause, the patrol leader identifies him and states the official reason for his presence in the area. He points out that the French forces have been granted free movement by the Ivorian authorities (the government and armed forces headquarters). But from where he is standing, he is out of radio contact with his superior office and in any case, can hardly pick up the handset with a gun being waved in his face. He is on his own.

At this point the gendarme notices the patrol leader's map of Abidjan. He tries to grab it. But the patrol leader manages to hang on to it, while continuing to talk to the gendarme.

Still angry, the Ivorian returns to his vehicle and starts talking on his radio. He comes back to the P4 jeep, again threatens the patrol leader with his weapon, and concludes with the warning: "If you come back here, we will kill you." He issues some orders and the two vehicles leave the area.

The crowd in the market then begins berating the patrol, telling them to leave. Fear is inscribed on their faces. They cannot take a stand against the French army without putting themselves in overt danger. Although relations with this section of the population have been very cordial up until now, the incident has completely changed the situation. "Go home, you have no business here!" The crowd gathers in large numbers. The patrol leader orders his men to continue. The patrol returns to Camp-Bouët.

The incident has lasted no more than ten minutes.

In this example, the patrol leader's coolness made it possible for him to get out of a situation that could have degenerated in a catastrophic way. This patrol leader has perfectly fulfilled his mission of interposition and preservation of peace in an unstable environment. Better than that, he gave all of his soldiers the example of a brave leader and master of his fear on which they can rely in all circumstances.

In so-called 'stabilised missions,' which can acquire a certain routine, the problem is that the situation can suddenly change when least expected. And fear can erupt out of nowhere and in an unexpected way. Strength of character and self-control are then more essential than ever to prevent the situation from escalating.

The Discipline of Dealing with Hatred and the Lust for Revenge

As well as being in command on operations and acting as a catalyst for his troops, the commander needs to keep a cool head and remain an example of emotional stability for his men. He must do everything he can to ensure that violence does not get out of hand, especially if it is exacerbated by an adversary seeking to force him into making a mistake – and particularly so when the media are present. The commander has a fundamental responsibility regarding any excesses on the part of his men – something, alas, that is always possible. Above all, he must never tolerate such excesses or, even worse, excuse them. In addition, there must be regular reflection with a view to respecting the enemy, controlling the use of coercive methods, setting behavioural boundaries, and ensuring that the rules of engagement are adhered to.

Since time immemorial, the military man has been the solely legitimate agent for the application of deadly force. But it is not his responsibility to be judge and jury when dealing with those who are just torturers and murderers, as opposed to legitimate combatants: he is not the righter of wrongs. His role is clearly defined in the mission he is given. The way the mission is undertaken is bounded on the one hand by the rules of engagement – we have already referred to this in a preceding case – and on the other hand by rules of good, morally permissible behaviour. He draws his legitimacy from the scrupulous adherence to these two standards, as well as from respect for his adversary and his human dignity.

To speak about the dignity of the enemy is also to affirm that all people, however abhorrent their views and their choices, always possesses inalienable rights. In the same spirit, this amounts to saying that those in society who have been given the power to use deadly force, also have duties towards those who confront them. They must therefore guard against any propensity to hatred and any temptation to act vengefully.

Action is given meaning through continuing explanation, education and example setting. The meaning thereby conferred enables one to struggle against unacceptable situations using morally and legally acceptable means, as exemplified by such examples as in the following encounter experienced by a French infantry captain in 1995.

Rwanda – 1995

My company was deployed on Operation Turquoise in Rwanda.

We soon found ourselves in the position of having to establish a secure humanitarian zone and having to protect the Hutus. It was the Hutus who had been responsible for the massacres, and were now attempting to flee to Goma, where there had been a terrible cholera epidemic. We were therefore in the paradoxical situation both of seeking out the Hutu killers, the perpetrators of atrocities and horrors for the past few weeks, and of protecting and freeing the few Tutsi survivors, who had been surrounded. At the same time, we also had to protect the Hutu population, many of them mortally ill with cholera, who were surging back towards our base. All this was happening partly in parallel with operations by humanitarian NGOs. The relationship with them was complicated and situated within a general framework that was becoming increasingly difficult to comprehend. The situation was evolving rapidly and radically. Our soldiers kept wondering about the point of our mission and we had continually to explain the rationale behind our mission and try and make our actions clear.

Our zone of responsibility extended over some 300 to 400 square kilometres – an enormous area for an infantry company of only 120 men to cover.

One day, with one of my platoons, while trying to repair a village dispensary, we discovered a mass grave of babies. About thirty tiny bodies protruded from the ground. Despite the horror of the discovery, we had to bury them afresh, to avoid any risk of contagion. The day after this disagreeable duty, the population of the village seized a man, claiming that he was one of the men who massacred the children. They were preparing to exact vengeance and lynch him, but I asked for him to be handed over. The villagers refused to do so. I therefore gave the order for the platoon to intervene. My platoon then went in to take the man from the angry villagers. It was our job to protect him, even though he had been identified as an assassin of the babies they had buried the previous day.

I arrived in the area an hour later. I found that the man extracted from the crowd was tied up and exposed to the blazing tropical sun. Not only that, but every time any of my soldiers passed by, they kicked him in the ribs. The prisoner was clearly not being given any water, despite the heat. My men were waiting for him either to die of thirst, or to attempt to escape, so that they could then kill him.

I didn't know whether he really was guilty, and no-one had given us any proof. If he was guilty, it was not for us to act as judge and jury; and if he were innocent, it was our duty to protect him. Objectively, he had the right to our protection, and we were under an obligation to respect his dignity as a man, whether he was guilty or not.

I therefore had to explain to my men why they had to act as his protectors. At that point I discovered and understood how easy it is to let oneself be taken over by this feeling of revenge, by this violence that brings with it war, death and crises.

In that situation, had not the captain held fast to the real meaning of what he was doing in Rwanda, and to his primary mission, which was specifically to put an end to the spiral of violence, his men would in turn have become actors in that terrible murderous game, they would have become torturers and assassins – one act of revenge inviting another. And how would the commander have been able to contain the spiral and to prevent his men from acting as judge and jury for the remainder of their mission? If one tolerates a first transgression, how then does one subsequently draw a line in the sand?

The only possible ethical attitude in such situations is to define an absolute standard of self-discipline and to remain committed to the greater requirement for dignity, to which every man has a right. The action taken by the officer in this example is the fruit of profound thought and the manifestation of great moral strength.

Case Study 2:
Discipline of Violence

Daniel Luna and Max Goldwasser

Introduction

Violence is a tool. It's the primary tool employed in the struggle between good and evil. It's used by both the light and dark, and in implementation therein lies its morality. Just like a hammer can be used as a tool to build, sculpt or create, in another application can crush a human skull and take life in its most brutal modality. It's the responsibility of the professional warrior to wield violence with the understanding and respect for its power and reach – to act with discipline and conviction, defeating their enemy and crushing their opponent without compromising their integrity, moral code or philosophy.

Our soldiers are not ready to conduct violence with discipline in its highest form. Knowledge of boundaries – the left and right limits of violence – is a prerequisite before true discipline can be achieved. Any thug can murder. Any child can hit his peer. Any animal can kill and eat another. Without understanding the boundaries intimately, it's easy to get lost and tear the psyche. Regardless of where you are anchored, your upbringing or relationship with violence, war is conducted in the gray area, the shadow. Because so many people don't understand it, we do more harm than good in sending people into the shadow without the mental preparation. We send soldiers to war with armor, but we fail in equipping them with armor for their character.

Violence is necessary in application. But that lesson must be transferred from those who have seen the underbelly of the beast so the appreciation and meditation on violence is constructive and nurturing for those who are called to commit it on behalf of their society.

These opinions will not largely be popular. The people we have lived with, trained with and operated with have seen and conducted violence at levels likely incomprehensible to most people living in western society. This is our philosophy driven by living in a world that has not been sanitized, where it's reinforced constantly that "natural law is tooth and claw. All else is error" (Redbeard 1890). These are our observations.

Awareness

"Somewhere, a True Believer is training to kill you. He is training with minimum food or water, in austere conditions, day and night. The only thing clean on him is his weapon. He doesn't worry about what it weighs, and he runs until the enemy stops chasing him. The True Believer doesn't care how hard it is; he knows he either wins or dies. You are already behind."

– Unknown[29]

Violence, in a vacuum, is merely a function of interaction. At face value, the function of violence is neither good nor bad. This is largely due to the broad range of actions taken by man and animal alike categorized as violent deeds.

Take fishing: For many, it's time spent outdoors with family. Maybe it's cathartic – you spend your weekends alone on the pond, angling for the catch of the day. Be it fly fishing, deep sea trophy fishing, or casting a line off the dock, the hunt is on as soon as the hook hits the water.

What seems innocuous on the surface is a genuinely violent event. You're setting a trap disguised as an appealing meal for an unwitting adversary. Should luck run your way, and your prey falls victim to the ruse, you snag them by the mouth, by the gut, through the gills with a barbed hook by which they are yanked from their habitat, possibly even after a struggle. At this point, the fish is either suffocated or broken, gutted and then prepared to be enjoyed at the dinner table by hungry mouths. Is this act – admittedly violent – a bad thing? Is fishing bad? You're providing food and life for your family. Survival is violent, but in a society that values life, survival is what we strive for.

The modern western society has lost its relationship with violence, even in the nature of things like fishing and hunting. We have outsourced

---

29 The exact source for this quote is unknown.

deeds that although inherently violent are paramount to survival. Roles traditionally held by the hunters and warriors are diluted and distributed – out of sight and out of mind for the average man and woman today.

It must be noted, however, that some cultures have sustained a healthy relationship with violence. By keeping livestock, maintaining cultural rites of passage and even preparing their own dead for burial, tribal societies have persisted despite facing threats to their survival – one of these threats being us, the warriors of a different tribe, a different culture. Our culture has routinely neglected the inclusion of violence as a necessary modality for survival in favor of money and power. Despite the wealth, engineering, and manpower behind our armed services, can we truly expect them to combat a culture rooted in violence without a similar upbringing?

This gap needs to be addressed. So much time is spent training our warriors to optimize mission outcome and efficiency. The Army's Basic Combat Training is 10 weeks long, and the Marine Corps Recruit Training lasts 12 weeks, at which point recruits are sent to various schools to hone their craft within their military occupational specialty (Hammons 2016). For the average enlistee, this is not much time to adjust from a society in which violence is shunned to a profession where it's celebrated.

Members of our society who have been raised under the notion that violence in any form is wrong are now being trained in weapons and tactics to conduct violence in the name of patriotism to support and defend the Constitution of the United States. This can be a difficult issue to reconcile without formally addressing that problem.

There are those who believe we've moved beyond violence. The core of that ideology is lack of exposure. Because these people aren't exposed to violence regularly, they presume society has the capacity to function without it. Behind the scenes of an otherwise peaceful neighborhood, however, lies the violent underbelly and foundation of its way of life. Law and order are only sustained through the threat of violence, punishment and imprisonment. And as such, there are those who have to defend the law (and their rights) at local and national levels. This fracture in social ideology is highly prevalent in western culture but much less so elsewhere in the world.

Those who choose to join the military or law enforcement professions will either directly support or participate in acts of violence. There is no way around this; it is central to the job.

The military and modern thinkers believe that basic training, standardized rules of engagement, and a code of conduct are enough to adequately prepare an individual to commit violence or support acts of violence and not be morally scarred. These people are wrong. To be successful in these professions, warriors must train their minds in conjunction with their bodies; they need to understand the history, philosophy, morality and stress that come with the job. The ultimate goal in any pursuit is mastery, and mastering violence is an operational imperative.

Preparedness

"There are but two powers in the world, the sword and the mind. In the long run, the sword is always beaten by the mind."

– Napoleon Bonaparte

In order to prepare for something, it's imperative to train in that domain. If the goal is to adequately study violence, you must first identify the ways to do so. A simple framework to categorize and prioritize training in the domain of violence is the Mental Food Formula. We have broken things down into three categories: healthy, unhealthy and poisonous. Think of it in terms of the food you eat, but the advanced application is in what you feed your heart and mind. You should analyze your own training through this filter.

Combat is three things: physically demanding, emotionally taxing and competition based. The emotional toll combat takes on an individual is often overlooked; thoughts of conflict and violence are often centered on the physical elements. When addressing training holistically, you have to take both the physical and non-physical into account. Outside of formal training delivered through the military, there are several avenues that allow for individuals to expand their capabilities toward a healthy exposure to violence and violent activities.

The majority of training the average person receives in violence stems from informal sources. For many, sports are the introductions to a violent activity. Historically, warrior cultures created games and activities to sharpen men for combat during peacetime. Even in the most junior leagues, activity is physical and competition based and therefore, the perfect experience for young people to use in war time down the road.

Complimentary in preparing the mind and body for violence are acts like hunting and fishing. At their core, these events expose their doer to killing and handling flesh after death.

These are low-consequence events, largely performed in the safety of friends or family who offer children exposure to otherwise violent activities in a constructive, healthy way.

Think through the hunting trip of a child and his father, and visualize just how closely it mimics tactical conflict. You wake up early. It's likely still dark out in the later months of the year. You move silently and listen to your environment. After scouting the area, you head to the most advantageous vantage point, set up your post and wait. The ambush is set, and your prey is unaware. A deer walks by just out of range. You call it closer, tempting your target into your crosshairs. That final moment before you pull the trigger or loose your arrow, you exhale, calm, and let fly death, killing your prey.

Ideally, this process is clean. The animal doesn't suffer, and you can field-dress and pack it out for processing. With the entrails and organs removed, you peel the skin from the muscle and carve the meat from the bone to cook, salt or save for later. It's a natural thing – albeit violent – something humans have done for millennia. You spill blood to feed hungry mouths, taking one life to support the tribe.

Historically, many cultures used the first hunt and kill as a rite of passage, considering it a step towards manhood and fulfilling the role of protector, provider and warrior. Looking at warriors in our own history – men like Carlos Hathcock and Chris Kyle – we see the best snipers (true hunters of people) have grown up hunting game and are therefore familiar and comfortable with taking life.

Even preparing for a profession of violence with sports and hunting, there are questions still to be answered. How does a soldier, one in the profession of violence, protect his heart and mind? He prepares for combat by donning physical armor on his head and chest, but what armor does he have for the psyche? Does he simply act justly within the Rules of Engagement? As the prevalence of veterans of PTSD becomes more apparent, we must work to equip the next generation of warriors with the psychological armor needed in wars of the future.

Policy makers who have never seen combat think it is 'cut and dry'; it's anything but. War is confusing, and those who have seen it often describe it in abstract, using words and phrases like "fog of war" or "working in the gray" or "moving in the shadows" versus more concrete definitions and descriptors. This mindset dates back to the Shinobi – a warrior class in feudal Japan – and likely farther back.

Preparedness requires action. It's by no means enough to be aware; you must also arm yourself with experiences to strengthen your capacity for violent deeds, helping you accomplish your mission, whatever that may be. Preparing for violence will always center on training, and training can (and should) start at a young age. If the first time you have to work through an injury to support a team, compete in something with consequence or take a life is in combat, it's too late.

Willingness

"The willingness of our citizens to give freely and unselfishly of themselves, in defense of our democratic principles, gives this great nation continued strength and vitality."

– Ronald Reagan

Willingness is difficult to learn. This integral discipline deals in personal integrity, predicated on the moral alignment of your mission, your group and yourself. Dissecting personal integrity is complex, but for the purpose of this study we will break it down into the internal alignment of thoughts, words and deeds. Understanding yourself in this way is the first step toward understanding your own levels of willingness.

First, you must be willing to enter the fray. Combat is messy. It's easy to get swept up in emotion in tense situations. Regardless of how many table-top exercises or scenario-based training you go through, there will always be the intangibles of human interaction. Soldiers are trained to constantly think of killing the enemy, beating opposing forces and emerging victorious in battle. Yet, as a group, very few conversations take place of the converse: what if we lose? What if we're all killed? That understanding and acceptance of the spectrum of outcomes is key to maintaining high levels of willingness in the face of adverse conditions.

Every society has those individuals predisposed to a willingness to kill. A percentage of those have the capacity to bind their willingness to law and regulation, all the while doing their utmost to kill the enemy on behalf of their nation and mission. Fewer still may even enjoy it.

Elite and specialized units have always attracted warriors like this. Like any organization, you will find people with different work ethics and dedications to the job. However, as the demands of the mission increase, so must the group's level of willingness to enter the fray and destroy the enemy.

When it comes to killing the enemy, some are quicker on the trigger than others. That is to be expected – the individual willingness varies across all groups. When a part of an organization deals in death and violence, it's crucial you examine your own willingness in comparison to the group and ensure both are aligned. You may have to dive deep into your own self-awareness and personal integrity to ensure you're capable of being part of that group and still achieve mission success. On the other hand, you may need to temper your own desires and levels of willingness to stay true to the laws governing your group and mission at hand.

Mission completeness is central to all that you do in uniform. That is not up for debate. What is encompassed within 'completeness' has broadened in an asymmetrical combat environment. If mission success is predicated on destroying the enemy, then the means to that end are irrelevant. However, there is an impetus on conducting war justly – it is not about using any means to achieve an outcome, but only what is necessary to achieve success. In a stressful environment, it is crucial to be willing to maintain discipline in the face exceptional stress and dangerous conditions.

Let's work through another analogy. It's now 2009 in Afghanistan, and you are on patrol on a moonless night, just outside Kandahar. You have been in country for less than 36 hours.

The desert is flat. Not soft sand but hard packed. You have on your body armor, and you are already perspiring because you have been walking a while. You thank yourself for packing extra water. The radio call passes that you are almost to the target. You are about to set up security around a village, moving into position at night. At first light you will start the clearance. This is done specifically because of the high IED and mine threat in the area.

The group you are with begins to break up to go to pre-coordinated security positions. Everyone is looking for a specific compound to move into and set up a security position. As you begin to move in, an explosion cuts through the night.

You look up … even in the inky darkness you see the size of the blast from the plume of dirt thrown into the air. You gasp. You know there is a team moving up on that hill, and your immediate thought is they are all dead. Working with explosives for as long as you have, the size and noise from the blast is so large, you are certain no one survived.

Finally, the earpiece you are wearing cracks with the voice of the troop commander. He breaks the silence with a calm: "Status." That word echoes as you watch the hill top. Again, more sternly: "Status." Once again, silence.

Your heart is still frozen, and now the feeling of nausea. The silence is broken again, this time with a different voice saying one SEAL is seriously hurt and needs to be flown out as soon as possible. Part of you is relieved only one person got hurt, but now your mind goes to your wounded teammate and brother.

With your mind racing, you and your team finish moving into position around the target. During that time, the small team formerly hidden in darkness is now exposed by the blast. Foregoing their night vision, the team is forced to turn on their flashlights. Weaving through the minefield, they finally make it to him and start to treat him. Both his legs had been shredded and he was starting to bleed out.

While waiting for the medevac, the team starts to move the injured SEAL down the side of the hill to get him ready to load and fly back to base. On this dark, moonless night, a stillness in the air settles back in, only to be torn apart by a sound you never thought another human could make. Sitting on a compound wall, the scream nearly knocks you off balance; the noise coming from that hillside echoing through the valley is the only sound heard for miles.

You can tell when the body is moved during the decent in the increase in volume. You keep thinking this noise could not possibly be human.

You continue to sit on that wall, holding security, looking up at the hill and listening to the sound of friend and teammate, Lt Dan Cnossen, USNA '02. Lt Cnossen will survive, and go on to have a successful career as a Paralympian and graduate student at Harvard.

You do not know that in this moment of extraordinary stress – and the anger starts to build.

You are looking out over the compound, in the dead of night, and all you can focus on is the upcoming mission at hand. It would be so easy to tear through the village and cut down anything in the way like a scythe in the night with blood and death in your wake.

But you do not do that. Your team does not do that.

You remain composed, set up security, and continue on with the mission as planned. Movement at first light.

Think of the range of emotion and confusion for those who were there. You had not seen the enemy yet, and were supposed to make first contact. Your team had barely unpacked their gear and were sending a teammate home not knowing if he would live or die. The whole world was on a razor's edge between control and chaos, and everything was hanging on the next move.

This story could have ended very differently – if the group's alignment had been off, or someone's personal willingness been incongruent with the mission at hand, it could have jeopardized everything that team was trying to accomplish. They did not lose composure. They did not indiscriminately reign fire and destruction down on this village. There was no bloodlust, there was no rage. All that remained was execution of the mission at hand. This was not the first time they had to work through these challenges, and they were all fully willing to continue to operate in the face of such outcomes.

The Rules of Engagement (ROEs) serve as a form of baseline for willingness in our military. They form the left and right limits of acceptable action for certain objectives. It is your responsibility to have awareness of your personal willingness to operate within those ROEs and not fall off on either end of the spectrum of allowable conduct.

The same is true for the team or group. As a whole, where does your team fall when it comes to willingness? Are they more willing to kill? Is your level of willingness restricting your team or encouraging them to go further than they would otherwise be inclined? These discussions are crucial to facilitate, especially for the officers and leadership, to ensure mechanisms are put in place to train, temper and foster alignment to avoid catastrophic outcomes in the face of stressful situations.

Conclusion

> "Evil will always exist, the only thing that is going to stop evil is good men that are skilled at violence."
>
> – Tim Kennedy

Have you taken the steps and put in the work to be physically fit, mentally sound and morally aligned? Have you adequately prepared to step into a profession which will throw you into areas of the world that are dark, dangerous and rife with conflict? Violence is central to it all – a tool used by the dark to destroy the light.

For good, for evil, out of love, fear or ego, violence is a tool we use to exert our will over others. The profession of arms is a noble pursuit. The application of violence together with a code of conduct requires a level of discipline that does not come naturally to most. As a member of the military, you will either participate in or support acts of violence against the enemies of our nation to meet a peaceful end-state. Thus, you must commit to training in this realm, in the gray, the shadow, that most people dare not enter.

Keep in mind: discipline goes far beyond simply, "do I kill this person or not?" or "*how* do I kill this person?" There is discipline in everything you do leading to that fatal, violent moment. There is discipline in training, discipline in action, self and group identity, all supporting the core task of staying on mission. This, more than anything else, is the most valuable lesson. The objective morality of your mission and identity supersedes the subjective morality of a kill-or-don't-kill moment. That is what the disciple should aspire to train towards, for then, in that unforgiving moment, they will not need to ask the question.

It is up to us to find the courage to commit completely to becoming a true disciple of violence in defense of our nation and way of life.

Remember, our enemy is training too. He is training with fewer resources but for a greater cause: survival. It is imperative we embrace the mindset of the True Believer. Remove unhealthy distractions and dedicate to training. Seek a teacher to help build your armor. Become the best version of yourself because our country's survival is on the line, and the enemy is at the gates.

So of you I ask, and consider your answer carefully: are you ready?

References

Duty with Honour: The Profession of Arms in Canada. Kingston, Ontario: Canadian Defence Academy – Canadian Forces Leadership Institute, 2003.

Foucault, M. *Discipline and Punish: The Birth of the Prison.* New York: Vintage, 1979.

Gabriel, R. A. *The Warrior's Way: A Treatise on Military Ethics.* Kingston, Ontario: Canadian Defence Academy Press, 2007.

Josephus. *The Jewish War.* Translated by G. A. Williamson. London: Penguin, 1959.

Madigan, P. S. "Military Neuro Psychiatry, Discipline, and Morale," *Journal of Criminal Law and Criminology* 32, no. 5 (1942): 491–97.

Olsthoorn, P. *Military Ethics and Virtues: An Interdisciplinary Approach for the 21st Century.* Abingdon: Routledge, 2011.

Osiel, M. J. *Obeying Orders: Atrocity, Military Discipline & the Law of War.* New Brunswick, NJ: Transaction, 1999.

Phang, S.E. *Roman Military Service: Ideologies of Discipline in the Late Republic and Early Principate.* Cambridge: Cambridge University Press, 2008.

Plutarch. *The Makers of Rome.* Translated by Ian Scott-Kilvert. London: Penguin, 1965.

Policy Sciences Division. *Military Self-Discipline: A Motivational Analysis.* Arlington, VA: CACI, 1978.

Polybius. *The Rise of the Roman Empire.* Translated by Ian Scott-Kilvert. London: Penguin, 1979.

Robinson, P. *The White Russian Army in Exile, 1920–1941.* Oxford: Clarendon Press, 2002.

Royal, B. *The Ethical Challenges of the Soldier, French Experience.* Paris: Economica, 2012.

Sabin, P., H. Wees, and M. Whitby, *The Cambridge History of Greek and Roman Warfare,* Vol. 1. Cambridge: Cambridge University Press, 2007.

Sherman, N. *Stoic Warriors: The Ancient Philosophy Behind the Military Mind.* Oxford: Oxford University Press, 2005.

Sukhanev, V. "Gallipoli." State Archive of the Russian Federation, fond 5881, opis 2, delo 612.

The Army Leadership Guide: An Introductory Guide. First Edition. Accessed April 13, 2018, https://www.army.mod.uk/media/2698/ac72021_the_army_leadership_code_an_introductory_guide.pdf

The Values and Standards of the British Army. No publication details provided.

Vegetius Renatus, Flavius. *Military Institutions of Vegetius, in Five Books, Translated From the Original Latin. With a Preface and Notes. By Lieutenant John Clarke.* London: W. Griffin, 1767.

Volkov, Col. I.N. (Ret.). "What is the Essence of Military Discipline?" *Military Thought* 11, no. 2 (2002): 118–22.

Volkov, Co. I. N. (Ret.). "Relationship Between Military Discipline and Self-Discipline," *Military Thought* 14, no. 4 (2005): 148–54.

Weber, M. "The Meaning of Discipline," in *From Max Weber: Essays in Sociology*, edited by Hans Heinrich Gerth and C. Wright Mills, New York: Oxford University Press, 1967, 253–65.

14

PROFESSIONALISM

Overview:
Professional Military Excellence
Through Practice

Daniel Lagacé-Roy and Carl Jacob

The Profession of Arms (PoA), as it is understood by authors such as Huntington,[1] is often described using professional values, such as loyalty and integrity, and requirements, such as competencies within ethical standards. These values, requirements, and standards are comparable with those mentioned in other traditional professions, such as law and medicine. While we recognize that listing the desirable professional value benefits and comparing them to other professions provides recognition in terms of belonging to a professional group, we also acknowledge that each profession, including the PoA, possesses particular fundamental professional guiding values (professional military excellence) – also referred to as *Ethos* – which form its distinctive hallmark.

This overview aims to discuss the meaning of the following terms: 'professional military excellence,' 'military identity,' and the 'being professional' state. By adhering to the PoA, members embrace a code of conduct which speaks to their professional military excellence. In doing so, they internalize an *Ethos* that transcends the mere profession's values. The internalization of one's *Ethos* process begins with one's knowledge of how the PoA is perceived and how one perceives it, in comparison to other professions. This concept will be discussed in the overview's first section.

---

1 Samuel P. Huntington, *The Soldier and the State: The Theory and Politics of Civil-Military Relations* (Cambridge, MA: The Belknap Press of Harvard University Press, 1957).

The overview's second sections will address the 'military identity' question as a desirable outcome when individuals become the PoA's members. Lastly, the overview speaks to the state of 'being professional' in the PoA significance. This 'being professional' state recognizes the virtuous qualities supporting the professional military excellence designation, and provides an answer to the question related to its meaning in practice.

Profession Amongst Professions

The concept of profession, used by professions such as law and medicine, is derived from an understanding that there is at least a specific and sophisticated knowledge body associated with its practice. Moreover, the distinctiveness that makes a profession a profession is not only based on the above-mentioned criteria, but also on particularities associated with social practices,[2] such as: a common language, vision, implicit and explicit knowledge,[3] values, standards, norms, rules and regulations, and ethical practices, all subordinate to civil authority.[4]

Since authors, such as Huntington,[5] Hackett,[6] and Janowitz,[7] began articulating the foundations on which is built the PoA, defining the military as a profession has been challenging because of its distinct nature. Moreover, the recognition of its members as 'being professionals' is, to a certain extent, a topic that needs constant revisiting. One may argue that this revalidation is unnecessary because the PoA has proven many times its raison d'être through its accomplishments at home and abroad, such as peacekeeping, peacemaking, as well as conventional and unconventional warfare. But the question remains whether these accomplishments are enough to make the military a profession.

While it might be the case, a constant reassessment of the military as a profession generates, at times, defensive arguments to justify its status. An example of such an argument is found in the article titled *A Profession*

---

2 George Lucas, *Military Ethics: What Everyone Needs to Know* (New York: Oxford University Press, 2016), 9.

3 Almeida, A.-M. De Oliveira, C. Vandenplas-Holper, and J.-M. De Ketele, "Revue critique de recherches sur les conceptions des parents à propos du développement de l'enfant," *Bulletin de Psychologie Scolaire et d'Orientation* 2 (1992), 1–2.

4 *Duty with Honour: The Profession of Arms in Canada* (Kingston, Ontario: Canadian Defence Academy – Canadian Forces Leadership Institute, 2003), 41.

5 Huntington, *The Soldier and the State.*

6 Gen. Sir John Hackett, *The Profession of Arms* (London: The Times Publishing Company Ltd., 1963).

7 Morris Janowitz, *The Professional Soldier: A Social and Political Portrait* (Glencoe, IL: The Free Press, 1960).

Like No Other[8] where the author suggests that the military profession is unique in terms of being "the most demanding of all professions."[9] While this statement maybe justifiable in the article's context, it creates an unnecessary tension between professions. We argue that there is an inherent flaw in this evaluation because a profession's uniqueness is not (and cannot be) assessed using a subjective label, since it is difficult to measure.

It is true that in the profession domain, the PoA is often described as a profession '*à part*' (distinct) because of its demands, especially the unlimited liability membership expectation. While such an expectation might raise the PoA to a uniqueness level amongst other professions, we argue that it entertains a discourse focusing on singularity, such as a comparison using similarities and differences, instead of aiming at discovering what each profession brings in terms of its professional excellence (*Ethos*).

One may dispute this argument by saying that the PoA's uniqueness doesn't preclude the above-mention statement. We agree, however, when the PoA, or any profession for that matter, is singled out because of some members' unethical behaviours,[10] for example, fingers are pointed to the members or the institution's lack of professionalism. By shifting the PoA discourse from its singularity to its professional military excellence, we consider that the military is recognized as a profession because of its members' conduct, and not because of its uniqueness. By adhering to a code of conduct that is grounded in professional military excellence, members define their profession using explicit knowledge about principles, expertise, and responsibilities, as well as implicit knowledge grounded in attitudes, beliefs, interpretations, opinions, perceptions, and values. They also define their profession using sociocultural identity concepts, and 'esprit de corps,' to name a few.

In retrospect, these values are not only the PoA's purview. They are shared by other professions which makes it difficult, according to Evetts,[11] "to draw a definitional line between professions."[12] We recognize that drawing a line between the PoA and other professions presents a challenge in itself. However, we also admit that this view is

---

8   Patricia Cook, "A Profession Like No Other," in *Routledge Handbook of Military Ethics*, ed. George Lucas (Abingdon: Routledge, 2015), 32–43.

9   Cook, "A Profession Like No Other," 38.

10 In Canada, the Somalia incident is a good example of this type of misconduct and unethical behaviours.

11 Julia Evetts, "The Sociological Analysis of Professionalism," *International Sociology* 18, no. 2 (2003): 397.

12 Evetts, "The Sociological Analysis of Professionalism."

not sustainable because commonalities, as well as differences should be viewed as part of each profession's raison d'être. Because attaining professional military excellence within the PoA doesn't happen by osmosis, its raison d'être defines the process by which members may work towards such excellence.

The process used to attain professional military excellence, from the initial membership to being professional, is described below using five concepts, namely: membership, professionalization, professionalism, professional, and Ethos (see Figure 14.1). To a certain extent, these concepts can be understood as part of a continuum; however, each one has a role to play in the professional military excellence's attainment (*Ethos*). When (1) joining the PoA, members are engaged into the (2) professionalization's social process where, as examples, they learn, through training, education, and socialization, how to become experts in their domain of expertise, such as combat engineering, and identify themselves as members of

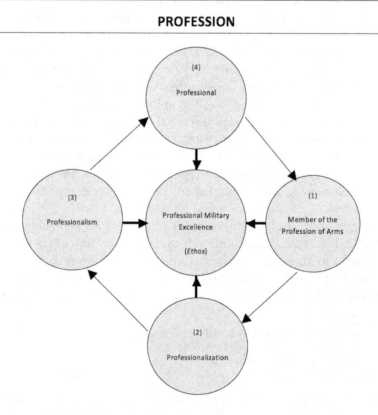

Figure 14.1   Professional Military Excellence (*Ethos*) Process

distinct elements, like the Royal Canadian Navy (RCN). Thereafter; (3) they display competence in their domain of expertise by the work they perform and the activities they complete. It is through others' recognition that (4) one may be deemed professional. Finally, the four concepts contribute to the building of a professional military excellence which also represents the *Ethos* of the profession. This is the reason for having it at the center of the radial graph.

Military Identity

The names used to designate a military member are numerous: warrior, leader of character, servant and professional,[13] warrior/peacekeeper, heroic leader/manager,[14] civilized soldier,[15] soldier diplomat, soldier scholar[16] and 'simply' soldier, to name a few. These names all contribute to the members' identity or identities. When one looks closer, one notices that each name possesses a specific conceptual framework within the larger PoA conceptual framework. In other words, each specific conceptual framework defines, in its own way, what it means to be a PoA member. Research suggests that identity development is a "lifelong process"[17] by which one becomes, over time, who they are as a person. The process of becoming who they are is the product of various factors such as biological blueprint (DNA), experiences, the environment, education and training. While identity development is often associated with the adolescence period where 'teenagers' are subjected to intense questioning about themselves in terms of who they are, it is also a period that can be experienced by adults, normally referred to as an identity crisis.[18] When it happens in adulthood, it can be the result of sudden changes, such as separation or divorce, cultural changes, for example diversity and inclusion, and/or environmental changes, namely

---

13 Don M. Snider, "The Multiple Identities of the Professional Army," in *The Future of the Army Profession*, ed. Don M. Snider and Lloyd J. Matthews (Mississauga, Ontario: McGraw Hill Custom Publishing, 2005), 139–73.

14 Marina Nuciari, "Models and Explanations for Military Organisation: An Updated Reconsideration," in *Handbook of the Sociology of the Military*, ed., Giuseppe Caforio (New York/London, U.K.: Kluwer Academic/Plenum Publishers, 2003), 80.

15 Patrick Mileham, "Military Virtues 1: The right to be different," *Defence Analysis* 14, no. 2 (1998): 186.

16 *Duty with Honour*, 18.

17 Richard M. Ryan and Edward L. Deci, "On Assimilating Identities to the Self: A Self-Determination Theory Perspective on Internalization and Integrity within Cultures," in *Handbook of Self and Identity*, ed. Mark R. Leary and June Price Tangney (New York: The Guilford Press, 2003), 254.

18 Erik H. Erikson, "Autobiographic Notes on the Identity Crisis," *Daedalus* 99, no. 4 (1970): 731.

different jobs or different postings.[19] The sense of identity is therefore challenged which leads to the inadequacy of one's identity.[20]

Sometimes individuals face obstacles that may prevent a strong identity development. This sort of unresolved crisis leaves individuals struggling to find themselves. At the other end of the spectrum, those who emerge from the personality development adolescence stage with a strong sense of identity are well equipped to confidently face adulthood.[21]

In addressing 'military identity,' emphasis should be brought upon two aspects associated with identity development: the construction of meaning and the organization of meaning. According to Kegan,[22] most adults have activities, like pursuing a career, and sharing similarities such as gender, lifestyle, and social position with others, that generate a variety of demands and expectations. He calls these activities and similarities: the curriculum of [modern] life.[23] It serves, in a sense, as the basis for his argument which suggests that individuals, in their life, have to construct the meaning of what is happening around them. In other works, they try to find meaning in their daily encounters, accomplishments, as well as duties and responsibilities, to name a few. According to Kegan, this process is needed in order to make sense of what they are accomplishing every day.

For Kegan, the making-sense activity, understood as "a meaning-constitutive activity,"[24] is important when one attempts to understand life's realities. In fact, this activity's importance is not that there is an attempt to understand, but that one is involved in the making-sense activity. To be more precise, the person is engaged in the activity as the actor, not a spectator. For Kegan, this engagement transforms the way one views, understands, integrates, and interprets a situation for the benefit of one's participation in an identity development.

For military members, what does it mean to engage oneself into the making-sense of one's environment process? How does this engagement inform their military identity? We mentioned in this overview's first section

---

19 William B. Swann and Jennifer K. Bosson, "Identity Negotiation: A Theory of Self and Social Interaction," in *Handbook of Personality: Theory and Research*, ed. Oliver P. John, Richard W. Robins and Lawrence A. Pervin (New York: The Guilford Press, 2008), 463.

20 Susan E. Cross and Jonathan S. Gore, "Cultural Models of the Self," in *Handbook of Self and Identity*, ed. Mark R. Leary and June Price Tangney (New York: The Guilford Press, 2003), 553.

21 Duane P. Schultz and Sydney Ellen Schultz, *Theories of Personality*, 9th Edn (New York: Wadsworth Cengage Learning, 2008), 216.

22 Robert Kegan, *The Evolving Self: Problem and Process in Human Development* (Cambridge, MA: Harvard University Press, 1982).

23 Robert Kegan, *In Over Our Heads: The Mental Demands of Modern Life* (Cambridge, MA: Harvard University Press, 1994), 5.

24 Kegan, *The Evolving Self*, 42.

that when members join the PoA, they must adhere to certain values, beliefs, principles, knowledge and expertise, roles and responsibilities. As well, they must develop a certain social and cultural identity, and an 'esprit de corps.' Moreover, members are also involved in a process that leads to professional military excellence. During that process, how do members perceive themselves? How do they make sense of what is expected of them in terms of values, attitudes and beliefs? Are these values, attitudes and beliefs congruent with theirs and the military identity that they have embraced?

These questions cannot be easily answered without the input from the members themselves because they are the ones who are constructing the meaning of what it is to be members of the PoA. They are the ones who have been experiencing and are now encountering ever changing realities and (un)certainties, such as diversity, inclusion, customs, traditions, and societal values, either at home or in theater. In that context, military identity will be built as an "evolution of meaning.[25] According to a research conducted by Gustavsen,[26] the meaning concept provides members with more insights into the nature of the events, activities, and work they perform, helping them to organize their understanding into a meaningful way.

Therefore, military identity is not a static concept. It is constantly 'in mouvance,' forcing members to pursue a personal and continual introspection in order to determine what they need to do when professional military excellence is not seen as a goal but as a virtue.

Professional Military Excellence

Charles Taylor,[27] a Canadian philosopher, argues that particular individual's dignity, such as a "warrior,[28] is dependent on the background understanding that there is some special value attached to these forms of life [warrior] or to the rank or station that these people have attained within them.[29] For this author, the sense of dignity bestowed on someone is the result of an attribution that some modes of life "[are] incomparably higher than others."[30] He suggests that the sense of dignity derives from an evaluation

---

25 Kegan, *The Evolving Self*, 15.
26 Elin Gustavsen, "The construction of meaning among Norwegian Afghanistan veterans," *International Sociology* 31, no. 2 (2015): 21–36.
27 Charles Taylor, *Sources of the Self: The Making of the Modern Identity* (Cambridge, MA: Harvard University Press, 1989).
28 This is the example provided by Taylor. However, we contend that this role attributed to the members of the PoA is no longer appropriate in today's context.
29 Taylor, *Sources of the Self*, 25.
30 Taylor, *Sources of the Self*, 19.

based on one's comportment/behaviour: the way they walk, move, gesture, and speak.[31] Taylor's explanation of how acknowledgment is accredited to a role, such as a warrior, gives the impression that the foundation of his reasoning is based on social attribution. In this case, social attribution may be explained either by internal factors, such as traits, or external factors, namely the environment the person is in.

This type of socio-psychological assessment has been criticized by Olsthoorn,[32] when he asserts that social attribution cannot provide or explain the meaning of something that belongs to other fields, such as the military for the term warrior. It is true that Olsthoorn's objection speaks specifically to the approach adopted by some military ethicists, which connects social psychology and moral philosophy, to explain ethical and unethical behaviours. According to Olsthoorn, behaviours with ethical and unethical consequences should be addressed using concepts that are rooted in moral philosophy, such as value and/or virtue, because they speak about the person's character. In other words, a warrior's dignity should be recognized not by their role but by the character they display.

The author's appeal to character is not new in the military training field[33] and, to a certain extent, the ethics domain, because of the means by which such character is achieved or built. The term character can be defined as "a set of acquired individual values that consistently influence the leader's behavior."[34] In our view, the building of character that is promoted here is not the same character type endorsed by Aristotle when he talks about moral virtues as character traits.[35] One may argue that building character in military training does lead to good behaviors which, in turn, lead to virtuous traits. While this objective is commendable, we argue that the driving force for character development which leads to professional military excellence is, in the long term, the practice of virtues that are associated with sound judgement, which is the use of sound, critical-thinking skills.

---

31   Taylor, *Sources of the Self*, 15.
32   Peter Olsthoorn, "Situations and Dispositions: How to rescue the military virtues from social psychology," *Journal of Military Ethics* 16 (2017): 1–2.
33   Roger Wertheimer, "The Morality of Military Ethics Education," in *Empowering our Military Conscience: Transforming Just War Theory and Military Moral Education*, ed. Roger Wertheimer (Farnham: Ashgate, 2010): 177–78.
34   Timothy T. Lupfer, "Leadership for Mere Mortals," in *Didactics of Military Ethics: From Theory to Practice*, ed. Thomas R. Elßner and Janke Reinhold (Leiden: Brill/Nijhoff, 2016): 135.
35   Martin Cook, "Military ethics and character development," in *Routledge Handbook of Military Ethics*, ed. George Lucas (Abingdon: Routledge, 2015).

Within the concept of virtue, as presented by Aristotle,[36] it is mentioned that one does not become virtuous solely because of the role one fulfills.[37] In other words, a person is not virtuous because of the societal role they play, physician or lawyers as examples. In fact, being virtuous is not tributary to an end, which could be determined by societal roles. The practice of virtues is an evolving goal as it encourages one to constantly revisit oneself in order to improve one's deep understanding of what it means to be courageous (*fortitudo*), prudent (*prudentia*), moderate (*temperantia*), and fair (*iustitia*).[38] These cardinal virtues should be understood as "pivot[al] [because] all other virtues pivot around these four virtues."[39]

At this point, it appears important to elucidate the meaning of the terms virtues and values in the context of professional military excellence (*Ethos*). On one hand, the practice of virtues, such as courage, is integral to one's individual military identity. While, on the other hand, values, such as duty, are integral to the military as a "social institution."[40] Values also contribute to defining professional military excellence (*Ethos*). In our view, both virtues and values influence military members' conduct in the "performance of their duty."[41] In fact, virtues and values 'go hand in hand,' therefore they cannot be separated at the risk of impeding the way members conduct themselves. Their combined "entity" bridges the "gap"[42] between what the military stands for in terms of values, and what members should aspire to in terms of virtues. Military members are therefore bound to these values, and are subjected to the practice of those virtues. Consequently, values and virtues would shape a mindset that would empower[43] them to adopt a disposition,[44] conducive to a 'good life,' which is characterized by

---

36 Janne Aalto, "Challenges in combining ethical education for conscripts and professional military: The Finnish point of view," in *Making the Military Moral: Contemporary Challenges and Responses in Military Ethics Education*, ed. Don Carrick, James Connelly and David Whetham (Abingdon: Routledge, 2018).

37 Aalto, "Challenges in combining ethical education," 112.

38 Hackett, *The Profession of Arms*, 42.

39 Th. A. van Baarda, "Forming a Moral Judgement Using a Dynamic Model," in *Military Ethics: The Dutch Approach. A Practical Guide*, ed. Th. A. Van Baarda and D. E. M. Verweij, (Leiden: Martinus Nijhoff Publishers, 2006), 282.

40 Bill Bentley, *Professional Ideology and the Profession of Arms in Canada* (Kingston, Ontario: Canadian Institute of Strategic Studies, 2005), 18.

41 *Duty with Honour*, 10.

42 Don M. Snider, "American Military Professions and Their Ethics," in *Routledge Handbook of Military Ethics*, ed. George Lucas (Abingdon: Routledge, 2015), 25.

43 Roger Wertheimer, "The moral singularity of military professionalism," in *Empowering our Military Conscience: Transforming Just War Theory and Military Moral Education*, ed. Roger Wertheimer (Farnham: Ashgate, 2010), 144.

44 James Eastwood uses the expression: "ascetic ethical disposition," in *Ethics as a Weapon of War: Militarism and Morality in Israel* (Cambridge: Cambridge University Press, 2017), 87.

professional military excellence (*Ethos*).[45] Such a good life implies "finding a balance"[46] between their own values and those of the institution. In turn, this balance would determine the practice of virtuous actions for their own sake[47] and not, as an example, for the sake of being perceived by others as virtuous.[48] If this is the case, members who are striving for professional military excellence (*Ethos*), as an end goal, would be committed to that goal not for the sake of a job or a career, but because of their attachment to military values. Such an attachment would lead to a virtuous conduct.

Conclusion

The concept of professional military excellence (*Ethos*) has been discussed in this overview by presenting the military as a profession amongst others, by addressing the military identity concept, and speaking to the state of being professional. We argue that professional military excellence (*Ethos*) is a practice guided by desirable outcomes[49] and grounded in the professionalization process. The importance of this process resides in the fact that it is during that journey that members internalize what it means to be a member of the PoA. In fact, we contended that this journey provides meaning to what the PoA entails.

We recognize that individuals wanting to join the military must reflect on the meaning of their membership to such an institution – traditional in nature, and endorsed by society,[50] as well as the reasons for joining and pursuing a profession within it. In our view, this question resonated throughout this overview, and tinted the way we envisaged professional military excellence (*Ethos*). Enrolling in the military means that one joins an institution which requires from its members unlimited liability, as well as service to one's country before self.

Second, this question also speaks directly to the internal and external motivators/reasons[51] one may decide to join the PoA. One may join because

---

45   Bill Rhodes, *An Introduction to Military Ethics: A Reference Book* (Santa Barbara, CA: ABC-CLIO, LLC, 2009), 8.

46   Th. A. Van Baarda and D. E. M. Verweij, "Military Ethics: Its Nature and Pedagogy," in *Military Ethics: The Dutch Approach*, 22.

47   T. H. Irwin, "Aristotle," in *The Shorter Routledge Encyclopedia of Philosophy*, ed. Edward Craig (London: Routledge, 2005), 63.

48   Christopher Coker, *Ethics and War in the 21st Century* (London: Routledge, 2008), 124.

49   Morris Janowitz, *The Professional Soldier: A Social and Political Portrait* (Glencoe, IL: The Free Press, 1960), 6.

50   C. J. Downes, "To Be or Not To Be a Profession: The Military Case," *Defense Analysis* 1, no. 3 (1985): 154, 156.

51   Charles C. Moskos, "The All-Volunteer Military: Calling, Profession, or Occupation?" in *Parameters* 7, no. 1 (1977): 2–9.

of career prospects; a 'calling,' or an aspiration, like a 'vocation'; or/and simply because it is 'a good job.' Whatever the motivation/reason one possesses for joining and pursuing a career in the PoA, it will determine, not only the importance one bestows on the PoA, but also one's professional military identity.

The concept of professional military identity, as it was presented in this overview, is central to the understanding of the said overview, because of its ramifications. In our view, the PoA depends on and benefits from members who possess a virtuous professional military identity, and who uphold the military institution's values. As for the practice of virtues, understood by some as special because of service demands required by the profession,[52] it is a *sine qua non* disposition for military members. While the practice of virtues is not only the purview of the military, because individuals in all walks of life[53] can be virtuous, military members are subjected to the practice of virtues throughout their diverse career experiences as members of the PoA. Consequently, these experiences become motivating factors for members in achieving professional military excellence (*Ethos*). They also help them define who they are as professionals, their professional military identity.

---

52 Shannon E. French, *The Code of the Warrior: Exploring Warrior Values Past and Present*, (Lanham, MD: Rowman & Littlefield Publishers, Inc., 2003), 7.

53 Hackett, *The Profession of Arms*, 45.

Case Study:
Professionalism in the Military

John Thomas

It is not by accident that 'Professionalism' is the final chapter in this book. This is because being a military professional means not only mastering all the virtues examined in detail in the previous chapters, but it also means having other qualities which fall outside the philosopher's strict definition of a virtue, for example technical skill, and physical and medical fitness. Crucially, professionalism also implies being accountable for one's actions. This notion of accountability is important. It means being personally accountable to one's comrades in arms, as well as being accountable under the law and, by extension, to society as a whole. This accountability is one key factor which distinguishes professionalism (as described in the context of this book) from the often unaccountable actions of mercenaries, paramilitary forces and criminals masquerading as military.

It is a very challenging expectation that every member of the armed forces, including those who are young and inexperienced, will master completely the daunting list of attributes explored in the previous chapters. What is remarkable is how close so many members of the military come to this ideal, and that so few of them fall seriously short. This is particularly so because the true test of military professionalism comes not in a debating chamber or during a classroom examination, but when personnel are exhausted, under great physical and mental pressure and sometimes – with good cause – frightened for their very lives.

The public perception of military professionalism is changing as society and technology are changing. For example, it is now completely accepted that the term 'military professional' applies to both men and women. Cyber warfare and drone warfare are also changing the definition of what it is to be a military professional. In the Second World War it would usually have been necessary to mount an air or commando operation to disable a factory or a headquarters behind enemy lines. Those who participated in such an operation would easily have met our definition of 'professional.' In the past, 'military professional' and 'warrior' were effectively synonymous, but technology is beginning to alter our perceptions. For example, is the software engineer who can disable an air defence system with a virus – and thereby potentially save many aircrew lives and hasten the end of an armed conflict – just as much of a professional warrior as members of a commando unit? Evidence also now suggests that these modern 'computer commandos' are as susceptible to PTSD as, for example, conventional military aviation pilots,[54] especially if they are combining kill missions with ordinary family life on a home base. (However, there is also some evidence that the main sources of stress for such cyber warriors are occupational, including low unit manning, rotating shift work, extra duties, administrative tasks, and long hours.[55]) While on the one hand, they might not face the same physical risks as their aircrew colleagues, they do get to 'know' their targets in a way that traditional aircrew never can and, as part of their mission, they also have to witness the often traumatic after effects of their actions.

Professionalism also differs from many of the other qualities in the previous chapters, because it can be as easily applied to an entire force – army, air force, navy or any smaller unit – in a way that honesty, integrity or perseverance, which are essentially individual virtues, cannot. For this case study, I want to look at two very different examples which fall within a traditional definition of military professionalism. However, even this seemingly innocuous reference to a 'traditional definition' raises a number of important issues. The first is that 'professionalism' is not an immutable concept in the military or any other environment, but one which evolves over time and is also to some extent context dependent. The behaviours and skills which made a soldier (or a teacher, or journalist) 'professional' in earlier centuries are not identical to those required today, even though we would expect to find large areas of overlap in respect of (for example) courage, wisdom and integrity. But whereas unquestioning obedience in

---

54 For example, see Jean L. Otto and Bryant J. Webber, *Mental Health Diagnoses and Counseling Among Pilots of Remotely Piloted Aircraft in the United States Air Force* (Medical Surveillance Monthly Report, March 2013), 3–8.

55 Wayne L. Chappelle, et al., "Symptoms of Psychological Distress and Post-Traumatic Stress Disorder in United States Air Force 'Drone' Operators," *Military Medicine*, 179, Issue suppl_8 (August 1, 2014): 63–70.

the pre-Nuremberg trials era was considered an essential military attribute, personal accountability for one's actions is now much more important.

The second issue is that 'professionalism,' like 'virtuous,' is a word for which there is no universally agreed definition. But when it comes to military ethics, arguments over the finer nuances of meaning are often of more relevance in an academic environment rather than as useful signposts to help military personnel make sound ethical choices. In my opinion, military professionalism, especially at the strategic level implies more than the accumulation of knowledge, and includes an ability to interpret political will and to exercise sound judgement to implement it in a way which is legal, ethical and effective and (crucially) to lead and inspire others to do likewise.

Furthermore, it is not enough to isolate (for example) a single act of courage, loyalty or obedience, however demanding or praiseworthy it might be, in order to label an individual as a professional. Professionalism is about sustaining all the military virtues over the long haul. Professionalism is not about perfection, because sustaining every virtue at the highest possible level, in all circumstances and at all times, is frankly an unrealistic ideal. It is rather about not lacking any of the virtues to a meaningful degree and having a permanent commitment to live and serve according to those virtues to the best of one's ability.

A military organisation, as well as an individual, can also display professionalism. Most of us would have no difficulty in describing an organisation that was corrupt, badly led and technically incompetent as 'unprofessional.' So, by the same yardstick, we would not be surprised to see an organisation that is well led, highly motivated and is technically highly proficient described as 'professional.' However, just as it would be unreasonable to expect an individual to sustain every virtue to the highest level at all times, so it would be unreasonable to expect every member of an organisation to behave similarly before it could be described as 'professional.' An organisation will demonstrate its professionalism by developing, advocating, encouraging and enforcing a set of behaviours which are intended to improve its competence and value to those it serves. It self-evidently has to do this in a way which is different from the way in which an individual motivates him or herself.

Organisations do not become excellent by accident. In her book *The Outstanding Organization*,[56] Karen Miller identifies four attributes that are required: Clarity, Focus, Discipline and Engagement. Although the book was written with commercial businesses in mind, these four qualities are no

---

56 Karen Miller, *The Outstanding Organization: Generate Business Results by Eliminating Chaos and Building the Foundation for Everyday Excellence* (New York: McGraw-Hill, 2012).

less applicable to a military organisation. A military unit that lacks clarity in its strategic objectives, focus in delivering them, is ill disciplined in its actions and does not fully engage the capabilities of its members will never become professional. However, these qualities might not in themselves be enough in the military environment.

The most obvious differences in the military context are the related and grave responsibilities that come with the authority, in some circumstances, to take life and the potential requirement to sacrifice one's own life. These are commitments which go way beyond achieving a sales or production target, however stressful these might seem to salesmen or production managers, and require a degree of training and maturity which is unique. To this burden must also be added the ability to perform sometimes delicate and difficult actions and to exercise sound judgement when under extreme stress. So, for a military organisation to be characterised as professional, it has to inculcate a range of qualities required of organisations in many other walks of life, but it also has to prepare its members to take life, offer their own lives and cope with often multiple and repeated extremes of stress. To this one must also add the accumulation of specialist knowledge, often in voluminous quantities. There is also a further important dimension – political control – which is highly relevant to military professionalism, as we shall see in my second example.

My first example of military professionalism is that of an infantryman, Warrant Officer Ian Fisher, a soldier in the Mercian Regiment of the U.K. Army. He did not conform to the gruff, unthinking caricature so beloved by civilians. He had an honours degree in Physics and Geology, loved to travel and doted on his wife and two young children.

He served first as a reservist with the Territorial Army, reaching the rank of Lance Corporal. His enthusiasm for and commitment to the Army was such that he volunteered in 1993 to join his Regiment as a regular private (an effective demotion) on an overseas tour of duty. He subsequently served on five operational tours, one in Northern Ireland, two in Iraq and two in Afghanistan. But the bald facts of his biography do not tell the story of the man and someone acknowledged by the many who knew him as the consummate military professional.

As a sergeant major and platoon second in command, he had a pivotal role as the link between the Regiment's officers and the fighting men of his platoon. Although he could be direct, even blunt, his men loved him, as did his officers, even those regarded as 'difficult' by the troops. Sometimes leading an officer without him realising is one of the greatest professional skills of a senior NCO and it was perhaps not for nothing that his nickname was 'The Colonel.'

He was obsessive in the pursuit of excellence, confident and with a meticulous eye for detail. Utterly reliable, dedicated and blessed with a huge personality, his professional knowledge was encyclopaedic. Morally and physically courageous, he was sought out by his commanders both as a source of knowledge – which can be learned from manuals – but more importantly as a source of wisdom, which is a much rarer quality. He had a mischievous sense of humour which is the oil which keeps armies running smoothly in difficult times and he was a pivotal figure in every aspect of the life of his battalion. He loved fun, when it was time for fun, but he knew when a professional persona had to be paramount.

There are many in the U.K. armed forces who aspire to be as professional as Ian Fisher – courageous, honest, wise, patient, and so the list could go on. The previous chapters in this book give examples of the theory and practice of military virtues. Ian Fisher probably knew the theory, or at least some of it, but his focus was on an instinctive delivery of what it meant to be a professional infantry soldier, in a sometimes rough trade and at a particularly difficult time for the Army. Military professionals like Ian Fisher are often unsung and unnoticed, except by those who know them well. No audiences applaud their motivational speeches, no big bonuses come their way after a hard year, no-one much notices the pride they take in seeing their subordinates succeed. But they are the genuine backbone of a fighting force and without them armies would founder when the going gets tough.

In a professional (as opposed to a conscript) army, military professionals have to make sacrifices long before they reach the battlefield. They agree to hand over many of their life choices – which most civilians would regard as inalienable rights – to the organisation which employs them. For example, at a social level, the organisation will decide where they will work (and often live), who they will work alongside and for how long. Their partner's employment opportunities may be severely restricted by enforced mobility or by living in a remote location. Leave might be cancelled at a moment's notice without redress or compensation.

At a professional technical level, they cannot simply decide that they are bored with their current duties and change to others, unless that happens to fit with the organisation's needs at that moment. And at the most fundamental level there is the notion of unlimited liability[57] and sacrifice. They may be required to work in physically dangerous and mentally demanding situations without the benefit of health and safety protections. Ultimately, they must accept that in some circumstances the

---

57   The term 'unlimited liability' was probably first used by Gen. Sir John Hackett in *The Profession of Arms*.

mission must take precedence over everything else, including their own survival. In many ways, the ultimate measure of military professionalism is measured by sacrifice and self-sacrifice. However, it must also include an ability to make sound and ethical decisions based on training and acquired skill, even in the most testing of circumstances. Being a professional means more than being a good person who displays military virtues; it also means living up to standards which have been established – perhaps over centuries – potentially at the expense of one's own wishes.

Sacrifice and self-sacrifice remain the ultimate legacy of too many military professionals, Ian Fisher included. He was killed by an improvised explosive device (IED) in Afghanistan on November 5, 2013. His commitment and courage sowed seeds of pride in the barren landscape of raw grief inhabited by his wife, sister, parents and children. For that is the reality of the true extent of military professionalism; the commitment to put the mission, and the safety of one's comrades, before one's own safety and even the happiness of one's family, and to keep doing it time and again, day after day, until the job is done.

Given the tremendous pressures of modern conflict, demonstrating continued professionalism at the individual level is a real challenge. However, achieving similar standards of professionalism at unit or capability level is self-evidently even more difficult. Individuals can self-motivate, but an organisation has to be motivated through leadership, clarity of strategic thinking and, from time to time, a determination to break down barriers of inertia and bureaucratic drag.

The U.K.'s recent involvement in the Iraq and Afghanistan conflicts presented some serious challenges to the Defence Medical Services (DMS). The U.K. had not been in a protracted period of overseas conflict since the Korean War, although there had been shorter periods of intense conflict. For example, in the operation to liberate Kuwait (1990–1991) when the U.K. lost 45 personnel to hostile action,[58] or the liberation of the Falkland Islands (1982), when 237 personnel were so lost.[59] Inevitably, both these conflicts and others gave rise to some serious trauma casualties and mass casualty incidents. But the duration of the conflicts and, to some extent, the nature of the injuries sustained, did not require the DMS (or its predecessor formations) to radically change treatment paradigms.

Any medical professional reading this case study should note at this point that this case is not a treatise on the science which underpinned many of the improvements that will be described here. There are a

---

58   "UK Armed Forces Deaths: Operational Deaths post World War II, 3 September 1945 to 28 February 2018," Ministry of Defence, 2017, 4.

59   "UK Armed Forces Deaths."

number of academic papers which cover such subjects as anaesthesia, haematology and emergency medicine in great depth. This case deals with the professionalism of the DMS, which assumes mastery of the underlying science, and looks more broadly at how opportunities were identified and exploited, as well as at issues such as courage and teamwork.

I mentioned earlier the relevance of political control in relation to military professionalism. Political control of the armed forces in a democratic society quite properly covers a wide spectrum of activities, ranging from shaping the outcome of a strategic defence review, through procurement to involvement in targeting decisions. However, in relation to the DMS, it is very instructive to examine how political decisions about the roles and resourcing of the DMS initially worked against fostering a climate of professionalism, before a reversal of some of those decisions had the opposite effect of dramatically promoting it.

Defence reviews[60] in the 1990s had significantly reduced the capabilities and resources (including people) of the DMS. Military hospitals were closed, specialisations such as obstetrics and gynaecology were abandoned and some military medical personnel were rusticated to work in civilian hospitals. The effect on DMS's operational capabilities was severe, as noted in 2004 by the retired Air Marshal Sir Timothy Garden and retired General Sir David Ramsbotham:

> As more and more specialist tasks were moved to the civilian sector, so the availability of uniformed, trained specialists fell. For some specialisations this trend could prove to be catastrophic in the long term. For example, the review resulted in the ability of the military medical services to support military operational deployments being virtually eliminated.[61]

However, lest the above comments be dismissed as no more than the bitter hindsight of the retired military commander, the findings of the House of Commons Defence Select Committee (DSC) were no less scathing.

In the 1996–97 Parliamentary session the Defence Committee examined the implementation of the changes announced in DCS 15. The Committee found that the DCS proposals had failed to enhance capability, and that staff levels and morale were dangerously low. They concluded that:

---

60   There were two such reviews, *Options for Change* in 1990 and the *Defence Costs Study* (DCS) in 1994. *DCS 15* was the study which related to the DMS. A brief description of these (and other U.K. defence reviews) can be found in the House of Commons Library document, *A Brief Guide to Previous British Defence Reviews*, dated October 19, 2010.

61   The original article, "About face: the British Armed Forces – Which way to turn?" appeared in *The RUSI Journal* 149, no. 2 (2004).

… the Defence Medical Services are not sufficient to provide proper support to the front line in all realistic planning scenarios and show little prospect of being able to do so in the future. A choice would have to be made between sending troops without proper medical support <u>or</u> only sending the limited number of troops who could be supported. Defence Costs Study 15 has not enhanced the front line but has seriously impaired it.[62]

This environment, created as a result of political priorities, not least of which was cost saving, was clearly one that was wholly inimical to fostering a climate of dynamic professionalism.[63] Morale was low and much of the DMS's 'esprit de corps' had been lost, with many clinicians dispersed in civilian hospitals.

However, the Strategic Defence Review of 1998 actively sought to address the deficiencies created by the two previous reviews and did so with no small measure of success. For example, the DMS manpower requirement was increased from 4,645 to 7,661,[64] specialist medical units were created, crucially including the Army Medical Services Training Centre (AMSTC) and measures were taken to 'remilitarise' personnel. By the time the second Gulf War started in 2003, the DMS was hungry to succeed with a new generation of young, energetic and capable clinicians looking to prove themselves.[65]

However, even fundamentally well resourced, highly motivated organisations are not able to make great leaps of progress by simply fixing one or two things that are going badly wrong. The issue for such organisations is to identify the areas in which improvements can be made and to pursue them with both rigour and vigour. Identifying such areas is

---

62 House of Commons Defence Select Committee (HCDSC) 7th Report *The Strategic Review: Defence Medical Services.* https://publications.parliament.uk/pa/cm199899/cmselect/cmdfence/447/44704.htm. See also HCDSC Fifth Report 1994–95, *Defence Costs Study Follow-up: Defence Medical Services*, 102 and Third Report 1996–97, *Defence Medical Services*, 142.

63 The cost saving measures, apart from the obvious direct implications, had an important negative effect on the execution of the U.K. Armed Forces command philosophy, known as Mission Command. In this type of command, the commander's *intent* is shared with subordinates, who are told what to achieve and why, but are then left to decide how to achieve it. Subordinates are encouraged to use their judgement, initiative and intelligence in pursuit of the commander's goal. (See HCDSC Fifth Report, 1994–95, para. 92 and Army Doctrine Publication 71940, Chapter 6.) However, it is an integral part of the commander's (or politician's) responsibilities to ensure that subordinates have adequate resources to achieve their mission.

64 HCDSC Fifth Report, 1994–95.

65 There is a plausible school of thought that the departure of so many experienced clinicians following *Options for Change* and *DCS 15* had the unforeseen positive consequence of allowing this new generation to move into positions of responsibility earlier than would otherwise have been the case.

not easy, especially if an organisation is running tolerably well, even if it is not achieving its full potential and having to sometimes relearn lessons from its own history. Transformation in these circumstances comes through an accumulation of small improvements and a constant desire to push the boundaries of excellence.

This is not a paradigm that is unique to the DMS, or even to the military, and a great deal of pioneering work was done in the world of sport, where hundredths of a second can mean the difference between success and failure. The precision and speed of Formula 1 pit stops would be one example, but perhaps the best is the dramatic improvement in British track cycling over the past decade. The analysis of where improvements could be made through marginal gains was aggressive, minute and intensely scientific. It reached the point when, as the U.K. track cycling team was dominating the 2012 Olympics, their French competitors apparently believed the U.K. team coach's comment (in jest) that the U.K. wheels were 'specially round.' Whether or not such a wheel is technically possible is not the issue, but the fact that it was at least superficially plausible to French ears speaks eloquently of the success of the strategy of small, but incremental, improvements.

It was a similar process which helped the DMS to revolutionise the treatment of combat casualties in Iraq and Afghanistan. A robust process of data collection and analysis was put in place,[66] a weekly teleconference between U.K. and deployed personnel in Afghanistan allowed trends (positive and negative) to be identified early, with lessons learned being immediately incorporated by the AMSTC into the training of those about to deploy. Similarly, detailed analysis of the nature and cause of injuries allowed suggestions for improvements to vehicle design, equipment and protective clothing to be made with a confidence born of robust analysis. No less important was a change which saw medical experts having a direct input into operational decision making, rather than as part of a wider logistics brief and this professional autonomy also allowed for faster analysis and implementation of improvements to care.

In terms of treatment protocols, an early turning point was the realisation that haemorrhage is the biggest cause of death in military trauma[67] and that it is potentially susceptible to life saving compression if

---

66 *Options for Change.*
67 Howard R. Champion, Ronald F. Bellamy, Colonel P. Roberts, and Ari Leppaniemi, "A Profile of Combat Injury," *The Journal of Trauma* 54, no. 5 (2003): s15. Quoted in T. Woolley, J. A. Round and M. Ingram, "Global lessons: developing military trauma care and lessons for civilian practice," *British Journal of Anaesthesia* 119, Issue suppl_1, (December 1, 2017): i135–i142.

swift action is taken, especially where the injury is to an extremity.[68] This contrasts with civilian trauma, where the biggest single cause of death is head injury. This difference in main cause of death arises directly from the obvious differences in the causes of catastrophic trauma injury in the civilian and military environments. Blunt trauma (for example in vehicle collisions) is the most common cause in the former environment whereas blast injuries, especially from IEDs became the defining injury in the Iraqi and Afghanistan theatres. During the period 2003–2012 in Iraq and Afghanistan 65 per cent of total U.K. casualties from hostile action were from blast injuries, as opposed to 31 per cent from gunshot wounds.[69]

This realisation that the nature of injuries was evolving resulted in several important changes to treatment. The first was to change the immediate action drills for treating casualties, from a sequential Airway, Breathing, Circulation (ABC) paradigm to a simultaneous Compression, Airway, Breathing, Circulation ('C'ABC) model.[70] This change required a number of significant consequential changes to both training and immediate treatment. A further significant change was the introduction of tourniquets to stem bleeding. This was a controversial decision with very strong and informed views both for and against the change, with a high-level decision ultimately required to authorise their use.

Most blast injuries were sustained in remote locations where specialist help was not immediately available. Generally, only two sources of help were on hand, either the injured person (where this was feasible) or his (or her) colleagues. This buddy care was essential, as without it, "the rest of the [care] chain is less viable."[71] New training regimes therefore emphasised the necessity of buddy to buddy help, how to attempt to stop catastrophic bleeding using tourniquets and the introduction of new haemostatic dressings (the introduction of which also carried a degree of risk) to aid blood clotting.

The remote and often hostile environments in which these injuries occurred required similarly dramatic improvements in the chain of care. Probably the most important of these was the creation of the Military Emergency Response Team (MERT). At the core of the MERT is a team of four military medical specialists – a consultant doctor, emergency nurses and paramedics. The team operated in the back of an armed Chinook

---

68   Champion and Bellamy et al., "A Profile of Combat Injury."

69   Jowan G. Penn-Barwell, Stuart A. G. Roberts, Mark J. Midwinter and Jon R. B. Bishop, "Improved survival in UK combat casualties from Iraq and Afghanistan: 2003–2012," *Journal of Trauma and Acute Surgery* 78, no. 5 (2015): 1014–20.

70   T. J. Hodgetts, et al., "ABC to <C>ABC: Redefining the military trauma paradigm," *Emergency Medicine Journal* 23, no. 10 (October 2006): 745–46.

71   Penn-Barwell et al., "Improved survival in UK combat casualties."

helicopter escorted by a helicopter gunship and accompanied by a small force protection unit in case of enemy action.

The underlying concept of the MERT is to take the emergency room to the patient, to provide consultant led treatment from the earliest possible moment – hence the fact that the teams were usually led by consultants in emergency medicine or anaesthesia ('seniority saves lives'). But in order to fulfil their mission, the medical team relied on the skill and courage of the helicopter crews, their force protection colleagues and significantly on the initial buddy–buddy actions of the injured person's comrades. The MERT was first introduced by 16 Air Assault Regiment, followed by the Commando Medical Squadron and it is no coincidence that both these units were unique in the U.K. order of battle in that they both 'owned' their medical specialists and were therefore able to exploit the MERT initiative quickly and effectively. However, this 'bottom up' initiative nevertheless required very high-level intervention to ensure that its long-term continued use was not jeopardised by the scepticism of senior NATO (non-medical) commanders.

The MERT itself fits into what is known is the operational patient care pathway (OPCP),[72] which aims to have critically injured personnel undergoing surgery within two hours and places great emphasis on the 'end of end' care of the patient. Severely injured patients would be medically evacuated to the Queen Elizabeth Hospital in Birmingham, for ongoing specialist care by a multidisciplinary team, at what is now a single centre of excellence for military trauma care in the U.K. The outcome of all these changes was that patients were increasingly surviving injuries when they would have been expected to die.[73] This might anecdotally be considered the ultimate validation and vindication of the changes put in place, but a more empirical assessment can be found in the U.K. Care Quality Commission's 2012 Review of the DMS, which found that the provision of trauma care in Afghanistan was 'exemplary.'[74] This is an extremely rare, possibly unique, assessment of the standard of trauma care in any U.K. medical environment, civilian or military.

In the context of this book, what does this hugely beneficial change tell us about the professionalism of the DMS, those who work within it and those who work alongside it? The first thing it tells us is that professionalism, like morale, is a fragile flower which has to be nurtured and actively

---

72 U.K. MOD Joint Service Publication 950 Leaflet 1-4-1.
73 Woolley, Round, and Ingram, "Global lessons: developing military trauma care," i135–i142.
74 Care Quality Commission Defence Medical Services, "A review of compliance with the essential standards of quality and safety," June 2012, 53.

encouraged. Such nurturing and encouragement has to take place at every level of the command chain. In our democracies, politicians decide the grand strategy and allocate (or not) the resources necessary to achieve it. At the most senior levels of military leadership, commanders have to develop a style of leadership which encourages constructive suggestion making and informed risk taking, but which nevertheless retains the authority for decisions made to be acted upon without dissent. At the operational level, middle ranking commanders have to be alive to new opportunities and have the confidence to articulate them, while at the same time not losing their grip on their many day to day responsibilities. The same is no less true of the tactical level of leadership, right down to the most junior non-commissioned officer.

The recent history of the DMS shows examples of all this. Politicians initially flunked the challenge in *Options for Change* and the *Defence Costs Study* but redeemed themselves in the *Strategic Defence Review*; their support was also often crucial in approving potentially high-risk medical initiatives during subsequent operations. Senior DMS commanders drove through initiatives – some of which like the MERT originated at the tactical level –which were sometimes initially controversial and not without risk. Energetic and intelligent clinicians collected and analysed data and lessons learned and fed the results immediately back into training and other areas of policy. And at the tactical level, a lot of people did a very difficult job very well indeed and were not afraid to speak up with suggestions for improvement.

But, as I mentioned at the start of these case studies, military professionalism is much more than an accretion of separate virtues, however laudable each one might be individually. Transforming an already highly proficient military organisation into one that is a world leader also requires vision, leadership, motivation and, perhaps above all, a burning desire not to accept anything less than the very best. Such qualities are contagious (no pun intended) and are what the military call a force multiplier, because they inspire others to behave in the same way.

There are many former patients and their families who have good reason to be grateful to the professionalism of the DMS and many of them have expressed their gratitude. The DMS and its members have quite rightly received many awards from a variety of organisations. But the accolade which gets right to the heart of all military personnel is that of being recognised as a consummate professional by the comrades with whom they share the risks and rewards of military life.

In this respect both Ian Fisher and the whole of the Defence Medical Services stand as equals. Both cases are different, one describing an individual, the other a whole capability, but the similarities outweigh the differences. You will find in them both an almost all-consuming desire for excellence, for improvement and a restless dissatisfaction with the average. You will also see common threads of enthusiasm, modesty and a willingness to share knowledge, as well as to acquire it. But above all, military people will recognise that these are the sort of inspiring people you want to have beside you when you have to draw on your last reserves of courage and strength in the most difficult of circumstances or when the worst happens and you are the wounded patient needing urgent care.

Finally, I should add here that the views and opinions expressed are those of the author alone and should not be taken to represent those of Her Majesty's Government, MOD, HM Armed Forces or any government agency. I must also add my thanks to all those who have assisted me with my research for these cases: I am grateful to them all.

References

Aalto, J. "Challenging in combining ethical education for conscripts and professional military: The Finnish point of view," in *Making the Military Moral: Contemporary Challenges and Responses in Military Ethics Education*, edited by Don Carrick, James Connelly, and David Whetham. Abingdon: Routledge, 2018.

Almeida, A.M. De Oliveira, C. Vandenplas-Holper, and J. De Ketele, "Revue critique de recherches sur les conceptions des parents à propos du développement de l'enfant," *Bulletin de Psychologie Scolaire et d'Orientation* 2 (1992): 1–2.

Army Doctrine Publication 71940 *Land Operations*.

BBC News. "Birmingham QE staff 'adapt to skills of the Taliban," November 15, 2012. https://www.bbc.co.uk/news/uk-england-20268734.

Bentley, B. *Professional Ideology and the Profession of Arms in Canada*. Kingston, Ontario: Canadian Institute of Strategic Studies, 2005, 18.

Care Quality Commission. *Defence Medical Services: A Review of Compliance with the Essential Standards of Quality and Safety*. Summary Report, June 2012. https://www.cqc.org.uk/sites/default/files/documents/20120621_dms_report_summary_final.pdf.

Champion, H. R., R. F. Bellamy, Col. P. Roberts, and A. Leppaniemi, "A Profile of Combat Injury," *The Journal of Trauma* 54, no. 5 (2003): s13–s19.

Chappelle, W. L., K. D. McDonald, L. Prince, T. Goodman, B. N. Ray-Sannerud, and W. Thompson, "Symptoms of Psychological Distress and Post-Traumatic Stress Disorder in United States Air Force 'Drone'

Operators," *Military Medicine*, 179, Issue suppl_8 (August 1, 2014): 63–70.

Coker, C. *Ethics and War in the 21st Century*. London: Routledge, 2008, 124.

Cook, P. "A profession like no other," in *Routledge Handbook of Military Ethics*, edited by George R. Lucas. Abingdon: Routledge, 2015, 32–43.

Cook, C. "Military ethics and character development," in *Routledge Handbook of Military Ethics*, edited by George Lucas. Abingdon: Routledge, 2015.

Cross S. E. and J. S. Gore, "Cultural Models of the Self," in *Handbook of Self and Identity*, edited by Mark. R. Leary and June Price Tangney. New York: The Guilford Press, 2003, 553.

Di Lauro, M. "The flight of angels: saving lives in Afghanistan's airborne A&E," *Daily Mail*, February 7, 2010. www.dailymail.co.uk/home/moslive/article-1248526/The-flight-angels-saving-lives-Afghanistans-airborne-A-E.html.

Downes, C. J. "To Be or Not To Be a Profession: The Military Case," *Defense Analysis* 1, no. 3 (1985): 154, 156.

Duty with Honour: The Profession of Arms in Canada. Kingston, Ontario: Canadian Defence Academy – Canadian Forces Leadership Institute, 2003, 41.

Eastwood, J. *Ethics as a Weapon of War: Militarism and Morality in Israel*. Cambridge: Cambridge University Press, 2017, 87.

Erikson, E. H. "Autobiographic Notes on the Identity Crisis," *Daedalus* 99, no. 4 (1970): 731.

Evetts, J. "The Sociological Analysis of Professionalism," *International Sociology* 18, no. 2, (2003): 397.

Fisher, L. Interviews, various dates 2018.

French, S. E. *The Code of the Warrior: Exploring Warrior Values Past and Present*. Lanham, MD: Rowman & Littlefield, 2003.

Garden, T. and D. Ramsbotham "About face – the British Armed Forces which way to turn?" *The RUSI Journal* 149, no. 2 (2004).

Gustavsen, E. "The construction of meaning among Norwegian Afghanistan veterans," *International Sociology* 31, no. 1 (2015): 21–36.

Hackett, J. *The Profession of Arms*. London: The Times Publishing Company, Ltd., 1963.

Hodgetts, T. J., P. F. Mahoney, M. Q. Russell, and M. Byers, "ABC to <C>ABC: Redefining the military trauma paradigm," *Emergency Medicine Journal* 23, no. 10 (October 2006): 745–46.

House of Commons Defence Select Committee. *Defence Costs Study Follow-up: Defence Medical Services*, Fifth Report, 1994–95.

House of Commons Defence Select Committee. *Defence Medical Services*. Third Report, 1996–97.

House of Commons Defence Select Committee. *The Strategic Review: Defence Medical Services*, 7th Report, October 1999.

House of Commons Library Document. *A Brief Guide to Previous British Defence Reviews*. Standard Note: SN/IA/5714, October 19, 2010.

House of Commons Library Research Paper 94/101. *Frontline First: The Defence Costs Study*. October 14, 1994.

Huntington, S. P. *The Soldier and the State: The Theory and Politics of Civil-Military Relations*. Cambridge, MA: The Belknap Press of Harvard University Press, 1957.

Irwin, T. H. "Aristotle," in *The Shorter Routledge Encyclopedia of Philosophy*, edited by Edward Craig. Abingdon: Routledge, 2005, 63.

Janowitz, M. *The Professional Soldier: A Social and Political Portrait*. Glencoe, IL: The Free Press, 1960.

Kegan, R. *The Evolving Self: Problem and Process in Human Development*. Cambridge, MA: Harvard University Press, 1982, 42.

Kegan, R. *In Over Our Heads: The Mental Demands of Modern Life*. Cambridge, MA: Harvard University Press, 1994, 5.

King's College London. "Life-saving treatments learnt from war being missed," March 20, 2015. http://www.kcl.ac.uk/newsevents/news/newsrecords/2015/March/Life-saving-treatments-learnt-from-war-being-missed.aspx.

Long, George, Interview, February 2018.

Lucas, G. R. *Military Ethics: What Everyone Needs to Know*. New York: Oxford University Press, 2016, 9.

Lupfer, T. T. "Leadership for Mere Mortals," in *Didactics of Military Ethics: From Theory to Practice*, edited by Thomas R. Elßner and Janke Reinhold. Leiden: Brill Nijhoff, 2016, 127–40.

Mileham, P. "Military Virtues 1: The right to be different," *Defence Analysis* 14, no. 2 (1998): 186.

Miller, K. *The Outstanding Organization*. New York: McGraw-Hill, 2012.

Ministry of Defence. "Warrant Officer Class 2 Ian Fisher killed in Afghanistan," November 5, 2013. http://www.gov.uk/government/fatalities/soldier-from-3rd-battalion-the-mercian-regiment-killed-in-afghanistan.

Ministry of Defence. *Joint Service Publication 950 Leaflet 1-4-1*, Edition 2. "operational patient care pathway," November 25, 2014.

Moskos, C. C. "The All-Volunteer Military: Calling, Profession, or Occupation?" in *Parameters* 7, no. 1 (1977): 2–9.

Nuciari, M. "Models and Explanations for Military Organisation: An Updated Reconsideration," in *Handbook of the Sociology of the Military*, edited by Giuseppe Caforio. New York: Kluwer Academic/Plenum Publishers, 2003, 80.

Olsthoorn, P. "Situations and Dispositions: How to rescue the military virtues from social psychology," *Journal of Military Ethics* 16, nos. 1–2 (2017): 78–93.

Otto J. L. and J. Webber Bryant. "Mental Health Diagnoses and Counseling Among Pilots of Remotely Piloted Aircraft in the United States Air Force," *Medical Surveillance Monthly Report* 20, no. 3, March (2013): 3–8.

Penn-Barwell, J. G., S. A. G. Roberts, M. Midwinter, and J. R. B. Bishop. "Improved survival in UK combat casualties from Iraq and Afghanistan: 2003–2012," *Journal of Trauma and Acute Surgery* 78, no. 5 (2015).

Porter, K. "Lessons learnt from the military," John Hunter lecture, London, Royal Society of Medicine, July 5, 2016. https://videos.rsm.ac.uk/video/john-hunter-lecture-world-class-trauma-care---lessons-learnt-from-the-military.

Rhodes, B. *An Introduction to Military Ethics: A Reference Book.* Santa Barbara, CA: ABC-CLIO, LLC, 2009, 8.

Ryan, R. M. and E. L. Deci, "On Assimilating Identities to the Self: A Self-Determination Theory Perspective on Internalization and Integrity within Cultures," in *Handbook of Self and Identity*, edited by Mark R. Leary and June Price Tangney. New York: The Guilford Press, 2003, 253–72.

Schultz D. P. and S. E. Schultz. *Theories of Personality*, 9th ed. New York: Wadsworth Cengage Learning, 2008, 216.

Snider, D. M. "The Multiple Identities of the Professional Army," in *The Future of the Army Profession*, edited by Don M. Snider and Lloyd J. Matthews. Mississauga, Ontario: McGraw Hill Custom Publishing, 2005, 139–73.

Snider, D. M. "American Military Professions and Their Ethics," in *Routledge Handbook of Military Ethics*, edited by George Lucas. Abingdon: Routledge, 2015, 25.

Swann W. B. and J. K. Bosson. "Identity Negotiation: A Theory of Self and Social Interaction," in *Handbook of Personality: Theory and Research*, edited by O. P. John, R. W. Robins, and L. A. Pervin. New York: The Guilford Press, 2008, 463.

Taylor, T. *Sources of the Self: The Making of the Modern Identity*. Cambridge, MA: Harvard University Press, 1989.

van Baarda, Th. A. "Forming a Moral Judgement Using a Dynamic Model," in *Military Ethics: The Dutch Approach. A Practical Guide*, edited by Th. A. Van Baarda and D. E. M. Verweij. Leiden: Martinus Nijhoff Publishers, 2006, 279–97.

van Baarda, Th. A. and D.E.M. Verweij, "Military Ethics: Its Nature and Pedagogy," in *Military Ethics: The Dutch Approach. A Practical Guide*, edited by Th. A. Van Baarda and D. E. M. Verweij. Leiden: Martinus Nijhoff Publishers, 2006, 279–97.

Wertheimer, R. "The Moral Singularity of Military Professionalism," in *Empowering our Military Conscience: Transforming Just War Theory and Military Moral Education*, edited by Roger Wertheimer. Farnham: Ashgate, 2010, 144.

Woolley T., J. A. Round, and M. Ingram. "Global lessons: developing military trauma care and lessons for civilian practice," *British Journal of Anaesthesia* 119, Issue suppl_1, December 1, 2017.

CONCLUSION

J. J. Stringer

This is a timely, perhaps overdue book and I am delighted to have been given the opportunity to provide some final thoughts in this conclusion. If the book began with reference to Aristotle and his influence and importance to fighter pilots, perhaps this rather tired and worn ex-fighter pilot might provide a perspective on why an expanded and reimagined set of military virtues is appropriate for the early part of the 21st century. My thoughts are informed by the tactical operator and operational staff/commander experiences that I have been fortunate enough to enjoy, and also by an enduring interest in the morality and ethics of the profession of arms, itself aided by studying under one of the contributors to this book. What follows is imperfect and will be – should be – open to challenge, but it does draw on those personal and collective set of experiences.

An earlier chapter spoke to the 'mano a mano' consequences of a particular course of action whilst conducting operations in Iraq in the period after Gulf War 2. There is something about our approach to the traditional military values that is somewhat classical: the clash of forces, pitched and lethal battles and the indisputable triumph of one side over another. The need to marshal and command large forces without sophisticated control, and the requirement to pass straightforward orders that required immediate acknowledgement and acceptance, drove a focus on the fewer original virtues. Existential fights such as World War II provide reinforcement for this view. As numerous contributors have noted, the context has changed considerably over the last 30 years: the period that could loosely be called that since the end of the Cold War.

My first operational tours were flown in my trusty (if a little underpowered) Jaguar, helping to enforce the No-Fly Zone over the Former Republic of Yugoslavia. As Brendan Simm and others have covered eloquently and forcefully, our operations in the Balkans were conducted against a most challenging humanitarian, political and international backdrop. The use of force required authorization by both military commanders and the United Nations, and I recall regularly flying over smouldering or demolished villages – our presence, devoid of the necessary will and mandate, was dangerously hollow. The contradiction was not lost on those commanding or participating, and the eventual forcing mechanism of the operations conducted in Autumn 1995 provided the means of forcing a negotiated settlement. Imperfect yes, but considerably better than allowing the situation on the ground to continue.

It did force much reflection within the military engaged on the mission. The certainties of the Cold War – from training, exercising and our alert postures, through to the certainty of oblivion if deterrence failed – were swiftly replaced by the more nebulous yet important aspects of Peacekeeping, Peace Support Operations, Operations Other Than War, and the numerous other descriptors that entered our lexicon. Attendant on almost all was the explicit, implied or derived requirement to render humanitarian assistance in a multitude of forms – keeping warring factions apart, protecting and distributing supplies, proto-nation building. In this new operational context, skill at arms in all its forms now needed to include personal control, swift and rational judgement, (at times, exceptional) grace under pressure, political understanding and 'savvy,' and Rules of Engagement that were becoming increasingly as reflective, if not more so, of national policies than of the Law of Armed Conflict. Coalition operations added further layers of Clausewitzian fog and friction, the need to understand allies' viewpoints, additional constraints and objectives as well as your own, and increasing and increasingly immediate media scrutiny, where the race to file or broadcast (and soon, post online) ahead of rivals prevented contextual description or reflection. Our education and training was in lag too.

In parallel, those with whom we might engage – in all forms – were expanding too. Small arms have always been available, but de facto private armies, bankrolled by the wealthy, by factions or even (without attribution) by states, were fielding increasingly complex and effective weaponry and with minimal scruples over their employment. And were Western societies willing to accept significant injuries or deaths, and considerable financial cost, to intervene in some or all of these fights?

Fast forward a few years to the late 1990s and very early noughties. I was now flying on Ops to enforce the Northern No-Fly Zone over Iraq, protecting the Kurds and enforcing UN resolutions on Saddam Hussein. These missions had been conducted for almost a decade (since the end of Gulf War 1) and there was a palpable sense of ennui in some capitals as to their continuation. Again, military personnel were aware that resolve was being tested back home and that there was no forcing mechanism: our operations could become endless, absent a change in the political weather. I would argue that we had become used to the swiftly evolving nature of our military operations, and that we could expect significant provocation that would not of itself warrant a response. If Professionalism is a military virtue in its own right, then that was the binding sense that underwrote and defined our operations. At this point, I might politely demur from seeing it in isolation: I have always felt that being professional encompassed the whole panoply of operational, specialist and personal skills and qualities that we seek in our servicemen and women – it connects rightly to the concept of the Profession of Arms, and I think we struggle to separate it from that broader and holistic sense of virtues and attributes. Certainly on a ship, regiment or flying squadron, being professional is seen as the prerequisite for all that follows; its absence is perhaps the cardinal individual and collective sin.

In the ten or so years after the end of the Cold War and victory in the Gulf shortly afterwards, the period since 9/11 has provided perhaps the greatest set of challenges for our militaries. National shock at the terrorist outrages in New York and those that have followed in other capitals and cities might be felt to generate a sense of retribution, where the required ends and that which has provoked them allows 'the gloves to come off.' Why seek to retain the moral high ground against opponents with little or no interest in its occupancy. Indeed, in Al Qaeda and in Daesh/ISIS, our opponents have actively sought to outrage and destroy: a nihilistic view of those they hold in contempt.

Yet we have rightly held ourselves to a far higher standard, even if at times we may have fallen short. I would argue that anything less would have been more than just morally wrong – it would have been deeply and fatally corrosive. Corrosive to the connection between the military and the people; corrosive to the cause for which we fight; and corrosive to our sense of ourselves and our own values. It might surprise a non-military audience just how often we reflect on the need to look ourselves in the mirror and be content with what we see, or the investigations, analysis and soul-searching undertaken when things do not go as planned.

On this score, it might be instructive to reflect on how the increasing use of unmanned systems could impact on the military virtues outlined by earlier authors. Using one highly relevant and much discussed example, I would disabuse anyone of any notion that drone pilots are somehow emotionally disconnected from the battlespace, engaged in a computer gaming world where they feel no personal involvement and any actions are consequence free. As Peter Lee writes here and elsewhere, this could not be further from the truth and all air forces are concerned by the longer-term issues that might arise from crews who are so closely connected with the tactical environment and their targets. The unstinting judgement, analysis and almost questioning culture that is central to their operations is worthy of quiet thanks. I am also not convinced that we had foreseen this at the start of their operational usage.

This questioning culture might pose some fundamental questions about the utility of force, and of its employment. Is there a risk that the skills, qualities and virtues that we ask of our Reaper pilots and that is mirrored across our forces might generate unintended consequences? Might we inadvertently generate and imbue a set of virtues and a mindset that risks us losing our warfighting edge? Are Orwell's 'rough men' a dying breed? And, allied to this, has the development of precision weapons and an emphasis on minimal collateral damage generated a way in warfare that is inimical to its true nature? Could it also see us losing through seeking to avoid the use of force?

Unsurprisingly, there is no simple answer. The elements noted above speak to ways in warfare, approaches to risk, national psyches and strategic cultures, political and public will and a host of other significant factors. What we cannot and must not lose sight of is that campaigning is not a risk-free, and ideally bloodless, undertaking. The nature of warfare has not changed and it continues to be brutish, violent and lethal when battle is joined. The weighing of risks versus benefits continues to be difficult, even with the LOAC framework to guide decisions on proportionality, necessity and advantage. We seek to generate, sustain and accelerate momentum in our campaigns, the better ultimately to prevail without unnecessary and extended suffering. We have also experienced a shift in our most recent engagements from largely rural settings involving limited numbers of individuals, to the complexity of fighting in dense urban areas. Global population growth and the inexorable movement of people to cities will probably see this trend maintained if not in fact accelerated. Rupert Smith's assessment of War Amongst the People was prescient, and those who saw an Afghan-esque future dominated by COIN were perhaps a touch shrill and over-reaching. Our armed forces must now contend with a variety of physical environments, all losing a different if overlapping set of problems. The almost total disconnect in values between some of our opponents and ourselves makes establishing a useful frame of reference difficult. At the extreme, the damage we will seek to avoid is actively sought by others such as Daesh, the better to support their narrative and discredit ours.

I noted previously that the immediate post-Cold War period saw significant military readjustment, both to the nature of threats and likely commitments and also within force structures and with the impact of Second Offset technologies. As our tactics evolved, so too did the command and control required, the emerging sense of whole of government approaches and the need to train and educate for this broader and more sophisticated context. Our assessment of morality and ethics needed rethinking too, and thematically this began to be woven into staff and command courses; at the U.K. Joint Services Command and Staff College, advanced course students could take it as specific MA module. The military instrument remained a key lever of national (and in coalition, collective) power but across a canvas that variously encompassed Soft Power (Nye) and Three-Block War (Krulak) perspectives.

Some of the strands and factors mentioned previously to describe the evolving geostrategic context of the last 30 years have been given additional oxygen and reinforced by two significant and linked issues: liberal democracy that is under numerous pressures and less certain in its structures, and the seemingly ever-increasing impact of the Information environment. We are in an era of persistent competition with states such as Russia and China, where a grey zone exists between what might be termed peace and conflict. Actions and activities that are below the threshold for a traditional political and/or military response are increasingly prevalent: the annexation of entire territories can be achieved through a variety of means, but where even the obvious and traditional – armed soldiers – can be made ambiguous and confusing through anonymous uniforms and uncertain ownership.

Given this, I would argue for the vital place for Judgement in supporting a number of the 14 virtues examined in this book. One could embody many of them, but in the absence of sound, consistent judgement, even the most virtuous can be undone. The complexity and interleaving of the persistently competitive environment within which we seek to Understand and Operate requires nothing less, and it is not axiomatic that it can only come with time and experience. They are helpful, but we ask much of some very junior personnel – we need to actively mentor and educate. During my tour as the U.K. Air Component Commander in the Middle East – from the start of operations to recapture Mosul through to the liberation of Raqqah – one of the key positions in the targeting teams that sat in the coalition's Combined Air Operations Centre at Al Udeid Air Base, Qatar was held by a very junior NCO. We asked much of that post and the individuals who filled it, and under exceptional pressure they delivered exceptional performances.

We also need to encourage a strong spirit of curiosity in our people, even if this might at face value look to pose problems for more traditional definitions of Obedience and Loyalty. At almost all levels, unthinking and/or blind applications of both might be just what we don't need. Equally, the days when even senior officers could excuse their approach or analysis by defaulting to claims of being 'a simple soldier/sailor/airman' are (or must be) well behind us. We need doers and thinkers, and they are not either mutually exclusive or different breeds; rather, we should be developing and championing those who are both. It was a little depressing to note media reflections on the appointment of retired General James Mattis as the U.S. Defense Secretary: a soldier who reads... who'd have thought? The reality is that nearly all our most successful commanders and military leaders have had a strong intellectual streak, even if the contemporary Service climates in which they served might not have been as conducive or supportive as they could have been.

Our own militaries have thus sought to understand and adapt: the U.K. is not alone in recognizing five distinct domains – Land, Maritime, Air, Space and Cyber – and we seek to recruit from an ever more diverse pool. We are less than five years separated from the then British drawdown from Afghanistan and the conceptual development of Information Advantage. Battalions, brigades and even distinct Commands have been established to understand and operate in this expanded landscape. For the British Army, 77 Brigade are in the vanguard of conceptual and structural development: 'Information Manoeuvre' has entered the military lexicon alongside its better established and more physical cousins. And the Forces themselves are changing with the advent of the Whole Force – regulars increasingly augmented (and in some fields, even replaced) by reservists, civil servants and contractors. We have professions within arms as part of the Profession of Arms. This shouldn't worry us, and it might finally put the correct descriptive wrapper around what we have been doing in some areas for many years. However, if we agree that an expanded set of Military Virtues are necessary for our forces, then it might also follow that these will need to apply to the Whole Force too.

I think that it might be useful to set this against what can be seen in changing ways in both warfare and war. To the long-established tenets and principles of *jus ad bellum* and *jus in bello* could now be added *jus post bellum*. It may no longer be good enough to establish the justification for any conflict and to behave legally and ethically once committed to the fight; we might now also ensure that we are setting the conditions for sustainable post-conflict reconciliation and reconstruction. Pity the commander balancing long term requirements whilst prosecuting a multi-domain campaign where numerous audiences, not just the enemy, have a vote.

Back to Al Udeid and the coalition Air Component role in the fight against Daesh. I mentioned earlier our Targeting Teams, and it would be useful to explore our military virtues through the perspective of those tasked with deciding whether or not to employ lethal force in some of the most challenging environments in which we have operated. I should also highlight that this is not the exemplar through which to conduct an assessment, but I do think it an exemplar and a good one at that. The battlespace was (and at time of writing, still is) exceptionally complex, congested and contested, with multiple nations and entities operating on the ground and in the air; the coalition dimensions added further tactical, operational and strategic complexity; numerous audiences were engaged and – via social media as well as more traditional forms of journalism – able to access numerous sources of information; Daesh posed a physical and virtual challenge that needed to be defeated; and the array of effects required, and/or the platforms from which they could be projected or defeated, spanned all five domains. Our partnering as the Coalition with the Iraqi Security Forces and the Syrian Democratic Forces generated further challenges and opportunities.

To make sense of what was going on, and to generate the necessary fidelity to underpin our targeting, required the most sophisticated fusion of multiple intelligence feeds from all sources that we have yet seen. Our intelligence picture was dependent on some leading edge technologies, and the coalition employed precision weapons as our default. Yet the human dimension remained central to everything: indeed, at times we probably over-controlled and were overly-restrictive as to the permissions we gave to our crews, precisely to ensure that we applied the closest possible assessment on targeting and weapons employment. I believe that the moral courage, personal and collective discipline, and integrity showed by all was both outstanding and essential. Nor was it age, rank or experience-specific, and everyone contributed their own thoughts and assessments.

As the fighting for Mosul and then in parallel Raqqah became more intense, and the demands on the Air Component intensified, we turned a fortnightly targeting team reflection period into a weekly event: a key part of our battle rhythm. Where previously we had discussed both actual events and hypothetical scenarios – the latter to attempt to pre-empt what we thought would be coming – these weekly sessions had ample real-world examples to dissect. In all of ours discussions, I was struck by a number of things: like all the best debriefs (and a staple of fast jet post-mission analysis), they were genuinely rank-blind and everyone had a voice and a contribution to make; and the fusion of lawyers, policy advisors, targeteers, senior leadership and intelligence analysts made for a comprehensive mix of everyone involved in targeting and approvals. I would offer that these sessions were professionally invaluable, an outstanding vehicle for challenge and personally and collectively cathartic for everyone involved. Much wisdom from young heads too, and humility, compassion, perseverance and patience in spades from everyone. I suspect that everyone involved will take the overall experience with them throughout their military careers and beyond; they will also be able to reflect on the framework of Military Virtues they employed and were guided by, even if they would not have perhaps have seen them as such at the time or since.

This has deliberately been a set of personal reflections devoid of footnotes or supporting embellishments (although they are all out their somewhere). I have been exceptionally fortunate to operate alongside some outstanding men and women, from the U.K. and our friends and allies overseas, over 25 years of frontline, command and staff experience. More importantly, I have learned much from all of them, as well I hope as imparting some thoughts and ideas of my own as to how to operate and to fight. We will need to remain focused on values and virtues, the more so as we utilize the military instrument alongside all other levers of national power, and the additional power (and challenges) offered by coalitions, within increasingly opaque and unpredictable contexts. And we will need to emphasize and educate all those who serve in why they matter, and the consequences from any deliberate choice to forego one or more for some perceived near term advantage. Rather like Franklin's cautionary words on the trade between liberty and security, it will be a false choice. It would also be one we would rue, as we have when making poor choices on values and virtues in the past. We are already facing adversaries and competitors who would be delighted if we joined them in a race to the bottom on ethics, values and virtues; at the extremes (such as Daesh) we face and fight those for whom amorality and perverted virtues are core elements of their beliefs and values. For our competitors, deceit, dissembling and disinformation – all done with a patina of believability that sows doubt – has proved fertile and productive. It would prove fatal for us.

INDEX

NOTES

CPSIA information can be obtained
at www.ICGtesting.com
Printed in the USA
LVHW081738020122
707667LV00001B/1

9 781912 440009